A Guide To Chess Improvement

THE BEST OF *Novice Nook*

DAN HEISMAN

EVERYMAN CHESS

www.everymanchess.com

First published in 2010 by Gloucester Publishers plc (formerly Everyman Publishers plc), Northburgh House, 10 Northburgh Street, London EC1V 0AT

First published 2010 by Gloucester Publishers plc

British Library Cataloguing-in-Publication Data
A catalogue record for this book is available from the British Library.

ISBN 978 185744 649 4

Distributed in North America by The Globe Pequot Press, P.O Box 480, 246 Goose Lane, Guilford, CT 06437-0480.

All other sales enquiries should be directed to Everyman Chess, Northburgh House, 10 Northburgh Street, London EC1V 0AT
tel: 020 7253 7887 fax: 020 7490 3708
email: info@everymanchess.com
website: www.everymanchess.com

Everyman is the registered trade mark of Random House Inc. and is used in this work under license from Random House Inc.

EVERYMAN CHESS SERIES (formerly Cadogan Chess)
Chief advisor: Byron Jacobs
Commissioning editor: John Emms
Assistant editor: Richard Palliser

Typesetting and editing by First Rank Publishing, Brighton.
Cover design by Horatio Monteverde.
Printed and bound in the US by Versa Press.

Contents

Acknowledgments

I would like to thank the following:

- Hanon Russell for giving me the chance to write the Novice Nook column.
- Mark Donlan for permission to turn the columns into book form.
- Mark, Byron Jacobs, and the other editors for making the material more readable.
- My students for providing material and examples (so long as I kept them anonymous!).
- Michael Montgomery for a needed second eye in reviewing the material.
- Grandmaster John Emms of Everyman Chess for encouragement, review, and guidance in putting the material into book form.
- Byron Jacobs of Everyman for helping with the finance and other issues.
- John Henderson of the Internet Chess Club for helping me get in touch with Everyman Chess.
- Everyman Chess for giving me the chance to get the material into wide distribution.
- The Chess Journalists of America for recognizing Novice Nook with two dozen awards over the past decade, including "Best Instruction", "Best Analysis", and "Best Column".
- Wife Shelly for support: "What are you doing?" "Working on my column for next month".
- Bobby Dudley – I struggled to get my first book published, and thanks to Bobby I am now up to my tenth...
- The masters and experts who told me how much the material has helped them, despite the name "Novice Nook".
- All the readers around the world who took the time to contact me about how much Novice Nook has opened their eyes about various subjects and aided them in their quest for chess improvement.

Introduction

It all started with Will Yu.

Will was a brilliant high school student, later voted Most Likely to Succeed in a high school filled with highly driven students. But in chess everyone has to start at the beginning and at this time Will was pretty much a beginner.

After a few tournaments Will's rating was below 1100. He showed great promise, but it wasn't coming through yet. Then Will played with some of my son's friends on a team at the 1999 US Amateur Team East event and posted a 5-1 record with a solid 1600+ performance rating.

I saw the games – they were no fluke; Will had improved dramatically in almost no time. But how is that possible, that an 1100 player can, all of a sudden, play like a 1600 player? That flew in the face of many things I had believed about chess improvement. So I talked to Will and thought about what I had learned for about three days. During that time I had an epiphany about chess learning and the associated thought process. But how to let others know?

I wrote and article about my findings and called it *The Secrets of Real Chess*. I had been following the new online magazine *ChessCafe*, so I contacted the publisher, Hanon Russell, about putting my article on the web. Thankfully, Hanon did and it got quite favorable feedback. I got several emails from people around the world basically stating "I have been studying chess for 20 years and was never a very good player. However, for the first time your article makes it clear to me why that is – why didn't someone write this a long time ago?"

Over the course of the next several months I wrote two more articles for ChessCafe: *Time Management During a Chess Game* and *Applying Steinitz' Laws*. Both were solid, but not the hit of *Real Chess*.

Then around New Year 2001 the phone rang. It was Hanon Russell:

"I am thinking of adding a column to help weaker adults learn how to improve. I think you would do a good job – are you interested?"

It was somewhat like asking Al Gore if he would help with global warming...

I was very grateful to Hanon. He decided to call the column "Novice Nook".

Of course, Hanon is a very strong player and most improving adults to him are relative novices. However, I quickly found that the ideas which help a player improve at one level can still be extremely helpful when elevated to another level. So Novice Nook ended up helping players of all levels get better.

This was illustrated by an email I received from a USCF expert (2000-2199), who wrote that he learned a lot from Novice Nook, but could not get his three lower-rated sons to read the column because they felt they were not novices! I passed his concern on to Hanon, who reasonably decided that the column had a following and changing the name would not make much difference. So Novice Nook remained somewhat a misnomer.

Meanwhile the column was attracting a lot of attention around the world. It annually won awards from the Chess Journalists of America. Besides winning the award for *Best Instruction* multiple times, Novice Nook also won the prestigious Cramer Award for *Best Column in Any Media* in 2005.

I think one of the cornerstones to Novice Nook's success is my desire to not pass along ideas that are easily found elsewhere. These include my crusades for Counting, time management, understanding the use of tactics study for determining the safety of candidate moves. There may be some ideas I thought were new but were accidental rehashing of old ideas of which I was unaware. Once my writing started to be compared to Cecil Purdy's, I purposely stopped reading Purdy because I did not want to even subconsciously steal any ideas!

Even the ideas which can easily be found elsewhere I hoped to package in a new or easily compartmentalized way. For example, the Novice Nook *King and Pawn and ? vs. King* tries to encapsulate all the possible exceptions where a king and a pawn and anything else on the board are unable to beat a lone king, because 99% of the time that material wins easily.

Have I succeeded? Well, I will let the reader judge for himself!

What is The Best?

By the time we decided to publish *A Guide to Chess Improvement: The Best of Novice Nook*, Hanon had sold ChessCafe to Mark Donlan, and thus Mark is also to thank for the permission to provide the material in book form. However, by late 2009 there was so much material that *The Complete Novice Nook* could not fit into a regular-sized book. In fact, limiting it to "Best" still only allows for about a third of the material to be presented. How to cut it down and still give the reader the flavor of the column? That led to some very difficult decisions:

- ♟ Less than half the columns are included. I tried to emphasize material that was most novel or helpful. This necessitated including a slightly higher percentage of theoretical vs. practical information but, like the column, there is still a heavy emphasis on what is practical.

- ♟ Out of necessity, material that was covered in some of my previous books was de-emphasized. That meant less tactics due to *Back to Basics: Tactics*, less thought process found in *The Improving Chess Thinker*, and less discussion of threats due to *Looking for Trouble*. All of these topics are still included, but not to the extent they would be if these books did not exist.

- ♟ When multiple Novice Nook columns overlapped a subject or were continuations of the same subject, I tried to combine the material into one column. This not only enabled me to include more original columns, but also allowed me to cut out quite a bit of redundant material. Moreover, combining columns also allowed me to provide some *new text* which properly links these previously separate Novice Nooks. For these reasons the combined columns are the ones most substantially changed from the originals, and I have made every effort to *update information* and provide consistency between columns. When columns were combined, the name of the secondary column is usually retained as a subheader and was also used in cross-references with the main header number. For example, if 3-2 is *The Two Move Triggers* and it contains the essence of the column *The Room Full of Grandmasters*, then *The Room Full of Grandmasters* will be a subheading and a reference to it would note that it is within 3-2.

I was also able to *correct some faulty analysis*, thanks to Mike Montgomery's laborious computer-checking.

Readers who wish to see the original columns can reference the archives of ChessCafe (http://www.chesscafe.com/archives/archives.htm#Novice Nook) or the same material crosslinked with comments via my website www.danheisman.com – click on "Novice Nooks". Similarly, Novice Nooks which are referenced for additional information but not included in this book, are referred to as "archived" and can be found at these websites.

♟ All Reader Questions were eliminated. This was a difficult choice because these provided natural clarification for some material. However, the questions usually addressed earlier Novice Nooks, and not always ones chosen to be in this book.

Importantly, some completely new columns, never published elsewhere, have been added. *Is it Safe? Quiz* is a natural extension of my emphasis on Counting and Safety. *The Three Types of Visualization* had been occasionally mentioned in Novice Nook, but never fully discussed. Ditto with *Ask the Right Questions*.

I decided to order the columns via sections, similar to how my website lists them by subject, e.g. General Improvement, Thought Process, and Time Management. Each section contains one or more numbered columns, which have been arranged to promote sequential understanding of material. Even so, there is some overlap in concepts from one section to another. For example, thought processes involving safety could just as well be categorized under tactics, or a time management concept like *The Two Move Triggers* is very helpful in thought process. Online I provided hyperlinks between the columns; for the book these links have converted to cross-references or references to "archived" ChessCafe columns on the web.

All ratings in this book are FIDE/USCF.

Ready for a trip to a place where Real Chess is a commonplace idea, micro and macro time management are key, Counting is the unbelievably overlooked tactic, and the mantra is "Checks, Captures, and Threats"? Then turn the page...

Chapter One

General Improvement

1-1) The Theory of Chess Improvement

"Even if they were born with incredible intellectual gifts, it still required about 8,000 practice hours to realize those gifts." – Kenneth A. Kiewra Ph.D. and Thomas O'Connor Ph.D. in "Developing Young Chess Masters: What are the Best Moves", *Chess Life*, May 2005.

Improvement at chess and similar activities consists of adding positives or subtracting negatives. It's as simple as that – and yet the ramifications are enormous. This simple idea suggests the following:

- ♟ Learning new ideas and chess patterns are examples of *adding positives*.
- ♟ Identifying your mistakes and misconceptions, and taking steps to minimize them are *subtracting negatives*.

To achieve improvement, your efforts must include a *balance* of:

A. theory and practice, and

B. adding positives and subtracting negatives.

"A" states that you must achieve some balance between theory and study and practice and play (for how to do this, see *An Improvement Plan* 1-2). By "some balance" I don't necessarily mean a perfect 50-50 division in time spent, but rather a sufficient ratio to address your study and practice needs. If you study and don't play, you can't apply what you are learning; and if you play but don't study, you are likely to keep making the same mistakes repeatedly. In order to effectively improve you should first learn something, apply what you learn by playing, learn from your mistakes during play, and then repeat the process as much as possible to provide maximum effectiveness. This is the *Improvement Feedback Loop* described in detail later in this column.

"B" states that your theory and study time must consist of *both* learning new ideas and patterns, and also eradicating your mistakes and misconceptions. If you study in such a way as to mostly add positives or only subtract negatives, you will eventually get diminishing returns on your time. When you reach a "roadblock" it is usually because you have to rebalance your efforts.

The above ideas are very important. For example, they help explain why you can't get better by just studying chess books. To improve you need both practice (slow games and some fast) and theory (adding new ideas and patterns, and identifying and minimizing mistakes). *Forgoing any ingredient can cause a lack of progress, and continuing to focus on one element will result in little progress.*

At many points in their career, a player needs to subtract negatives in order to improve. That is why all good players either took extensive lessons or had strong chess friends to help them.

Let's consider what it means to add a positive or subtract a negative in more detail.

Adding a positive means that you learn a new principle or new pattern (opening, tactical, endgame, etc), read an annotated game, or discover a new way to manage your time or improve your thought process.

Subtracting a negative means that you replace a misconception or a bad thought process with something better or more correct. For example, if you think that all pieces, *on the average*, are worth exactly an integer multiple of a pawn (bishop/knight=3, rook=5, queen=9), then that is no more correct than thinking everyone in your town is exactly an integer multiple of a foot tall! Those numbers are easy for a beginner to remember, but they are not the actual averages. Trading a bishop and a knight for a rook and a pawn is usually a mistake because bishops and knights are both worth *slightly more* than three pawns (on the average)!

Or suppose you play too fast because you don't have a good thought process, or you never realized that pacing yourself to use almost all of your time is a better way to manage your time. Then once you achieve a better thought process or attain proper pacing, you are subtracting a negative (playing too fast) and replacing it with something superior. You get better.

The personalized study book that I suggest in *Reviewing Chess Games* (1-3) differs from all other chess study books in that it emphasizes the subtraction of negatives, while almost all other books and videos emphasize the addition of positives.

The more you can subtract negatives *and* add positives the better off you are. But not all negatives and positives are of equal value. You get a much bigger impact from adding large positives (such as learning commonly occurring tactics; better analysis methods; and proper time management) than you do from small positives (like a new 12th move in a given opening). *Improving things you do on each move* (analysis, time management, and evaluation skills) *gets a much bigger bang for the buck than improving things that occur occasionally* (how to mate with a bishop and a knight against a king).

Give a man a fish and you feed him for a day. Teach a man to fish and you feed him for a lifetime.

I teach my students how to add positives by themselves, so they can study and absorb new information efficiently and independently. I concentrate most of our lesson time on subtracting negatives, which is much harder for students to do by themselves. One negative they *can* subtract without my help is to look up the opening after they play each game and find out what they would do differently the next time that sequence is played. But for most other negatives, such as time management or thought process mistakes, it is much easier if a good instructor helps you identify your misconceptions.

So how does one go about maximizing adding positives and subtracting negatives? In the remainder of this column we are going to deal with those issues in a more global manner. For example, how does one find as many "big" negatives as possible within a short period of time? And how do you identify what causes the negatives and how to minimize or replace them? Each is a separate issue.

Let's start with subtracting negatives, since most chess books are filled with adding positives (new opening information, guidelines, endgame patterns, and tactical problems). In "Developing Young Chess Masters: What are the Best Moves", *Chess Life,* May 2005 the authors state:

All the young chess masters have been coached by titled players and most began regular instruction of one or two hours per week soon after learning the game.

This was so important and effective for those strong young players *because most of the roadblocks to improvement are from the failure to eliminate errors, rather than the failure to add new information.* I would estimate that 75% of my students' errors are from not following concepts they already know. Only about 25% are because of something they did not know and need to learn. Of course, if you only eliminate errors and never learn new information that will surely stifle your improvement as well, so both methods of improvement are important and necessary.

You probably know several weak chess players who have read hundreds of chess books and strive to find more books to ignite their stalled improvement. I would bet that almost everyone in that situation would get more out of identifying and minimizing their recurring errors than they would by learning new information.

A person's ability to identify his own errors – not just in chess – is somewhat suspect. That's why we have teachers, quality assurance personnel, and proofreaders. Moreover, *identifying an error versus doing something about it are totally different capabilities.* While a good coach can do more than just help you find your negatives, one of the best and most common ways to identify your mistakes does not require an instructor. How is this possible?

You can't lose a chess game without making a mistake. Moreover, strong players bring out – and take advantage of – mistakes of weaker players. Therefore a great way to find out what you are doing wrong is to play higher rated opponents and allow them to highlight your mistakes. It's a simple concept.

You make similar mistakes against *lower* rated opponents but, of course, they are less likely to punish your mistakes, and they give you less opportunity to make them. For example, suppose you are playing someone rated 300 points below you and you quickly win a piece. Then it is unlikely that your opponent will generate enough pressure on your position to force meaningful mistakes – unless you don't follow the guidelines presented in *When You're Winning, It's a Whole Different Game* (7-3). Then you probably have made some enormous mistakes that you can correct in future situations! But otherwise you are so far ahead that there will be many reasonable paths to victory. To make matters worse, weaker opponents may even play so badly as to *justify* your mistakes and *reinforce your misconceptions*! So a steady diet of weaker opponents can definitely be harmful to your game.

You need a method for identifying mistakes, determining how serious they are, what could have been done instead, and how to prevent them in the future. Yet every player has one potentially great tool for that – your opponent! If you can get a higher-rated opponent to review the game with you then he likely will be able to help identify (sometimes too gleefully!) what you did incorrectly. Players are often "not in the mood" to go over a lost game, but this only compounds your mistakes by overlooking a great opportunity to improve. Almost all strong players took advantage of such critical "post-mortem" opportunities on their road to improvement. Luckily, the possibility to play stronger players is plentiful, as most tournaments allow you to play "up" against higher rated opponents. Online servers allow you to challenge higher rated players – sometimes asking them to play "non-rated" is an enticement.

When going over your game with a stronger opponent, you should discuss:

- ♟ Where you could have improved in the opening. If you made a move that was "incorrect", then your opponent can likely tell you what would have been more acceptable.
- ♟ Any tactics that either of you overlooked.
- ♟ Any moves you made which converted the game from a win to a draw (or loss), or a draw to a loss (the losing move). It is a great exercise to identify the losing move in each decisive game – in other words, analyze with your opponent to find the spot where an alternative move would have saved the game.
- ♟ Any other tips your opponent will offer. He may not be a super strong player, but even players at your own level know things that you don't – it would be almost impossible that your knowledge and his are identical!

So whether you are at a chess club, an over-the-board tournament, or just playing online, don't overlook opportunities to go over your games with your opponent *or any strong player who is willing to chime in* – think of these as golden opportunities to improve.

Any negative which can cost you a game is important, but the negatives that cost you many games are the most important. Therefore, repeatable errors are the ones you most want to eradicate. In my experience, some of the most common errors include:

- ♟ Playing too fast or too slow.
- ♟ Having bad thought processes – such as playing "Hope Chess" (making a move without analyzing whether you can safely meet any forcing reply), seeing a good move and not looking for a better one, or not looking for *all* your opponent's threats from his previous move.
- ♟ Not following general principles, such as not developing all your pieces in the opening or not activating your king quickly enough in the endgame.
- ♟ Misunderstanding the value of the pieces. For example, thinking that trading a rook and pawn for a bishop and knight is usually an equal trade.

- ♟ Psychological errors, such as not playing with confidence, or avoiding higher rated players for fear of losing.

- ♟ Analysis errors, like "retained images" (you analyze and visualize a piece as still on a square from which it moved earlier in the imagined sequence) or making "quiescence errors" (stopping your analysis to evaluate a position when there are still tactics to be resolved).

- ♟ Evaluation errors – thinking a position is good when it is actually bad and vice versa.

Some errors are very easy to identify, and possibly even to correct. For example, if you think you are learning as much from playing weaker players as playing stronger ones, reading an article such as this one may be all you need to set yourself straight. Other errors require much more work and time to fix. Suggestions for many of these problems will be made throughout this book.

However, some errors are difficult to correct, even when properly identified. Suppose you're experiencing an abnormal number of retained image errors. In this case, although just practicing "long" analysis will help somewhat, it will not cure that particular error. Therefore, in addition, you must become more aware that this particular error can occur in your analysis and "wire your brain" to be more alert for its presence. This should result in being more careful when you mentally move the pieces. Another beneficial action you can take is to start more long analysis lines from the initial move instead of from the most recent branch. This method reduces retained images but it is also time consuming.

Another error is playing too slow, consistently take seven minutes to decide where to put your knight on move six. Even if someone pinpoints this problem, it may be extremely difficult to break what has become a bad habit. It's not so easy to convince yourself that your impending time trouble will cause more harm than putting your knight on an inferior square. However, you must correct it, or you will lose five or more games because of time trouble for every one you might save by playing too slowly in non-critical situations.

This brings up an interesting point: fixing one problem can give rise to new problems. Many actions involve a trade-off: taking less time *here* and more time *there* surely means that "here" may be harmed. Spend less time in studying the opening and surely you will know less about the opening. Yet harming the less critical areas is precisely what you must do in order to maximize improvement. After all, your time and resources are limited, so spending them wisely, even at the cost of other areas, is your best plan.

Improvement is not a black and white situation – grey is often best. For example, playing all fast games is certainly better for your chess improvement than playing no chess at all, but likely not as good as playing all slow games. However, the best mix is to spend most of your practice time playing slow games, but augment that with a reasonable dose of fast games. There are many examples of the "grey is best" in chess improvement, just as in real life.

One proven way to identify negatives and help minimize their effect is by hiring a good chess instructor. Even if you, without any help, were able to identify all your negatives –

and this is unlikely – it would be difficult to assign the proper level of their effect and identify how to minimize their recurrence. If you're interested, refer to *Finding a Good Instructor* (1-6).

Finally, let's briefly address the issue of making the most of adding positives. Since almost all chess books attempt to add positives, this is a much more common method of study. Some positives yield far more beneficial results than others. For example, playing over instructively annotated master game books is a great source of learning general principles, how to analyze correctly, and how to play many different types of chess positions. For annotated game book suggestions see *An Improvement Plan: Theory* (1-2.2).

Working on your Counting skill, a major aspect of tactics, is another way to add a major positive. See *The Two Types of Counting Problems* (5-5) and the first chapter of my book *Back to Basics: Tactics.*

Another important point about adding positives is *you must know almost all of the ideas that would be normal to learn at a level before you can attain a capability two or three levels higher*. For example, if you don't know almost all the basic patterns that a 1200 player should know, then you won't understand the material that is geared towards 1700-1800 players. At *some point* in your improvement, the holes in your learning will catch up to you. This also helps explain why studying basic tactics, even if you already know 80% of the material, may be very helpful, because the missing 20% can be crucial for further development. This is known as "having a good foundation".

The Improvement Feedback Loop

The key to learning is setting up a system for continuous improvement.

The tried and true method for teaching in schools is to:

♟ Introduce new material by explaining it and providing examples;

♟ Give (sometimes repetitious) problems addressing this material as homework;

♟ Check homework for accuracy and correct any errors/misconceptions;

♟ Test material to see if student is ready for further new material. If the student is not ready, look for new ways explain/learn the problematic material.

This method of learning is generally very good and almost necessary. When applied to chess, it would look something like:

♟ Learn new material (or remove misconceptions) via drills, reading, or reviewing games with stronger players;

♟ Play slow (and fast) games to try to apply the new material;

♟ Review the games with your opponent, instructor, and/or stronger player to see if the new material fuels improvement (see *Reviewing Chess Games* 1-3). In the review you may learn something new (first point above) and also see how well you have implemented recently learned material (third point). Reviewing your games is thus pivotal to any improvement plan. If you identify problems, take measures to either improve your capabilities or eliminate similar mistakes;

♟ See if your rating and results are improving in the long run.

The most difficult aspect of this loop is the availability of good players to provide feedback on how well you are doing. My theory is that the stronger the player is, the more important it is for even stronger players to be available to play, analyze, or instruct. It is possible for a 900 player to lock himself in a closet, set up his own feedback loop, and come out a year later at 1200-1300. But it is virtually impossible for a 2100 player to attain 2400 without extensive interaction with stronger players.

For the average player between 900 and 2100 the importance of the availability of a stronger player lies in between. Having a strong player or two as a friend, club member, opponent, or instructor/mentor is a key asset. Even a friend who is at a similar level (a "study friend") is a great bonus, because they will share different knowledge, views, strengths, and weaknesses – at least be a sounding board.

Let's examine the improvement feedback via some examples.

Example A

You are playing too quickly and not using all your time during slow games. Therefore, you:

♟ Become aware you are playing too fast, resolve to slow down, determine actions that should help (see *The Case for Time Management* 3-1), and make a resolution to implement these;

♟ Record the number of minutes remaining after each move, review each game, noting how much time you took on critical moves and how much time remained at the end of each time control. Note where you played too quickly, so that next time you get closer to using all your time.

Example B

You miss many tactics because you stop analyzing too soon, missing easy wins of material in games that you would find in a "play and win" problem because of *quiescent errors* (stopping analysis too soon). Therefore, you:

♟ Become aware of this error from reviewing your thought process with strong players, peers, or a good instructor;

♟ Review applicable positions to see how and if you can avoid such errors, then try to implement this better thought process in slow games (much more difficult in fast games, but not impossible!);

♟ Review the games played to see if the quiescent errors you were formerly making are now being caught. For example, you now consider sacrificing material as long as the potential reward is greater than the risk. If this is not happening, perhaps you don't understand the concept of risk/reward, or perhaps you do not have the tactical vision to recognize potential follow-ups to pseudo-sacrifices (sacrifices where there is no risk because all the material sacrificed or more can be recovered by force).

Example C

You play well on offense because you efficiently search for possible combinations, but you allow very basic tactical motifs to be played against you. Therefore, you:

♟ Become aware that you are not paying as much attention or devoting sufficient time to what your opponent can do in reply to your candidate moves. Resolve that for every candidate move you consider, you will systematically search for forcing moves (checks, captures, or threats) in reply that cannot be met and, if there is one, eliminate that candidate from consideration (see *Is it Safe?* 5-3);

♟ Play slow games, at first consciously checking each candidate move for safety, and later try to incorporate this check "automatically" as it becomes habit;

♟ Check your games to see if you are still allowing basic tactics against you (or at least at a lesser rate). If you find that you are still allowing such tactics, take additional steps (such as repetitious basic tactic drills to more readily recognize dangerous patterns) that may eliminate candidate moves because they are not safe.

As a final check in each example, after a reasonable number of tournaments and games, analyze your results to see if your actions have caused noticeable improvement.

The key to any improvement loop is the awareness and identification of the problem. Many players think they can identify their own problems, but it is difficult to be objective and easy to rationalize that the causes are under your control. That is why almost every good player at some point spent considerable time around other good players who pulled them up to a high level.

Another common misconception is that all you need do is find a good software engine to review your games. See *Finding a Good Instructor* (1-6) for many reasons why this is not so.

Any good feedback loop should enable you to minimize previous errors and identify new ones to minimize. Sometimes it is necessary to "step outside" your study, game play, and review cycle to perform special improvement exercises, and to identify special psychological and physical needs, such as not getting discouraged after a mistake or eating better during long games.

If you are trying to improve, be aware that your results or rating will fluctuate quite a bit. No one improves monotonically – slumps and ruts are normal and the goal is to take two steps forward for every one back instead of one step forward for every one back. In my experience I have found that perseverance is a much more difficult and rewarding trait than determination (see *Traits of a Good Chess Player* 4-1). Anyone can be determined to improve, but to persevere by consistently overcoming discouragements is much more difficult.

However, if your rating stays low despite your best efforts, there is usually a reason your improvement process is flawed. Perhaps you are ignoring an important aspect such as time management or position evaluation, rely too much on computer analysis, are reluctant to play stronger players, or don't get a chance to practice openings properly through speed play.

Even a good feedback loop won't always produce the desired results. The loop may be designed to help improve certain areas, but it won't function as well with others. Or you may have reached a point in your life where you are getting diminishing returns for your chess time. Most players don't reach anywhere near the potential playing strength they would have if they had started young and become a full-time chess player. But that is normal and we all have restrictions in many areas besides chess, so worrying about these is counterproductive.

No matter how you wish to improve, your feedback loop should be the basis of your improvement plan. It can be simplistic or fairly complex, but your understanding of your loop and how it works can be just as important as your study material or your ability to practice.

1-2) An Improvement Plan

No one gets good at chess quickly and without a lot of work; if that was possible I could not be a full-time chess instructor. There are no full-time tic-tac-toe instructors.

One of the most popular ChessCafe articles was Michael de la Maza's *400 Points in 400 Days*, now expanded into the book *Rapid Chess Improvement*. The reason for the article's popularity was its title and subject: in the chess community almost everyone is attracted by the prospect of becoming a much more respected and capable player – especially in a short period. I would estimate that over 90% of the chess media is purchased with this goal at least partly in mind.

I generally agree with Michael's theory about tactics being the number one component for any improvement program. However, I do not agree with all of Michael's theories, so I thought it might be interesting to publish a general improvement program and readers could make a comparison. Everyone is different, so what works for one person may fail with another. Modifications to fit a particular reader's lifestyle or learning preferences can be made. For example, some people process information more effectively via auditory means (ear) rather than visual (eye), so watching videos rather than reading similar books is more beneficial for them.

I consider the method in this article a good "middle of the road" strategy. One thing Michael's theory and mine have in common is the premise that "To make an improvement program work correctly, it requires quite a bit of dedication and effort." Doing a program halfheartedly, especially the basic tactics study and following the Real Chess discipline (see Section 2: Thought Process), is likely to result in much less improvement per unit time.

This column will cover practice, a plan for studying theory, and a special section on chess books and prerequisites. More specifics on how to best use your improvement time will be covered in *Reviewing Chess Games* (1-3).

1-2.1) Practice (The Road to Carnegie Hall)

A young man walks Broadway and asks an elderly gentleman: "What is the best way to get to Carnegie Hall?" The old gentleman raises his cane and says, "Practice, practice!"

The overwhelming majority of chess literature is about theory: opening theory, improvement theory, tactical ideas, how to think, etc. Good stuff.

But the flipside to theory is practice. How good would you be at golf if you only took lessons and never played? Just about as good as you would be if you only played golf and you did not get any golf "theory": no lessons, golf books, nor visits to the driving range. You need both theory and practice in tennis, golf, chess, math, or just about any subject of sufficient complexity. That is why college graduates are not as good at their profession as they will become with experience – they primarily have theory.

Slow Chess is Necessary Chess

Let's start with a notable "problem": with the proliferation of internet-based chess, more and more people play primarily online and not over-the-board. But a slow online game is often considered to be 30+5 (30 minutes with a five second increment added each move), a time limit which is considered pretty fast over-the-board!

Who are the best fast players in the world? Answer: The best slow players.

So how did Carlsen, Kramnik, Anand, and Nakamura get to be the best fast players in the world, by playing slow or playing fast? The answer is by primarily playing slow (even blitz specialist Nakamura has played hundreds of slow events), so you should, too, if you really wish to improve. Only by playing slow do you have time on each move to:

♟ Think about specific types of positions and candidate ideas really deeply, so that you learn and, when you encounter similar patterns again, you will be able to both recognize them and also apply what you have learned. This builds up your mental chess "database" in a important way fast chess never can; and

♟ Consider which *previous* positions (or aspects of a position) you know that are similar to the one you have now, and whether those similarities are pertinent to the current position. Then use your knowledge to both save calculation time and also feel more confident that your observations are correct. For example, you see this position and notice the e-file:

White to play

...you can ask, "In similar positions in the past I have played Re1 followed by d2-d3, winning the pinned knight for a pawn. Does that work here?" Once you have worked that out in slow games you can quickly apply it in fast games.

So you want to both *remember what you have learned and recognize and apply that learning in the future.* Therefore you need to play slow enough to be able to implement this learning. Patterns need time to resolve and get implanted in your long-term memory. Even online you should try to play as slow as your available time allows; not just 30+5, but games of G/90 or slower.

Not convinced? Then consider that chess is a thinking game, and if you don't learn how to think correctly, then you will never be a good player. Most players learn better thinking methods by taking lessons from strong players who know how to correct thinking deficiencies. To think "correctly" (see Section 2), like anything else, requires theory and practice: you learn what to do, and then practice it every move you play. The point is that thinking correctly in most positions takes time. Playing almost exclusively fast games precludes practicing correctly, and so you will never get very good! Sure, fast games are fine and even *necessary* for practicing openings, developing decent tactical vision and improving critical-ity assessment, but the kind of thinking it takes to plan, evaluate, play long endgames, and find deep combinations is just not possible in quick chess. So *why study planning, evaluation, endgames, and deep combinations if you primarily play fast games and can never get to properly use that knowledge?* Yet so many do!

This is worth repeating: *While fast games are fun and actually necessary for serious improvement, the one requirement for serious improvement is to learn how to think correctly, and to consistently play many slow games to practice good thinking habits.*

As I originally wrote in the archived *The Secrets to Real Chess*, thinking correctly (or at least something close to it) is necessary, but not sufficient for great improvement. In other words, if you don't learn to think correctly, you likely never will get a lot better, but just doing that and ignoring everything else (like time management, and learning basic tactics and guidelines/principles cold) is not enough in itself.

Whom to Play?

It is usually better to play opponents who are enough better than you to push you hard, but not so difficult that you have no chance. This generally means playing those about 100-200 Elo points above you. Is it best to play *only* those in that range and, if so, isn't that impossible because then no one who is following the same guideline would ever play you?

Luckily, the answer is that playing *only* players 100-200 points above you is not optimum. *It is also important to occasionally but consistently play those within 200 points below so that you can learn "how to win".* Those techniques that work when you are ahead a piece or even a pawn against the lower rated players are the same techniques you use in those situations against stronger players. But if you are only competing against players rated above you and not often playing for a win, then you will not get enough chance to develop your "technique".

Only seeking out players rated above you is also not good for your chess psychology. While the object of each *move* is to find the best move, the object of the *game* is usually to win. But if you only play those above you, you sometimes change your objective to just holding on for a draw, and in the long run this kind of mentality is self-defeating. So I would recommend *playing about 2/3 of your games against competition that is 100-200 points above you and 1/3 equal to or below you.* If you are playing in large, open, over-the-board (OTB) tournaments this would translate to playing "up" a section two times out of three and playing in your own section one time out of three. Players should especially play in their own section in championship tournaments, where it is possible to win titles you will cherish for the rest of your career. If your rating is toward the lower side of your section (say you are rated 1405 in a section that is Under 1600), then playing in the U1600 section is sufficient since you are playing mostly "up" in the U1600 anyway.

Internet players should be patient and wait for reasonably rated opponents who will play a slow game. I tell my students that if they put out a challenge they should limit the lower rating of potential opponents to no more than about 50 points below theirs. It is better to play one 60+5 game against a player around your rating than four 15+0 games against players 50-200 points below you, even though those type of games are easier to find. There are internet slow leagues and tournaments at many servers, all of which guarantee you at least one good slow game each week.

Where and How Often?

When playing slow games on the internet, if staring at the screen for long games is bothersome, consider using a regular chessboard, and only resorting to the monitor to input your moves and receive your opponent's.

A large percentage of my readers play on the internet almost exclusively. But there is a strong case for at least augmenting internet play with some OTB play, whether in a club or, better yet, a tournament. Tournament play gives you the kind of concentrated, slow chess that often helps improve your game, especially if you are inexperienced at slow play. I would guess that *players who have never played OTB usually gain 50-100 points of playing strength just from competing in their first long weekend tournament, assuming they play five or more rounds of very slow chess.* Socially there is no comparison; the players on a server might be friendly and chatty, but being in a live OTB event is just much better unless you are the shy type who can chat online but never says a peep to those same people when they are standing there! Sure, an occasional weekend event takes a lot more of your time, but the benefits are comparatively greater if improvement is your ultimate goal. Don't have two days? Try a one-day quad (a round-robin among four similarly rated players).

How often should you play? If you are trying to improve that means as often as you can, but playing lots of slow games can be tiring and time consuming, so most people are not able to play an OTB tournament every weekend even if one was convenient. *A minimum of 8 OTB tournaments and about 100 slow games a year is a reasonable foundation for ongoing improvement.* If you join a local club and play one slow game a week, then 10 additional 5-round tournaments would give you that 100. Of course, many good players improved rapidly by playing much more than that, so additional play will likely help even more.

Can't make 100? Then try for 60. However, if you only play three or fewer tournaments a year and do not play slow chess regularly at a club or online, then you are only playing a couple of dozen serious games per year, so do not be surprised that you are not really improving. If you wanted to be really good at basketball, would you only play full-court games a few times a year and the rest of the time just shoot in your back yard? That would not make any sense, and neither does the expectation that playing only a few slow games each year would be sufficient for dramatic improvement. More likely you will find yourself "rusty" at each event and be lucky to play yourself into shape before the final round!

Of course, there is a limit to how much chess you can tolerate. Some players can play tournaments every week, but they are certainly the exception.

Other Helpful Hints

Suppose you *are* at a tournament. (*If you are not playing in a formal environment, you should still play as if you were: record your game, play with a clock, follow all tournament rules, etc. No sense in practicing one way and then playing "for real" another way.*) What can you do to enhance your experience? I will not get into the "non-chess" factors that could take up an entire column, like get plenty of sleep, eat during long games, etc. Instead, I will concentrate on "chess-stuff".

Before you play a game, fill in all the information at the top of your scoresheet. This accomplishes several things, not the least of which is to get you mentally prepared in the same way to play each game, somewhat like a foul shooter taking the same number of dribbles before a foul shot in a basketball game.

Don't play too fast or too slow. To help rectify this later, during the game write down how much time you – and your opponent, if you wish – have left after each move, with the possible exception of "book" opening moves. See Section 3: Time Management.

Should you walk around while you are playing? While it is probably not good for your back or bladder to sit in your chair for several hours, excessive strolling is not good, either. The old adage is to think about tactics (analysis) on your time and to think about strategy (planning) on your opponent's time. If the position is sharp and your opponent only has one or two dangerous moves, you should start analyzing them while he is thinking.

What openings should you play? When you first begin serious competition, play sharp openings so that you can strengthen your tactics. Several weaker students have told me they play "dull" openings because they are not very good at tactics. Bad strategy! Since tactics are such an integral part of the game, getting better at them means improving overall, so work on your weaknesses and see if you can minimize them. Gambits are great to play when you and your opponents are not advanced players. The reason is clear: you often get a "free" attack and your opponents probably don't have the technique to win up a pawn anyway if you misplay the position and lose the initiative.

More experienced players should play the openings that they either know best or are attempting to learn. The key is that you should look up your game in an opening book later so that you can confidently answer the question: "What, if anything, would I do differently next time if an opponent made all the same moves?"

This is an excellent way to strengthen your mental "opening database", especially if you play frequently. It works even better with fast games(!). Suppose your opponent played a move that was not in any of your books. In that case, try giving the position to *Rybka* or *Fritz* and see what it would have done. If the move was not in a book, it was not likely to be a lot better than the book move and it may have been a lot worse. If your opponent takes you "out of your book", don't panic, but see if the move is either a possible mistake or, more likely, a move that will cause you no problems and you can just develop without any pressure.

Draws? *Think of a draw offer as an offer to remain ignorant about anything you might have learned during the rest of the game.* The more you are in "learning" mode the more you don't want a draw. Only consider a draw under the following circumstances:

- ♟ You are very tired or ill and cannot play your best;
- ♟ The position is so dead drawn that you cannot learn anything, and playing on would waste everyone's time, insult your opponent, and result in a bad reputation for you;
- ♟ It is the final round and a draw ensures you of a prize or a "goal" you need for the tournament; or
- ♟ Your position is so lost that you cannot understand why your opponent offered the draw. It is considered rude for *you* to offer a draw in this case!

Bobby Fischer immediately declined almost all draw offers. He benefited from that extra experience and also gained the reputation of a fearless opponent, which in turn enhanced his results in the long run.

In most cases it is better to play on, lose, and learn something than draw and learn nothing. Learning is what will make you a better player, not getting the extra ½ point.

Learn the more common rules. For example, most players don't know that a threefold draw by repetition of position has nothing to do with what moves were made or that the repeated positions do not have to be consecutive. Or they erroneously believe the 50 move rule only goes into effect when one player only has a king.

Should you play the man or the board? Players who participate in open, swiss events often do not know their opponents as well as international and club players do, so playing the board is always safer. On the other hand, if you know your opponent has a strong predilection toward something, like enjoying tactics or endgames or the Sicilian, avoiding those might be beneficial. The best advice is to not worry about your opponent and each move try to do what the position requires.

1-2.2) Theory

Theory includes activities such as reading books, taking lessons, watching videos, or doing problems on software.

At the start, concentrate on *The Big Five* (1-4), the five major things a "beginning" chess player should learn first: safety/tactics, activity, thought process, time management, and understanding and applying general principles.

If you can do all five of those decently well, then you are likely already a pretty good player. Here is a big secret: *if you don't do each of these five at least moderately well, you can read 1,000 chess books and never get much better!* Too many players make the mistake of glossing over important basic skills as if they now know them and then spend a lifetime reading things that provide diminishing returns and almost no improvement.

Don't believe me? I have heard about instructors teaching players rated 1200-1300 Philidor and Lucena positions. Yet I lost an easily drawable Philidor position because I did not know the technique. My point? I had been playing tournament chess for 5½ years and my USCF rating was about 2100! Sure, if I had known the technique I would not have lost, but the point is that I got to 2100 without knowing the Philidor draw because such specific knowledge is only marginally useful (not useless!) and I was pretty good at each of the Big Five.

If you are not the naturally careful type, you will have to work extra hard at trying to be careful. The attributes of carefulness, perseverance, confidence, enjoying chess study (and not just play), and willingness to tolerate and learn from losses cannot really be taught (see *Traits of a Good Chess Player* 4-1). However, all of these traits can be improved with self-discipline and the realization that getting better is usually a lot more than just playing some games and reading some books.

With that background, how do we begin the study part of our improvement program? First I will have a section listing suggested books of different types, then a section on improvement steps and when to use those books.

Opening Books

The first thing to learn about openings are general opening principles; see *Learning Opening Lines and Ideas* (6-1). One classic book on general opening principles is *How to Open a Chess Game* by seven grandmasters, now out of print. Fine's vintage *The Ideas Behind the Chess Openings* tells you how each opening's pawn structure dictates where the pieces should go and what kind of pawn advances would be called for in the middlegame. Soltis' *Grandmaster Secrets of the Opening* is a great book full of practical advice. An advanced book of this type is Suetin's *Modern Chess Opening Theory*.

I also recommend a one-stop encyclopedia like *Modern Chess Openings 15*. These books won't tell you how to understand the chess openings, but they can't be beat if you want a recommendation as to which moves might have been better. It takes a little practice to use an encyclopedia – see the archived *How to Use MCO-14*. After you learn how to use it, refer to your encyclopedia consistently to slowly build up your opening tree.

Once you identify an opening you really like and wish to learn in more depth, then should you pick up a book on a particular opening or variation. Start with ones that explain the opening variations, like the fabulous *Starting Out* series from Everyman Chess.

Be aware of the difference between a repertoire book and a regular one. A repertoire book champions either the Black or White side of an opening and only gives one (or possibly two) recommendations for moves in a particular position for that side, while showing most of the opponent's possibilities. A regular opening book does not champion a side, and may show multiple possibilities for either player on each move, while still pointing out which of those possibilities it thinks may be best. Thus a repertoire book can be "thinner" while concentrating on the themes for one side.

Tactics

I think the best tactics set is in Bain's *Tactics for Students*. Other good basic books include Wollum's *The Chess Tactics Workbook*; Coakley's *Winning Chess Strategy for Kids*; *Bobby Fischer Teaches Chess* by Fischer and Margulies; and my *Back to Basics: Tactics*. Software includes *Chess Mentor 2.0* or *Chess Tactics for Beginners* by Convekta. Study a set until you can do each problem quickly (see *A Different Approach to Studying Tactics* 5-1). I recommend non-mate books first, since checkmates are rarer than tactics, which can occur on almost every move! For checkmates, Polgar's *Chess: 5334 Problems, Combinations, and Games* and Renaud and Kahn's *The Art of the Checkmate* are great, in different ways. At the intermediate level I think the best book is Coakley's misnamed *Winning Chess Exercises for Kids*. It has the highest approval rating of any book I have ever recommended, and is good for players with ratings up to 2000 and beyond. Reinfeld's *1,001 Sacrifices and Combinations* is a classic in descriptive notation and a very good one is Alburt's *Chess Training Pocket Book*. Software at that level includes Convekta's *CT-ART 3.0*. Khmelnitsky's *Chess Exam and Training Guide* covers tactics and other types of puzzles. For advanced players, Nunn's *Chess Puzzle Book* and Vukovic's *The Art of Attack*, a non-puzzle book, are highly recommended.

Instructive Game Anthologies

The most helpful game books are the ones written for instruction. A great one to start is Chernev's *Logical Chess Move by Move*. A next step would be the same author's *The Most Instructive Games Ever Played*. Modern texts in this vein include McDonald's series, starting with *The Art of Logical Thinking*, and Giddins' *50 Essential Chess Lessons* and his follow-up book(s). Euwe and Meiden's *Chess Master vs. Chess Amateur* is a classic. A recent book that fits in here is Crouch's *Modern Chess Move by Move*; for a more advanced book, try Nunn's *Understanding Chess Move by Move*. A more general work, Nunn, Burgess and Emms's *The World's Greatest Chess Games* is also fairly advanced. Bronstein's *Zurich 1953* is considered by many to be the best chess book ever written; it is good.

Personal Game Collections

The general theory, which I believe is correct, is that individuals learn chess ideas in roughly the same order that these ideas were discovered by the top players over the past few centuries. Following that reasoning, beginners should start their studies with players who lived in simpler chess times, but also players with a tactical style. Therefore, starting with the games of Morphy is not a bad idea; *A First Book of Morphy* by del Rosario bridges the gap between instructive anthologies and personal collections. In general, game books with annotations by the player are superior, such as *Marshall's Best Games of Chess* by Frank Marshall. To study players with a more universal style, start with Lasker and Tarrasch, and then Spassky and Fischer. The more dynamic school might follow the order Alekhine, Botvinnik, Keres, Tal, and Kasparov. The more subtle positional school starts with Steinitz, followed by the clear play of Capablanca, and then the murkier Petrosian and Karpov. There are many other very fine game collections: Korchnoi, Bronstein, Larsen, Gligoric, Shirov, Speelman, Anand, Timman, and Nunn, to name a few. If you get through all of those, you are probably quite a good player just from osmosis!

Positional Texts

There are two major sub-categories:

- ♟ Static considerations such as pawn structures
- ♟ Planning (and evaluation)

Some books attempt to cover the whole range from beginner to advanced, and Nimzowitsch's famous *My System* starts the list – it even covers non-positional topics.

Probably the best "beginner" positional books are the most general chess instruction books. So GM Wolff's great "first" book, *Complete Idiot's Guide to Chess,* would qualify. Coakley's *Winning Chess Strategy for Kids* has an excellent basis for players of any age. Anyone who starts with these two simple books in parallel with basic tactics books is getting a great start in chess! Several classics, such as Lasker's *Common Sense in Chess* and Capablanca's *Chess Primer*, are in this category (Yes, I know there are the diehard Tarrasch, Réti, and Tartakower fans...)

There are several classic "intermediate" positional texts. One of the most basic is Horowitz and Mott-Smith's little-known *Point Count Chess*. Kmoch's *Pawn Power in Chess* is terrific, but see *Breaking Down Barriers* (4-3). Other well-known works are Pachman's *Modern Chess Strategy* and *Euwe and Kramer*'s two-volume set, *The Middle Game*, covering static and dynamic features.

Modern treatments of the subject include Evans' interesting *New Ideas in Chess*, my *Elements of Positional Evaluation* (enlarged edition in 2010), and Watson's superb and very advanced *Secrets of Modern Chess Strategy*.

A "pure" planning book is Euwe's *Judgement and Planning in Chess*. A recent series that does it by puzzles are Ward's *It's Your Move*.

Thinking Process

An excellent book is *How to Choose a Chess Move* by Soltis. The following are varied works that I found interesting: the best known is Kotov's series, which starts with *Think Like a Grandmaster*; Abrahams' *The Chess Mind*; the opening chapters of Dvoretsky and Yusupov's *Attack and Defense*; and the granddaddy of them all, de Groot's thesis-like *Thought and Choice in Chess* and its offshoots, my *The Improving Chess Thinker* and Aagaard's *Inside the Chess Mind*.

Endgames

A good beginner endgame book, once you correct the typos, is *Pandolfini's Endgame Course*. Hall's *Endgame Challenge* contains many crucial positions, and many of these basic ideas are explained in Averbakh's *Essential Chess Endgames*. A recent superb contender is *Silman's Endgame Course*. More advanced players would love Soltis' *Grandmaster Secrets of the Endgame* and Fine's encyclopedic *Basic Chess Endgames* is the classic.

Principles

An adult book for learning principles is Alburt and Lawrence's *Chess Rules of Thumb*. A more recent and comprehensive guide is Soltis' *The Wisest Things Ever Said About Chess*.

Practical Advice

One that comes to mind is *Chess for Tigers 2nd Edition*, by Webb. There is also quite a bit of practical advice contained in many fine books, such as the advanced *The Seven Deadly Chess Sins* and *Chess for Zebras* by Rowson. Besides my *Everyone's 2nd Chess Book*, which offers both practical and theoretical advice, my *A Parent's Guide to Chess* has practical advice for not only parents, but anyone wishing learn about the world of chess. Reading good advice on practical play often gives you a better "bang for the buck" than studying ten new opening books.

Others

Everyone might enjoy some of the following: Chernev's *Fireside Book of Chess* or *Bright Side of Chess*; Assaic's *The Pleasures of Chess*; Soltis' *The Art of Defense in Chess*; Rimmer's *Castling to Win*; Tim Krabbé's award-winning and wonderful *Chess Curiosities*; or even my *The Improving Annotator*. It might be a good idea to have a copy of *The Official Rules of Chess*.

Authors

For my money, GMs John Nunn and Andrew Soltis are the best of the prolific chess authors. I have already expressed my admiration for Silman and Watson. Some earlier authors like Ludek Pachman and Max Euwe are justly renowned.

Did I leave out any great books and authors? Of course, but these are only suggestions...! Do you need to read all these books? Heavens, no!

Improvement Steps

Let's assume you are a beginner and you will be using books, software and, eventually, a good instructor. For each step, I will provide an approximate end rating and an estimated amount of time it would take from before step 1 until the end of that step, assuming ~10 hours study time per week for homeworks #1-3 below, excluding practice.

At each step, limit yourself to four parallel, ongoing homeworks:

- ♟ Play slow and fast games (approximately 90% and 10% of practice time respectively). About 55% of your overall chess time is this practice.

- ♟ Do an appropriate puzzle book, usually a tactics book (because that is key).

- ♟ Read through many annotated game books quickly to pick up general principles and planning. The goal is to develop a "chess conscience" where many authors advise you on how to play various positions.

- ♟ Read "talky" books to learn all other chess information.

Step 1: Getting a Good Start (800-900; 1 month)

Make sure you have learned to play correctly. This includes all of the basic rules (castling, *en passant*, draws, etc), as well as moving the pieces. The book I recommend is *The Complete Idiot's Guide to Chess* by Wolff. The first two thirds of this book is full of good tips for beginners and near beginners. For adults, this should take their rating to 800-900.

This is a great time to practice board vision (de la Maza calls these Chess Vision) exercises. You can find examples in *Everyone's 2nd Chess Book*, *Chess Mazes* by Albertson, and also in *Rapid Chess Improvement*. Exercises are a great way to increase your understanding, in terms of both possibilities and quickness, of what pieces can do on a chessboard. There are excellent board vision problems in Coakley's *Winning Chess Puzzles for Kids, Vol 2*.

Step 2: Starting Down the Paths Correctly (1100-1200; 6 months)

This may be the key Step, because if you take the important points in this Step lightly, the remaining steps may seem slow and stifling.

My homework suggestions at this level are:

- ♟ *Chess Tactics for Students* by John Bain, followed by *Bobby Fischer Teaches Chess* by Fischer and Margulies.
- ♟ *Logical Chess Move by Move* by Irving Chernev, then starting the McDonald series with *The Art of Logical Chess Thinking*.
- ♟ *Winning Chess Strategy for Kids* by Jeff Coakley, and (as a second "talky" book) *Everyone's 2nd Chess Book* by Dan Heisman.

Step 3: Tactics are not the Only Thing in Chess (1400-1500; 18 months)

At this point you should learn more about positional play, endgames, opening principles, etc. There are several basic positional texts and everyone likes different ones. For example, Ward's *The Improver's It's Your Move* can be read after *Winning Chess Strategy for Kids*. For tactics Woolum's *Chess Tactics Workbook* is good, as is my *Back to Basics: Tactics*. Another rare but interesting book is *The Logical Approach to Chess* by Euwe, Blaine and Rumble. For thought process my *The Improving Chess Thinker* should provide plenty of thought!

Instructive game books should include Chernev's *The Most Instructive Games of Chess Ever Played*, *Chess Master vs. Chess Amateur*, along with continuing the McDonald series and Giddins *50 Essential Chess Lessons*.

At this point you have learned many general principles, but may often get confused as to how they are used. Two books that should help straighten out what is important and what is not in the important areas of evaluation and planning are *The Amateur's Mind* by Silman and my *Elements of Positional Evaluation*.

At this point you can also start to learn opening lines more formally. I would start by picking some lines that are either tactical or you have fun playing. As a reference you can use *Modern Chess Openings 15* by Nick de Firmian *or any number of tabiya* (standard table-setting moves) *books that cover all the major openings, but far fewer lines in more detail*. Take a few minutes to learn the tabiyas of the main lines in your openings (see Section 6).

At this point you might consider hiring a decent instructor (see 1-6) to enhance your *Improvement Feedback Loop* (page 17).

Step 4: Consolidation Phase (1600-1700; 30 months)

A more advanced positional text is Pachman's *Modern Chess Strategy*. Game books might include more of McDonald and Giddins and Crouch's *Modern Chess Move by Move*, as well as individual game collections such as Marshall, Lasker, or Alekhine. Despite its arcane nomenclature and descriptive notation, a wonderful text at this level is *Pawn Power in Chess* by Kmoch. For tactics Coakley's terrific *Winning Chess Exercises for Kids* is not as easy as the title sounds. I think you will find my unique puzzle book *Looking for Trouble* fits in nicely here.

At this point you are adequate tactically and, if you want to improve further, need to be well balanced in the Big Five: If you are not playing enough slow games against strong competition, you will probably never get much better if you do not start doing so regularly. If you are still losing pieces to simple combinations more than you should, then reading additional positional and endgame texts will be counterproductive. This is also the reason why a person with a 1300-1600 rating "jumping in" to this improvement program in the middle may not work – you may think you are "too strong" to learn the early phase information that forms the solid basis for any real improvement!

At this level openings start to play a bigger part, so having an opening book specifically addressing each opening you normally play is often *de rigueur*.

Step 5: Intermediate Play (1700-1800; 48 months)

The biggest difference between intermediate play and beginner play is that not all games are (or could be) won on tactics. Michael de la Maza is right that if you are a better tactical player you are likely going to win no matter what your rating, but there are many games played at the 1600+ level where the game is won without the losing player just making a *bad* tactical mistake. Tactics still predominate, so don't forget to keep studying them.

Tactics books for this level include *The Art of Attack* by Vukovic, Alburt's *Chess Training Pocket Book*, and Khmelnitsky's *Chess Exam and Training Guide*.

Another overlooked point is that while many books are on offense, just as often you are on the other side playing defense, so *The Art of Defense* by Andrew Soltis is a worthwhile text, as is his *How to Choose a Chess Move* and *The Wisest Things Ever Said About Chess*. If you need advanced general opening encyclopedias, then a step up from *Modern Chess Openings* is the five-volume *Encyclopedia of Chess Openings*. Game books at this level could include Capablanca, Botvinnik, Keres, Tal, and Larsen.

Step 6: On towards Expert (1800-2000; 60+ months)

For players approaching "A" class, such books as Silman's *How to Reassess Your Chess* (after the first 52 pages, which are much more basic) and the follow-up *How to Reassess Your Chess Workbook* are very good. Soltis' *Rethinking the Chess Pieces* is an excellent insight into advanced evaluation. The modern, comprehensive *Fundamental Chess Endings* by Mueller and Lamprecht can be augmented by Soltis' *Grandmaster Secrets: Endgames*. To help improve your evaluation and planning skills, consider Euwe's *Judgement and Planning in Chess* and Ward's *It's Your Move*. For dessert try Watson's wonderful *Secrets of Modern Chess Strategy*. Continue your game book study with games of Fischer, Kasparov, Speelman, or Shirov. It's time for the classic *Zurich 1953* by David Bronstein. Soltis' *Pawn Structure Chess* augments opening study.

There are lots of other good books and you don't have to read them all. If you feel that you can easily substitute a book or three for the ones I mentioned, by all means do so. These are my opinions only and no one agrees 100% with anyone's opinion... But please don't read 200 more at the expense of really learning and applying the lessons in the more important ones.

Don't forget to augment all this theory with the practice discussed in 1-2.1; essential activity for players who are nearing expert is to play regularly against experts (and masters, if possible) and analyze your games with strong players. Once your rating gets within earshot of 2000, the need to play carefully on every move becomes apparent, and the best way to learn to do this is to play against players who will punish you each time you don't.

1-2.3) Chess Books and Prerequisites

Players often debate which books and videos are the most instructive, good for beginners, most unique, etc. It is important to understand how this dynamically growing set of material can be used, especially which material either requires (or is better understood) by learning other material first. This knowledge is similar to understanding prerequisites for high school or college courses.

Just because a book contains lots of information that you don't know, it doesn't necessarily mean that it will be extremely helpful in making you better at this point in your development. As an analogy, take a student from Spanish I and put him in Spanish IV, or a middle school student studying social studies and put him in graduate school microeconomics. In both cases it is easy to see that the student is now in an environment where there is lots of unknown information, but it will not be very helpful to him.

Much more subtle is the case of chess books, because any intelligent adult can pick up a well written chess book and both understand the material and see that it contains information he does not currently know. The problem is that, unlike Spanish IV, he may not be able to tell that the material, while understandable, is not the right kind of information that will help take him to the next level. In many cases, this information may even be somewhat counterproductive .

Let's consider Jeremy Silman's excellent book *How to Reassess Your Chess*. This book is more advanced than his similar great work *The Amateur's Mind*. Both deal with fairly advanced positional and planning subjects – advanced for beginning adults. These players are still making basic tactical mistakes and will get diminishing returns for studying positional and planning niceties. It would not be possible to fully use these books without having absorbed some of the basic positional ideas and thinking guidelines they intend to correct. So, for example, you might first read a text like Coakley's *Winning Chess Strategy for*

Kids to learn about positional ideas before you read *The Amateur's Mind* to see how beginning and intermediate players often incorrectly prioritize this information and thus misapply it.

Many players who are not yet ready for *How to Reassess Your Chess* mistakenly think that just because it is well written and contains a lot of good information that they understand and do not already know, that it must be able to help them immensely. I have run into dozens of players who feel this way about Silman's (and others') books. However, when I look at their rating and their games, it quickly becomes obvious that they play "Hope Chess" (see Section 2) and are not sufficiently familiar with "removal of the guard" or other similar basic tactical motifs, to play a reasonable intermediate level game, say 1500-1700 USCF. Instead, they have "adult beginner" ratings of 900-1400.

Yet many of them swear by *How to Reassess Your Chess* because they learned so much from it. The problem is that knowing when a bishop is superior to a knight or how to identify the static strengths and weaknesses of your opponent's position is not much use if you lose pieces regularly, or don't understand the principles you need to win a game when you are ahead a piece.

As IM Silman wrote to me in an email on this subject: "*...and yes, you have to start people out with tactics and the basic mates else they will get shredded instantly.*"

At this point in their development these weaker adults would improve more rapidly learning about a good thought process (Section 2), the more basic guidelines found in my *Everyone's 2nd Chess Book* or from (re-)studying a book on tactical motifs (see *A Different Approach to Studying Tactics* 5-1).

There is no universal guide to the intended audience of chess books, nor even unanimous opinions. Most reviewers (and some book introductions) do a good job in describing a book's intended audience. Sometimes internet user groups have interesting discussions on this point. But it is still difficult for inexperienced chess players to figure out which books they should probably explore next. At least check with your coach or a strong player or two before plowing ahead with a text that may be inappropriate or even somewhat harmful.

1-3) Reviewing Chess Games

Every good chess player has played over lots of annotated and unannotated master games, including the most famous games.

One of the most common questions I am asked is, "What is the best way to play over a chess game to get the most out of it?" This is quite a complex query because the answer depends upon:

What are you trying to get out of the game? Maximum improvement? Maximum improvement per unit time? Maximum enjoyment? Try to identify your goals, if not specifically, at least in general.

Whose game are you going over? Yours? An amateur's? A grandmaster's?

How heavily annotated is the game? Not at all? Light notes? Lots of voluminous lines? Heavy instructional text?

What tools do you have available? A chess engine like *Fritz* or *Rybka*? Is the game already in electronic format so it can be played over automatically, or is it in a book and if you wish to analyze it electronically you have to enter the game manually.

For the sake of simplicity, let's assume you are playing over the game *for instruction*. We will consider two cases: *Playing over the Games of Others* and *Reviewing Your Own Games*.

Playing over the Games of Others

Let's start with two basic premises:

- ♟ The more master level games you play over, the more you intuit how masters play chess.

- ♟ The more text annotations you read, the more information about chess you receive.

The following can also be added: The more times you play over the same game, you get diminishing returns on what you learn on each replay.

From these premises we can conclude:

In a given unit of time, it is better to play over lots of annotated games, each with a certain level of learning, than it is to use that same time to play over fewer games repeatedly. The more annotations you read, the more you learn about how to play certain positions and apply certain principles. *The goal is to create a "chess conscience" where you have dozens of expert authors whispering in your ear while you play.* Having only one author or just your instructor whispering is usually somewhat narrow and biased. So playing over lots of annotated master games by many different authors is extremely helpful.

There are two extremes to the approach of replaying games, both of which can be very useful if used in moderation:

♟ The "Ken Smith" fast-approach. IM Smith suggested in *Chess Digest* magazine that you should gather hundreds of unannotated master games and play them over as quickly as possible to get an "osmotic" feel for where the chess masters put their pieces, especially considering the pawn structure. It is easier than ever to implement this approach if you have a tool like *ChessBase* because it has what I would call "movie mode" where you can use the menu option Game-Replay to watch a game and you can indicate how long a pause you want in between moves. This approach is especially helpful for learning how to play an opening line by following many games of good players.

♟ The "Excruciating Detail" slow-approach. In this approach you take hours to review a game, painstakingly reading each annotation note (sometimes using multiple boards for variations), playing out every annotated variation, guessing the moves of both players, and checking the moves with a computer chess engine, etc. At this extreme you spend lots of time on each position, such as I suggest in the Stoyko Exercise (see the archived *Chess Exercises*).

Both of these extremes are definitely helpful – and almost necessary for drastic improvement – if applied cautiously. If you have never done either, you are surely missing something in your chess education.

Despite the obvious advantages of occasionally going to the extreme, I suggest a norm of getting out a chessboard, playing each move, reading what the author has to say about the move, and then making the next move. At this rate, it should only take 20-40 minutes to play over an annotated game. I am often asked, "But should I play out all the analysis lines?" The answer is, "If you want to, but it is not necessary." I would play out any analysis line that answers a question you don't understand. For example, if you wonder why one player did not capture a pawn and the variation explains it, then by all means play out the line (use a separate board for analysis moves if that makes things easier or quicker).

At 20-40 minutes per game you should be able to go through most game collection books in a reasonable amount of time. Going through games quickly and efficiently means you can read more annotated game collections and the more, the better. I played through about 30 in my first two years of serious play and it helped me greatly. That's about 2,000 annotated games.

As for which books to study, see *An Improvement Plan: Theory* (1-2.2) for a list.

Books that contain no text, but just Informator-style symbols are not very good for helping you learn general principles, no matter how in-depth and accurate their analysis. It is worth stating that these books can be excellent for their intended purposes – we are only considering their instructive value for improving players.

Reviewing Your Own Games

The main goal of reviewing your own games for instruction is clear:

To identify your mistakes and take whatever steps necessary to minimize – or elimi-nate – their recurrence!

Besides going over the games yourself, there are many other aids available: strong play-ers/instructors, chess programs, databases, books, etc. You want to make use of as many of these as possible to achieve your goal.

No matter which aids are available, you should first review the game, preferably with your opponent, and especially if the game was played at a decently slow time limit and your opponent is willing! If your opponent is a much stronger player, reviewing the game together will kill multiple birds with one stone, as not only will you be able to discuss the game when your motivations and thought processes are fresh, but you are also getting a free lesson! If you are not currently in the habit of asking your opponent to review your game, especially your losses, then you are missing out on a golden opportunity. I was lucky enough to acquire this habit when I first started tournament play. I thank all my stronger opponents and higher rated friends, especially at the Germantown Chess Club in the late 1960's, who were patient enough to explain to me why I should not do this or that – I loved it and asked for more! I was never defensive in going over my games; I expected that I made mistakes and I wanted to uncover them, understand them, and minimize them. I was never embarrassed by mistakes unless I made one repeatedly – and I think the fear of repetition made me all the more determined not to do so.

If your opponent is not available to review the game, then you should still do so yourself at least once before showing it to stronger players or submitting it for computer analysis. There are several reasons for this quick private review. First, you should form your own opinions about what you did wrong and what you should have done differently. Initially you won't be too successful, but that is OK; you need to hone your skills at self-evaluation and you will improve each time you do so. Secondly, when you play an over-the-board game, it is important that your scoresheet makes sense before showing it to stronger play-ers or an instructor.

One advantage of going over web-based games, from an instructor's standpoint, is that the game is recorded perfectly and every move is time-stamped: both are greatly beneficial in helping me aid my students. Reviewing an over-the-board game while it is fresh in your memory will help you find discrepancies and ambiguities in your scoresheet (which rook went to d1?) so that the better players will be able to help you more efficiently. A third rea-son to review your game yourself is to solidify your memory of what happened, so that when/if the stronger player asks you about it, you will feel more comfortable. When I re-view a game I often ask questions such as, "Why did you take so much time on that move?" and "What was your reason for choosing this move?" or "Did you consider playing this al-ternative?" If you have already reviewed the game, then your answers are usually both fresher and reinforced.

Whether the "once over" is alone or with your opponent, you are now ready to make use of any aid available. It may be more effective to use a physical board to review games, but sometimes easier to view a game electronically, especially if the game was played and stored on the computer (online or against a computer opponent).

With regard to the opening, I will repeat a common *Novice Nook* mantra: After each game (or series of blitz games), review the opening(s) to ascertain, "If a future opponent makes the same moves, where would I differ to improve?"

For example, suppose as White you got into a Two Knights Defense:

1 e4 e5 2 Nf3 Nc6 3 Bc4 Nf6

White to play

...and then played 4 d3. While 4 d3 is a reasonable move, you might find, after investigation, that 4 Ng5 (Classical) or 4 d4 (Max Lange Attack) are both more rigorous.

After each game you should find the tabiya (main line) of each suggested variation, decide which you want to learn (based on what looks more interesting, fits your style, or meets whatever criteria you wish), then do whatever is necessary to learn it (such as playing out the line several times) so that if the sequence happens again, you will know it. After this, you should be able to play the appropriate move(s) next time that sequence arises.

If you can't find the sequence in a book or don't know what to do (a common complaint), you can either analyze the position with a chess playing program or ask a stronger player what you should do. The most likely scenarios are:

- ♟ One player made an innocuous move that causes the opponent no trouble and you can continue to develop unimpeded.

- ♟ The move that can't be found is an outright blunder whose refutation can be spotted by the program/strong player.

- ♟ One player played a rare line that is perfectly acceptable but is not in your book/database. In this case you can either learn the rare line (by getting additional material or following the computer's suggestions) or avoid it by playing a different move.

Learning Opening Lines and Ideas (6-1) contains additional useful advice on learning openings.

If you don't take the steps to learn what is correct *you will repeatedly make the same opening mistakes, or innocuous moves, and will improve at a much slower rate.* Repetition of opening miscues also makes it difficult to compete with others who may be currently competitive with you, but are doing more to identify and minimize their errors. Moreover, it is just as effective to perform the instructive opening search after fast games; since re-searching opening moves is not dependent on the speed of the finished game and, with quick games, you can play more frequently and experiment more freely with the openings than you can in "more important" slow games.

No matter how much players want to improve, many don't do the simple tasks that would be quite beneficial. My suggestion to "look up each game after you play it, to make sure you are not repeating your mistakes" is also one of my most ignored pieces of advice. I am not a big fan of weaker players memorizing lots of opening lines they will never play. However, it is quite a different issue to spend a small amount of time learning how to play your openings a little better each time they occur. A long journey begins with a single step.

Recently a prospective student admitted that he had played thousands of online speed games, but his rating had remained about the same. It turned out that he owned *Modern Chess Openings (MCO-15)*, but had never researched *any* of those games to see where he could improve. Contrast that to my chess beginning: when I was 16 and played in my first tournaments, I bought *MCO-10*, then *the* English language Opening Bible, and it was *de rigueur* to "look up your opening in *MCO*". Subsequently my copy became overwritten with notes; someday it may become a collector's item...! So which one of us was doing a better job of learning from our games and improving more rapidly?

As for the reviewing the remainder of the game, there are several helpful hints:

♟ If you have recorded the remaining time after each move, you can review your time management to see if you were playing too fast, too slow, or not recognizing critical moves and giving them the proper allocation of your time.

♟ If you own a program like *Fritz*, which has an overnight analysis mode (see the archived ChessCafe article *The Fritz Fairy Analyzes and Annotates While You Sleep*) you can use this great feature, which is especially helpful for iden-tifying tactical errors. For more general advice about using the computer, reference the archived *Using the Computer to Improve*.

♟ Suppose that during a game you chose a continuation without sufficient thought because of time restrictions. Then, after the game is a great time to mull over these decisions, especially for non-critical but interesting positions. The principle is common sense, but logical and powerful:

The closer the decision, the more time and effort it takes to differentiate on what you should do – yet the closer the decision, then the less difference it makes *and the less time you should take!*

Admittedly there are two problems with this truism: First, if you are an international level player, then making a series of second best decisions may be enough to cost you the game. So, on that level, even close decisions have to be taken very seriously. Secondly, weak players often don't recognize when a decision is clear cut or close. Because of this mis-evaluation, they may end up making a bad move quickly, believing the decision does not matter when it is actually critical. Nevertheless, you should save a reasonable amount of your time for critical decisions – especially when there is a large penalty for playing the second best move. So, *if you want to learn something by spending a lot of time studying those close non-critical decisions, the proper time to do so is after the game!*

When reviewing games with a strong player or instructor, indicate the moves where you had difficulty choosing, analyzing, or evaluating, even if you eventually arrived at the correct decision. The strong player may have some useful guidelines or tips on how you could have come to the decision more quickly, accurately, or easily. You should also analyze the most complicated tactics with the stronger player, so they can show you key patterns that are likely to recur in future games when you find yourself facing a similar attack – or defense! Sometimes good players like to spend hours trying to find the "truth" of the position: whether an attack was sound or a sacrifice could have been made. Whenever possible, it is both fun and educational to go along for the ride.

Another post-game agenda is to identify all the moves where the evaluation changed drastically. The last point where the game changed from drawing/winning to losing is called *The Losing Move*. If it is a move that takes you from drawing/winning to losing (it is impossible for you to make a move that takes you from drawing to winning or losing to drawing; see the archived ChessCafe article *Steinitz, Zermelo, and Elkies*) but later your opponent blunders and lets you off the hook, then your previous error is only a Would Have Been the Losing Move! The attempt to prove all of these transition points is usually very beneficial, as it requires careful analysis using instructive logic such as, "Is that move really forced?" or "Is that move really best?" and "Is the position no longer salvageable with best play?" You can benefit enormously by doing these investigations with stronger players!

Personalized Study Book

Make note of areas for further study when reviewing your game. For example, you may lose an easily drawn king and pawn endgame because you have never studied king and pawn endgames. This may be a good time to do so! Or you may miss a common *removal of the guard* tactic, so it is likely time to hone up on that particular type of tactic. If you got into unnecessary time trouble, try to identify the causes, so that your future time management is better. Remember, your goal is to minimize repetition of future mistakes!

Catalog the mistakes you have identified and wish to avoid repeating in your own *Personalized Study Book*, using a three ring binder. For each page, print a diagram where you made a mistake and underneath describe What you did wrong, Why it was wrong, and What you should have done. You can add positions from almost every game you have played! Then study the book every few weeks to avoid repetition of these errors. Very effective!

Identify what type of annotated master games would be beneficial for future study. For example, if you are making basic mistakes, try Irving Chernev's *Logical Chess Move by Move*. If you need to play more speculative sacrifices, try Tal's games. Not getting your pieces out efficiently? Paul Morphy may be the one. Need to play more straightforward and logical? Try Capablanca. Give up too easily in bad positions? Then Emanuel Lasker or Victor Korchnoi might be for you. If you are already a very good player but need to understand modern grandmaster play? Then I recommend Watson's *Secrets of Modern Chess Strategy*. One word of warning: don't study a book which is over your head, even if it contains something indicated. For example, a well-annotated Morphy game might be helpful for everyone, while Watson's book is not really recommended until you are tactically sound and can implement all the basic guidelines well, say a minimum FIDE rating of 1800.

In conclusion, studying your games and annotated master games can be one of the best ways to improve. Of course, continue to evenly mix theory (study) and practice. Going over games is great, but if you don't consistently try to apply what you have learned – to see if you can minimize those same mistakes – may yield diminished returns on your time. So play lots of slow chess – and throw in some fast chess as well – to enhance and reap the benefits as well as providing more fuel for future study.

1-4) The Big Five

If you have read 200 chess books and you are still not that good; then reading a random 201st is not likely the key to getting better!

The most important aspects to concentrate upon to start playing good chess ('The Big 5'):

1. Safety
Tactics; especially important are *counting* and basic motifs.

2. Piece activity
Use all your pieces all the time.

3. Thinking process
Real Chess, efficient analysis.

4. Time management
Pace yourself to use almost all your time every game and allocating more time to critical moves.

5. General guidelines/principles
Learning them, and how and when to apply them.

Bonus
Make your chess learning fun.

If weaker players would concentrate on just these five, they would improve quicker. Plus, most of the remaining information can be acquired much easier if it is studied later in the learning process, when it has The Big Five as a baseline to build upon.

1. Safety

What is it?
Basic Tactics. I define *tactics as the "chess science" of piece safety*. It involves forced sequences that win material or checkmate; preventing these are *defensive tactics*. See *The Five Levels of Tactics* in *A Different Approach to Studying Tactics* (5-1).

Why is it on the list?
See *The Three Show-Stoppers* on page 48.

How do you improve at it?

The first and most important step to becoming proficient at tactics is understanding safety and counting, followed by repetitious study of very simple problems, those involving counting and single motifs (pins, double attacks, removal of the guard, etc). This repetitious study mimics the "Seven Circle" tactics drills suggested by de la Maza in *Rapid Chess Improvement*. See *An Improvement Plan: Theory* (1-2.2) and *A Different Approach to Studying Tactics* (5-1).

Learning basic tactical motifs "cold" in order to do harder problems better is similar to learning multiplication of one-digit numbers as the basis for all multiplication. The following example shows how a more difficult tactical problem may consist of basic components:

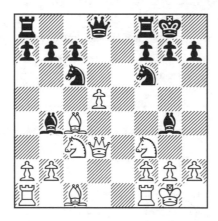

Black to play and win a pawn

1...Bxf3

Temporarily giving up the bishop pair, but achieving removal of the guard on the e5-square!

2 Qxf3

If 2 dxc6 Bxc6.

2...Ne5

Fork and *removal of the guard* on d5!

3 Qe2 Nxc4

Getting rid of the bishop pair, as a bonus to removing the bishop's guard on d5.

4 Qxc4 Bxc3

Removal of the guard again!

5 bxc3

Or 5 Qxc3 Nxd5 winning the pawn, but not 5...Qxd5 6 Qxc7, which is not as good.

5...Nxd5 6 Rd1

A pin that had to be foreseen by Black as harmless to make the combination work!

6...c6 7 Qb3

To threaten both 8 c4 and 8 Qxb7.

7...Qc7

Sidestepping both, and Black is up a pawn.

Although the analogy of tactics to multiplication is not perfect (some difficult tactical problems are *not* just combinations of single motif problems), in general it is necessary to be able to solve the common, easy patterns quickly and accurately to have a decent chance to identify and solve difficult problems.

Amount of time required:

Fairly extensive – at least 100+ hours.

How do you know when you are sufficiently skilled?

If you have a set of easy non-checkmate problems, with at least 400 (preferably more) positions, containing all types of tactical motifs and you can do 85%+ correctly within 10-15 seconds per position, then you are probably fairly capable at that level. A real test is to be able to score that same result with a set of random problems that you have never seen before, and the best indication is if you can recognize those same tactics in game situations!

2. Piece Activity

What is it?

Piece activity means that the piece not only has raw mobility (number of squares to which it can legally move), but also plausible, safe moves. For example, a piece may have ten moves, but if all ten squares are not safe, then it may have no practical activity; *the more activity, the more powerful the piece*. A more active army is both more powerful, relative to the total value of your pieces, and likely more flexible. Why is a queen worth more than a rook? Because it can also move diagonally, thus potentially giving it more activity.

Why is it on the list?

If you lose a piece it cannot do anything, so the reason you keep your pieces on the board is so they can do something. Conversely, a piece that is always doing nothing is almost worthless, so it is almost as if you don't have it. So therefore *you must keep your pieces both safe and active, else neither is worth anything*. As Garry Kasparov has been known to say, "Chess is all about piece activity." For more, see *The Three Show-Stoppers* on page 48.

How do you improve at it?

You *can* improve at keeping your pieces active quicker than almost any item on this list. Yet, my experience shows that weaker players have more difficultly with this than with many of the other items! Following many of the piece activity guidelines requires discipline more than knowledge. It is easy to acquire knowledge but for many it is much more difficult to acquire discipline. The temptation to make a premature attack, "save your rooks for the endgame", or follow any number of bad habits that leave some pieces inactive or awkward at best, is too great for many. Sometimes these bad habits are rewarded and psychologically reinforced with an undeserved victory over weak opponents. It is important and helpful to consistently follow guidelines such as:

- ♟ "In the opening, move every piece once before you move any piece twice, unless there is a tactic";
- ♟ "In the endgame the most important idea is often to activate your king";
- ♟ "A premature attack is doomed to failure";
- ♟ "If you don't know what to do, identify your worst piece and make it better".

When I first started playing chess and was instructed to develop each piece efficiently in the opening, I initially thought, "So what? If I get a tempo behind, I can always catch up later. My opponent can't conduct an entire attack with only one extra piece out for one move." But I was wrong. Once I started playing stronger players and fell behind in development, they used their superior force to make threats – *taking the initiative* – and I was usually so busy addressing those threats that I could *never* catch up in development and lost in the end! So I became much more cognizant and efficient in getting each piece into play.

Amount of time required
Theoretically, very little time is required, but in practice sometimes quite a while.

How do you know when you are sufficiently skilled?
This probably occurs when, game after game, you are aware that *every* piece needs to be active, *and* you consistently attempt to orchestrate that activity throughout the game.

3. Thinking Process

What is it?
Thinking process is the method you use when you are given a position and are asked to generate a move. In a sense, thinking process consists of not only the events and their sequence, but can also be expanded to include its two most important *contents*: **analysis** and **evaluation** (See *Analysis and Evaluation 2-4*).

Why is it on the list?
Chess is a mental sport and, from that perspective, nothing can be more important than the method by which your brain processes positions and formulates moves. Sure, good players all think somewhat differently, but they all use certain essential features that allowed them to become good and without which they would not have become so skilled. A player with a good thought process can often beat a player with superior knowledge and experience, but an inferior thought process.

How do you improve at it?

- ♟ Listen to good players analyze a position;
- ♟ Read books and articles about thought process (e.g. *The Improving Chess Thinker*);
- ♟ Read annotated master games where thought process is discussed;
- ♟ Take lessons from a good chess instructor who works on thought process.

Amount of time required

Theoretically, little time is required once you know the minimum criteria needed to practice. However, suppose you begin with bad habits and only much later learn better ones. If you need to consciously think about your process during your move, then it takes a bit of practice until you can perform the better thought process subconsciously.

How do you know when you are sufficiently skilled?

One key indicator is if you are rarely surprised by an opponent's good move during a slow game. One of my students got to the expert level and I asked him when was the last time he was surprised by his opponent's move in a slow game. He smiled and wisely asked if I meant a *good* opponent! I said yes, and he replied that it had been *six months* since he had encountered a move he had not considered during a slow game against a good opponent! Also, if you play too slow or too fast for the time limit, obviously something is wrong with your thinking process since neither of those is optimum.

4. Time Management

What is it?

Time management is both the ability to pace yourself so that you play at the "right" speed and use almost all your time by the end of the game, plus the ability to recognize critical positions and allocate more time to them. See Section 3: Time Management for details.

Why is it on the list?

See *The Three Show-Stoppers* (page 48).

How do you improve at it?

Improving thought process (the remainder of Section 2) definitely improves time management. For other tips see *Time Management Suggestions* (page 154).

Amount of time required

Theoretically, little time is required, but to hone your skill requires experience and practice at different time controls. Since that kind of experience requires many different events, this takes some time.

How do you know when you are sufficiently skilled?

If you go to tournaments and are consistently finishing your game near the end of the time control, that is an excellent sign. Occasionally there will be games that end abruptly with resignation (or an early draw) where you have plenty of time left, but these should not be games where you get into trouble, play fast, blunder and resign. If you get into difficulties, slow down, or you may end up with lots of time left on the clock that you could have used to try to get out of trouble. However, in general *it is better to use your time to avoid problems than to try to extricate from them!*

5. Understanding and Prioritizing General Principles

What is it?

Much of each player's knowledge is encapsulated in bits of data that help guide your move choice or other chess-related decisions. This data is referred to as *general principles*, *guidelines*, *heuristics*, or *rules of thumb*. What differentiates a principle from a rule is the strictness of its application. A rule should almost always work; if there are exceptions, they can be delineated. A rule differs from a principle, which is much more judgmental and may have many exceptions. An example of an opening principle is "Move every piece once before you move any piece twice, unless there is a tactic." A principle which is *generally* useful can be inapplicable or even harmful if applied in the wrong situations. Because principles are so variable, learning how to apply and prioritize them becomes at least as important as learning them in the first place (see *The Six Common Chess States* 8-3).

Why is it on the list?

Many players rely heavily on principles to help them understand what to do in any given position. For example, while it is impossible to memorize every opening line ever published, it is quite a bit easier to learn most opening principles and apply them to applicable positions. Because in almost every game you are "out of book" at some point, the answer is not to learn more opening lines, but to consistently and wisely apply opening principles.

How do you improve at it?

When you read books or review games with stronger players, the author (or stronger player) often quotes helpful principles for certain positions, or explains why a given guideline might not apply or is superseded by a more important guideline. Any well-annotated master game usually includes several principles, so reading at least hundreds of annotated master games is extremely helpful. Alburt and Lawrence's *Chess Rules of Thumb* and Soltis' *The Wisest Things Ever Said About Chess* are devoted exclusively to guidelines. Many other books (such as my *Looking for Trouble*) put general principles in italics, bold, or in a box to bring these important ideas to your attention. My website has a "Guidelines/Principles" page.

Amount of time required

A moderate amount of time is required to learn the guidelines; and a great deal of time (longer than any other of the Big Five by far) is required to learn how to weigh and prioritize them based on the situation.

How do you know when you are sufficiently skilled?

You are never as good at understanding and prioritizing guidelines as you can be. But don't be discouraged; there are ways to tell if you are adequate. For example, if you are comfortable in the opening each time you are out of your "book", then you probably have a sufficient understanding of general opening principles. Similarly, if in the endgame you are comfortable knowing how your goals and plans differ from those in the opening and the middlegame, then again you have probably achieved a passable level of understanding.

Make Your Chess Learning Fun

If you already find chess learning fun, great! But if you don't, see if you can find ways to do so. More in *Chess, Learning, and Fun* (4-2).

What's Not on the Big Five List

There are many important ideas not in the Big Five. They may not be included because they don't sufficiently aid lower rated players' improvement, or are not important enough, or are just areas that can wait until you master much of the Big Five. These include memorization of opening lines, psychology, development of physical traits (stamina, memory), how to play particular pawn structures, advanced tactical patterns, and learning many advanced endgames.

Being good at any one of the Big Five is necessary but not sufficient for improvement. For example, knowing all the basic tactics does not help if you don't keep your pieces active. Your playing strength "chain" is usually only as good as your weakest Big Five "link".

The Three Show-Stoppers

No sense in laying out a grand strategy and then losing a knight.

Suppose you're a baseball batting instructor and a new student wants to improve his hitting:

"Grab a bat, get into the batter's box, and I will help you learn to set up and swing correctly."

But instead the student grabs a basketball and stands on first base! How much can you help him?

This is analogous to what happens when aspiring chess players want to forego the most fundamental basics, but still want to improve. You need to become competent at three of the Big Five before you can reap the major benefits of studying most other chess strategies:

- ♟ Time management
- ♟ Basic tactics, and
- ♟ Activity

Many weaker players fail to realize the necessity of doing all three consistently. If a player consistently fails to follow any of the three, then playing above ~1600 FIDE is very difficult:

♟ Play very fast in slow games and it will be virtually impossible to find better moves than the first one you choose (see *The Fun of Pros and Cons* 2-7). Play much too slow and you will be forced to play fast later with disastrous results.

♟ Don't check before your move to make sure all your pieces would be safe after that move, then you will often lose material and strategy will not matter (see *Is it Safe?* 5-3).

♟ Use a subset of your pieces and you have as much chance as a football team using seven players instead of eleven. *You are the coach of your chess army and everyone is required on the field!* Only if your opponent is a weak player too (and also doing some of these three incorrectly) will you be able to survive. Want to get that outpost knight by moving it a second time? – usually it is best to wait until the rest of your army can support it. *Don't play the opening like the middlegame!*

Many players rated under 1600 approach me for lessons complaining they don't know their opening well enough or they don't know what to do after the opening but, in almost all cases, their perception is a by-product of the three base problems.

Almost everyone gets to a point in the opening where they do not know what to do. I am a master, and in almost all my games at some point my opponent or I have taken one another out of our "book". Yet when weak players get to a point in the opening where they don't know what to do and then ignore basic safety issues and lose material, they usually blame their failure on not knowing the opening well enough rather than playing "Hope Chess". When I point out that if they could consistently play safe moves they would not have this problem, they sometimes counter that they would also rid them of this problem if they just knew their opening much better. However, this problem does not go away for *any* student who plays unsafely, no matter how much they study the opening. Their "opening problem" only disappears after they consistently practice a thought process that allows them to play consistently safe moves.

Some students are of the opinion that I, too, doggedly pursue a particular issue throughout multiple lessons. As it turns out, this issue is always one of the three! The reason is clear. As in math, some consistency in base issues is required before anyone can benefit from the multitude of advanced possibilities. A graphic of this issue:

Slow –> Safe –> Active –> *Explosion* to all other strategies

Since the base three issues are such critical "show-stoppers" (i.e. chokepoints), we need to at least minimally pass them first before the main learning fun can fully bloom.

If a student has a clear problem in any one of the three areas, that is the show-stopper and, unless I am directed otherwise, I have little choice but to attempt to correct that weakness with whatever suggestions, exercises, and psychological help are at my disposal. It's a little like telling that guy on first base with a basketball that he must grab a bat and get in the batter's box; if he does not, it is difficult to help him hit better!

Therefore, some of my weaker students, who have one or more of these major stumbling points, perceive (correctly) that I am working primarily on their show-stopper(s). Stronger students who at least do each of the base three decently never have that same perception of my teaching "weakness"! These stronger students work with the entire possibility of strategy, openings, endgames, positional nuances, time management, etc.

When I first ran into this perception, I felt that something was wrong. However, over the years I began to realize it was because I was doing something right! I could "fix" my teaching weakness by downplaying or ignoring the student's base weak point(s) – that might make those lessons more fun for both me and my student (see *Chess, Learning, and Fun* 4-2). Unfortunately, it would also be shirking my duty.

Therefore, in order to best serve my students, I do – as best possible – try to get them over these show-stoppers. Teaching students who are past the three show-stoppers is more fun than helping those who are not, just from a matter of diversity. There are so many interesting learning issues and chess ideas that jumping around and covering a wide set – depending on student need – keeps the student and instructor fresh. *On the other hand, solving one of the show-stoppers gets the most bang for the buck (rating points in a short time period) and is thus very satisfying for both the student and myself!*

Not coincidentally, show-stoppers seem among the most difficult issues for players to overcome. Players who move too fast often cling to their habit no matter how well I can demonstrate it is damaging and/or readily fixable.

The following example is from a student who plays extremely fast in slow games. He was Black and the time limit was G/45 + 45:

1 d4 d5 2 Nf3 Nc6

Blocking his break move (see *Break Moves: Opening Lines to Create Mobility* 8-4).

3 e3 Bf5 4 c4 dxc4 5 d5 (see following diagram)

White threatens 6 dxc6. Although he would lose castling rights after 6...Qxd1+ that is not even an issue if a piece can be won. *Often weak players have trouble weighing plusses and minuses that do not all involve material*, but the overwhelming majority of non-beginners would correctly win the knight even if they lose the right to castle.

Black understood he should move the knight. His options are limited, as 5...Ne5 and 5...Nd4 are clearly not safe. 5...Nb8 is safe, but many weak players dismiss similar retreats even if it were the only safe move and thus clearly best! Less obvious is 5...Na5, when 6 Qa4+ (always see if you can meet your opponent's checks, captures, and threats safely) 6...c6 saves the knight by guarding it with the queen. This common safety pattern is often missed by beginners. On the other hand, 5...Nb4 is clearly unsafe as 6 Qa4+ picks up the knight without any special fuss.

Black to play

These safety issues would be the first thing to go through a strong player's head, and *he would take time to decide if the best position that White could achieve after 5...Na5 is better than the one after 5...Nb8.*

However, my student *almost immediately* played **5...Nb4??**. I asked him why he made this move so quickly and he replied, "My plan was to attack c2." When I pointed out that 5...Nb4 was unsafe as the queen check wins the knight for nothing, he replied "Yes, I know. That's what happened, but you asked me why I played this move and the answer is that I wanted to attack c2."

It is instructive to examine this student's thought process and see how we can minimize the chance of similar train wrecks in the future. The student:

- ♟ Played extremely fast, almost immediately.
- ♟ Wanted to make an "aggressive" move despite any safety issues.
- ♟ Wanted to make an "aggressive" threat no matter that the threat was easily defended.

All of the issues listed below are characteristic of weaker play:

- ♟ There were quite a few safety and strategic issues that need to be resolved, but the student did not take the time to examine them. What's worse, he did not even seem interested in the fun of finding and comparing the various issues. He just wanted to play a move and see what happened, despite the enormous amount of time on his clock. There was no issue of *if you see a good move, look for a better one.* 5...Nb4 attacked c2, and that was all that mattered.

- ♟ The student played complete Hope Chess and did not make any attempt to see if 5...Nb4 could be refuted by any checks, captures, or threats. White's only check after 5...Nb4 won the knight, so it could be easily spotted, but the student admittedly made no attempt to determine the safety of his move. The idea of aggression is completely nullified if the aggressor's piece can just be won for nothing, thereby eliminating the threat!

- ♟ White has defenses to 5...Nb4. Besides the best defense of 6 Qa4+, he could defend with other moves such as 6 Na3. The fact that his threat was easily met was of no consequence to Black. He completely ignored the ideas expressed in *The Three Types of Reasonable Threats* (page 338), not only making no attempt to see if the defenses made 5...Nb4 look bad, but not looking for any defenses at all. This lack of concern for the opponent's reply may be characteristic of extreme blitz play, but is hardly conducive to good play in a slow game.

This type of mistake is not uncommon with weaker players. When I point out what they did wrong and how they could fix it, they are often much more interested in learning new moves in the Caro-Kann! In other words, they wish to skip the three base issues and get right to the "fun" strategy subtleties. For these players, it is as if the problems caused by playing too fast in dangerous positions will be solved by learning a new opening move or how to attack an isolated pawn.

In this example the student did not seem overly concerned playing so quickly and seemed nonplussed over my attempts to get him to first take some time to address the safety issues. Thus, it is not surprising that he continued to play fast in subsequent games, resulting in many similar disasters. I am doing my best to convince him that many of his troubles will disappear if he slows down and attempts to follow the two most basic principles: *If you see a good move look for a better one*, and *When you select a candidate move first determine if the move is safe*.

Instead of just suggesting "Don't play fast", I constructively attempt to explain what the student should do next time in a similar situation. In this case I suggest "When faced with alternate ways to save a piece, first take the time to figure out all the possible moves that *might* save the piece. Then determine which of those candidates are safe by asking 'If I make this move, can I meet all my opponents' replies of checks, captures, or threats?' Once you determine which moves are safe, take time to analyze what your opponent is likely to do on each, and finally evaluate to determine which resulting position you like best."

If over subsequent slow games the student makes no attempt to slow down and follow the most basic principles, it is counterproductive to ignore these important issues and go on to new ones. If someone has trouble with addition, you don't skip to multiplication!

The challenge for me is to get the student to slow down. If constructive suggestions – and other conventional wisdoms – don't work, I can't resort to the football coach's ultimate solution of benching the player! For this reason I kidded with one of my students, a psychologist:

"Suppose I have a student who has a basic problem and I not only identify what they are doing wrong, but also make several suggestions on how to correct their problem and the benefits of doing so. They are willing to make the correction, but unable to do so. Then the issue is no longer one for a chess instructor, but rather one for a chess psychologist, and I will subcontract them out to you. After you get them over the hump, give them back to me and we will proceed!"

This was stated tongue-in-cheek, but only partly so! If a student is having trouble overcoming one of the basic issues, then this is usually more frustrating for them than it is for me. They understandably want to get past the problem and get on to the more strategic challenges of chess.

It takes more than just determination to do the basics correctly. To show how difficult it can be to overcome one of these issues, take the main opening goal to *safely, effectively, and efficiently develop all the pieces*.

I estimate that approximately 500 of my students, when they first began lessons, did not know to – or could not – develop all their pieces, move after move, game after game. To each student I suggested an important principle to help achieve this goal:

In the opening, move every piece once before you move any piece twice, unless there is a tactic (see *Strong Principles vs. Important Principles* 8-1).

If you had asked me before I began instructing what percent of players who do not follow this principle, after being familiarized with it, would be able to successfully apply it and start developing all their pieces somewhat consistently, I would have guessed twenty-five percent or so. My guess would not have been close.

The correct answer is that only *one student* was able to do so right away. The rest either took a while or were never able to consistently activate their army. Of course, all students who became much better players were eventually able to do so, but that is the point: for most players, it is difficult, but necessary, to overcome the most basic bad habits. I am well aware of this difficulty and, while it may seem repetitive to students, I think that unless directed otherwise (the student is, after all, the boss), a good instructor should patiently work on these areas to best serve their students' needs.

1-5) Getting the Edge

You can lead a horse to water, but you can't make him drink.

Below I list my *least* followed advice: the suggestions I make that are followed by the smallest percentage of students. By turning this around and following all – or almost all – of the advice, the reader will surely *Get the Edge* over most of their rivals on future improvement!

For each I will provide:

- The advice;
- Why it is helpful;
- Why players are sometimes reluctant to follow the advice;
- The consequences of not following the advice.

Decide for yourself if the subsequent advice is both worthwhile and sufficiently fun. If so, reap the benefits!

1. The advice

Review each of your games, identifying opening (and other) mistakes with the goal of not repeatedly making the same mistake.

Why it is helpful?
One of the most meaningful things someone can do to improve at anything is to identify your mistakes and misconceptions and set up an "improvement loop" to help avoid repeating those mistakes (see *The Improvement Feedback Loop* 1-1 and *Reviewing Chess Games* 1-3). For example, look up opening lines to see what you would do differently next time.

Why players are sometimes reluctant to follow it?
Reviewing is not as much fun as playing, and it can be somewhat time consuming. This is ironic because so many players love buying opening books, sometimes taking enormous amounts of time trying to memorize lines that rarely occur in games. It is far more efficient to learn not to repeat one's mistakes. Looking up an opening after a game involves learning how to use a book like *Modern Chess Openings-15* (see the archived *How to Use MCO-14*) or a database, finding a strong player, or loading your game into a chess engine.

What happens when it is not followed?
The player repeatedly makes the same mistakes and doesn't learn the proper patterns. That player's improvement either halts or suffers serious setbacks.

2. The advice

Read many annotated game collections (review each game relatively quickly).

Why it is helpful?
Many of the best players and instructors have written books and articles to help future generations. By looking at entire games, the aspiring player learns about openings, middlegames, and endgames all at one fell swoop. Playing through annotated games spurs improvement as the reader learns how good players consistently handle common positions and problems. It is the best way to learn planning.

Why players are sometimes reluctant to follow it?
It takes quite a bit of time (even more so, since players often read these games too slowly) and, for some, it is not fun. Treating each game like a mystery tale, where you find out how the winner takes advantage of his strengths and his opponent's weaknesses, is a good way to maximize the fun of reviewing each game.

What happens when it is not followed?
A player who does not read annotated game collections is slower to learn how to handle common positions and problems, good planning, and technique. On the other hand, playing over the same game repetitiously, or too slowly, has two drawbacks:

♟ A player gets diminishing returns on multiple reads of the same game; and even more importantly,

♟ It is far more beneficial to read how multiple authors describe similar situations. One author's text in a particular game can be prejudiced, incomplete, or even incorrect. However, if you read works from a dozen authors, it is not only more interesting and memorable, but also probably likely homing in on the "truth" of the situation. *The goal is to develop a "chess conscience" where these authors whisper in your ear about how to play all kinds of positions.*

3. The advice

Play as many very slow games as possible. The game should be played with a clock, and each player has at least one hour to complete the game.

Why it is helpful?
Slow chess is still the dominant form for providing prestige and titles. Moreover, slow chess has superb instructional value. Slow chess improves visualization – moving the pieces around in your head for 20 minutes on a move reaches analysis depth not possible in fast chess. Slow chess also affords opportunities to practice good criticality assessment and related "micro" time management, and builds knowledge of positions into long-term

memory for later retrieval in all types of games. It teaches players the rewards of patience and the ability to live with their decisions. Playing "slow" games without a clock loses many of the key benefits, while playing games at a slow time control, but playing much too quickly, loses almost all the benefits.

Why players are sometimes reluctant to follow it?
Blitz players often think that they can get much better playing exclusively fast games. Slow chess does not have the addictive adrenaline rush of blitz games and requires considerably more time at one sitting. In addition, sometimes the player needs a little knowledge and/or proactive searching to find appropriate opponents, both online and at local clubs.

What happens when it is not followed?
Players that do not play much slow chess – or play slow time limit games quickly – have poor time management when they do, have trouble with visualization and, in general, don't improve as rapidly as those that can play a steady diet of good opponents in slow games.

4. The advice

Use about ten percent of playing time for fast games.

Why it is helpful?
Because playing all slow chess or all blitz chess misses the best instructional benefits offered by both. Playing fast chess provides:

- Great opening practice per unit time (and less "penalty" for falling into traps);
- Practice of time management for time trouble aspects of slow play;
- Practice for building technique (winning won positions);
- More practice per unit time for pattern recognition (both for general board vision and specific patterns);
- Help for developing a quick feel for danger;
- Opportunity to develop criticality analysis skills to help a player decide which moves require more thought.

Why players are sometimes reluctant to follow it?
Slow players often resist quick games because either it is not "real" chess, it is "too fast for me", they are disgusted with their mistakes rather than embracing them as learning opportunities, or feel the clock is not an important part of chess, so playing fast is antithetical to making "good moves".

What happens when it is not followed?

The player does not get enough chance to practice their openings. Time trouble in slow games remains a terrifying place never to be conquered. Practicing varied board positions is more difficult as there are less "fun" games to practice technique and experiment with unclear sacrifices to evaluate them better for more important games. The player slowly or, more likely, never fully develops the criticality analysis skill necessary for properly deciding how much attention each move deserves.

5. The advice

Play fast games with the same increment as in meaningful games.

Why it is helpful?

If your goal is to be a good over-the-board player (such as to get titles or championships), then you need to play over-the-board chess at some point. But each federation has suggested time limits. For example, the United States Chess Federation has a preference for digital clocks and a five-second time delay in slow games. But many serious games come "down to the wire" where quick thinking is rewarded, and learning how to best pace yourself is very important. If you cannot play intelligently with little time on your clock and a five second time delay, you are at a huge disadvantage. Online play offers increments, which are similar to time delay. Anyone who can play accurately with a five-second increment can probably play just about as well with a five second time delay. So to best get accustomed to this important skill, fast games, over-the-board and online, should primarily be played with the same increment as required by your national federation.

Why players are sometimes reluctant to follow it?

Older experienced players are used to "five minute" chess where there is no time delay. This "race condition" play is more difficult than time delay and requires a somewhat different skill set. Others like the adrenaline and randomness of bullet games. Another reason is that online services have no proactive program to encourage online games at that time limit. For example, the Internet Chess Club, by popular demand, has a separate rating system for five minute play, but none for more helpful games with a five second increment.

What happens when it is not followed?

Depending upon their experience, players who practice the wrong speed time controls and then get into time trouble in important over-the-board games either play too fast (because they are used to zero increment games where every extra fraction of a second counts) or play too slow (because they are playing games with either too large an increment or possibly not playing the fast games at all). Either way can be equally disastrous to your results, since errors can easily occur in very critical situations.

6. The advice

Go over your games with your opponents.

Why it is helpful?

Even if your opponent is not as strong as you are, it is likely you can learn something from him. For example, you might be a better analyst, but he might be a better evaluator, or know the opening better. Asking your opponent "What would you have done if I had done this?" or "What do you think was the losing move?" gives you insight into how others think: their fears, their misconceptions, and their differing perceptions. Also, going over the game with your opponent gives you a chance to analyze without a computer or a very strong player, so you can test your "moving the pieces" analysis skill before getting skilled information that will prejudice your thinking. This gives you more raw data with which to improve your analysis and evaluation skills. Of course, when a stronger player does chime in, it is usually so much the better.

Why players are sometimes reluctant to follow it?

Some players have legitimate reasons: a more pressing engagement or they have no desire to improve. But, for the most part, weaker players do not go over the games with their opponents because they don't realize how much it will help in the long run, are afraid they will have a bad social experience, or they don't know what they are looking for.

What happens when it is not followed?

An amazing opportunity is lost. I can't tell you how much I learned from the many hours going over my club and tournament games with my opponents and others. I was like a sponge, absorbing what everyone had to say, and comparing it to my feelings during the game. Lacking this vital feedback about your thoughts and play is definitely a drawback in any rapid improvement plans.

7. The advice

Study general opening principles, not lots of lines in opening books.

Why it is helpful?

In almost all the games you ever play, you will find yourself "out of book" – on your own – at some point, no matter how much you try to learn or memorize opening lines. And once you do, your playing strength reverts to your normal rating. Many intermediate adults either know little about general opening principles or just don't follow them consistently: they don't know where to safely place their king, when to push a rook pawn, or when to get their pieces in front of or behind pawns. Yet they think the answer to their problems is to buy another opening book, lock themselves in a closet, and memorize it for the next event. When their opponents inevitably either avoid the opening directly or play some rare line that is just bad, they have no idea how to take advantage of it because "it is not in the book".

Why players are sometimes reluctant to follow it?

Learning opening principles seems too vague. Besides, the most palatable way of doing this is to review many annotated master games and, as we have seen in #2, they don't find this interesting either!

What happens when it is not followed?

Once a player gets out of their "book" they start to play inferior moves and their game often deteriorates. Then they complain either "I need to study the book more" or "I got all my pieces out, but then I did not know what to do". The latter is not uncommon since, by not following good development principles, the pieces are often developed to unpromising or inactive positions.

8. The advice

Practice Good Time Management.

Why it is helpful?

Both micro and macro time management are very underrated as to their importance toward improvement. Proper micro time management ensures that you apply more time to the moves where you get more "bang for the buck": critical or complicated tactical positions. Proper macro time management (using up almost all your time each game, assuming it is not a miniature) ensures that you could not have spent any less effort on the entire game. You did the best you could, using up all your time and avoiding severe time trouble.

Why players are sometimes reluctant to follow it?

Many players grew up playing chess without a clock, and so don't understand the importance of the clock in competitive play. Others play way too fast or too slow, and changing these bad habits is sometimes very difficult: fast players find slowing down to be boring or don't know what to think about; slow players often have excessive fear of making a mistake, even in non-critical positions where the tenth best move is almost as good as the best move.

What happens when it is not followed?

The main results are either ruinous time trouble (for slow players), playing way below your potential level (for fast players), or making enormous mistakes on critical moves (for those that can't recognize criticality correctly or play too fast even if they understand the entire game is on the line).

9. The advice

Don't worry about your rating or losing rating points.

Why it is helpful?

Ratings are no more than an accurate reflection of your playing strength. If your rating is too low, it will improve just by normal play. If it is too high, then it is not deserved, so unless you want to quit forever, the only way to get it to that level is to improve. Not worrying about your rating, and instead concentrating on your playing strength, helps you make intelligent decisions about how to improve your game instead of "protecting" or artificially manipulating your rating. In general, playing makes you a better player and eventually raises your rating, while not playing, for whatever reason, is usually counterproductive.

Why players are sometimes reluctant to follow it?

Because ratings are so accurate, over-the-board and online chess has become a "class" society, where a player's rating grants prestige and status. Most new players, who start out playing for fun, unfortunately soon fall victim to the lure of rating status, and begin worrying about their rating instead of playing for fun and learning. It is ironic that *if you play for fun and learning, then your rating will eventually go up, and if you worry about your rating and try to protect it, then it probably won't!*

What happens when it is not followed?

Players who worry about their ratings often start playing to protect their rating, for example taking draws against stronger players when winning to garner a few precious rating points. They might agree to a draw in an endgame with a higher rated player to gain rating points rather than continuing to play, which results in learning and increased strength. Or, even worse, they stop playing altogether because they become so rating conscious. I had a college roommate who loved chess, but stopped playing because he got his rating up to 1800 and wanted to maintain it forever.

10. The advice

Repetitively study easy tactics until you can do them quickly and accurately.

Why it is helpful?

The main reason is defense (see the third section in *Odds and Ends* 9-3, page 375)! In my experience, most intermediate players find basic tactics "too simple" – so long as there is a sign saying "White to play and win" and they are White! But turn that same situation around: don't put up any signs and make the same tactic *the opponent's possible reply* to their candidate move. Now the question becomes "Is it Safe?" (5-3) and those same intermediate players have to find their opponent's tactic before committing to their move, without warning, and often miss it. *But if you are so familiar with the pattern that you know it upside down and inside out, then you can see it upside down from your side of the board and won't play that losing move.*

Why players are sometimes reluctant to follow it?

Many players find repetitively drilling basic tactics boring. But one can always make it into a game by taking statistics, trying to break your timing or percentage records, etc. Just as importantly, they may figure such study is unnecessary because "they never miss those tactics", but they are not missing them *on offense*. Those tactics are not too easy to study if those players consistently miss them on defense.

What happens when it is not followed?

Players don't recognize basic safety patterns sufficiently and end up losing material by playing unsafe moves via Hope Chess.

11. The advice

Be proactive about attending clubs or becoming involved in chess. Support chess through your national chess federation.

Why it is helpful?

Chess includes everything from grassroots at the local level through the national federations and grandmasters. While few suggest that average players should start a support fund for a country's grandmasters, joining a national federation supports chess in general. This support extends not only to grandmasters but all the way back to those same grassroots players. For example, players who would never join the USCF still wanted to root for Bobby Fischer in Iceland in 1972 or Hikaru Nakamura today, but don't stop to think that these players would not be able to represent the US without the members of the USCF supporting them via their dues.

Why players are sometimes reluctant to follow it?

They think "it's not worth the money" or "I don't play enough over-the-board to justify joining", instead of "by joining I am supporting chess in my country and around the world."

What happens when it is not followed?

National federations need a consistent number of members to develop and support ongoing programs. If programs are constantly being funded and then cut back or cancelled, not only do the targets of those programs suffer, such as scholastic groups, the national magazine, and strong players, but eventually so do all chess players.

12. The advice

Create your own personalized study book of positions from your games.

Why it is helpful?

Most players believe that the primary way to improve is by reading chess books, but that approach only "adds positives" (see *The Theory of Chess Improvement* 1-1). When your rating gets stuck, it is often because you are not subtracting negatives: you repeatedly make the same mistakes and never shed your misconceptions. One way to help minimize the recurrence of mistakes is to identify and study them by creating a unique Personalized Study Book (see *Reviewing Chess Games* 1-3).

Why players are sometimes reluctant to follow it?

It takes a little impetus to get started. Today most players either play games online or put their over-the-board games into a computer program, so printing out positions where you made mistakes should be easy. Of course, you need a way to identify your mistakes. For basic tactical patterns a chess engine will do, but other mistakes may be more difficult to recognize. For example, suppose your mistake was taking seven minutes to decide where to put your bishop on move six and then you got into unnecessary time trouble and lost. Hopefully you can recognize that taking that much time was a big mistake and will be able to put that position in your book, noting that taking less time and using general principles to guide your decision would have left valuable extra time for later.

What happens when it is not followed?

The chances of making the same mistakes are increased.

13. The advice

Until you get to be a fairly good player, *don't have a "better idea"* than following well-known principles/guidelines.

Why it is helpful?

You have to learn how to walk before you can run. In elementary school there is no sense in attempting to learn multiplication before addition. Similarly, in chess there is no sense in spending huge amounts of thinking time figuring out when there are exceptions to general principles if one doesn't understand *and routinely follow* general principles. In my experience, a player has to be fairly highly rated (1700+) before it becomes worthwhile to spend time investigating the violation of principles. Players rated any lower are much better off just learning and following principles than wasting time trying to break them.

Why players are sometimes reluctant to follow it?

Because it is more "fun" and "creative" to try to break principles, and more restrictive and methodological to follow them. Unfortunately, if you are trying to improve, it is sometimes better to start with something methodological until you develop enough basic skills to try to be creative. For example, I am not a good enough golfer to try to slice on purpose. I should first learn to try to hit the ball straight as much as possible, and only if I become proficient at that should I try to learn how to intentionally slice or fade.

What happens if it is not followed?

Players waste too much time looking for "creative exceptions" to the principles, which usually just results in taking too much time for moves *and* choosing inferior moves.

14. The advice

If you are a fairly weak player, you can almost completely forget about positional nuances like weak pawns and concentrate solely on safety/tactics (material and king safety).

Why it is helpful?

Too many weak players read advanced books and decide to follow Capablanca's or Karpov's lead by subtly trying to pressure his opponent's isolated pawn, but then make an oversight that allows their opponent a basic winning combination. On the average, an isolated pawn might lose a tenth or two (-0.2 pawn) of its value, while even a small amount of material is worth much more. Therefore, tactics dominate play until both players are very strong (see *The Principle of Tactical Dominance* 2-6). Instead, it is much more helpful to follow the advice in *Is it Safe?* (5-3). Most weaker players are OK at finding basic combinations, but are much less proficient at taking the effort to make sure their move does not allow their opponent those same combinations.

Why players are sometimes reluctant to follow it?

There are almost no chess books about how to prevent simple combinations ("Can my candidate move be defeated by any check, capture, or threat?), but chess literature is filled with wonderful master victories over great opponents, who would never allow a simple tactic to win the game. Those games feature superb tactical play and/or subtle positional finesses. Readers get the erroneous idea that the way for *everyone* to win games is to be a brilliant tactician or great strategist. Nothing could be further from the truth when weaker players are involved. In that case the proper – and most effective – approach is to mostly concentrate on safety, and follow basic strategy and principles.

What happens if it is not followed?

A player ends up spending most of their time looking for subtle positional and strategic ideas and then loses game after game to simple tactics they might have seen if they had looked for them. This misplaced emphasis on nuances also leads to bad thought process habits, as a weak player thinks anything but safety first, and has to learn to prioritize the more important issues.

1-6) Finding a Good Instructor

"The best thing you can do to improve your game is to hire a good instructor...But if you can't take criticism, I suggest you take up something more tame, like solitaire." IM Jeremy Silman (paraphrased from Chess Life).

Why an Instructor?

A few times I have been asked "What can a good instructor do for you that you can't do for yourself by going over your game with *Fritz*?" Each time I smile and begin, "If I can't answer that, I am out of a job!..."

Before I give the remainder of my answer, an important point: no one has ever gotten really good at chess without some top-flight instruction. Bobby Fischer boasted that "The Russians had teams but I did it all myself", but where did Bobby go after school when he was growing up in Brooklyn? The "Hawthorne Chess Club" at John Collins' house, which featured some of the best players in the US: William Lombardy, Robert Byrne, Donald Byrne, etc. If you hang out with some of the top players in the country, analyzing with them amounts to pretty good instruction!

One way to answer the question is to turn it around: What are the primary aids software *can* provide that an instructor cannot?

- ♟ It can work for free – or at least a fixed purchase cost – even while you are sleeping (e.g. an overnight analysis mode);
- ♟ If directed, it can perfectly identify all your tactical errors;
- ♟ It can quickly list the best knight moves in order of how good it thinks they are;
- ♟ It can provide a database of opening moves with associated information about each line.

What does that leave? Almost everything. A good instructor can:

1. Look at your games and see what you are doing wrong. He (or she!) can not only point out missed tactics, but every possible weakness, such as misconceptions about how to play positions, planning and position errors, etc.

2. Talk with you and find out what you know and what you don't. If you don't know that both sides should try to attack the opponent's king when castling opposites sides with queens on the board, an instructor will find that out and quickly teach you.

3.   Answer questions and explain things that you don't understand. Suppose you read in a book, "Passed pawns must be pushed" and you don't know when or why. If you ask a good instructor, he should be able to explain it to you until you are satisfied.

4.   Work on your thought process. Listen to you think and make constructive suggestions on how to improve your content, order, priorities, and technique.

5.   Suggest a practice routine, including what media to study, which tournaments and events to participate, how to prepare, and what time limits would be the most helpful.

6.   Suggest a way to learn new information and patterns, whether it be through reading books, watching videos, listening to tapes, etc.

7.   Work on your time management. He can show you in what kind of positions it is important to take your time and in which ones you are wasting your time if you think too long.

8.   Provide psychological support. He can teach you that you will not go straight up and that setbacks are normal and to be expected; teach you how to deal with and learn from your losses. He can encourage you when you are down and keep you on an even keel if you get overconfident.

9.   Help you pick an opening repertoire if you need help. He can teach you what moves you will encounter the most frequently and the most practical ways to expand your knowledge.

10. Help you judge your progress and figure out what that means for your future play, practice, and study.

11. Show you themes and patterns that occur frequently so you know how to handle them when they do.

12. Listen to your concerns and desires and help you decide what are reasonable expectations; when you just need to accept what is happening and when you might need to do more.

I think you get the idea. However, if you do decide to hire and instructor, the following should be very helpful.

Where to Locate Instructors

There are many places to find instructors, but not the Yellow Pages. First you should decide if you wish to have a "live" instructor you can visit (or will come to your home) or one who is "outside": via phone, email or, preferably, the internet augmented by phone. There are several pros and cons to "live" vs. "online":

Internet lessons are usually more flexible since you don't have to travel, nor possibly pay extra for an instructor to visit your home. However, internet lessons may have hidden charges if you simultaneously talk with the instructor on the phone or have to pay for extra web access time (not too likely today). And your or your instructor's computer may occasionally have technical difficulties and you may not be able to get access at lesson time.

Internet lessons offer a much wider range of really good (and bad) instructors. Unless you live near a major chess center, the better instructors on the internet are probably much more competent than your local instructors. In my case I have hundreds of internet-stored puzzles, so getting out a puzzle to fit any occasion is easy for my online lessons.

In-person lessons are, for similarly competent instructors, more effective because you get the full benefit of the instructor's body language, tone of voice, etc. In addition, a live instructor can show you supporting information, such as what a particular book or chess video looks like, how to set a digital clock, or how to fill out a scoresheet. Of course, live lessons do not require a computer with internet access.

If you decide to look for a live instructor, contacting local chess clubs will usually result in a recommendation. If that fails, you can contact your regional affiliate via your national chess federation. If you decide to use internet instruction, then your options for finding instructors widen considerably. Federation magazines have ads for instruction in their classified sections, and there are several lists online, such as at the Internet Chess Club or via general chess sites with specific instructor link pages. A quick search on Google for "Chess Instructors" or something similar should yield a large harvest.

If you can do phone lessons via the internet instead of just typing back and forth, you get a lot more out of the lesson. I have unlimited long distance calling in the US and Canada for that reason. When I was teaching a speech class to engineers, my co-instructor found the following meaningful statistic: "Only 30% of information in speech is contained in the content – the other 70% is divided between voice tone/inflection and seeing body language". So with that information you can see that live lessons are best for communication, followed closely by internet augmented by voice, and dead last is internet/typing or email. Most of the lessons I give are internet augmented by voice, and that works extremely well in almost all cases.

As an example of the problems one might run into via internet/typing, suppose an instructor punches in *"What were you thinking?"* He likely means "What was your thinking process that led you to make that move?" However, some students might misinterpret and think it means "You idiot! What could you be thinking to make such a move?!" This would be an honest mistake, but such a miscommunication can be ruinous. It does bring up another important point: an instructor should always offer *constructive* criticism, never *destructive* criticism.

Choosing an Instructor

When selecting an instructor, feel free to ask for student references and check them. Ask the reference specific questions about how he likes the instructor, what he has learned, how they interact, etc. Most references are happy to give out this information.

Keep in mind that *there is only a weak relationship between the two skills of being a good player* (which requires little or no interpersonal communication skills) *and the ability to instruct* (which requires excellent communication skills). Just as Michael Jordan or Shaquille O'Neal are likely not the best basketball coaches, many top players are not the best instructors (to be fair, several are top-notch). Of course, if for a similar price you can choose between a high quality instructor who is a very good player and another high-quality instructor who is a much weaker player, you should choose the instructor who is also a very good player!

Picking the playing strength of your instructor also depends on what you want to learn. If you are obtaining lessons for your son, a weak player who only wants to learn to compete at the beginning scholastic level (but doesn't want to listen to dad), then you probably don't need a 2500 player; an amateur instructor who is 1700 might be just as good or better. In my experience, players lower than 1700 often inadvertently teach bad habits – or don't know to detect and correct them. Similarly, if you are 1200-1500 and want to learn what it takes to be 2000, probably any decent instructor rated over 2200 is fine, and it may likely be overkill to pay extra for someone over 2500. On the other hand, if you are already 2300 and wish to be 2400, it is much more likely that a high quality GM coach will help you more than a good instructor near or just above your level – the GM will be able to spot your subtle misunderstandings.

Be reasonable with your cost expectations. Full-time instructors have to make a living and you are not paying them benefits like health insurance, so expecting a professional instructor to give you lessons for $8 per hour is not reasonable (don't laugh – some players think this *is* a reasonable fee!). But you don't always have to pay exorbitant prices; it may be possible that an Expert level coach who charges X/hr is better suited for you than a GM who charges 2X/hour. Any top-flight name instructor is likely to charge more, and if they are a top-flight instructor (as opposed to a top-flight *player*) they have earned the right to charge a premium. Be careful, because the instructor field is not so public that it is "efficient" – you don't always get better instruction when you pay more.

Budget in a reasonable amount and be honest with your instructor as to how often you can afford lessons, and hopefully a long-term relationship will develop. Ask the instructor if he gives a discount for multiple lessons, but don't commit until after a lesson or two, to make sure such an investment is wise. For example, maybe after the first couple of lessons you wish to continue and are interested in a long-term discount. You can offer to pay up front for "N" lessons and receive "N+1" lessons, or some other similar deal. Asking an instructor to just lower their prices puts them on the spot, so making a specific offer is much more amenable. Note: you are more likely to get a discount if your lessons are frequent.

If you do work with the instructor only once every month or two, be aware that although your lessons may be vivid to you, he may not remember each word he told you a month ago! On the other hand, a good instructor should take notes so that he does not try to teach you the same thing every month, or completely forget who you are and what you know.

Chemistry between student and instructor is very important. For example, a similar sense of humor is helpful – if you are deadly serious, you probably don't like an instructor that is often lighthearted, and vice versa. The way the instructor handles giving criticism is another key area. Since a student is paying the instructor to help them identify and minimize weaknesses, an instructor must be able to "masterfully" offer constructive criticism in a way that will most help the student, and not make them defensive or depressed. Again, what works for some does not work for all, so an instructor's style is important.

There is another aspect to chemistry that may be worth noting. Just as one can play the man or the board, one can look at chess as a puzzle or a fight (or a science or a ...). If you are someone who is not interested in crushing your opponent's ego, you might not want an instructor with a "winning is everything" attitude, who promotes "you against the world". So if you are looking for an instructor who wants to "lead you into battle", that may be different than looking for someone to lead you to higher proficiency.

During your first lesson or two, issues of discussion should include expectations, goals, and how you feel about methods of getting to those goals. For example, some people learn better via hearing/listening than reading, so the instructor might be able to assign DVDs, videos, and audio tapes instead of books. Other players cannot easily get away for enough time to practice "over the board", so if the instructor feels that slow game play is necessary, he should be able to help you find it, possibly over the internet, without forcing you to drive two hours every week.

Make your expectations reasonable – and known – and expect only reasonable assurances. If you tell your instructor, "I have a rating of 1200. If I take lessons from you every week for a year then I want you to get me to 2000" that is not reasonable and any instructor who promises you such a result is also being unreasonable. Even if he promises the much more achievable result that he can take you from 1200 to 1600 in one year – much more likely, but nothing that could be *promised* – then either that instructor is not trustworthy or your requirements for his business have put him in a corner where he felt he had to make such a promise – which he should not have done anyway. On the other hand, if he says that going from 1200 to 1600 in one year is *possible*, that is not unreasonable – but chasing improbable goals may be very difficult for both of you, especially if you don't play enough games to make your rating move that much even if your playing strength does improve markedly(!).

There should be some synergy between the instructor's methods and views compared to those of his students. For example, I often use the Socratic ("questioning") method and that can be frustrating for some. If this gives a student a problem I adjust, but at the beginning I use this method because it usually helps one understand and not just memorize. Many competent instructors are strong believers that students should study opening principles, but not memorize a lot of lines until they are at least 1300-1400, and even then just start minimally. Emphasizing tactics instead of opening lines is consistent with the "study lots of basic tactical motifs until you get to be a pretty good player" philosophy. So if you are a student rated below 1300 and all you want to learn are opening lines, some instructors are likely more willing than others ("the customer is always right"), and you might be better off with one who emphasizes opening line memorization.

Aspects of Instruction

There are pros and cons about instructors that use primarily "canned" lessons, but mostly cons.

First of all, most canned lessons are aimed at a given rating range. For example, teaching how to play king and one pawn versus king is suitable for players rated 1000-1500, while Philidor and Lucena rook and pawn endgames are not likely helpful unless a player is at least 1500. Similarly, one learns simple openings, guidelines, and tactics before complex ones, so teaching the same canned lessons to everyone is not fair nor especially helpful for those who are not at the intended level of competence.

Secondly, everyone has different weaknesses, so spending a lot of time in an area where the student is already strong is also not helpful. Finally, an instructor should be able to best pinpoint student weaknesses by examining their slow games, so going over those games gives the most "bang for the buck" in my opinion; giving a canned lesson often ignores the important information available in those games, which identifies what the student needs to learn now.

On the pro side, there is certain information that almost everyone needs to have to achieve a certain level, and canned lessons allow and instructor to make sure the student has that knowledge. So every instructor should have some "canned" lessons which he should use when you have appropriate needs.

Two of the most important features of chess instruction for players rated under 1600 are "thought process" and "time management". Therefore any long-term instructor that does not spend at least some time listening to his student think out loud is likely not addressing an important aspect of that student's needs. And since managing one's clock is also very important, that too needs to be strongly addressed in any improvement plan, especially if the student is consistently too slow or too fast. In my opinion, bad time management is a far more serious problem than not knowing the difference between the Sicilian Four Knights and the Kan Variation or not knowing how Botvinnik beat Capablanca in their famous game at AVRO in 1938.

Always question your instructor if you do not understand something he says, he is going too fast or too slow, or he assumes you know something that you do not. After all, *you are paying for one-on-one lessons, so the pacing of the lesson must be optimized for your benefit*!

For example, suppose your instructor says, "That move is questionable because it leads to a backward pawn" and you really aren't sure exactly what a backward pawn is. Then say, "Stop. I have heard of a backward pawn, but I am not sure exactly what one is. Can you define it for me and show me an example?" If you fail to do this, then you are reinforcing your instructor's erroneous assumption about your knowledge, and this may lead to further problems. To defend your instructor in this situation, no one can read minds, and *just because your proficiency is at a certain level does not mean you know exactly all the things the average player at that level knows*. Almost everyone knows more of some things and less of others than the mythical "average" player at your level of competence. So your instructor, especially when you start working with him, may expect that you do have that knowledge, but other than his inquiring each time (which may sound condescending), he will likely make a reasonable assumption. Therefore, if you do not know something you should tell him and not feel embarrassed.

Give your instructor a chance. Chess is a big subject and it takes time, practice, and quite a bit of knowledge flow to noticeably improve. So if you are serious about getting better you will need a steady flow of lessons (part of the "theory" to complement the practice of a lot of slow games) over a period of time. If this is not your intention, you should be honest with your instructor so he knows that you are only taking a few. Often students hint to their instructor that they are in for the long term only to stop after 2 or 3 lessons. If the student knows this in advance, they are doing both themselves and their instructor a disservice by not saying so, as the instructor might have taken a more "short-term" approach he knew the student was not going to continue.

Therefore, if you know ahead of time that for any reason you are only taking a few lessons, by all means say so and your instructor will be able to adjust accordingly (but don't have high expectations of big results!). Reasons for only a few lessons include:

- ♟ You are only out for "a few tips" and not serious improvement;
- ♟ The instructor, for whatever reason, shows himself to be definitely not what you wanted;
- ♟ Costs/budget;
- ♟ You are a raw beginner and just need a "push" to get started – learn the rules, some basic strategy, how to record games, where the local clubs and tournaments are, etc.

Be patient. It will take time for your instructor to both recognize your weaknesses and work with you on them. Moreover, what is not a weakness of concern when you are 1200 may become a big concern if it is not improved by the time you are 1500.

If you do wish to stop taking lessons from a particular instructor, tell him the truth. Don't say "I will call you next week to schedule" when you have no intention of doing so. Truth is a good basis for any relationship, even one that is ending.

Chapter Two

Thought Process

2-1) Making Chess Simple

Some players make chess seem way too difficult.

How does one play "simple" chess? Let's list some key ingredients:

- ♟ Look at your opponent's move to see *all* the reasons why it was made. This includes, but is not limited to, "What are his threats?" Don't forget to look for discoveries and squares that are no longer guarded.

- ♟ Look at what moves you might play (candidates) and what might happen after each of those moves, then determine which one leads to the position you like the best. Always assume the best or most dangerous moves by your opponent. When picking candidates, start with the forcing moves: checks, captures, and threats, for both sides.

- ♟ Look for the Seeds of Tactical Destruction (piece configurations that *may* allow a tactic; see the archived *The Seeds of Tactical Destruction*) for *both* sides. If you have a tactic consider playing it; if your opponent has a tactic, strongly consider stopping it. If there is no tactic, what are you trying to do? If you don't know, consider improving the placement of your least active piece. Try to use all your pieces all the time! Similarly, try to minimize the activity of your opponent's pieces.

- ♟ If you see a good move, look for a better one – you are trying to find the best move that you can in a reasonable amount of time.

- ♟ Manage your time so that you spend much less than average on non-critical moves (use general principles), which allows you to have more time to spend on critical moves (use precise calculation). Try to use almost all your time in each game.

We can summarize good, simple chess in one (!) sentence: *"First, see if there is a tactic for either side; if so, address it; if not, maximize the activity of your pieces and minimize your opponent's."* You can play pretty well, if you just follow that advice! A similar statement is *"Take your time to do the best you can at keeping your pieces as safe and active as possible – while doing the opposite for your opponent's pieces."*

What can go wrong in trying to follow this "simple" advice? Everything! Let's list some of the most common errors:

- ♟ You don't consistently look at what your opponent could do in reply to each of your candidate moves. *Result*: You make a move and he replies with a threat you can't meet. I have dubbed this problem "Hope Chess". Almost every player rated under 1500 plays Hope Chess at least once or more per game and often gets burned.

♟ You see a good move and don't look for a better one. *Result*: You end up playing too fast and making a series of second and third best moves that unnecessarily throw away the game.

♟ You don't try to activate your whole army. *Result*: You end up moving the same pieces over and over again and never fully get *all* your pieces into action.

♟ You don't pay attention to your opponent's moves and mostly concentrate on what you are doing. *Result*: Your opponent often surprises you with threats that you are unprepared for – or did not even see.

♟ You constantly play too fast for the situation. *Result*: Even if you have plenty of time, you overlook simple ideas, often squandering big leads; completely missing what is going on for both sides. Suppose you play a match in which you have 5 minutes and your opponent has 60. What percent of the games would you win? So what makes you think you can play well, if you do not take the time to be consistently careful?

♟ You play too slow during non-critical stages of the game, agonizing over minutiae, such as whether your bishop belongs on e2 or d3! *Result*: When the game finally does become tense, you find yourself running short on time and have to make a critical move quickly. Too bad; you should have saved some time for when you needed it. See the excerpt by GM Rowson (page 75).

♟ You don't repetitively study basic tactics, so instead of recognizing these situations when they occur, you count on your renowned ability to "figure them out". *Result*: You take much more time than you should and you're more likely to overlook a basic tactic for your opponent!

♟ You stop your analysis of candidate moves without trying to determine what your opponent can do to you. *Result*: Your evaluation is superficial and based upon incomplete information. You end up evaluating the wrong positions, come to the wrong conclusions, and make the wrong move. See the archived *Quiescent Errors*.

♟ You *misevaluate* the position – you think you have a superior position when you actually have an inferior position. *Result*: Another wrong, possibly disastrous, move.

♟ You misunderstand why your opponent made a move. *Result*: After you move, your opponent shows you the reason he made his previous move. Oops! This oversight is enough to lose another game. I devoted a chapter to this concept in *Everyone's 2nd Chess Book*.

♟ You don't consider your opponent's best or most dangerous reply to your move. *Result*: You play bad moves and hope your opponent plays worse ones.

Related Problem: You assume your opponent's move is good or safe without doing any analysis. *Result*: You are giving your opponent too much credit! *While analyzing your move, you have to assume your opponent will make the best move; however, when your opponent makes a move, you have to assume it might be a mistake.*

♟ You don't play enough slow (and possibly fast!) chess to develop the necessary board vision to be able to recognize common patterns and get the experience on how to best play them. *Result*: Both the probability and the effect of many of the previously noted problems are enhanced.

If you find yourself a victim of one or more of the above problems, you are not alone! There are plenty of players out there who are nowhere close to master – or even expert – strength, and there is likely some reason besides just raw talent that they are not as good those rated 2000+. You may think the reason you are not as good as the titled players is that they know the Caro-Kann better, but I will bet you a dollar to a donut that your problems are more likely one of the above.

So, by not properly implementing the basics, many players end up making the game of chess much harder than it is! Someone may think they are being clever, because an advanced positional text tells them not to trade pieces when their opponent has an isolated pawn, but then they overlook a simple trade that would win material! Sound familiar? Unfortunately, I see this kind of "penny wise and pound foolish" thought process all the time. In many cases, it would have been better for the player not to even know about positional weaknesses until their rating got to 1400+!

However, this does not mean that chess is an easy game! Let's list a few of the more difficult tasks:

♟ Finding a combination that would make Shirov or Kasparov (or *Fritz!*) proud. These are the kind of tactics featured in *The Magic of Chess Tactics* by Meyer and Müller or *Nunn's Chess Puzzle Book*. There is practically no limit to the difficulty of this part of chess.

♟ Deciding between two subtle but consequential evaluations between similar-looking positions. Not often easy, but sometimes critical. A slight difference can sometimes determine a winning or losing position. This happens all the time in the endgame. Getting it right requires skill, patience, and a good eye.

♟ Deciding on the right plan when none look promising or when many look equally so. It takes experience and judgment to choose the right plan. And, if you go down the wrong track, it could be decisive in the other direction.

♟ Winning a won game, when the margin for victory is razor-thin, and the opposition is putting up optimum resistance. This is sometimes the equivalent of finding a needle in a haystack. This ability is called *technique*. This is different than the ability to win an *easily* won game, as discussed in *When You're Winning, It's a Whole Different Game* (7-3).

Thus, there are many difficult aspects of chess that give the game its deserved reputation for skill and mental challenge. The problem is that too many players think these situations come up almost every move, and they make easy decisions way too difficult. A good example of how to identify and combat this is illustrated by GM Rowson in his excellent book *Chess for Zebras*, when writing about his choice of 18...Rc8 in the following position. His challenge was to avoid playing too slowly at a non-critical juncture of the game:

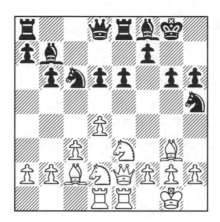

Miles-Rowson
British Chess League (4NCL) 1996-97
Black to play (18...Rc8)

"Generally quite useful, but my opponent was playing very quickly, and it's important not to fall too far behind on the clock without good reason. In this case I have lots of decent moves, and the key is just to play them, and not worry, at this stage, about getting them in the right order. Any problem resulting from getting the order wrong is likely to be less significant than a serious time-shortage later in the game."

Great practical advice! The point is that White is not threatening anything serious – the two armies are still somewhat at arm's length. What Black needs to do is to activate *all* his pieces. His rook on a8 is his least active piece. It can either go to d8 (after the queen moves) or to the semi-open file on c8. Rowson quickly chooses the latter. Notice that if he had chosen a committal move like 18...e5, then there is no way he could have played it as quickly as he did 18...Rc8. The important point is that Rowson identified that he needed something simple and solid and he played it quickly.

If a strong GM like Rowson is not worried about making a minor inaccuracy early in the game against a world-class opponent, can you see how ineffective it is if lesser players spend too much time worrying about the same thing? So don't make chess harder than it needs to be – sometimes playing reasonably good chess is relatively easy. Of course, *if you are not sure your move is non-critical, you must assume the worst case – that it may be critical – and play slowly and carefully. Moreover, for every Novice Nook reader who plays too slowly there are likely two that play too quickly and carelessly* (see Section 3: Time Management).

A Simplified Thought Process

I am occasionally asked to describe a simple thought *process* for slow chess that covers all the possibilities. While this is impossible, interested readers can see more detail in the archived *A Generic Thought Process* and *The Goal Each Move* (2-2). Here is a five step process based on the "simple" ideas expressed above:

1. *What are all the things my opponent's move does?* In other words, what are all the things he can do now that he can't do before, what are his threats (see *It's Not Really Winning a Tempo!* 8-5), and did how did his move parry my previous threat? Don't forget the important step discussed in *Is it Safe?* (5-3). Also, don't stop when you find one reason for your opponent's move, because the ones you miss may cost you the game.

2. *What are all the positive things I want to do?* This step also primarily includes executing or stopping tactics! But it also includes planning; your decisions should be based on both sides' threats, strengths, and weaknesses. See the archived *A Planning Primer*.

3. *What are all the moves that might accomplish one or more of my goals?* In *Initial and Final Candidate Moves* below, I dub these the *initial candidate moves*. I believe World Champion Alexander Alekhine once stated "Don't look for the best move; look for the best plan and the moves that accomplish those goals." He was describing steps 2 and 3.

4. Which *of those initial candidates can I reject immediately because they are not safe?* (See *Is it Safe?* 5-3.) In other words, are there any checks, captures, or threats that can quickly defeat an initial candidate? Once you have eliminated these "unsafe" candidates, the remaining candidate moves are *final candidates*. I call doing this step consistently *Real Chess*. Not doing it is *Hope Chess*. (See *Real Chess, Time Management, and Care* 2-3.)

5. Of the final candidates, which one is best? This requires visualizing the positions each would likely lead to, comparing, and choosing the one that evaluates as best for you.

Interestingly, strong players usually perform steps 1-4 very quickly and then spend the overwhelming majority of their time on step 5. In a sense, many "improvement" chess books (except those on planning) are about performing step 5. However, most weak players omit one or more crucial steps, or else spend way too much time on them! Performing *all* the steps at least moderately well in a reasonable amount of time usually means you are on your way to becoming a good player.

Initial and Final Candidate Moves

The most important moves to consider – for both sides – are the forcing moves.

A candidate move is any reasonable move that you should consider playing. We can define two sets of candidates which occur as part of a normal thought process during a slow game:

- ♟ The *initial* candidate moves that serve some positive purpose, like stopping a threat, starting a tactic, initiating/continuing a plan, or improving the position of a piece;

- ♟ The *final* set of candidate moves from which you must decide "Which one is best?"

The main difference is that you should perform the check *Is it Safe?* (5-3) on each initial candidate move and, if it is not, discard it. The safe ones make up the final candidate list. Sometimes your analysis might add safe moves to the final list that were not on your initial list.

Forcing moves are *checks, captures, and threats*, in roughly descending order of force. Therefore, to be most efficient, they also represent the order in which you should search for candidate moves for both sides: first checks, then captures, then threats, and finally all other moves.

While the phrase "checks, captures, and threats" is snappy, we can delve a little deeper and create a more extensive list of candidate move ordering criteria, roughly in decreasing order of importance:

1. Checks
1a. Checks where there are few possible responses
1b. Checks which bring more pieces into the attack
1c. Checks which bring powerful pieces – especially the queen – closer to the king

2. Moves which meet the *opponent's* threats to checkmate by force

3. Threats of mate in one or threats of a forced mating sequence – especially if the possibilities to parry it are limited

4. Captures
4a. Captures of unguarded or inadequately guarded pieces
4b. Captures of enemy pieces by pieces of lesser value
4c. Captures of enemy pieces by pieces of equal value
4d. Captures of enemy pieces by pieces of greater value

5. Non-Mate threats
5a. Threats to pieces by pieces of lesser value
5b. Threats to pieces by pieces of equal value
5c. Threats to pieces by pieces of greater value
5d. Threats to make an attack on the king
5e. Positional threats: control files, ruin pawn structures, etc.

6. Moves which meet the *opponent's* non-checkmate threats

7. Moves which are not any of the above, but meet some type of positive goal or plan, like developing a piece in the opening, or making a piece better in the middlegame or endgame, or stopping an opponent's piece from getting better, etc.

Let's see how candidate move identification and selection works in practice via three examples, in increasing order of criticality/difficulty.

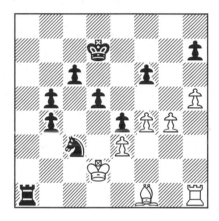

Example #1: Black to play

The first level candidate moves are the ones that carry out some plan or goal. In the above position Black has such a strong position that he might have several plans or goals with corresponding initial candidate moves:

Plan 1: Push the white king into a possible mating net or force a tactic. Candidates: 1...Ra2+ 1...Rd1+, 1...Nb1+
Plan 2: Get the black pawns rolling. Candidates: 1...b3, 1...c5, 1...d4
Plan 3: Get the king into a better position to help the pawns. Candidates: 1...Kd6, 1...Ke6
Plan 4: Stop the white pawns from creating counterthreats. Candidates: 1...h6, 1...Ke7, 1...Ke8, 1...Ke6

Of these choices, Plan 1 would be the most attractive, primarily if it results in an immediate tactical win. Otherwise, the second, which can also win right away, and the fourth, which follows the dictum *when winning easily, think defense first*, are the most attractive. If

Black can stop White from mobilizing his kingside pawn majority he should, with a little care, be able to win as he pleases on the queenside.

However, not all of the initial candidates are viable, even the ones which correspond to the most positive plans. For example, it should be easy to see that although pushing the most advanced passed pawn 1...b3?? would be nice, the immediate reply 2 Kxc3, which also stops 2...b2, puts an end to further consideration and knocks 1...b3?? off the final candidate list. It does, however, introduce a new candidate, 1...Na4, which would allow a safe 2...b3 next move. Another pawn push, 1...d4, initially *looks* refuted because of 2 exd4. However, that is superficial analysis, since after 1...d4 2 exd4, 2...e3+ is a winner as either the b-pawn promotes or the bishop is lost because of the deflection of the king or a further 3...e2. Missing this, and thus dismissing 1...d4 as a viable candidate moves, would be a quiescence error (see the archived *Quiescence Errors*).

In the actual game Black spent three minutes on his move and played **1...c5??**, not checking to see if it should have gotten onto the final list at all (Hope Chess!). Black woke up quickly when White made the not-too-difficult reply, **2 Bxb5+**. This discovered attack won the exchange and a pawn after **2...Nxb5 3 Rxa1**, turning an easy Black win into a difficult fight!

Yet it should not have been. Why spend three minutes on a move if you are not going to spend at least a few seconds to ask: *Is my proposed move safe?* i.e. *if I make this move, what are all his checks, captures, and threats, and can I meet them?* All the other time spent may be wasted if you don't develop the discipline to ask this on every move. In this case 1...c5 fails to *the only check the opponent has in reply, which therefore should have been the* first *reply Black considered when deciding if 1...c5 was viable.* But he missed it completely! With a proper thought process, 1...c5 should have been quickly eliminated and never placed on the final candidate list! This failure to consider even the most obvious reply is a common problem of weaker players, so it follows that they must not be consistently asking themselves the most basic, required question.

Black has many winning ideas, but the computer's choice for best move is the straightforward 1...Ra2+.

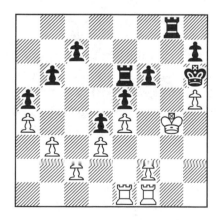

White to play

In this position White is in check, and plays the "active" move 1 Kf5, without seeing if this is safe. Why might it not be? Black replies by saving the rook and attacking the c-pawn with 1...Rc6. This leads to our second example. What does White do now?

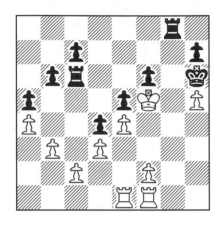

Example #2: White to play

White wrote 2 Rc1 on his scoresheet and then did a sanity check, causing him to erase 2 Rc1 and instead play 2 Rg1, with a total thinking time of about three minutes. This indicated that White had a serious error in his thought process. Why?

Although moves that guard the c-pawn like 2 Rc1 and 2 Re2 should make your *initial* candidate list, you should immediately look for forcing replies and discover that they both fail to Black's only check, 2...Rg5 mate! Therefore, *only moves which prevent mate should make the final candidate list*. For the move 2 Rc1 to make White's scoresheet indicated he did not find 2...Rg5 mate until his sanity check. This is way too late for an efficient thought process. Much better would have been to think:

1...Rc6, what does that do? It saves the rook and attacks the c-pawn, but it also removes my king's only flight square, e6. Suppose I save the pawn on c2. What happens then? What are all Black's checks, captures, and threats? His only check is 2...Rg5+. But that's checkmate! Whoops! That means my only moves are ones that stop checkmate. Which are those? 2 f4 and 2 Rg1. Now what would Black do after each of those, so I can figure out which is better...?

With this correct thought process White would discover 2...Rg5 mate *early* in his thought process and save lots of valuable time by quickly identifying his final candidates as 2 f4 or 2 Rg1, both preventing checkmate. Moreover, with a good thought process, he would have seen 2...Rg5 mate on the *previous move* and made sure he had a good defense; e.g.

If I play 1 Kf5, Black has to save his rook. He will probably move 1...Rc6, also attacking my pawn on c2. Then suppose I try to save my pawn. What would be all Black's checks, captures, and threats? His only check would be 2...Rg5+. But that is checkmate! Whoops! That means my only 2nd moves are ones that stop checkmate. If I don't have one, then 1 Kf5 cannot be played! Also, Black is threatening both checkmate and the pawn on c2, so I had better be careful about playing 1 Kf5 because even if I don't get checkmated I am allowing a double threat which may lose a pawn...

The first two examples were from a weaker player, but, of course, even strong players mistakenly eliminate initial candidate moves, often because of faulty analysis.

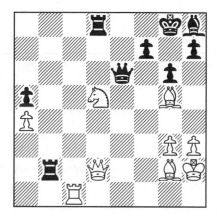

Example #3: White to play – what would you do?

Black has just played **1...Rb2**. The game was played at a G/70 time limit with a five second time delay. White's time was running short and he had 7+ minutes left to complete the game! Let's see what White was able to do in the three minutes or so he took to make this move, which he recognized as very critical.

Material is unbalanced, but with all the hanging material and pins, the "plan" is clear: *Find which tactic – or forcing sequence – gets you the most material (or loses you the least!).* This is not the kind of position where you look for something subtle!

Existing threats: White had threatened Bxd8 with his previous move, and Black had countered by threatening White's queen with ...Rb2, so any move that White considers should either save the queen, give check or checkmate, or attempt to win equal or more material for the queen.

Initial Candidates:

- Checks: 2 Nf6+ and 2 Ne7+
- Captures: 2 Qxb2, 2 Qxa5, and 2 Bxd8
- Threats: 2 Re1, 2 Rc2, 2 Nc7, 2 Nf4
- Moves that save the queen: 2 Qd3, 2 Qe1, 2 Qe3, 2 Qf4, 2 Qd1

Whew! How to proceed with such an array of potential tactics? Well, *in tactical positions almost always start with checks!* One principle is "Always check, it might be mate" but that's bogus. Better is "Always consider a check – it might be the best move." The opposite principle "patzer sees check, patzer gives check" is also not very helpful, although it describes the penchant for weak players to give check, no matter how awful the result. Nevertheless, if a check works, it is very forcing and perhaps no other move can match it. So it's best to check those first (pun intended).

So the first check is 2 Nf6+, then 2...Qxf6 seems bad for Black because of 3 Qxd8+. Notice how the bishop guards the queen right through the opposing queen! That's easy to miss. After 3...Qxd8 4 Bxd8 White is up a piece. But just because one line is good doesn't mean they all are. We need to find Black's best reply to 2 Nf6+ and, of course, it is the natural 2...Bxf6. Now 3 Qxd8+ Bxd8 4 Bxd8 is completely winning for Black. White's other third move try, 3 Bxf6, fails miserably to 3...R2xd2 4 Bxd8 Rxd8. And finally, 2 Nf6+ Bxf6 3 Qxb2 is just a piece worse than the immediate 2 Qxb2, so 2 Nf6+ is a terrible move.

How about the other check 2 Ne7+, does that make a difference? Moving the king in response can quickly be eliminated as either king move allows a rook to be taken with check: 2...Kg7?? 3 Qxb2+ and 2...Kf8?? 3 Qxd8+. So Black must play 2...Qxe7. After this capture, it may seem that recapturing the queen is reasonable for White, but 3 Bxe7 loses to 3...R8xd2 since 4 Rc8+ Kg7 wins for Black. So instead of capturing Black's queen, White needs to look for something better. Because White's queen is also attacked, it makes sense to look at capturing a rook and capturing the black queen afterwards. White considered 3 Qxb2 but he saw that after 3...Qxg5 Black is nicely up a pawn and threatening White's queen – not the bad 3...Bxb2? 4 Bxe7 Bxc1 5 Bxd8 when White is up a piece. That only left the capture of the other rook with 3 Qxd8+, which White, in time trouble, dismissed because of the superficial guarding of the d8 by Black's queen. That caused White to abandon the entire 2 Ne7+ line, dismissing this check from his candidate list. But that was the fatal error! If White had more time, he would have seen that the g5-bishop is – again – guarding the d8-square *through* the opponent's queen. So 3 Qxd8+ Qxd8 4 Bxd8 would leave White up a piece for a pawn. Thus 2 Ne7+! would have been the winning move. Instead, it was eliminated from the final candidate list!

After that mistake, it turned out the less forcing candidate moves also failed. The capture 2 Bxd8 is not very promising, as after 2...Rxd2 White has no great continuation, e.g. 3 Ne7+ Kf8 or possibly even 3...Kg7 should work.

A counterattack with 2 Nc7 would allow Black to play 2...R8xd2 3 Nxe6 Rxg2+ 4 Kh1 and now the simple 4...fxe6 is more than sufficient. So this type of counterattack is out. Even the similar 2 Nf4 R8xd2 3 Rc8+ fails to 3...Qxc8, while 3 Nxe6 transposes into the above losing line.

So White thought the checks and counterattacks did not work. However, he also correctly concluded that saving the queen by moving it off the second rank would allow combinations on d5, since then the rook on b2 would pin the bishop on g2. For example, 2 Qxa5? allows 2...Rxd5 since the pinned bishop is not able to capture. Therefore, White decided he could not check nor move the queen, and thus had to settle for the purely defensive final candidate **2 Rc2??**, even though he saw this would lead to a draw after the forced sequence **2...Rxc2 3 Qxc2 Rxd5 4 Bxd5 Qxd5 5 Qc8+ Kg7 6 Qc3+ Kg8**, which is what quickly followed. After a short, but less than perfect time scramble, the game was soon drawn with 17 seconds remaining for White and 13 for Black.

In this example White considered the candidates in the correct order, but came to the wrong conclusion in his hasty analysis and the correct move was not even on the final list! Moral of the story:

Even if you find all the candidate moves correctly and analyze them in the correct order, you can still make mistakes if you don't do the analysis correctly!

By the way, *I* was White in this game and was not a happy camper when the overlooked tactic was discovered! Even though I am an "old master" and my clock was running down, I should not miss something of this level of difficulty. But it only takes one mistake to cost you a game and in this instance I gave away a half point – let's attribute it to rust!

Finally, note that although a candidate move must pass the "Real Chess" test to keep it under consideration, *passing that test is not sufficient to make the move*. In order to play a final candidate, you should prove that it is at least as good as the other final candidates, and doing so is a different story...

2-2) The Goal Each Move

"Many, if not most, of the people who play serious chess often don't try to find the best move and, when they do, don't know what that requires."

What are you doing when you are playing chess?

You are using your brain to think – to play a game whose moves reflect those thoughts. The goal is to use your skills to try to defeat your opponent. In that sense chess is a mental sport. Yes, it has elements of a fight, a science, and an art, too.

At the start of the game both players have the same overall "game goal": winning the game (unless you are playing for a draw for some reason, such as needing a half-point to clinch first prize, etc).

Because serious, slow chess is played with a clock, in order to achieve that game goal, you face a series of "move goals" which, on each of your turns, is to *find the best move you can in the time available*. Unless you are already winning easily or in severe time trouble, you are not just trying to find a move that is reasonable.

Almost everyone knows that they should try to find the best move each on every move, but in practice most players often don't try to do it! This amazing fact is a prominent reason why many weak players are not a lot better; they cannot advance no matter how many chess books they read or, to put it another way, no matter how much chess knowledge they acquire. They confuse chess knowledge with chess ability! Sure, if you learn more that *may* help your playing strength, but *if you don't attempt to take your time and apply what you have learned to find the best move possible, move after move, you will never be a good player and will get severely diminishing returns on your study time*. After all, what good is learning something new if you are not going to apply it when needed?

There have been numerous occasions when students have showed me a move from their games, and I asked, "What made you think this was the best move?" They often mention things like "This move forced him to weaken a square" or "I threatened to win a pawn" but those answers are usually irrelevant!

In order to find the best move they had to prove, or at least attempt to show, that *their move is better than any move*! Whether the move they are considering – their candidate move – would entice a weakening of an opponent's square or threaten to win a pawn is only an aspect *of that move*: in order to properly answer the question it is not sufficient for them to show why their move is good; instead they need to show that their move is better than all the others, and this requires at least some *comparisons*.

As a follow-up, I become more specific and ask: "For example, what made you think your move A was better than move B?" The usual answer is that they did not even consider move B! And even if move A *was* better than move B that does not mean that A was the best move – just that B was not! If the student's game was played on the internet and the clock indicated that they used (say) only 17 seconds on the move (which is fine in a five-minute game but potential disastrous in any critical position in a slow game), then I know they could not have compared move A to move B, much less considered moves C and D nor analyzed all the possible dangerous replies to A! If you don't want to use almost all your time, play a faster game. Otherwise do your best and try to use most of your time finding the best moves you can.

I often use the clone argument: Suppose a player is cloned and plays a match against his clone. In each game he has to give the clone time odds, say 10 minutes to 2 hours. Assume both sides use almost all their time for the game. What percent of games would he win? Almost everyone answers anywhere from 0-10%. Suppose the player wins 5%. According to the rating tables, that is about a 500 rating point difference. So that means *if you play much too fast for the time limit you could be giving away as many as 500 rating points in your potential playing strength*! Keep in mind that enormous handicap next time you play a 60-minute game quickly and leave yourself more than 50 minutes at the end.

Let's consider what it theoretically takes to try and find the best move. Suppose there are 30-40 moves from which to choose on each move, as in the average middlegame position. Then, in order to find the best move, you need to evaluate what will happen after each, and to choose the evaluation that is best for you. It is extremely important to note that you can only evaluate *positions*. When you "evaluate a move", it really means to evaluate the likely positions that can occur from that move, as we will discuss later. But in order to evaluate which move is best, you need to assume that your opponent will also be trying to maximize his chances. *So it is not enough to look at each move and evaluate the position immediately after each of the 30-40 moves and to choose the evaluation that is best for you.* That would only work in the unlikely case that after each move, your opponent's move can have no meaningful effect on the position! You need to consider your opponent's most dangerous replies, like checks, captures, and threats. Later we will also consider the obvious impracticality of considering all 30-40 moves.

Let's take a couple of absurd examples to show that considering your opponent's reply is usually necessary:

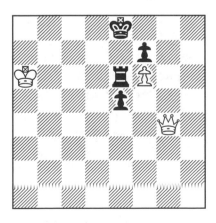

White to play

Without considering the opponent's reply, the move **1 Qxe6+** looks fantastic. It captures a rook, gets you out of check, and puts the opponent in check. Unfortunately, Black can reply **1...fxe6**, winning the queen. However, without further analysis that may not be too bad, since the recapture doubles and isolates your opponent's pawns as well as gives you an advanced passed pawn. But with even a little more analysis you should be able to see that Black has a winning endgame and 1 Qxe6+ is not a strong candidate move. (Would you know how to win this game for Black after 1 Qxe6+?. If not, see the archived *K&P&? vs. K.*)

You may laugh at this silly example, but in my instructing experience this is exactly what many players do. They don't even realize this mistake because, in most positions, the consequences are more subtle than an obvious recapture losing material. Let's take another absurd example, but one that is not a capture:

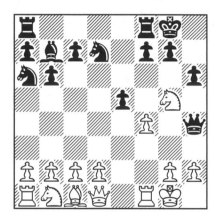

White to play

Black has just played ...h7-h6. Here the reply **1 g3** is superficially terrible: it leaves the knight *en prise*, weakens the white squares in front of the king in a position where Black has a light-squared bishop and White does not, and it neglects development with White already behind in that critical area. On all these "one-ply" issues – the ones that just look at the position after the move and ignore what is going to happen – 1 g3 just doesn't make sense. However, 1 g3 is of course the right move because it traps the black queen and is the only move that gives White a winning position.

The obvious conclusion: In analytical positions, you can't evaluate a move without considering your opponent's best reply (and also what you might be able to do about it!). How can we do this systematically?

In slow games, your goal each move is usually to find the best move, and the principal way you do this is to be careful each move to:

1. Identify *all* the things your opponent could do to you if you would "pass" – his threats;

2. Identify your candidate (reasonable) moves;

3. Analyze what would likely happen after (all) your candidate moves (*considering your opponent will try to play his best move, of course*);

4. Evaluate the resulting positions, compare them, and choose the *move that leads to the position that you feel is the best for you.*

This *Prime List* differs slightly from the five-step list in *Making Chess Simple* (2-1) because here we are focusing primarily upon the narrowing down process, allowing one to compare final candidate moves, and not on the overall process, which in *Making Chess Simple* included the important safety checks to differentiate initial and final candidates.

It takes great skill to do some the tasks in the list *well*, especially the very difficult skills:

♟ Properly analyzing difficult combinations (the part of chess laymen recognize as difficult);

♟ Knowing in each line when it is safe to stop analyzing and start evaluating;

♟ Evaluating positions with the same amount of material and roughly equal king safety.

However, to follow a similar *process* each time you move (assuming an analytical position and with sufficient time on your clock), even if you have to start by doing it poorly, is easier. Nevertheless, my testing of hundreds of players revealed that, while strong players consistently perform a thought process something like the list above, hardly any weaker player does! This finding is a prime aspect of my book *The Improving Chess Thinker*.

Some strong players don't think they perform a process like this but, when questioned, actually are doing similar steps rapidly and somewhat subconsciously. For example, strong players often use deductive logic and their experience/judgment to dismiss the remainder of the candidate moves once they find one that is so good, it is a waste of time to look for anything better, but weaker players should be careful when doing this! Players looking to improve who begin to take their time and use a process similar to the list above seem to have a much higher ceiling than the ones that don't. You can, too; it just takes a little care, practice, and willpower.

You don't have to play chess for years to implement at least the main aspects of a basic proper thought *process* – of course, it does take years to learn to recognize all the critical patterns and the proper way to play in the most commonly occurring positions. I believe the best way to begin to understand this recognition of commonly occurring positions is first by recognition of basic tactical patterns, by understanding what to do with specific pawn structures, as per the books *Pawn Power in Chess* by Kmoch, *The Ideas Behind the Chess Openings* by Fine, and *Pawn Structure Chess* by Soltis, and to know the most basic endgames, e.g. via *Essential Chess Endgames* by Averbakh.

While the extreme of not considering any opponent's replies to potential candidate moves does not work, of course neither does the other extreme of analyzing all possible sequences of moves for the remainder of the game. Except for late endgames, the number of possibilities is so astronomically high that it is impossible even for computers. So one key is to *at least make sure you can safely meet all your opponent's most dangerous possible replies on your next move.*

Occasionally, even during a slow game, your goal might *not* be to find the best move:

a.   You're winning quite easily. Then if you *think defense first* and none of your opponent's moves can hurt you, then playing any reasonable move in a moderate amount of time is usually sufficient.

b.   You are losing badly and, further, your opponent is good enough to easily win in the given position. Then, since all your moves clearly lose, rather than finding the best move, it is often more pertinent to find the move which gives your opponent the best chance to go wrong; in other words find a move – or plan – which gives you a chance to get back in the game by creating complications, setting a trap, etc. You have nothing to lose by playing a second-best, tricky move since you are lost already and normal resistance is just hopeless.

c.   World Champion Alexander Alekhine wrote that the right idea is not always to directly find the best move. He felt that often you must find the best plan and then find the move that best fits this plan. While this is another reasonable way of looking at your "per-move" goal, theoretically the best move will be the one that implements the correct plan. Therefore, for the purposes of this article, we will assume you are looking for the best move and *the idea of finding the best plan is a method to help identify the best move.*

In serious slow games there is a clock running and players have limited time. Therefore, the best you can do is use almost all your time and your practical move goal is then modified: it is *to find the best move(s) in the given time available.* Adding the dimension of time means:

1. Your important time management skills tell you how much time is reasonable to take for a move. This is a function of:

a.   The time control for the game;

b.   How many moves you have left in the time control (indefinitely many for "sudden death" time controls);

c.   How much time is left to the time control;

d.   Is there a time delay or increment;

e.   How critical is the move;

f.   How difficult is the move?

While you do *not* have to consciously figure all of this out each move, you should at least periodically look at the clock and the board and ask yourself "*Do I need to slow down or speed up on each remaining move to use almost all my time?*"

2. You have to know *how* to find the best move possible *in that time*. A big subject, but one we have explored in some detail in other *Novice Nooks* and will review again below.

When you are playing chess, you should be playing a series of moves where you are trying to find the best move you can on each one, given the time constraints. The question remains, "With the time factor what does that require?"

First, you need to take a practical approach that can be applied in the available time. This means you might consider the following shortcuts (taking into consideration the Prime List discussed earlier), depending upon the time constraints:

1. You must identify any threats made by your opponent's last move and only consider moves that either meet the threat, make an equal or greater one, or allow you to properly ignore it. Moves that just allow the threat(s) and give you no hope for something equal or better can be immediately discarded.

2. You should consider all (or as many as possible) of your moves that are checks, captures, and threats. If none of these are decisive, you also need to consider moves that either increase the power of your army (such as ones that activate a dormant piece or take advantage of an opponent's weakness) or ones that restrict your opponent's army in some way.

3. For each candidate move you should still assume that your opponent is trying to play his best move. For example, you cannot just envision a candidate and then evaluate the position after that move is made if your opponent has something forcing that he can do on his move (i.e. the position is not *quiescent*). You need to resolve the most important tactical sequences until things "settle down" before you can evaluate them. But chess is a rich game, and often *it is not possible in the given time available to evaluate all possible forcing continuations to quiescence*. The following two cases are worth noting:

   a. If the position is unclear, use your judgment to decide how good the continuation is. Your judgment becomes more effective with more experience in similar positions. *Players looking to improve should choose unclear continuations over ones they judge as about equal.* By doing so you improve your judgment and positions you previously judged unclear may eventually be given a more and more accurate assessment;

   b. If the potential gain from a sacrifice is less than the amount sacrificed, stop your analysis and evaluate the line as inadequate. For example, if you analyze a possible sacrifice of your queen for an unclear attack and if checkmate looks impossible to force or the amount of material/compensation you can possibly win back is worth clearly less than a queen, there is no sense analyzing further.

From all of the above we can see that with very few exceptions (like the late endgame or getting out of check), even in slow games a good player cannot and does not consider all his moves in order to arrive at the best one.

Let's consider the Prime List from the standpoint of evaluation. In a slow game a player attempts to find the best move by identifying the candidate/reasonable moves ("You can't play what you don't see") and then looking just far enough ahead after each to determine how good that line (sequence of moves) is. He must determine whether the opponent has any forcing moves that will "kill" the line and if not, then, time permitting, what the opponent is likely to do.

For example, suppose you are in an analytical position, and are considering a candidate move where your opponent has three "forcing" replies, two of which are threats and a third that is a capture. Then you need to look far enough in each of the three to determine how good those lines are for your opponent and which one he is likely to choose (i.e. the best one for him). *Then the sequence that includes his best reply is the likely one that will happen should you choose that candidate move. You should assign an evaluation to your candidate move equal to how good your position is after the line starting with your opponent's best move.* In other words, for each candidate move you assume both sides will then make the best moves and that will tell you how good that line is for you.

But assuming that sequence of best moves is OK for you does *not* tell you to make that candidate move, although many beginners would make it without further thought. *When you see a good move, look for a better one – you are trying to find the best one you can, given the time constraints.* You need to repeat the above thought sequence for each candidate move (as always considering candidate moves which are forcing for you or which follow some sort of "plan" which is called for by the current position). Then once you figure out the most likely line, assign an evaluation to the position at the end of that line and *compare it to the position at the end of the "best" line you have found so far.* If the evaluation of the new line is better for you, then it becomes your "King of the Hill" – the best move you have found so far. If not, the previous King of the Hill (line and evaluation) stays in place. Once you have done this for all your reasonable moves, the one with the most appealing line (which can be as short as one ply if your opponent has nothing that worries you, or as long as many moves in a long forcing capturing or endgame sequence) becomes the move that you will play.

If you are not sure which line is best – and weaker players are often sure but wrong! – you need to evaluate your best possibilities carefully and weigh them against each other (and eventually improve your evaluation skills). Strong players, thanks to their experience and good judgment, can usually find what they think is the best move in most unfamiliar positions in less than 10 minutes. Even when a position is complicated, if there is one clearly best move, most good players will play it fairly quickly once they have proven to themselves that it is, indeed, best. You don't always need to see everything that will happen – *once you know a move is best, nothing else needs to be done. Your goal is to play the best move in the time available, not completely try to predict the future!*

You may not be able to always find the best move, but if you don't even look for it, your odds of stumbling across it go way down. So next slow game, take your time and go get 'em!

It's Your Move!

A fun and helpful set of instructional books are GM Ward's *It's Your Move* series. I was using *The Improver's It's Your Move* during a lesson and gave my student the following:

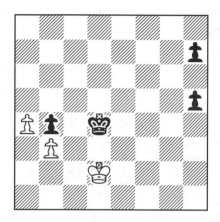

White to play

Like all the problems in this series, you are given five different answers and are asked to choose the correct one. GM Ward's answer seems to imply that White is winning. If Black is not careful, White will:

a) 1 Ke2 Kc3? 2 a5 Kxb3 3 a6 Kc2 4 a7 b3 5 a8Q b2 and White wins with a queen vs. a b-pawn on the seventh rank, e.g. 6 Qc6+ Kb1 (6...Kb3 7 Qd5+ Kc2 8 Qd3+ Kc1 9 Qd1 mate; see the archived *Going to Sleep in the Endgame*) 7 Kd2 Ka2 8 Qa4+ Kb1 9 Kc3 and White wins quickly.

b) 1 Ke2 Kd5 (suppose Black does nothing) 2 Kf2 Kd4 3 Kg3 Kd5 4 Kh4 Kd4 5 Kxh5 Kd5 6 Kh6 Kd4? 7 Kxh7 Kd5 8 Kg7 Kd4 9 Kf6 Kd5 10 Kf5 Kd4 11 Ke6 Kc5 12 Ke5 Kc6 13 Kd4 Kb6 14 Kc4 Ka5 15 Kc5, when Black is in *zugzwang* and must lost his pawn and the game.

But all is not so simple! Suppose in line 'b' Black plays for the distant opposition with 6...Kc6 or 6...Kd6, or the direct opposition with 6...Ke6. Then White can make no progress:

1 Ke2 Kd5 2 Kf2 Kd4 3 Kg3 Kd5 4 Kh4 Kd4 5 Kxh5 Kd5 6 Kh6 Kd6

The distant opposition.

7 Kxh7 Kd7! 8 Kg6 Ke6 9 Kg5 Ke5 10 Kg4 Ke4 11 Kg3 Ke5!

The diagonal opposition.

12 Kf3 Kd5! 13 Ke3 Ke5

But not 13...Kc5? 14 Ke4! and wins.

14 Kd3 Kd5

And White is making no inroads, e.g. 15 Kc2 Kc6.

In middlegame positions we often speak of "White is better", but in the late endgame it is either a win or a draw! In this case White is "better" because it is Black that has to be careful, but it is a draw!

2-3) Real Chess, Time Management, and Care

"Your game is only as good as your worst move."

I commonly run across the sad case of a student who wants know more about the 9th move of some variation of the Sicilian, but loses because he moves too quickly and overlooks the loss of a material to simple double attacks. This is being "penny wise and pound foolish".

When I suggest reviewing the thought process that caused him to lose the material, he often brushes it off with a statement such as, "Oh, I just moved too fast" or "Yeah, I just overlooked his check". They are much more interested in my opinion of the 9th move. I try to politely say "But you don't get it! The reason you are 1200 and not 1600 has *much* more to do with the carelessness or bad time management that caused you to lose the piece than it does from your lack of knowledge of the Sicilian." Want proof? Take a 1600 player and make him play an opening he never has before in his life – he still plays close to 1600; take a 1200 and let him play his favorite opening and he still usually plays like a 1200.

While it is true that most players under 1400 don't know a great deal about openings, endgames, or positional play, a great majority of their games are (or could have been) lost not because of some opening trap, bad plan, endgame subtlety, or complex combination, but because of some basic tactical oversight. That is why the repetitious practice of basic tactical motifs, in all their guises, is *by far* the most important thing you can do when first studying chess.

Learning new patterns is necessary for improvement, but not the only way to improve. Ask yourself the following question, "Of all the games I have lost recently, what percent were lost because of something I did not know, and what percent were lost due to something I *already* knew, but was not careful to look for?"

If you are like most non-advanced players many, if not most, of your losses are due to a tactical oversight on a pattern that *you already knew*: putting a piece *en prise*, miscounting the safety of a piece, missing a simple double attack or fork, allowing a back-rank mate, etc. Since you already are familiar with those tactics, that means either that you played carelessly, did not practice "Real Chess", had poor time management, or have no consistent thinking pattern.

The key to Real Chess is making sure you don't make a move before establishing that your opponent cannot easily defeat it with a forcing move: *check, capture, or threat. Many readers have indicated to me that this is the single most important chess tip they have ever received!*

For most positions, this requires consistently asking "Is it Safe?" (5-3) about each candidate move. *Tip: One good way to discover your opponent's threats are to assume that you "pass" – make no move – and see what he could then do to you next move.*

Time Management means to use your time wisely. For the game this means pacing yourself to use almost all your time without getting into unnecessary time trouble. For a move it means allocating more time to critical moves and less to non-critical moves (see *The Case for Time Management* 3-1).

The interesting part about both Real Chess and Time Management is that both have to be practiced 100% of the time – 98% does not nearly work. For example, if on 98% of the moves (49/50) you play correctly, but on one move you decide to just relax and "see what happens", that can be a disaster. *By missing that one move each game you will consistently play hundreds of points weaker than your strength would have been if you had played every move carefully.* It is similar with time – if you play even one move fast that may be enough to cause you to lose, and if you play too slowly and then have to play quickly during time pressure (as many top players do), then again just one big slip at the end may easily be enough to cost you the game.

Playing Real Chess and practicing good time management requires being careful, but not pedantic. The ratings of two equally knowledgeable players may be separated by hundreds of points if one is more careful. A careful player need not be indecisive – those are two different qualities. But a player who is naturally not careful at other things may find that in chess that lack of care results in sudden catastrophes. We all know players who say, "I am 1600 and I was beating that 1900, but then he got lucky..." The explanation is that the 1600 may be better in all technical phases of the game, but the 1900 may have learned to be careful on *all* his moves every game, while the 1600 player is one of those 98% types.

So if you are not the careful type or don't know how to manage your time, what can you do?" The following suggestions should help:

1. If you do not buy into the idea of being careful every move, you are likely to remain below your potential. Learn to pace yourself to take almost all your time each game. When you see a good move look for a better one. See *The Case for Time Management* (3-1) for several additional helpful tips.

2. Your opponent's previous move should never contain any "secrets"! Make sure to ask "What are *all* the things my opponent's move does?" If you take your time and look around, sometimes you might be surprised at how it changed the position and what kind of measures you should be considering.

3. Play each move and each game with pride, care, and optimism:

    Pride because your game represents your accomplishment, and each move should be a representation of the best thoughts you have about the position, which you are hopefully proud to show everyone.
    Care because without care you probably won't be so proud. Examples of playing with care: taking your time, looking for the total effect of your opponent's moves, creating a PV of at least 3 (on most moves), and "If you see a good move – look for a better one!"
    Optimism because chess is a mental game and if you feel you are going to make bad moves or play a bad game you will probably make it a self-fulfilling

prophecy! In the first game that I ever played a master my thoughts were not "I am probably going to lose", but rather "I'll do the best I can and see what happens". I won.

4. Use a "Sanity Check". After you decide on your move, write it down and take a deep breath or close your eyes for a second. Then take a fresh look at the board and say to yourself, "Is my planned move insane? Will the piece be safe? Am I just missing an easy checkmate – for me or him? Can someone just capture a queen?" If you still don't see anything, make your move and hit your clock.

5. Tactics is the science of chess safety. You can go a long way being careful and just concentrating on two things: safety and activity. And these two are really related because *you keep pieces safe so that they can do something, and if pieces are not doing anything it is almost as if you lost them.* You will be surprised what your army can do when it is safe and all the pieces are doing something.

6. Unless you are really good already, don't fool yourself into thinking you don't need any of this. If you never make a bad mistake in a slow game, maybe you are that good already. A high percentage of readers would be much better if they just paced themselves better and played more carefully than if they study 100 more opening books.

A caveat: Will doing all the above make you an expert or master? Not very likely! If it were that easy, then lots of players would be really good. All that other stuff with openings, endgames, positional play, planning, combinations, etc is still required to attain high level play. It is just that without instigating Real Chess and decent time management, none of the other stuff will matter much.

2-4) Analysis and Evaluation

In the long run your rating will always follow your playing strength.

Many players confuse analysis and evaluation. Here are my definitions:

♟ **Analysis** is the process by which a player takes the current position and generates candidate moves by visualizing "I move here, he moves there" possibilities. This process creates a "tree" of moves that lead to possible positions to evaluate. This contrasts to the *strategic* thinking process, which is used to arrive at a plan, although these two processes are not completely independent. Analysis makes use of many skills, such as deductive logic and visualization.

♟ **Evaluation** is the process of examining a position and deciding *which side is better, by how much, and why* (the "why" is usually the key to your *plan*). Evaluation occurs after some candidate moves are generated, at the *nodes* of analysis (c.f. quiescence below).

Analysis is inherently *dynamic*, while evaluation – and planning – are primarily *static*. A dynamic process involves "mental" movement of the pieces, while a static process works with a particular "unmoving" board position. For example, a combination or a knight maneuver is dynamic, while a bad pawn structure or an open file is static.

To evaluate a position before any analysis can be considered *static evaluation*; evaluate a position that might occur during analysis is *dynamic evaluation*. When you analyze a position, you sometimes need to dynamically evaluate dozens of positions to compare the relative merits of each. How you choose which moves to analyze (candidate moves) is outside the scope of this article; when to stop analyzing and evaluate is discussed below.

How do you decide when an evaluation of a foreseen position is required and meaningful? The answer is the concept of *quiescence. You cannot evaluate most positions until they are "quiet"*; that is, all the most forcing moves, such as checks, captures, and strong threats, have been resolved ("the smoke is cleared").

As a trivial counterexample, it would be silly to think, "I will capture his queen with my queen and I will be ahead a queen" and not consider his obvious recapture that restores material equality! See the first two diagrams in *The Goal Each Move* (2-2) as examples.

When should you stop analysis because you cannot reach a desired goal? This is complicated, but for sacrificial lines *you should usually abandon your analysis as fruitless when the material sacrificed becomes greater than the potential gain*. At that point it is not likely you will attain a reasonable goal, so the sacrifice should be rejected. For example, if you are conducting a mating attack you would not stop analyzing after sacrificing a queen unless you are sure that there is no possible mate in that line. If you are analyzing a line where you sacrifice a queen and all you might possibly win back is a pawn, no further analysis is necessary. On the other hand, if you find a line where you *do* get back your sacrificed material and more by force, your goal is reached and you have an excellent candidate move!

However, you may still sacrifice even if you do not see that you get all your material back. With some sacrifices, your compensation may be long-term, such as your superior piece play, the opponent's unsafe king, or his badly wrecked pawn structure. You just have to make sure the potential gain is greater than the sacrifice. Since checkmate is greater than any sacrifice, a sacrifice that may likely lead to mate, even if you have no hope of calculating all the lines, is always worth consideration. Further, some positions have either unclear quiescence or such complexity you cannot achieve quiescence – they still have to be evaluated, even though doing so may require a "feel" or "intuition" based on your experience in similar positions.

When you analyze, if possible, consider and resolve the all potential checks, captures, and threats for both sides, and try for each to eventually arrive at a quiescent position. Evaluate the position using your knowledge of positional aspects – see *Evaluation Criteria* below.

You should do much of this for all candidate moves, *assuming each side will choose his best moves*. However, in many/most cases, a conscious determination of each side's best move is not always necessary or practical – being able to deal with the opponent's most dangerous replies may be all that is required.

Examples of Analysis and Dynamic Evaluation

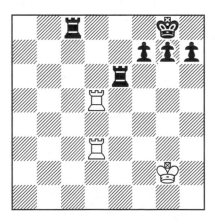

White to play

Analysis: A static evaluation shows White is down material. If he does nothing he will surely lose, so he looks for a back-rank mate, which is reasonable given the three pawns blocking in the king. If **1 Rd8+,** 1...Rxd8?? 2 Rxd8+ Re8 3 Rxe8 is mate, so **1...Re8!** is forced and White has nothing since the black rooks guard each other through the white rook – a good pattern to remember!

Evaluation: Count the material at the end of the critical line 1...Re8!. Black has three extra pawns – this is such a large lead that smaller positional considerations, if any, don't matter too much. Since 1 Rd8+ is the only line to worry about and after 1...Re8 White has no mate, Black has an easy win.

In the King's Indian Defense, after **1 d4 Nf6 2 c4 g6 3 Nc3 Bg7 4 e4 d6 5 f3 0-0 6 Be3 c5!? 7 Nge2 Nc6 8 dxc6 dxc6 9 Qc2** what is Black's best move?

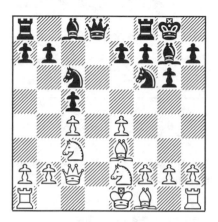

Black to play

Analysis: Black has no reasonable checks and the capture 9...Nxe4 leads to little after either recapture, so he should look for reasonable threats and, if he does not find one, just develop. The most interesting threats are 9...Nb4 and 9...Nd4. But notice that 9...Nb4 has the additional follow-up that, after the queen moves, 10...Nd3+ may lead to a discovered check if White does not play 10 Qd2. But then **9...Nb4 10 Qd2 Nd3+ 11 Kd1 Nxb2+** wins material. When looking ahead, did you see that the queen was pinned and that this was possible? After **12 Kc2** Black wins yet another pawn with 12...Nxc4 or **12...Qxd2+** followed by **13...Nxc4** as played in the game.

Evaluation: Count material at the end of the forced line: After 13...Nxc4 Black is up two pawns and has no noticeable weaknesses; White's exposed king, which would be a big detriment should the queens still be on the board, may actually be somewhat a benefit in the upcoming endgame, but is not nearly enough to compensate for the loss of two pawns. Therefore, Black is winning easily.

In the King's Indian Attack, after **1 Nf3 d5 2 g3 Nc6 3 Bg2 e5 4 d3 Be6 5 0-0 Qd7 6 e4 d4 7 Nbd2 Bh3** who is better and why?

(see following diagram)

Analysis: Start by looking at checks, captures, and threats and, if there are none, look for a way to develop the pieces, for example by planning the thematic "break" move f2-f4. There are no checks and the two captures are 8 Nxe5 and 8 Bxh3.

White to play

8 Bxh3 looks questionable as the g2-square is weak, but it is always worth looking to see if, say, 8...Qxh3 9 Ng5 traps the queen. It does not, so there is nothing to recommend 8 Bxh3. **8 Nxe5** does not look too promising, but you always have to check these things out, and not stop just because **8...Nxe5** seems to win a piece because the position is not yet quiescent: **9 Qh5** double attacks, and the knight cannot guard the bishop nor the bishop the knight, so 9...Nxd3 or 9...Bxg2 looks forced. But 9...Nxd3 10 Bxh3 attacks the queen (followed by c2xd3), and the main line **9...Bxg2** allows **10 Qxe5+** and then 10...Qe7 11 Qxe7+ Bxe7 12 Kxg2 or other Black moves allow **11 Kxg2**, so the surprising 8 Nxe5 is best, winning a pawn.

Evaluation: Count material: after the principal variation starting with 8 Nxe5 White sneaks away with a pawn and is left with a better position as well, including an imposing kingside pawn majority that will get rolling after a later f2-f4. **The general rule is that an evaluation of +1 pawn is about the dividing line between a theoretical win and a draw.** If the opponent has compensation for the pawn you are not likely winning yet, but if he has no compensation (or you have some!) then you are winning.

How far ahead do you need to see?

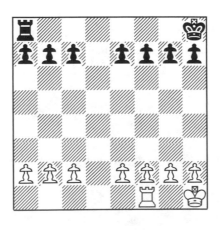

White to play

Analysis: Whoever gets to the open file first has a big advantage. *Since the goal is almost always to find the best move, and not necessarily to tell the future* (although sometimes that is necessary to find the best move), here **1 Rd1** grabs the file and threatens to penetrate to the seventh rank, so I can make this move with no other calculation at all. When asked how far he looks ahead, Capablanca wryly answered: "Just one – the best one." I prefer another famous reply, "As far ahead as necessary!"

Evaluation: Count material: level so far, but with the prospect of possibly winning a pawn once the rook gets to the seventh rank. As the best move is obvious, a detailed evaluation is not necessary since I don't have to compare this line with any other. However, after I get to the seventh rank the black pawns are weak, but capturing them too soon gives Black the d-file and the threat of a back-rank mate, so I am likely winning but some care is required. I will figure out what to play and whether it is a forced win when I get there...

Funsy Finish: In case you have not seen it, the shortest possible stalemate is **1 e3 a5 2 Qh5 Ra6 3 Qxa5 h5 4 h4 Rah6 5 Qxc7 f6 6 Qxd7+ Kf7 7 Qxb7 Qd3 8 Qxb8 Qh7 9 Qxc8 Kg6 10 Qe6**.

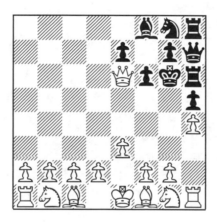

Black to play

Black never gets to make his 10th move!

Evaluation Criteria

When measuring "How much one side is better?" there are really only three mathematically correct answers: White is winning, Black is winning, or it is a draw. However, humans are not able to calculate this level of certainty except for easily won positions and endgames. Therefore we have invented other ways to state how much better one side is than another.

Originally we used a system like "=" for equal positions, "±" to mean White is distinctly better, "∞" to mean unclear, etc. However, with the growing advent of computers, we now see evaluations like "White is +0.32 pawns at 12 ply", meaning that the computer is looking six full moves ahead for both sides and thinks White is better by about a third of a pawn, where a pawn advantage or more is likely winning. These evaluations are augmented by human commentary, with the traditional "I don't think White is winning yet, but I would be very happy with his position."

Static evaluation is performed on a position as it currently stands; *dynamic* evaluation is made after analyzing moves to see what is possible. I believe that the following are the four dominant evaluation criteria:

1. Material
2. King Safety
3. Total Army Activity/Mobility
4. Pawn Structure

It is interesting to compare these criteria to the ones presented in Evans' *New Ideas in Chess* or Dorfman's recent *The Method in Chess*. Any comparison will immediately bring up questions about the commonly-used criteria "time" and "space". With these criteria, the key is whether these provide your army extra mobility/activity: *space is not useful if it does not provide you with more activity than your opponent and, similarly, extra tempi are not good if they are not used to make your army more menacing – so these are really just means to the ends* of more mobility and activity (as well as coordination or flexibility). To a lesser extent, this explanation also holds with "center control". And a "lead in development" is just well-spent time in the opening, again with the goal of creating superior piece activity. There are strong similarities in all theories, since the major components of material and king safety are always included.

The above four criteria also differ from the seven "Elements" in my book *Elements of Positional Evaluation*. The Elements are primarily used to evaluate the power of each piece in a particular position; not positions in general.

There is one other major evaluation criterion – although this one is not position dependent. It is remaining clock time per move. For example, if you are playing a sudden death time control and have a dynamically equal position against an equally strong opponent but have 15 minutes remaining to your opponent's 5, this represents a big advantage. I estimate a 15 to 5 minute advantage without time delay is equivalent to about 200 rating points, or about a 3 to 1 favorite.

Material

Watch any two little kids playing and ask them "Who's winning?" They will almost always answer just on the basis of material. Here are GM Larry Kaufman's scientifically derived average piece values from his March 1999 *Chess Life* article "The Evaluation of Material Imbalances":

- ♟ Bishop ≈ Knight ~ 3¼ pawns
- ♟ Rook ~ 5 pawns
- ♟ Queen ~ 9¾ pawns
- ♟ Advantage of the bishop pair ~ ½ pawn bonus

...and I might add the king's *fighting power* is about 4 pawns – its *trading value* of course is infinite. At the start of a game a tempo is worth about ⅓ of a pawn (for a pawn gambit you like to get three tempi), but that quickly escalates in most positions. In fact, in most complicated positions an extra tempo can be worth a queen or mate. Just try giving someone odds of an extra move anywhere in the game!

The base unit is always pawns – calling the base unit "points" is unnecessary. Since a pawn is by definition worth one "point", then a pawn must be the unit; using points instead is like saying a foot is worth one hoobley and measuring everyone's height in hoobleys.

It is worth emphasizing that the above values are *averages; there are no absolutes.* The numbers vary greatly with position (see Soltis' *Rethinking the Chess Pieces*). For example, even though pawns are the measure, not all pawns are worth one. Kaufman noted that rook pawns were only worth about 85% of an average non-rook pawn. Similarly, a pawn that can unstoppably promote to a queen next move is worth a queen minus a tempo, and two connected passed pawns on the sixth beat a rook. Kaufman also stated that of all the pieces, the queen's value varies the most from its average. In my opinion a bishop or a knight is probably worth closer to four pawns in the opening and is often worth less than two in the late endgame.

When evaluating material, don't count up all the pieces and convert to total equivalent pawns. Just look at the differences. For example, if you have an extra rook and your opponent has an extra bishop or knight, you are "up the exchange"; if you have one extra rook and an extra pawn and your opponent has an extra bishop *and* an extra knight, he has "two pieces for a rook and pawn"; if you have an extra knight and he has two extra pawns, you are "up a piece for two pawns".

You have a nice advantage if you have the bishop pair or, even slightly better, two pieces for a rook and a pawn. Both imbalances represent about ½ pawn advantage, but before the endgame the latter is often enough to win, as the two pieces can be used to win additional pawns.

King Safety

King safety, of course, is sometimes more important than material, especially if someone is about to get mated. But in most positions the safety of both kings is either similar, or the difference is more long-term. For example, if you are castled on opposite sides with queens on the board, then whoever's attack can get to the opposing king first is likely winning, despite small material imbalances, so in this case king safety is very important. Similarly, if one side sacrifices material to expose the enemy king while there is still enough material around to form a likely mating attack, then king safety becomes a dominant factor.

Total Piece Activity

The third criterion is the activity of all your pieces. This is distinctly underrated by weaker players, who often consider pawn structure as more important. In testing hundreds of adults, weaker players are much more likely to make a statement similar to "White is better because Black has an isolated d-pawn" than they are to say (in the same position) "Black is better because his pieces are much more active". Yet strong players almost always get this correct, so beginner's books have done a poor job of selling the dynamic possibilities of piece play versus the "easier-to-categorize" properties of static strengths and weaknesses.

In my opinion Garry Kasparov is the best player ever at evaluating and using total piece activity; he often pitches a pawn or even the exchange to make sure his army is the one with all the play. In fact, he has occasionally stated something to the effect of "piece activity is what chess is all about."

I might add that total piece activity has an extremely high correlation with the sum of the pieces' actual mobility. Think of activity as being subjective while mobility is strictly objective: counting moves. In activity, there are more factors involved, such as the value of the real estate where the activity is present (e.g. more important around the enemy king and near the center), the flexibility of the army, and its coordination.

Pawn Structure

The final criterion is pawn structure. See the archived *A Positional Primer* for more on well-known features such as weak squares, passed pawns, isolated pawns, and open files. Although pawn structure is relatively least important of the four, it is still important! If the other factors are roughly even but one side's pawns are sufficiently worse, this alone can easily be the cause of defeat.

These four are not the only criteria for evaluation. Others exist, or could be broken out from the above. For example, in queen and pawn endgames one of the most important criteria is who has the most advanced passed pawn, or the best chance of getting one. You might consider this part of pawn structure, or separate. As another example, with a locked center, the player who has the more dangerous pawn breaks on the flank is usually better.

Let's evaluate four positions:

(see following diagram)

Material: Even

King Safety: It looks roughly even since White has pushed the kingside pawns and Black is not castled. But of course *king safety* is not always independent of *army activity* when the enemy army is knocking down the doors of the king's barricades, as White is doing here to the black monarch.

Piece Activity: Black has dilly-dallied with moves like ...h7-h6 and ...Qc8 and a bunch of queen's knight moves. In return, White has been much more efficient, with the finely posted knight on e5 and his centralized army backing it up. Enormous advantage: White.

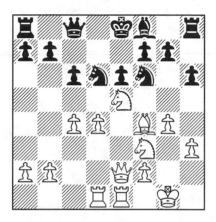

Position #1: White to play

Pawn structure: The structures are roughly even. White is slightly looser on the kingside, but this also provides a space advantage. Since pawns that advance are usually more vulnerable, having more space (a pseudo-element that may give more piece activity) and having more vulnerable pawns usually go hand-in-hand.

Conclusion: White has a massive advantage and should not waste time.

The game finished:

1 d5!

Again, opening the position with a break move, to accentuate/take advantage of the big lead in activity. An "attacking" move like 1 c5 would be the wrong idea.

1...cxd5 2 cxd5 Be7?

Understandable, but allowing a further infiltration. However, White still has a winning advantage after the ugly 2...Rg8 3 dxe6 fxe6 4 Rc1.

3 dxe6 Qxe6

3...0-0 doesn't change anything anymore: 4 Nd7 Nde4 5 Nxf8 Qxf8 6 Rd4.

4 Nd4!

It's all over.

4...Qc8

4...Qxa2 is not the saving move due to 5 Ng6!.

5 Ng6!

Threatening mate.

5...Nxg6 6 Nxg7

White misses the pretty 6 Qb5+! Qd7 7 Nf5 fxg6 8 Nxg7+ Kf8 9 Rxd7 but still wins a piece.

6...Kxe7 7 f3 Qc5 8 fxe4 Rhd8 9 Be3 Kf8 10 Ne6+ 1-0

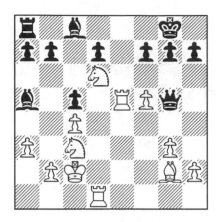

Position #2: Black to play

If it were White's move, the evaluation would be trivial: there is a mate in one with 1 Re8. But it is Black's move, and we have to evaluate the position assuming mate will be prevented.

Material: White has a rook and two knights for a queen, a bishop (and the bishop pair) and a pawn. This would normally represent a big advantage to Black, except dynamically it is easy to see that *Black cannot both stop mate and hold his bishop on c8*, which will change the static evaluation quite a bit as soon as this unstoppable dynamic feature is taken into account. Again, that is why non-quiescent positions, such as the one above, are much harder to evaluate because you have to take any forced play into account. *Trying to evaluate without quiescence can be very dangerous to your game's health.* The exception is a speculative sacrifice, which you usually evaluate on judgment, but using the same criteria, where you trade off material for the other factors.

King Safety: It looks as though white's king is exposed and, after black's king creates *luft*, it has better pawn cover. But this is an illusion since white's king has plenty of places to hide from Black's only two active pieces. Big advantage: White.

Piece Activity: Enormous advantage to White, who not only has more pieces in play, they are also working toward their maximum capability, while Black's queenside rook and bishop are spectators.

Pawn structure: This is not a big factor here. One of the reasons pawn structure is fourth in priority is that, when the difference in any of the other criteria becomes great, it almost disappears as a factor.

Conclusion: Big advantage to White, which should translate into a quick win.

The game continued:

1...h5

As good as anything else. If 1...g6 2 Re8+ Kg7 3 Nce4 Qh5 (other moves get mated or lose the queen immediately) 4 f6+ Kh6 5 Nxf7 mate is pretty.

2 Re8+ Kh7 3 Rh8+

Irresistible, but the computer-like 3 Rd5 is even better, as is the simple 3 Nxf7 because 3...Qxf5+ gets the queen pinned with 4 Be4.

3...Kxh8 4 Nxf7+ Kg8 5 Nxg5

And White won easily.

This is an instructive one from the archived *A Counting Primer*: **1 e4 e5 2 Nf3 Nc6 3 Bc4 Bc5 4 0-0 Nf6 5 Ng5?!** (an "unreasonable threat" – see *The Three Types of Reasonable Threats* in 8-5, page 338) **0-0 6 Nxf7? Rxf7 7 Bxf7+ Kxf7**:

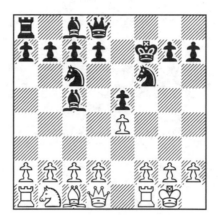

Position #3: White to play

Material: Using old "Reinfeld" values, it looks like rook plus pawn vs. bishop plus knight is about even ("six pawns to six") but bishops and knights are worth closer to 3¼ pawns each. That puts Black ahead 6½-6, and by GM Kaufman's value system, the bishop pair is worth ½ pawn bonus, so that makes it 7-6.

King Safety: It may look like Black's king is more exposed, but this is largely an illusion since ...Kg8 is looming. Actually White's king is slightly *less* safe due to Black's piece activity (see below), but we do not want to double-penalize him so we will call it even.

Piece Activity: Big advantage to Black. In the opening a pawn sacrifice is usually worth 2-3 tempi, so a (worthwhile!) tempo is worth about ⅓ of a pawn. Black is up 2-3 very-well-taken tempi, so that adds up to almost another pawn lead in activity.

Pawn structure: White's extra pawn gives him more solidity, but neither side has any pawn weaknesses.

Conclusion: Normally it takes a greater than one pawn advantage to have a winning position, especially if it is early. Here Black is ahead well over one pawn, so Black should expect to win. This is a far cry from the erroneous beginner evaluation "Material is about even but Black's king is exposed so White is better!"

(see following diagram)

Material: Even

King Safety: Both perfectly safe – neither is in any danger of being mated until a pawn promotes.

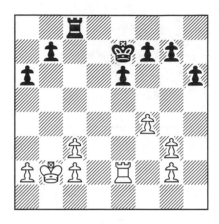

Position #4: Black to play

Piece Activity: Advantage to Black, especially because White's king is cut off guarding the c3-pawn. In most endgame positions king activity is a big factor.

Pawn structure: White's pawns are a mess. Besides the isolated queenside pawns, the doubled g-pawns may allow the black king to threaten inroads there as well.

Conclusion: Big advantage for Black; it should be enough to win for most intermediate+ players.

With practice, you will learn to evaluate with increasing skill and accuracy, and your move choices will correspondingly improve.

2-5) Improving Analysis Skills

The two most important thinking process skills are analysis and evaluation.

Improving analysis skills is important because analysis most highly correlates with chess strength, especially for players below rating level 2000. It may be the single best thing you can do to improve your chess play.

Let's start with an example from a recent tournament:

White appears to be in deep trouble. Black has the extra pawn, a lead in development, and the bishop pair. White's kingside light squares are a mess.

Black to play

1...Qe2

OK, this move is a stunner! Your job is to analyze and decide: brilliant, bad, good, unnecessary, terrible? Provide the Principal Variation (PV) and any other pertinent lines to back up your decision. The answer appears after the next diagram.

Black sees back-rank possibilities if 2 Rxe2 Rd1+. When this type of shocking move occurs, White *should adopt a positive attitude* and think "OK, Black wants to sacrifice the queen for a back-rank mate, but since he is human *I must assume he may have erred in his analysis, so how can I play so that I can safely capture it?*" Then he should leisurely try to analyze accurately; it is important not to miss any chances during this critical period. White did play slowly, but instead of looking for opportunity, he simply believed that Black's play was correct (a bad mistake!) and replied:

(see following diagram)

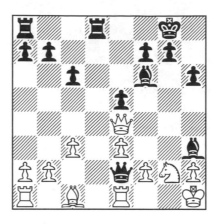

White to play

2 Bd2??

White believes the back-rank danger is real and that the rook on e1 needs to be guarded, so he allows Black to win a piece with 2...Qxd2.

But White should not have given his opponent so much credit. Here is how he should have analyzed:

"If I can take the queen and survive – even returning some material – I should be able to win, as long as I stay ahead in material and don't get mated. So I will start my analysis by assuming I can take the queen and trying to prove that I can get away with it – after all, if prove I can win the queen, then I will likely win! So suppose I capture the queen with 2 Rxe2.

"Now 2...Rd1+ is the only move that I am worried about, and after that check I have two legal moves: 3 Re1 and 3 Ne1. If either move works, that's enough information for me to capture the queen. Normally I don't want to move into a pin with 3 Ne1, but here that general consideration is moot because a pin on the knight is relatively meaningless compared to being ahead a queen. So let's try 3 Re1 first. But the "knight on g2 is attacked and guards the rook on e1", and *a piece that is guarded by another piece is susceptible to a removal of the guard tactic*. Since the knight can be captured with check, Black will not play the innocuous 3...Rxe1 4 Nxe1 when I am ahead a queen, but rather the 'dangerous' 3...Bxg2+, removing the guard on the rook. Now I have two ways to capture: 4 Kxg2 and 4 Qxg2. 4 Qxg2 allows 4...Rxe1+, when I have to interpose with the queen, and after 5 Qg1 Rxg1+ 6 Kxg1 I am again behind a pawn. So therefore I have to play 4 Kxg2, and after 4...Rxe1 I am ahead a queen for a rook and a pawn. I can then break my back-rank bind with an eventual b2-b3 and Bb2. So 3 Re1 looks pretty good!"

This analysis indicates that 2 Rxe2 is safe and a quick glance shows that *no other move can possibly be better*. It is not necessary – or even good time management – to determine your best third move at this point. If I had loads of time I could decide whether I am going to play 3 Ne1 or 3 Re1, but it is more efficient to decide that on the next move. I am just trying to find the best move, and I know that 2 Rxe2 is it, so *I should stop analyzing and play 2 Rxe2.*

Let's assume that 2 Rxe2 is *now played* and, after 2...Rd1+, White has to determine whether 3 Re1 or 3 Ne1 is correct. First, *I must not assume my previous analysis of 3 Re1 is correct* (a bad mistake) and then either just play it (not even trying to find the best move!) or skip to 3 Ne1. Instead, I should verify the previous analysis (see "Not as Simple as ABC" in *Odds and Ends* 9-3, page 374).

Upon verifying my analysis from the previous move and reaching the same conclusions as above, I might now continue:

"How about 3 Ne1 - ? At first it looks like Black's attack is stopped dead in its tracks and I am just ahead a queen! But this line is critical; if I analyze this correctly the remainder of the game should be rather simple. See the guidelines in *When You're Winning, It's a Whole Different Game* (7-3).

"So upon careful examination of Black's potential replies to 3 Ne1 (as always, looking for the checks, captures, and threats), we find the dangerous removal of the guard idea 3...Bf1. Now what should I do? I can move the rook and lose the knight or I can guard the rook with the queen, losing the exchange. Normally I would much rather lose the exchange, which is worth about half a piece, but since I am ahead a queen, it doesn't make that much difference, so I am going to play the one that gives me the least problems. Let's first look at losing the exchange: I can guard the rook with 4 Qf3, 4 Qg4, 4 Qc2, or 4 Qc4.

"But 4 Qc4 looks tricky because of 4...b5, attempting yet another removal of the guard, so I won't analyze that further unless I am desperate. Both 4 Qf3 and 4 Qg4 look a little 'loose' since Black can try to attack me with pawns, again using the removal of the guard idea. For example, 4 Qf3 e4 5 Qg4 g6 threatens 6...h5, pushing me off the diagonal. However, after 4 Qc2 neither 4...Bxe2 5 Qxe2 Rad8 nor the immediate 4...Rad8 look very dangerous because I am eventually going to play the freeing b2-b3 and Bb2. Analyzing further, in the line 4...Bxe2 5 Qxe2 Rad8 White can play 6 b3 g6 7 Bb2?! R8d2? (much better but insufficient is 7...R1d2) 8 Qxd1! and Black can resign in good conscience.

"OK, so 4 Qc2 looks pretty safe but, unless I am in time trouble, I should check out 4 Rd2 to see if it is even easier, because that would mean that 3 Ne1 might be better than 3 Re1. But after 4 Rd2 and then 4...Rxe1 Black threatens a discovered check, leading to one of those big tactical situations you can only allow with the greatest of care; other Black threats include double check and a desperado piece. Here the discovered checks contain the dual threats of 5...Bh3 mate and 5...Bd3+ winning the queen, and these are very strong because I have no move that stops both! Any queen move to a dark square to avoid a bishop discovery allows the mate threat. Suppose after 4...Rxe1 White tries 5 Qg4; then 5...Bc2! 6 Qg1 and now not 6...Rxg1+?? 7 Kxg1 when Black's bishop pair, pawn, and some minor factors more than make up for the exchange, but – when you see a good move, look for a better one – 6...Bf3 mate. Therefore, I reject 4 Rd2 and my best line with 3 Ne1 Bf1 appears to be 4 Qc2 with a large advantage to White. So while either 3 Ne1 or 3 Re1 appears to win, why give him the free rook? I will play 3 Ne1."

So, not only was White winning by capturing the queen, but on the next move he could not even be mated no matter what he did, had he analyzed 2 Rxe2 carefully to try to justify it instead of acceding with 2 Bd2??. When opportunity knocks, you have to be there – mentally and otherwise! And, we can also conclude that instead of 1...Qe2?? almost any other safe move, like 1...Qg4, was better; the best move would have been the killer 1...Rd1.

OK, that was fun and instructive stuff. You want to experience as much of that as you can, so at tournaments and clubs, listen to good players analyze to pick up their skills. Books on this subject include Kotov's classic *Think Like a Grandmaster*, Aagaard's *Inside the Chess Mind*, Soltis' excellent *How to Choose a Chess Move*, and my *The Improving Chess Thinker*.

The following is a list of the most important skills used in analysis. The aim is to help you identify areas that need to be improved to become a better analyst.

Analysis Skills

- *Deductive Logic* – The goal is to see which moves are candidates (for both players), and what is forced and what is not. For example, "If I go here, what moves would my opponent have to make?" or "If my opponent has these two threats, what moves can meet both of them?"

- *Memory* – What is a player supposed to do in a position like this one? What guidelines apply to this type of position? What does theory say about this opening or endgame?

- *Pattern Recognition* – What kind of position is this? Is it similar to something I have seen before? Is there a Seed of Tactical Destruction (a defect in a position that might allow a tactic; see the archived *The Seeds of Tactical Destruction*)? If I have seen a tactic in a position similar to this, does the tactic still work here?

- *Carefulness* – This is a greatly underrated skill. One has to be very careful during analysis, since one mistake can result in choosing a line which is bad for you. It just takes one bad move to lose a game, and thus a single analysis error can easily lead to a loss. I am sure it has happened to you...

- *Micro Time Management* – You are trying to find the best move you can, *given the time constraints*. So knowing how much analysis you can do via the criticality of the position and the time situation is an important skill. For example, taking too much time in non-critical positions, or not enough time in critical positions, or failure to recognize what is a critical position, can all be fatal errors.

- *Will* – to analyze the position correctly, move after move.

- *Patience* – to analyze the position thoroughly.

- *Thought process* – to know what steps to take.

- ♟ *Board vision* – to see what is happening (statically) across the entire board quickly and accurately.

- ♟ *Visualization* – to keep the imagined patterns correctly in the mind's eye when looking ahead.

- ♟ *Quiescence recognition* – to know when to stop analyzing lines and evaluate.

- ♟ *Criticality assessment (awareness of danger)*, plus the recognition of *The Seeds of Tactical Destruction*.

A related skill: *Evaluation* at the nodes of the analysis tree. This is technically not part of analysis, but pertinent to the discussion; see *"Using evaluation with analysis to determine the best move"* in *Chess is Decisions* (2-7).

Some are better than others at these various "innate" skills. However, that does not mean that you cannot improve these skills greatly! For example, I could not play blindfold chess when I started to play tournament chess at age 16; yet two years later – without any practice – I could do so fairly easily. I got "better" at this visualization skill primarily just by playing many slow games and going over numerous games in chess books. Similarly, when I first started out I played "Hope Chess" (did not attempt to find my opponent's forcing replies to my candidate moves and how I could safely meet those replies) and used only about 20-30 minutes out of the allotted two hours. Yet, before I had played one year, I had worked out a much better thought process and, by doing so, also learned to pace myself so that I took almost exactly all my time in every game, which is the "only" correct speed of play. So again I was able to improve crucial skills through awareness, determination, and practice.

I even improved at carefulness, and this was primarily a result of awareness. Once I learned that good chess players could always beat you if you made one bad mistake, I made the commitment to play every move as if it were to be published in every magazine in the world: I may make many mistakes, but I never purposely play a move with less than my best effort.

The above generic skills lead in turn to "chess-specific" skills. These include the ability to:

- ♟ Quickly generate reasonable candidate moves.
- ♟ Accurately identify threats and basic tactical patterns.
- ♟ Discern which aspects of the position are relevant and which are not.
- ♟ Stop the analysis without looking too far at unnecessary moves but far enough to not be surprised.

At the heart of analysis is choosing candidate moves, including yours and your opponents, eventually creating the entire analysis tree. One way to examine one's tree-generation capability involves categorizing moves into the following types:

1. Checks

2. Captures

3. Threats

4. Moves that increase your piece's activity or decrease the opponent's pieces activity

5. Forced moves, like "the only legal" ones, or necessary recaptures

6. All other moves

Whenever you select candidate moves, you should consider forced (#5) and forcing (#1-#3) moves first. Suppose your opponent is attacking your queen with a piece of lesser value and you have no in-between forcing moves that would cause him not to capture it; then you are forced to save it in some way.

However, in most cases you should consider your forcing moves first, usually in the order of checks, then captures, and then threats. The reason is that *even if your opponent is threatening something, you might have an even more forcing sequence that you would otherwise miss by just addressing his threat*. For example, if your opponent is threatening your queen, but you can checkmate him with a series of checks, then you don't need to save your queen. Many players miss opportunities because they concentrate too much on their opponent's threats and overlook their own greater opportunities.

There is one major exception to the "forcing sequence" order of *checks, captures, and threats*.

Threats to checkmate by force, especially *threats of mate in one*, are *more* forcing than captures, and sometimes even more forcing than checks, and so deserve higher priority in your search for reasonable moves.

In positions where there are no forcing moves (for example, early in many openings), then the primary goal should be to play a move of type #4: moves that increase your army's activity or decrease your opponent's activity. The guidelines "Find your worst piece and find a way to make it better", "Trade off your opponent's most active pieces", and "Find your opponent's worst piece and see if you can find a way to make it permanently bad" are all aimed at this type of move.

You don't have to identify *all* your candidate moves at the start, although for players who move too quickly doing so will help them slow down. If at any point you can prove that your move must be best, then you can immediately make your move! However, if you have adequate time, the game is close, and there are multiple analytical possibilities like captures, then any good move will not do – if you see a good move, look for a better one. The following are common analysis mistakes made by weaker players:

♟ They don't try to find the best moves for each side. For example, they "assume" their opponent will make an inferior move and then are surprised when faced with a much better one.

♟ They don't apply the ideas in this article to both players' moves, but rather only to *their* candidate moves. They don't next consider the opponent's checks, captures, and threats, etc. (So they play too fast.)

♟ They waste time in analytical positions without comparing the positions that could occur after one move with the positions that could occur after another, to see which is preferable. This is a very common and big error!

Each time you identify a forcing sequence, make sure it is as forcing as you think it is, and try to analyze to quiescence. Of course, *it is not always possible to analyze to quiescence*. For example, suppose you are contemplating the "classical bishop sacrifice" 1 Bxh7+ and you analyze that Black must play 1...Kxh7 (else he will just be down a pawn for nothing with his king somewhat exposed), and that after 2 Ng5+ he must play 2...Kg6 (the normal move), when you then have 3 Qg4. It may not be possible to calculate all the possible defenses for Black from that point. So you have to use your evaluation skill – your judgment of how good the position is for you, which in turn determines how good you feel the move 1 Bxh7+ is. If you evaluate the move as unclear and otherwise think you can play a move that leaves you better, then 1 Bxh7+ is likely not best and should not be played. However, if you find that 1 Bxh7+ is unclear, but otherwise your other "best" moves lead to an equal position, then *if you are trying to learn, play the unclear lines over the equal one*. That way you will improve your judgment and next time you will have a better feel as to whether the sacrifice in similar positions is good or bad.

Here are additional tips for analyzing:

Small considerations rarely overcome big considerations. For example, wrecking your pawn structure is usually a small price to pay for winning material – see *The Principle of Tactical Dominance* (2-6).

Another big issue is being able to see the entire board as accurately and as quickly as possible ("board vision") so that you can analyze better – see *The Three Types of Chess Vision* (4-4).

When the time limit for the game is shorter, all analysis suffers. This leads to an important point: *a significant way to get better at analytical skills is to play a great many games at time limits long enough to practice and improve those skills*. That way when you do play shorter games it is much easier to "shortcut" a good analytical practice than it would be if you never played those long games and do not have good analytical practices. With regard to analysis, practice will not make perfect, but it sure can make for dramatic improvement, even in visualization!

Outside of playing, other types of analysis practice are a great way to improve. For example, after a game, analyzing with stronger players is a surefire way to improve your skills. Playing correspondence (email or snail mail) allows you to move the pieces, and this can also help develop analysis skills, except for visualization! A book series specifically designed to improve visualization is *Chess Visualization Course* by Ian Anderson. Self analysis of your game – preferably before you give it to a computer program – is yet another common and effective practice (see *Reviewing Chess Games* 1-3).

Managing your time so that you spend most of it when the position is critical is an important skill. Alburt and Lawrence's book, *Chess Rules of Thumb*, lists five characteristics of a critical position:

1. When the game changes from known theory into unknown territory, from opening to middlegame, or from middlegame to endgame.

2. When any pieces are exchanged, especially queens.

3. When there is any change, or possible change in the pawn structure – especially in the center.

4. When you have a tactical (short-lived) advantage which will disappear if not exploited now.

5. When you see a move which seems to win.

Their next principle is: "a critical position is one about which you should think long and hard". For example, in a quiet position a computer rates your best move as giving you a +0.21 pawn advantage, the second best +0.18, and the third best +0.16, then that move was likely not too critical. But in another position where the pieces were flying around the board, you find that your best move was rated at +3.26, the second best +0.60, and the third best -2.13. In these complicated, analytical positions, realizing the position is critical and taking time to find the best move is usually the difference between winning, drawing, or even losing.

So *if you can at least allocate most of your time to the moves that need it most, then even if your overall analytical skills don't improve much, your results will.*

Bootstrapping Analysis Skills

When you work on improving the analytical skills listed earlier, through practice and exercises, you need to "bootstrap" them as a group. Concentrating on one or two will eventually result in diminishing returns on those skills and leave you woefully short on your overall analytical capability. Therefore, if you are especially weak at one or more of these areas, you should concentrate on strengthening those areas to get the most out of your study time. Your analysis chain is only as strong as its weakest link.

Examples

1. Suppose you are an experienced player with good board vision, but have not extensively studied basic tactical patterns. Then you can see what is happening on the board, but instead of quickly and accurately recognizing basic tactical possibilities for both sides, you have to figure them out. In doing so, you are not only slower, but less accurate, because knowing the solution reduces error in trying to figure it out. See *The Three Types of Chess Vision* (4-4).

2. Suppose you are fairly good with deductive logic, but use it only to figure out

what *your* pieces can do – your application of this skill to your *opponent's* possibilities is minimal. That means you will be able to find good moves for yourself, but will consistently allow your opponents easy tactics. You can never become a good player until you give approximately equal weight to both players' possibilities.

3. Suppose you neglect the area of evaluation and concentrate only on analysis. Then you will be able to figure out what might happen, but, since you don't know how good a particular position is, you will consistently choose the wrong move. Everyone knows how to evaluate positions where a king is being checkmated or there is a clear material imbalance, but evaluating positions where the material is even and both kings are safe is key. Many weak players think that pawn structure is more important than the activity of the pieces or the advantage of the bishop pair, but that is usually incorrect (see *Evaluation Criteria* 2-4). Take the following position, from the archived *Evaluation Quiz*:

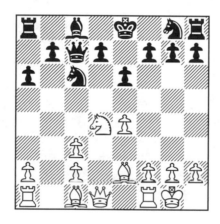

White to play

White's queenside pawn structure is ruined: his a-pawn is isolated and his c-pawns are doubled and isolated on a semi-open file (about as bad as it gets). White has three pawn islands to Black's two, and both sides have two pieces in play, although White is castled. Many intermediate players think that Black is better, but nothing could be further from the truth. White to play has a sizable, likely winning, advantage, primarily due to three factors: the bishop pair; the presence of Black's weak dark squares, coupled with White's monstrous dark-squared bishop; and Black's inability to castle while holding the d6 square. (Don't believe me? Have a computer play this position against itself or, if you are very bold, with White against you!) This misconception illustrates a very important and often overlooked principle: *If one player is weak on a color complex, has no bishop of that color, and the opponent has that color bishop, and the queens are on the board, that weakness is likely worth more than one pawn.* In this example all those criteria are present, and that is the fuel for White's advantage.

If, as Black, you purposely go into positions such as the one above because you think you are better, then you will consistently find yourself defending bad positions, even if you were properly able to analyze all the possibilities.

4.   Suppose you are good at all the other skills, but your micro time management (see Section 3) is terrible. This results in one of three problems:

♟   You play too fast and could have played much better if you had taken more time;

♟   You play too slow and get into unnecessary time trouble, whereupon you make hasty moves that cause you to lose;

♟   You play inconsistently where your total time used (macro time management) may be reasonable, but you spend too much time on non-critical moves and too little time on critical moves, the latter usually resulting in terrible mistakes that cause you to lose.

Therefore, if you are proficient at all the other analytical skills except for this one, you will still end up making enormous mistakes that could have been avoided (see *The Three Show-Stoppers* in 1-4, page 48).

The moral of the story is clear: your analytical chain is only as strong as its weakest link. To continually work on the same links and to neglect others will result in severely diminishing returns on your study time and – once again – explain why so many players keep doing "the same good things" and don't make any progress.

If you can improve each of your key analysis skills and also recognize which associated actions, attitudes, and approaches are the most effective, then your improvement will be noticeable. However, *even with the knowledge of how to proceed*, improving is a slow process.

Interestingly, when a player asks me, "I have been playing for twenty years and have not made any improvement in the last fifteen. What should I do?" and I explain how to identify and work on some of the above skills, many reply with reasons why it won't be effective! Yet it does work for those players who have high perseverance and are proficient at *Breaking Down Barriers* (4-3).

Let's put your analysis skills to work. What should White do in the following position?

(see following diagram)

The first question to ask is *"Am I playing to win or am I playing to draw?"* In this position White is ahead a pawn, so normally White would be playing to win.

On this assumption, the next thing you should *always* ask in such positions is, "Can I simplify by exchanging rooks to win the king and pawn endgame?" If the answer is 100% "Yes", you should go ahead and do it. But you must be sure you are winning. *Don't trade down into a king and pawn endgame where you are not sure that you are getting the result you want*, unless not doing so would clearly give you even fewer chances. The corollary is that unless you have some trivial checkmate, *you should always trade into a winning king and pawn endgame, since that is the easiest endgame to win.*

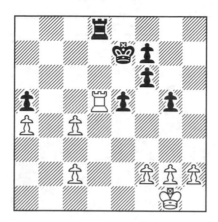

White to play

In amateur games it is amazing how often the player who is worse trades or offers to trade into a losing king and pawn endgame, or players who would have an easily winning king and pawn endgame often refuse to enter into it (especially if that trade involves a "sacrifice").

Therefore, in the diagram, the first line you should analyze is 1 Rxd8 Kxd8. One could argue that perhaps the first move you should examine is winning material "free" by 1 Rxa5, but *almost always a winning king and pawn endgame is even better/easier than a rook and pawn endgame where you are ahead an extra pawn.* Of course, in this case, 1 Rxa5?? is met by 1...Rd1 mate so the question about taking the pawn becomes moot.

In this position, trading rooks cannot be played quickly on general principles. Although White is ahead a pawn, his crippled pawn structure means that you can't just rely on a weak guess, such as "White is ahead a pawn so he should trade rooks". A king and pawn endgame is usually deterministic, even for humans: either White wins or he doesn't. You don't find king and pawn endgames where one side is "a little better"; one can have the better side of a draw, but that's about it.

Returning to our analysis, after 1 Rxd8 Kxd8, what should White do? The most obvious try is to activate the king, so 2 Kf1 makes sense. After 2...Kd7 3 Ke2 Kd6 4 Kd3 Kc5 5 Kc3, White's king arrives in time to prevent Black from either capturing on c4 or winning the a-pawn, but now which side can make progress?

It turns out that Black's potential passed pawn is on the e-file, so 5...f5, with the idea of ...e5-e4, ...f5-f4, and then possibly ...e4-e3 to create a passed pawn is thematic. Similarly, White's potential passed pawn – on the outside! – is possible after 6 h3 (but not 6 g3? g4! making the h-pawn backward) and then g2-g3 and h3-h4.

But wait! This should ring a bell, courtesy of your deductive logic skill. Why does the white king have to go to c3 at all? Can't White just create unstoppable passed pawns on the c- and h-files immediately after the rook trade? Indeed, he can! The one difference is that Black's king is now free to wreak havoc on the queenside. So now you just have to count tempi to see if Black can counterattack by capturing on a4 and getting his own passed pawn: **1 Rxd8 Kxd8 2 h3!**.

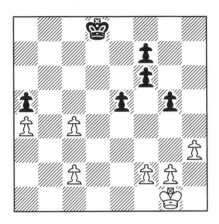

Black to play

 2...Kc7 3 g3 Kc6 4 h4 Kc5 (or 4...gxh4 5 gxh4 first with the same relative tempi) **5 h5 Kb4 6 h6 Kxa4** (the race is not even that close, but, unless you are in time trouble, it never hurts to confirm!) **7 h7 Kb4 8 h8Q a4 9 Qxf6 a3 10 Qxe5** and White wins easily. Again, 2 g3?, trying to save a tempo, fails miserably to 2...g4! when, because of the backward h-pawn and the possibility of *en passant*, White cannot create a passed pawn on the h-file.

 Since White wins with 1 Rxd8, there is no need to find a better move. Therefore, we should make one last re-check just to be safe. *This extra caution is justified since the proposed move is critical, a potential winner, and after it there is no turning back.*

2-6) The Principle of Tactical Dominance

Never apply tiebreak criteria to non-tiebreak positions.

Weaker players often make the process of choosing certain moves far more difficult than it should be. Consider the following:

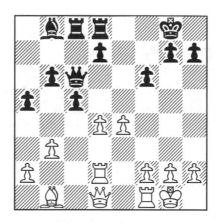

White to play

White plays 1 dxc5. How should Black recapture?

If Black plays 1...Qxc5? then White plays 2 Rxd7 winning a pawn. So Black should play **1...bxc5**, allowing the queen to continue protecting the d-pawn. Yet in a similar position, a student played 1...Qxc5? because he "didn't want to get an isolated pawn on the a-file"(!). When I analyzed the position, I never got so far as to consider the isolated pawn; I did not consider any positional features once I realized there was only one way of recapturing without losing a pawn.

The student's thought process is a good example of (mis)applying tiebreak criteria to non-tiebreak positions.

Tiebreak criteria are any single or set of minor, positional considerations. In GM Larry Kaufman's excellent *Chess Life* article on isolated pawns, he stated that the single worst positional disadvantage was doubled isolated pawns on a semi-open file. Such a ruined pair of pawns was worth, on the average, only slightly more than one pawn – they had lost almost a full pawn in value. This is an interesting observation which allows us to draw an important and practical "powerful" conclusion:

The single *highest valued* positional factor is worth *slightly less* than the *least valued* tactical factor (a pawn). In other words, *tactics almost always take precedence over a positional consideration*, since even the smallest material loss may be more valuable than the largest positional one. We can even make this the...

Principle of Tactical Dominance

Tactical criteria dominate positional criteria. Therefore, use of positional criteria is almost always useless if there is a tactic that wins material or checkmates; decide tactics first and only apply positional criteria if no tactic exists.

In other words, *when considering candidate moves, first decide if there are any tactical considerations that cost either side a pawn or more. If there are no tactics that would conclusively indicate a particular move, then use strategic and positional considerations as a "tiebreak" to decide between the moves that involve no material gains or losses.*

This powerful knowledge makes many difficult-looking chess decisions easy and saves valuable clock time! For example, in the above position, a player can disregard whether the a-pawn becomes isolated in deciding how to capture since a tactical consideration – the loss of pawn – is involved. In other words, tactics decide – if there are no tactics then positional considerations are the tiebreak – they usually only decide if the tactics are absent or neutral. (Note: This idea is closely related to the principle: *When you are way ahead in material, don't worry about the little things.* Because most little things *are* positional nuances, when one side gets far enough ahead these fractional values are secondary factors and needn't be strongly considered.)

Let's consider another example. Black has just played **1...g4**. What should White do?

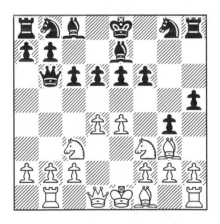

White to play

In a similar position a student immediately played 2 Nd2, with the analysis: "If I play 2 Nh4 or 2 Ng1 then my knight is not well placed – *a knight on the rim and your future is dim* – so I must play 2 Nd2." But this overlooks the obvious – and much more important – fact that after 2 Nd2? Black can simply capture the pawn on d4 with 2...Qxd4, so the "bad" 2 Nh4 is correct (being much more active than the other rim move, 2 Ng1). By choosing the "centralizing" 2 Nd2?, this student was erroneously applying tiebreak criteria in a non-tiebreak position.

I have found that many students often play similar bad tactical moves after wasting several minutes agonizing over arcane strategic and positional factors. *These players could save themselves from making a bad move, and quite a bit of time on the clock, if they first consider the question, "is my candidate move safe?" Or, more comprehensively, "Is my candidate move tactically justified?" and reject it if it allows a forcing reply that loses material.*

This failure to realize that tactics take precedence over other considerations is an epidemic among *weaker players, who are filled with useless opening knowledge and overweighted* (for them!) *positional information, but can't count or calculate correctly.* Tactics – and careful analysis – are more important! The applicable phrase for their deliberations is: "Penny wise and pound foolish". The result of this misguidance is that players rated below ~1400 often make decisions that look crazy to a stronger player because they would rather give up small amounts of material (a large concession since a clear pawn advantage is often enough to have a winning position!) rather than make a tiny positional concession.

¹White to play

In this position White can save the attacked e-pawn in many ways. Instead, White chose to lose the pawn by playing **1 Nxc6?** and after **1...Qxe4+ 2 Qe2 Qxe2+ 3 Bxe2 dxc6** the material was even. After the game I asked White, "Why not save the pawn with 1 f3?" 1 Nc3 is even better (not 1 Qd3 Qb4+ 2 Qc3? Nxd4! 3 Qxb4 Nc2+ 4 Kd2 Nxb4 winning the knight. although sacrificing the b-pawn with 2 Nc3! is strong), but I was curious as to why the plausible 1 f3 had been rejected. Interestingly, White saw that 1 f3 was safe, but rejected it immediately because "it was better to give up the pawn than weaken the future castled kingside position with 1 f3." However, 1 f3 hardly weakens the future king position – Black no longer has a dark-squared bishop and the only weakened square, e3, is not a problem. But just the fact that White *thought* that it was better to lose a pawn than create the "weakness" with f3 shows that White was unaware of the *Principle of Tactical Dominance*, and thus valued a minor positional weakness more than a pawn!

Suppose you stumble across the following position after **1 e4 c5 2 d4 cxd4** (or even 1 d4 c5 2 e4 cxd4) without realizing that the "book" idea is to play the Morra Gambit with 3 c3:

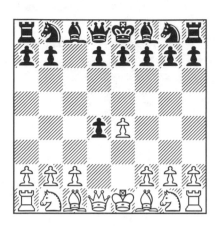

White to play

Assuming you don't know that 3 c3 is a decent gambit, you could play 3 Nf3. That's a very good move, especially if you know that after 3...e5?! you should play 4 c3! with a favorable Morra Gambit (but not 4 Nxe5?? which loses the knight to 4...Qa5+). But *if* you don't know that 3 c3 is the normal move, you probably also would not understand the nuances of 3 Nf3 either, so we can assume you should not play 3 Nf3.

One of my students recently arrived at this position and thought: "OK, I can't take the pawn with the queen because then my queen is developed too early and Black will win a tempo after 3 Qxd4 Nc6." So my student played **3 Nf3 e5 4 c4?** (4 c3!) when if Black had simply played 4...Nc6 or 4...d6 or even 4...Nf6 (5 Nxe5? Qa5+ again wins the knight) he would already be ahead a protected passed pawn after four moves!

So this is a case where the *Principle of Tactical Dominance* clearly held again. White's position is *much* better after 3 Qxd4 Nc6 than it is after 3 Nf3 e5 4 c4? Nc6. Although 3 Qxd4 is *not* better than 3 Nf3, it *is* better to win back the pawn with an even game than to lose a pawn. My student clearly gave too much "evaluation weight" to losing a tempo after 3 Qxd4 Nc6 compared to the much bigger problem of being down a pawn for nothing. So, once again, we find a weak player regarding minor positional considerations as being worth more than a pawn.

To some extent, this under-evaluation of a pawn's value by less experienced players *is* understandable.

When you first start playing, your opponents are also weak, and losing a pawn is no big deal since more valuable pieces are so loosely tossed around. Moreover, getting your queen out early and having it kicked about can often lead to quick and devastating losses, so no wonder a beginner might conclude that bringing their queen out to a square where it might be attacked *could* be worse than losing a pawn. But eventually, as you and your competition improve, your respect for an extra healthy pawn starts to grow in proportion to you and your opponent's ability to win with it. At the start of the game, *before the opposing forces clash*, a tempo is usually worth about a third of a pawn, so regaining a "free" pawn at this early stage is clearly superior to saving a tempo.

pawn at this early stage is clearly superior to saving a tempo.

OK, the *Principle of Tactical Dominance* is only a principle – a guideline, and not a rule. There *is* a material advantage that can result from a mini-tactic that is worth less than a pawn: the bishop pair. The bishop pair (the full terminology is "the advantage of the bishop pair", meaning one side has two bishops and the other does not), is a material value, but only worth about ½ pawn, on the average. Therefore any "tactic" winning the bishop pair might easily be outweighed by positional values. Consider the following:

1 g3 c5 2 Bg2 Nc6 3 c4 Nf6 4 b3 b6 5 Bb2 g6

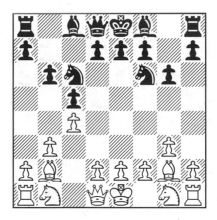

White to play

Here, with the golden opportunity to permanently weaken the d5- and d6-squares and dominate d5, White gladly gives up the bishop pair with **6 Bxf6! exf6** and Black can no longer guard the d5- or d6-squares with a pawn since the e-pawn has moved to the f-file and the c-pawn has already advanced. After **7 Nc3** the domination – and eventual occupation – of the important d5-square more than compensates for the bishop pair.

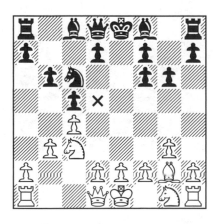

Black to play

Keep in mind, however, that *most positional features are worth less than half a pawn* as well, so winning the bishop pair is a "mini-tactic" that takes precedence over most positional features.

Moreover, there are times when a single positional weakness creates long-term tactical opportunities. For example, suppose the queens are still on the board and you can weaken a square or pawn in front of the opponent's king. In these cases it is not just the compensation of the positional weaknesses that allows one to sacrifice material (say the bishop pair, a pawn, or possibly in rarer cases even a piece!), but rather the additional longer-term tactical opportunities to create a mating attack.

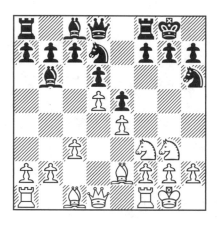

White to play

In this position White should seriously consider giving up the bishop (and thus the bishop pair) with 1 Bxh6. But it is not just the doubled isolated h-pawns that are the compensation; his other minor pieces are well placed to support a kingside attack.

On the other hand, in the Advance French after **1 e4 e6 2 d4 d5 3 e5 c5 4 c3 Nc6 5 Nf3 Qb6 6 Be2**, IM John Watson suggests **6...Nh6** as a main line.

White to play

Here, in comparison to the previous position, with the black bishop on f8 and Black's king in the center, **7 Bxh6** is certainly a reasonable move, but hardly a killer. Both sides have chances – and Black may even castle kingside in many lines after ...Bg7!.

Earlier we suggested that before the pieces clash, a tempo is only worth about ⅓ of a pawn (after they clash a tempo can be worth a piece or more!). But that is less than the ½ pawn value of the bishop pair. Therefore, *near the start of the game it is usually correct to preserve the bishop pair at the cost of a tempo.* For example, in the King's Indian Defense, after **1 d4 Nf6 2 c4 g6 3 Nc3 Bg7 4 e4 d6 5 Be2 0-0 6 Nf3 Nbd7** (6...e5 is the main line) **7 0-0 e5 8 Be3 Ng4**

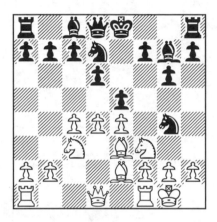

White to play

...the correct move is not to guard the bishop with a developing move such as 9 Qd2, allowing 9...Nxe3, but instead preserve it with **9 Bg5**. Similarly, in the Najdorf Sicilian, after **1 e4 c5 2 Nf3 d6 3 d4 cxd4 4 Nxd4 Nf6 5 Nc3 a6 6 Be3 Ng4**

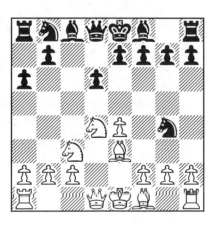

White to play

...the main line is **7 Bg5**, preserving the bishop pair.

Although a pawn is almost always worth more than a *single* positional feature, it could be worth less than *multiple* positional features. It is possible that multiple positional considerations can add up to more than one pawn's worth of value, so of course it is possible to sacrifice a pawn (or more!) for positional considerations. It is important to note that it is more likely one would sacrifice a pawn for your army's *piece activity* (as you do in most opening gambits) or to weaken your opponent's *king safety*, which are different issues.

Since multiple positional criteria can have larger value, we can state an exception to the Principle: *If more than one positional criterion is affected, it is possible, although unlikely, that the total value could add up to more than one pawn, so it may be possible to "win" a pawn, but at too great a positional cost.* But, although this exception can occur frequently in practice, the percent the Principle does apply is so high that weaker players can – and should – forget about balancing positional factors against material loss until they achieve at least intermediate status.

As an *ad absurdum* example, suppose White initially has a perfect pawn structure, but in the course of his combination (several moves) to win a black pawn, has to accept the doubling and isolation of *all* white pawns:

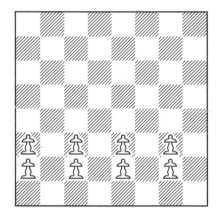

In almost all cases, such a disaster would be worth far more than a single pawn, so White would not even consider accepting such a trade-off. Nevertheless, this general domination of positional features by tactics helps explain why someone's playing strength – especially for players rated less than 2000 – is closely related to their ability to analyze. Since tactics are the most important component of analysis, other factors such as planning and evaluation become "tiebreaks" to playing strength, only when analytical and tactical ability is similar (as we see in many players rated 2000+). For most players rated below 2000, the better the analyst, the better the player.

2-7) The Fun of Pros and Cons

How many people would have fun flipping a coin all day to see if more heads or tails came up?

Anyone who wants to become a better player and does not understand the idea of decision-making is doomed to have a "low ceiling" in their quest for improvement. Adding chess knowledge, such as learning to play the Caro-Kann better or win the Lucena endgame, is only going to get you so far.

The following applies to anyone who wishes to improve their game:

♟ If you want to be a better player, you have to make better moves.

♟ If you want to make better moves, you have to make better decisions about the moves you play.

♟ If you want to make better decisions, you have to at least compare different moves to see how good they are (based on your evaluation of the positions resulting from those moves).

♟ If you want to compare different moves, you can't just consider one move or idea.

Conclusion: *If you want to be a better player, you have to consistently make decisions and compare moves, and not just act upon the first move you see.* You also have to learn how to make *better* decisions. This requires making at least one, if not multiple, comparisons between your choices!

Many players often choose their moves instantly – or with very little decision making – in positions where they should take more time. *This tendency to jump to conclusions in positions with multiple choices is found even among players who might not otherwise play that quickly.*

In a slow game I don't "hand wave" and make analytical decisions based on general principles. For most good players, including myself, much of the fun in playing slow games is "controlling the environment": analyzing carefully to ensure the right choices are made. It would be no fun to make a non-forced move in eight (!) seconds, as was done in the example below despite Black having 45 minutes remaining.

If I moved that quickly and it turned out I either threw away a chance to get a better game or, even worse, lost one I should not, then I would feel terrible. That would be like deciding games via a coin toss. On the other hand, if I took my time, tried my best, and still made the same mistake, I would not feel nearly as bad. It's not the mistake that hurts the most, but rather the knowledge that I might have prevented it if I had played the way I knew I should.

Moving without comparing the possibilities would be no fun at all; old-timers called players who did this "woodpushers" because they were not really thinking and making decisions – just pushing wood. In positions with distinct choices it's an intellectual challenge to try to "do the puzzle" and figure out which lines come out best; to pick a line quickly just because "it looks good" or "maybe it wins" leaves too much to chance.

Take look at that eight-second move from a student's slow game on the internet:

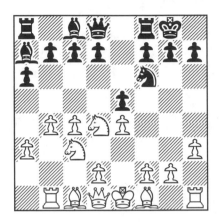

Black to play after 9 Nxd4

Black has to decide whether to recapture with the pawn or the bishop. There are pros and cons for each capture. If this were a speed game, I would quickly recapture with the pawn because it is the oft-missed removal of the guard tactic: **9...exd4** and, after the white knight moves, **10...Nxe4** and I *seem* to win a pawn. Since tactics dominate positional considerations (see *The Principle of Tactical Dominance* 2-6), it would seem that this would be enough to choose 9...exd4. But in slow games good players require more information – they ask themselves "Is it really so?"

Let's have some fun and give our brains a challenge by considering the pros and cons of each recapture:

- 9...Bxd4 – This centralizes and seemingly activates the bishop. It avoids doubling pawns on the d-file. It attacks the knight on c3, which is guarding the e-pawn, and it prevents the bishop from possibly being shut out of the game with c5.

- 9...exd4 – This immediately attacks the defender and loosens the e-pawn. Besides removing the defender it may cause the knight on c3 to go to a better or worse square. It opens the e-file for the rook on f8, and after a further 10...Nxe4, the white king is exposed in the middle.

However, the above considerations are not enough to make the move! They are only halfway past "hand-waving". In order to determine the best recapture, I need to analyze the likely lines of play and see which I like better.

For example, after 9...exd4, where would the white knight go?

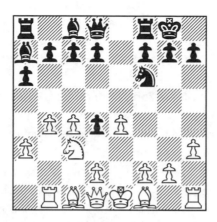

White to play after 9...exd4

If 10 Ne2, it attacks d4, but that square is guarded and the knight on e2 blocks the light-squared bishop. 10 Ne2 does cover the king, but, after 10...Nxe4 11 g3 (to develop the bishop), Black is doing very well; while after 11 c5 (to remove the guard on the d-pawn), Black can guard it indirectly with 11...Re8, when 12 Nxd4?? loses the queen to the "Petroff trap" 12...Nc3+.

If White plays 10 Nd5, he can't stay there forever since ...c7-c6 can't be prevented. Moreover, after 10...Nxe4 11 c5? (to block in the bishop), 11...Re8 wins. Moving away from the center with 10 Na4 or 10 Na2 is certainly no better. The counterattack 10 e5 is interesting, but, after 10...Re8, Black is not only pinning the e-pawn, he is also attacking both that pawn and the knight on c3, so it seems to fail as well. Therefore, after 9...exd4, Black is doing fine.

But if you see a good move, and have the time, look for a better one! To play 9...exd4 without even comparing it to the alternative would be a crime. Put 9...exd4 in your pocket. You can always play it if 9...Bxd4 does not look as good. Let's look at 9...Bxd4.

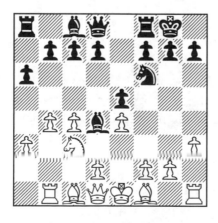

White to play after 9...Bxd4

If 10 Be2, then Black can still give up the bishop pair and play 10...Bxc3 11 dxc3 Nxe4, although winning a pawn for nothing (with 9...exd4) is much better than giving up the bishop pair for the pawn. However, White does not have to give Black the e-pawn at all. For example, after 10 Qc2 Bxc3 11 dxc3, the pawn is guarded and White preserves his bishop pair. Note 10 d3 won't do, since the pawn was guarding the knight and 10...Bxc3+ wins the knight.

One has to consider the problem long enough (see *A Room Full of Grandmasters* 3-2, page 162) that the amount of time taken would be reasonable for finding the best move in the given circumstances. How long is reasonable here? It depends on the time limit and the criticality of the position. In this case the game was 45 minutes with a 45 second increment, so the average time for a move is about two minutes. These two minutes can make a big difference. Thus, based on the above, I would likely have played 9...exd4.

Let's give this position to *Rybka* and let it run for several hours: at 23 ply it gives 9...exd4 as -0.85 pawns (Black is almost a pawn ahead) and 9...Bxd4 as -0.21. So Black is over half a pawn better with 9...exd4 than 9...Bxd4, and winning the pawn, as suspected, was easily correct.

Now let's return to my student, who played 9...Bxd4 in eight seconds even though he had over 45 minutes left on his clock. In my experience this student is very typical of many intermediate players: they are not so much interested in finding out whether 9...Bxd4 is better than 9...exd4. They make many moves on general principles (e.g. capture 9...Bxd4 because it doesn't double pawns; activates the bishop, and attacks the knight) and then "see what happens".

Yet, not weighing the pros and cons, and not doing the requisite analysis is enough to keep one a weaker player forever. *Almost all weaker players would be hundreds of rating points higher if they would just consistently do three things*:

1. Take their time on each move, as dictated by the time control and the situation;

2. Make sure their move is safe and, if the opponent's move is not safe, consider just taking the material;

3. Make sure all their pieces are always active and not play with a subset of the pieces.

Easier said than done, but some of the best chess advice you will ever get.

A big part of the above is to enjoy the decision-making process of doing the analysis and weighing the pros and cons. If you have fun doing the analysis, you will always take your time. If you always take your time, you will be more likely to avoid making simple blunders and more likely to catch your opponent's safety errors (see *Chess, Learning, and Fun* 4-2).

Unfortunately, examples like the one above are commonplace. Take any timed game between two weaker players and you can usually find several moves where one side played too quickly and missed an easy win of a pawn or more. Yet good players only need a pawn advantage to win the game. So a pawn advantage is usually a big lead – and once weaker players come to this realization it is often a sign that they are improving.

Any move can be the one that loses the game, so playing too fast and "flipping the coin" – even once during a game – is often what keeps players from achieving a higher rating category.

Here is another example from the same game, a few moves later.

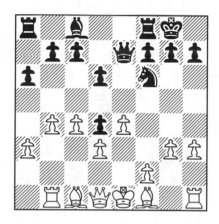

Black to play after 13 g3

Keep in mind both players started with 45 minutes on their clock and have a 45 second increment each move. The times at this point were White: 52:09 (!) and Black 45:53. Considering both players have been out of "book" since move two, we can say that Black is "only" playing much too fast, while White is playing super-fast.

Black now considers the capture **13...Nxe4**. Is this a candidate? Of course! Any move that might do something positive should be a candidate (see *Initial and Final Candidate Moves* 2-1, page 77). Black quickly reasons: if White captures 14 dxe4, then after 14...Qxe4+, I am attacking both unguarded rooks. If White does not capture 14 dxe4, then I win a pawn and threaten a discovered check. What could be better than that?

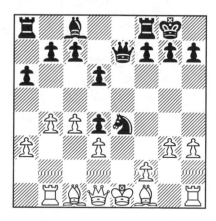

White to play after 13...Nxe4

Unfortunately, Black only thought about this for eleven (!) seconds, ignoring Alburt and Lawrence's sage advice in their handy book *Chess Rules of Thumb*: "When you see a move which seems to win, that is a critical position...A critical position is one about which you should think long and hard."

To White's credit, he thought for over four minutes on his reply. Unfortunately, he could not find an answer and so acquiesced (see the archived *Acquiescing*) with **14 Bb2??**. This lost his queen to the "Petroff trap" **14...Nc3+**. While four minutes can hardly be criticized as a quick think, if White missed this simple discovered check and had over 50 minutes on his clock, then taking more time surely would have been helpful. No sense saving all that time for a completely lost position. It also shows that being familiar with basic tactics – such as discovered checks – is extremely helpful, *especially when applied to your opponent's replies!*

But suppose White had played the correct 14 Qe2:

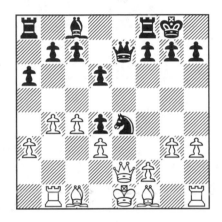

Black to play after 14 Qe2!

In retrospect, the eleven seconds that Black took for move 13 can now be seen as Hope Chess – you make a move without analyzing all your opponent's checks, captures, and threats, and then you hope you can meet his reply. Unfortunately, there seems to be no good answer to this pin. For example, if 14...Re8 15 dxe4 (but not 15 Qxe4?? Qd8 and Black wins the queen – it is always necessary to be careful!) 15...Qxe4 16 Qxe4 Rxe4+ 17 Kd1 (but not 17 Be2?? d3 – there is that careful thing again), and White is ahead a piece for two pawns plus the bishop pair and is well on his way to winning.

Truth in advertising department: I let *Rybka* analyze this position and, after 20 ply or so, it found a wonderfully deep and clever line for Black that guarantees an advantage after 14 Qe2! Bf5!!. But that does not negate my point – the lesson is still sound!

Here is another example of pros and cons:

(see following diagram)

It seems like Black has only six choices to not lose a piece:

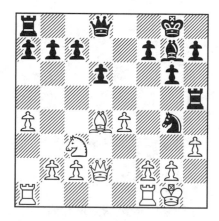

Black to play after 14 h3

- Save the knight with 14...Ne5, 14...Nf6, or 14...Nh6.

- Capture the bishop with 14...Bxd4.

- Counterattack with moves like 14...c5 (which, by Counting, fails to 15 Bxg7) or 14...Qh4 when 15 hxg4?? allows mate.

However, to his credit, Black came up with yet another way to save the knight, **14...Be5!?**. White can't take the knight. Do you see why? Answer below.

Yet, despite the fact that this is the kind of position that consumes a master's time, Black took less than 30 seconds on this move! I am not sure he was even aware of the possibilities in that short period. Further, just because 14...Be5 is tricky does not necessarily make it good (or bad).

The answer is that 14...Be5!? 15 hxg4 loses to 15...Rh1+! 16 Kxh1 Qh4+ 17 Kg1 Qh2 mate. However, White can just play 15 Bxe5, so 14...Be5 is not necessarily better than the other possibilities.

The point, as before, is that with sufficient time a good player weighs the pros and cons of each possibility. He analyzes each to see which might lead to the best position, and assumes good play from the opponent. When you have time and so many choices, quickly playing a complicated line such as 14...Be5 is bound to backfire sooner or later.

On many, if not most, moves you have more choices than may first meet the eye. So the duty is doubly difficult: to identify these interesting possibilities and then weigh the pro and cons. Doing both is important, and hopefully forms a foundation for good play and the enjoyment of the mental sport.

You won't get better at weighing the pros and cons by avoiding the task! Practice may not make perfect, but it sure will make you better. Another way to improve your judgment is to play over plenty of annotated master games; even better is consistently reviewing your decisions with strong players and listening to their comments.

For the players that make these considerations consistently, they are the pros. For the ones that don't, we can call them the cons.

Chess is Decisions

If you are not spending your chess thinking time making decisions, what are you doing?

Let's concentrate upon a thought process that facilitates making candidate move decisions more effective.

Chess is a thinking game. When good players take a long time on their move, the one thing they are likely doing is making decisions.

The two *biggest* decisions you have to make are:

♟ What moves are worth considering? (See *Initial and Final Candidate Moves* 2-1)

♟ Among those moves, which is the best I can find in a reasonable amount of time?

Yet, the *first* decision you have to make, consciously or subconsciously, is "how much time is reasonable to take for this move?" If you are playing a one-minute game, the answer is easy: "Almost none: make the first move that your experience tells you to consider." Whoever plays fastest without getting checkmated will then win.

But most games are played at longer time controls, and that is where micro time management becomes involved: how much time is reasonable for a move, given the circumstances? For example, suppose you are playing at the time limit of 40 moves in two hours, followed by one additional hour to complete the game, with a five second time delay. Then:

♟ A book move (but only one where you are 100% sure!) should be played very quickly;

♟ A non-critical move, such as where to develop a piece, should take about a minute;

♟ A super-critical move like whether to sacrifice a bishop or whether to trade into a close king and pawn endgame, takes whatever time is necessary, maybe 10-25 minutes.

If you end up taking way too much time or way too little time than the circumstances suggest, the result could be disastrous.

Most other decisions involve move choice. Here are some of the major choices you should make:

♟ After you look for *all* the things your opponent's move does, you must decide what to do about them. You can try to prevent them in various ways or even ignore them.

♟ Then you have to decide what you are trying to do. If what you are trying to do is tactical, then you are trying to win (or prevent your opponent from winning) material or checkmate. If tactics – or at least forcing lines – are not involved, then this is where strategy and planning come into play.

♟ Once you have an idea of what you and your opponent are trying to do, you have to decide which moves do something positive for you. Then you have to include the step that most weaker players do not, which is to find out which of those moves are safe (See *Is it Safe?* 5-3).

♟ Now comes the hardest part: Which of the final candidate moves is best? This usually involves some very difficult decision making and, even for the best players, can consume quite a bit of time. But at the very heart is the most important decision on the chessboard: *Is the move I am considering at least as good as any other move I can play?*

Using evaluation with analysis to determine the best move

How do you know whether one move is better than another? This is one of the most important things you could ever know at a chessboard...

The answer is: "One move is better than another if, assuming the opponent makes the best moves (best play), the position that will eventually be reached after the one move is better than the position that can would arise after the other move."

Let's present a theoretical method for deciding whether one candidate move "A" is superior to another move "B" in an *analytical* position:

1. Visualize the position after move "A" and see if the position is quiescent (see the archived *Quiescence Errors*). If so, evaluate it (or hold it for comparison; see *Evaluation Criteria* in 2-4, page 99). If the position is not quiescent, and thus the opponent has relevant forcing moves, assume the best move and continue analyzing to attempt to reach quiescence. Again evaluate the quiescent position or hold it for comparison. Let's call the quiescent position A* and its evaluation E(A*). Then E(A*) is how good move A is.

2. Do the same for move B. Obtain E(B*).

3. Now comes a hard part: compare E(B*) to E(A*). Whichever evaluation is better for you, with the key assumption that you did everything correctly, implies the corresponding move is better. *When strong players think, they are often comparing positions to see which ones they like better.*

(see following diagram)

In this position it is easy to tag candidate moves. Black has just captured on g3, so White must recapture. In this case A = 1 hxg3 and B = 1 fxg3. The position is quiescent after each move, so we don't have to find Black's best move.

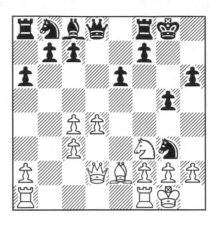

Example #1: White to play

The position after 1 hxg3 is A* and the position after 1 fxg3 is B*

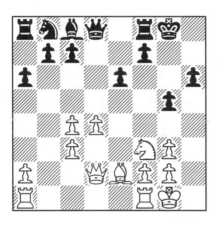

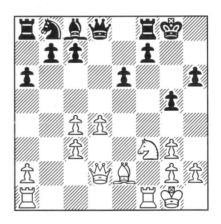

A*: Black to play   **B*: Black to play**

The hard question is: *Which is better for White, A* or B*?* Here is another way of stating this: *Is E(A*) > E(B*)?*

There is a fairly strong principle (see *Strong Principles vs. Important Principles* 8-1) that helps us in this position, which is *when two pawns can capture on the same square, unless there is a tactic or it is the endgame, capture toward the middle.* This principle is even more likely to be correct when applied to the b- and g-files rather than the c- and f-files.

Therefore, since this is not the endgame and there are no immediate tactics, the guideline suggests that A* is better than B*. Certainly the *pawn structure* in A* is better than the pawn structure in B*.

If you only use this guideline, then our decision is easy: play move A. However, while weaker players should follow guidelines and not spend too much time and effort looking for exceptions, that does not mean there are no exceptions. So, assuming you have sufficient time, you can't just go by general principles; you still need to analyze to see which move is better.

Moreover, there is another less-known guideline that might suggest the opposite. It says that *if your opponent has weakened his king and there are still many pieces on the board (especially queens), you want to open up as many lines as possible to that king.* Here the black g-pawn has advanced, making the f-pawn slightly backward and a target. If the black f-pawn advances, then the king is further exposed. Therefore, there are some modifying reasons that would indicate 1 fxg3 is not as bad as it usually is (taking with the f-pawn in similar positions, but where the black pawn is still on g7 is a common beginner misjudgment).

I used *Rybka* to assign a value to E(A*) and E(B*). *Rybka* is not the world's best evaluator, but it is pretty good, and it can assign specific valuations to positions (unlike humans, who mostly evaluate with words: White stands slightly better, etc.). At 19 ply *Rybka* rates White better by 0.68 pawns after 1 fxg3 and 0.49 pawns after 1 hxg3. *Rybka* indicates, by a small margin, that this example *might* be an exception to the "capture toward the middle" principle.

To extend this analytical method from "How is one move better than another move?" to "Which is the best move?" add the following step: The first time you compare two moves, save the better move as the "King of the Hill". When you analyze another move, compare its quiescent position's evaluation to the quiescent position resulting from the King of the Hill. If the new move's position is better for you, replace the King of the Hill with your current candidate. If the new move's position is not better, retain the current King of the Hill. When you are finished looking at candidates, then, assuming you have time, re-check your King of the Hill to make sure you are not missing something critical (somewhat of a "Sanity Check") and if not, then your King of the Hill now becomes the move to make.

Example #2: An Analytical Decision

Black to play

White has just played **1 Ne4** attacking the queen. What can Black do? As always, he wants to play the best move, but how does he go about finding that? After identifying this type of serious threat, Black should list all the moves that may make the queen safe, and it seems that there are seven "initial candidate" possibilities:

- ♟ Save the queen with 1...Qd8, 1...Qc1, 1...Qe7, 1...Qe5, or 1...Qa5
- ♟ Counterattack the white queen with 1...Bxc4
- ♟ Pin the attacking knight with 1...Bf5

However, initial safety analysis reveals that both 1...Qe7?? and 1...Qe5?? lose to White's only safe check, 2 Ng6+. This type of refutation should be routinely found immediately after identifying a candidate by asking the crucial question "Can my opponent reply to my candidate with a forcing move that I cannot meet?" To not make this analysis and to move without searching for 2 Ng6+ would be "Hope Chess" (see *Real Chess, Time Management, and Care* 2-3). To do the safety check later in the thought process after examining other aspects of the candidate move often is a waste of time.

Deeper analysis shows that 1...Bh3?! is also possible, since 2 Nxg5 Re1+ will win back the queen. That leaves Black with six final candidates:

- ♟ Save the queen with 1...Qd8, 1...Qc1, or 1...Qa5
- ♟ Counterattack with 1...Bxc4 or 1...Bh3
- ♟ Pin the knight with 1...Bf5

But which one is best? Unlike the previous example, the position is not quiescent after these moves, so, given sufficient time, each should be analyzed at least a little further before they can be evaluated and compared.

The purpose of the above discussion is not to analyze the position; it is to show the kind of decisions that should be weighed before a good move can be played, always assuming one has the time. A poor alternative is to just play fast and see what happens, but that is not what good players do. In order to make good decisions, the work has to get done somehow.

On the other hand, do good players use shortcuts, alternate methods, and draw on their experience as much as possible, so they don't have to do all that work? Of course! That's a subject worthy of an entire book; I recommend Soltis' *How to Choose a Chess Move*.

An interesting study was done several years ago to determine which part of the brain was being used during a chess game by players of different playing strengths. If I recall correctly, the method used electroencephalograms. *The data showed that the level of player that analyzed the most was expert (FIDE/USCF 2000-2199).* As the ratings dropped the players did less and less analysis, either because they did not know how or because they did not wish to work that hard. But higher rated players also did less analysis, as they relied on their memory to recall the correct ideas in similar positions. It is much better to know what to do than to figure it out by analysis – less room for error and much less time used on the clock – but it seems that you must be at least master level before playing chess this way is efficient!

Don't feel that if you fail to use the above analytical method on every move of a slow game that you are doing something wrong. In many quiet positions, such as those that occur in the early opening, there may be several moves that result in a similar evaluation. Once that similarity is determined, use your experience and judgment to quickly select the best one you can, making sure it is safe. It is important to save your time for more critical and/or analytical positions.

2-8) Ask the Right Questions

Alice: "Would you tell me, please, which way I ought to go from here?"
"That depends a good deal on where you want to get to," said the Cat.

Chess involves making good decisions, but which questions are the right ones to decide. Some are quite obvious to ask, like:

- ♟ "What is the best move to play?"
- ♟ "What am I trying to do in this position?"
- ♟ "Do I have a tactic?" or
- ♟ "How much time do I have on my clock?"

Just because a question is easy to ask doesn't mean the answer is easy or even possible!

I often find that my students either do not ask many questions at all, or ask the wrong ones. A very common example is the erroneous "How can I defend my piece?" when something is attacked and needs defending. For example, consider what happens when I show a relative beginner the main line of the Two Knights Defense **1 e4 e5 2 Nf3 Nc6 3 Bc4 Nf6 4 Ng5** and ask "What are all the things that **4 Ng5** does?"

Black to play

The student will quickly say that it attacks the pawn at f7 and threatens a fork with 5 Nxf7 and possibly 5 Bxf7+. They don't usually say that it also defends e4, but that should be included since it is a relevant safety issue. It is not necessary to state that it clears the d1-h5 diagonal for the queen and unblocks the f-pawn, but in a similar position either might be important. After the student mentions the attack on f7, I will ask "What are all the ways to meet these threats?"

Even though I was careful not to word the question "How can you defend this pawn?" I often get an answer like "I don't see how I can defend the pawn – 4...Qe7 does not seem to work." The student automatically goes into "defend" mode and overlooks the most common defense, the blocking move 4...d5. Of course, only an advanced player would be aware – from previous knowledge and not calculation – that counterattack with the double-edged Traxler move 4...Bc5 is also possible.

This same problem occurs when determining the safety of a move. Good players often ask "Superficially move X looks unsafe, but is there any way I can make it work?" Weaker players don't even attempt to do this and just assume the worst. In the following position my student just assumed that he could not move his bishop on c1 because it had to stay and guard the b-pawn.

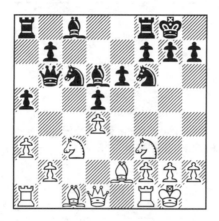

White to play

My student asked himself if the pawn would be unguarded if the bishop moved. That was the end of his reasoning. But I knew that I wanted to move the bishop if at all possible and was searching for ways to make it work. As a shortcut I asked *Rybka* what the best move was and it gave 12 Be3, with the further 12...Qxb2?? impossible due to 13 Na4 trapping the queen. My student had not only failed to see that the possibility to play 13 Na4 made the pawn safe – he did not even consider the idea of making it safe indirectly without the necessity to guard it with the bishop. As a final irony he was never able to develop either his bishop or queen's rook and resigned later with neither having made a move. That was not a coincidence.

One of the most common "question errors" is asking "Why did my opponent do that move?" instead of "What are *all* the things that move does?" Here is a typical example; Black has just played **1...Bf5**

(see following diagram)

White responds to the threat on his rook with: **2 Rxe8 Qxe8 3 Rc7+**

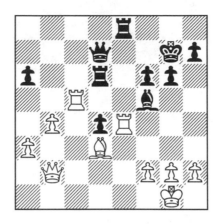

White to play

3...Kf8?

There is no reason to allow White to continue to attack the h-pawn. After the game Black said that he was not worried because 4 Rxh7? allows 4...Bxd3. The problem with this logic is that after White resolves the threat on d3, Black will still have to worry about h7. Just because White cannot take it now does not mean Black should not worry about future tempi.

So White resolves the problem on d3 with **4 Qd2**

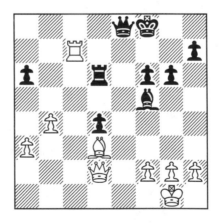

Black to play

Here Black asked "Why did White play 4 Qd2"? and was satisfied it must be to protect d3 while still keeping an eye on the back-rank squares e1 and f1. So he duly captured **4...Bxd3??**, fully expecting the mundane recapture 5 Qxd3, but was caught completely by surprise with **5 Qh6+**

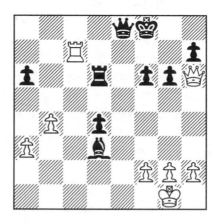

Black to play

and **Black resigned** as it is mate next move.

From asking hundreds of students about the reasons for thousands of mistakes I have a pretty good feel for which causes are frequent. And asking the wrong question, especially omitting the "all" in "What are *all* the things my opponent's move does?" is a fairly common culprit.

IM Jeremy Silman had a correct idea when he instructed students to view future patterns, and ask if possible continuations to achieve these are both *feasible* and *effective*. In other words, you have to ask whether your opponent will allow your pieces to get to those spots and, if so, whether once they get there they will achieve the desired effect by force. For example, take the following mating pattern:

White to play (potential Black defensive pieces not shown)

How often have you seen weaker players play **1 Bh6**, threatening 2 Qxg7 mate no matter how easily met? For example, suppose Black has a knight on f6, then 1...Nh5 might effectively attack the queen, guard the mate, and make it awkward to keep the pin saving the bishop. Or suppose Black has a queen on d8. Then the defense 1...Qf6 not only defends g7, but also threatens to capture the bishop. Occasionally White can play 2 Bg5 to effect, but that is not the point. The point is that players who automatically play 1 Bh6 whenever they get into similar situations rarely ask whether it is effective. They know it is feasible, but I guess the lure of the possibility their opponent might miss the threat is too much to overcome and they play it no matter how easily defended or how awkward their position might be after a defense.

The President of our chess club is a very weak player, about USCF 1100. But he has a lot of fun trying to checkmate his opponents every game. He ignores Steinitz' Theory ("You can't attack somewhere unless you have an advantage...in that part of the board") and just throws his pieces at his opponent's king whether the position justifies it or not. Consequently, he forms a superb example of flouting Silman's suggestion because his continuations are often feasible but almost never effective. For example, he will spend several tempi setting up a mate in one but, when his opponent sees it and defends, he has to start all over and find something else to do. If spending those tempi turns out to be a complete waste, he is not concerned until the defense is played. I am sure that rather than asking "If I spend tempi on trying to achieve that position, is it feasible that they will get there and, if so, will the setup be effective?" he asks "Wouldn't it be fun to go for that setup and see what happens? Maybe I might be able to checkmate him..."

In the following position White is ahead the exchange and has a fairly easy technical win. Instead, he asks the wrong question, "Can I safely attack his knight with a pawn and force it to move?"

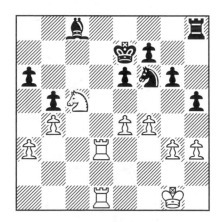

White to play

The answer is "Yes", so White plays **1 e5?** virtually forcing the knight to occupy the strong square d5 after **1...Nd5**. The knight now blocks both white rooks on the open d-file.

But a much more logical set of questions would have been:

- ♟ "Is the knight better on f6 or d5?"
- ♟ "If I don't push the e-pawn is it still safe?"
- ♟ "If I push the knight to d5 does that help my pieces more or my opponent's pieces more?"

The answer to these questions would all indicate that playing 1 e5? makes negative progress. Instead, White should also ask "How can I infiltrate with my rooks to make them much stronger?" The answer to that question is Rd6-c6-c7. The next question would be the Silman-like "If I try to do that, is it feasible; i.e. can Black easily stop me?" The answer to that is "No", so White should have played 1 Rd6.

In the opening when weaker and intermediate players get taken out of their "book" they often continue to play fast, sometimes playing "their" book moves even though the opponent has entered a completely non-book continuation. Sometimes continuing as suggested makes perfect sense, but other times it is completely disastrous. The player may ask "Is that a book move? No. Then is my book continuation safe?" Occasionally he asks "...is my book continuation logical given that his move is not the same?" However, rarely does a player at that level jam on the brakes and ask "OK, now that I am out of book, where does it look like *all* my pieces should be going?" This takes extra effort, and is why Alburt and Lawrence in their book *Chess Rules of Thumb* state that the first move out of book is critical and usually demands quite a bit of time.

Another helpful opening question is "Do I have to do that move now, or is there a more flexible continuation?" This idea goes hand in hand with the helpful principle "Make the moves you need to make before the moves that you want to make." The longer you wait, the more information you have as to where a piece may be effective. This is one driving force behind the principle "knights before bishops".

On the other hand, you should always ask "In the course of this game, where is my king going to be safe?" If you answer this question incorrectly, such as "castling into an attack" then that one strategic error may be enough to cost you the game. A corollary is "Is there a place where my king will be safe?" Often intermediates and weaker players make a bunch of "aggressive" moves without regard to allowing some king shelter for the coming middlegame.

In the endgame the king has to come out and fight, but weaker players often delay this so they can "do something better", often to their detriment. If you are winning and plan to finish off the game without the king, ask if you are far enough ahead to justify not using his majesty. Often the answer is "No" and his participation is required. In that case, the sooner the better!

With most pieces you ask "Where would this piece be best placed?" but with knights that is not always sufficient. Knights are path pieces, and in addition you often have to ask, "If I move my knight here, is there a viable path that would get it back in the game?" or "...get it where it is well placed?"

Sometimes meta-questions about the game are important. For example, "Am I playing for a win or a draw?" will often dictate how you play the endgame. I have often seen very strange endgames by weaker players who have a secure draw but don't recognize it and "do something active" and just lose miserably because they are trying for a win in a position that does not justify it.

Another meta-question is "Am I playing for fun, to learn, or to win a title/prize?" Answering this question will go a long way towards determining how you play. For example, if you are playing only for fun, then it is OK to play "too fast" or "try stuff" but if you are playing for the other goals then these transgressions can be quite costly.

Lesser/better question pairs

In the following pair of questions the second one is usually more helpful or accurate:

- How can I defend my piece? How can I make my piece safe?
- Where can I move my king out of check? How can I get out of check?
- Which piece should I move next? How can I make sure all my pieces are doing something?
- Where should I castle? Where would my king be safest in the long run?
- How can I meet his threat? What is the best way to deal with that threat?
- What does my opponent's move threaten? What are *all* the things my opponent's move does?
- Where do I want to go? What position am I aiming for and will it be feasible and effective?
- Why should I bring my queen out early? Is it too early to activate my queen?
- What is a good check? How can I bring a piece closer and/or get another piece into the attack with tempo?
- What is my next move? Where are all my pieces going to go in this opening?
- How can I stop a back-rank mate threat? How can I fix it so I can never be back-rank mated?
- How am I going to solve this problem? What is a reasonable amount of time to think before I should pick the best solution I have found so far?
- What might be the book move here? Am I 100% sure I know the book move? If not, time to start thinking hard.

Additional common good questions

- Is there another move that is even better?
- Are there any other pieces and squares affected?

- ♟ Where is my extra pawn and how can I make it a dangerous passed pawn?

- ♟ Do I need to win more material or can I just win by trading off?

- ♟ If I castle on opposite sides, whose attack will be fastest and strongest?

- ♟ If I get my piece to that square, what can it do from there?

- ♟ Which is the next piece I need to move to make sure every piece is active?

- ♟ If I were my opponent, what tactics would I try to set up to get back into the game?

- ♟ If I start a promotion race, who will queen first?

- ♟ What are all my pieces currently doing and which ones are free to move?

- ♟ If my opponent threatens that, how will I be able to stop him?

- ♟ Have I been in similar positions before and what did I learn about what works and what doesn't?

- ♟ If my opponent tries to trap that piece by attacking it, where would it move next?

- ♟ If I open that file, who will be able to control it?

- ♟ If I block my bishop with my pawn, how will the bishop become active later?

- ♟ Can I create an outpost square where I can place my knight?

- ♟ Can I use a pawn break to blast open my opponent's pawn structure?

- ♟ Where can my rooks go so that they will be effective when a fight breaks out?

- ♟ Am I playing too fast? Too slow? At what speed do I need to play so that I can efficiently make the time control?

- ♟ How critical is this move? If it is very critical, I need to take my time; if it is not critical at all, I can play relatively quickly using general principles.

- ♟ If I can trade two pieces of equal value, which one in this position is the better piece? If it is mine, maybe I should not trade; if it is my opponent's, maybe I should.

Finally:

Questions that are almost always wrong to ask

- ♟ Why did I blunder that pawn back on move 12?

- ♟ Why should I be careful here? I am so far ahead that nothing bad can happen.

- ♟ Why shouldn't I ignore my opponent's moves? He has no worthwhile ideas.

- ♟ Who am I going to play next round after I finish off this loser?

- ♟ What am I going to do 20 moves from now, if he somehow opens the h-file and gets his rook and queen on it?

- ♟ How can I keep moving the same few pieces over and over to maximize their effect, while ignoring the rest of my army?

- ♟ Why should I look for a better move? The first one seems good enough.

- ♟ Why should I think I have a chance to win? My opponent is rated 200 points higher than I am.

- ♟ I wonder if I should offer a draw? I am up a piece, but my opponent is higher rated so I will gain rating points!

- ♟ Why should I show this game to my instructor? I played so badly he is going to find much fault with my play.

If you can avoid any questions similar to the last group, you are probably doing pretty well!

Chapter Three

Time Management

3-1) The Case for Time Management

The Joker (Batman I): "*So much to do, so little time...*"

Karl Dehmelt is an "amateur" player here in Pennsylvania. He is really no amateur, as he obtained three International Master (IM) norms. We went to the same high school, but he was six years younger. When I met him, Karl's rating was only about 1400, but he easily got to master level before he graduated high school. I noticed something very interesting about his play, and it related to his time management:

Whenever there was a complicated-looking position where, nevertheless, one could quickly deduce the best move, Karl would play that move quickly. In that situation most class A and B (1600-2000 FIDE) players would see the complications and play slowly. On the other hand, if there was a simple-looking position where it looked like the best move was obvious but, beneath the surface, there was more than met the eye, Karl would play slowly. In similar situations those same A and B players would play the "obvious" move quickly.

I was quite impressed with young Karl's time management skills, including his insight on the amount of difficulty in determining the best move. It was not the first time that I realized how critical it is to manage your time well, but it is a sterling example.

With the advent of sudden death time controls, digital clocks with time delay, and more events at various fast time limits, time management has become increasingly important.

The Most Effective Skill to Master

I have been a full-time chess instructor for over 10 years. Although it is clear that the most *used* – and likely most important – skills are analysis and evaluation (a player usually utilizes these several times on every move), possibly the most effective skill to master *first* may be time management. It is particularly useful to learn the following two time-management skills:

1. *Macro Time Management*: How to pace yourself to use almost all your time every game; play neither too fast nor too slow for the time limit. The best time to check your pacing is during your opponent's move.

2. *Micro Time Management*: How to identify the critical situations. Then allocate more than the average time to critical moves and less to non-critical moves.

If you can do even the first of these – the second is more difficult – then everything else seems to fall into place faster because *the proper pacing is equivalent to doing the best that you can*. It follows that if you do the best that you can, no one can ask for more! Another way to look at this same issue is as follows: if you are not properly applying what you know (in order to apply the correct amount of thought to play at the proper speed), then learning other new things results in diminishing returns until you do so.

So if you do not already know how to pace yourself, get started today ...

After giving lessons to hundreds of adult students, I can authoritatively say that most show poor time management. They don't understand that pacing your moves in chess is much like running a foot race – you must try to pace yourself at close to the right speed each and every time. If players don't take their time each move to try and find the best move possible in the given time, they are very unlikely to become good players. When I see a player who thinks he can play fast some of the time, and thus consistently obtains poorer results than he should, my comment is "He just doesn't get it!" The consequences of playing too fast (and for others, too slow) may be as devastating, or more, when compared to the other two big impact issues of learning – recognizing basic tactical motifs and having at least a minimal "Real Chess" thought process.

I often advise my students to play slow games for several reasons. One big reason is that in order to improve, you need to continually learn how to play different types of positions better and better.

By playing slow on each move, you are able to put what you are learning into your long-term memory and, just as importantly, you are able to retrieve what you learned about similar positions in the past and ask yourself, "Which information I have learned about playing similar positions applies to this position?"

For example, if you see a familiar Seed of Tactical Destruction (see the archived *The Seeds of Tactical Destruction*), like a potential winning pin, with past experience and pattern recognition you can recognize the pin and determine more quickly if utilizing it will be successful. It's not that fast time control games are bad for you – they are not – but just that slow games are clearly more effective for most long-term learning purposes.

Many adults who strongly wish to improve make the silly mistake of playing a slow time control, but then not pacing themselves throughout the game to use almost all their time. They play too fast and end the game with lots of time on the clock. This would be fantastic if you were paid a large amount of money for each minute you have left on the game, but since you are not, it is a complete waste! You don't want to risk running over on time and lose a time forfeit, but the opposite – playing much too fast for the time control – is almost as bad. If you play a game with a time control of 90 minutes for the game and finish with 74 minutes left, that is not playing a slow game. That is playing a slow time control, but a relatively quick game!

The problem of playing too fast – or its cousin, playing too slow and getting into time trouble and then having to play too fast – is so prevalent among lower rated players as to be an epidemic. Part of the reason is that playing fast time controls and fast chess is very much the vogue on the internet. Players see the grandmasters playing fast games online to relax, figure that fast play must be the way to go, and emulate them. Or you don't have much time, or energy, and log on "for a few quick ones to relax". The result is that the same 30 minute game which is considered fast over-the-board is considered "too slow" for internet play. Yet the reason why all the best fast players in the world are all the best slow players is that they learned how to play positions from playing slow games and studying with other good players. Once you play enough slow games to know how to play a position, you can play well quickly since you are making many of your moves – and plans – from memory ("I know how to play this position!").

Go to any slow time control, over-the-board tournament and you will see that the strong players are also the best at pacing themselves to use all their time, game after game. This suggests that the skill of time management is very important, and that weaker players should try to emulate the pacing of the stronger players. The potential benefits of pacing yourself correctly are enormous.

It almost goes without saying that a correct pace includes varying the amount of time spent on each move according to need (time control, time left, complexity of position, etc), and not just taking the "average" amount of time each move!

Let's consider some reasons why time management is so important:

1. *Why Study and Not Apply?* If you are going to spend time studying chess, what good is all that knowledge you accumulate if you are not going to try to apply that same knowledge, as best time allows, to each position you reach? Many players read dozens, if not hundreds, of chess books and then go out and play too fast for the time limit. They certainly 'don't get it', and I think it is ironic they thirst for all that chess knowledge and then don't even try to take the time to apply it!?

2. *The Clone Argument:* Suppose you played a 100 game match against your clone, but had to give 10-1 time odds, say two hours for your clone and 12 minutes for you. Assuming both you and your clone used almost all your time and did the best you could, how many games would you win? The average answer is about 2%. But this translates into about a 600 rating point difference! That means if you play much too fast for the time limit, then you may be giving away hundreds of points in playing strength!

3. *The National Congress Observation:* A few years ago I was leaning against the post in the middle of the ballroom at the National Chess Congress. It was exactly halfway through the four-hour session and that year all the sections were playing 40/2 (40 moves in two hours), so half of each game's time control had passed. To my left were the higher rated sections: Open, Under-2200, U2000, U1800, U1600; to my right were the lower rated sections: U1400, U1200, U1000, U800, and U600. Approximately what percentage of games do you think were still being played on each side of the room?

♟ Good player (left side): 95%

♟ Weak players (right side): 25%

Is this coincidence? I think not!

4. *The Infinite Time Argument:* Suppose you were playing a game with a clock against someone rated about the same as you and the winner would get $10,000. How much time would you take on each move, on the average, if there were no clock, and you did not have to move until you were pretty certain that you had found the best move? I think the answer is that most decent players would take quite a bit of time, say 10 minutes, 15, or much more – as the greatest players in the world did before they started using clocks in international tournaments around 1883. Yet if you would take that long on a move, how long should you want to take in a 60 minute game or any other slow game time limit? The answer is that it should always be easy to use all your time, since you would take even longer if the game was important and you could do so.

5. *The de Groot Observation:* I once had a player who said he always played too fast and he could not help it. So I administered to him the de Groot exercise, where he had to think out loud and find the best move. Doing this exercise, which requires one to find a move as usual, but to do so while thinking out loud, may take longer than normal by a factor of about 2-1. This extra time is due to two reasons:

   a. thinking out loud slows you down;

   b. analyzing a position that you 'come into cold' requires some acclimatization.

I instruct every student not to "show off" for the exercise and to only spend as much effort analyzing as they would in an important World Open game. This student took 23 minutes on his move, and he only moved after I reminded him a second time that he was not supposed to show off for the exercise! He took longer on that one move than he had taken for many 60 minute games where "he could not help himself" to play slower! So obviously he could play slower if he wished. This player was not atypical, in that only a few students who took the de Groot exercise played a move quickly, and most were youngsters. Weaker adults often took more (adjusted) time for a move in this "meaningless" exercise than they did on similar, important moves in their meaningful games! Does that make any sense?

6. *The Marathon Analogy:* Suppose you were a jogger and you were going to run in your first marathon. What pace should you try? The extreme cases of running as fast or as slow as you can are clearly ridiculous. For example, if you run as slow as you can then it might take days to go 26+ miles and everyone else, including the officials, would have finished long ago and gone home. So, there is only one clearly correct pace, and that is to run about as fast as you think you can to cover the entire 26+ miles so that when you are done, you feel you could not have run any faster. One way to do this is to run conservatively for 20+ miles and then if you feel that you have some energy left, speed up slightly for the final few miles. In any case, something similar to this would be your optimum strategy.

Here the chess analogy is very strong – how fast should you make your moves? Surely going as slow as possible would leave you still contemplating which opening to play when your clock falls, but playing as fast as you can, say one second per move, is not likely to result in very good moves and all that extra time on the clock is completely wasted. So instead the clearly correct strategy is to pace yourself to use about all your time each game. Then adjust your time to be slower or faster according to the complexity of the position, the amount of time left on your clock, your evaluation of how the game is going, the time limit, etc. As you gain more experience, your adjustment will be better and better and you will learn to "pace" yourself so that you are always using about the optimum time, no matter what the time limit.

I think any one of these reasons is convincing, but together the evidence and proof is overwhelming. Time management is an extremely important part of chess, and these days, with faster and varied time limits, it is more important than ever. Yet I have trouble convincing some very intelligent adult students how important it is.

Part of the answer lies in the 'chicken or the egg' question I first raised in *Everyone's 2nd Chess Book*:

Which comes first?

1. Coming upon the realization that playing slow and careful is much better for your game, and thus you slow down; or

2. Learning the extra chess knowledge you need to consider in determining a move (a better process for determining the best move, more sophisticated positional evaluation information like pawn islands, etc) so that playing slow becomes more necessary to process correctly?

Clearly both factors are at work simultaneously but, whereas many years ago I thought that reason #1 would be the most likely, I now see that reason #1 is rarely sufficient in itself, but neither is reason #2! Instead, it takes a combination of these reasons plus a *third* strong force – the "peer pressure" of playing in a tournament and seeing that all the strong players are taking longer than you are, and thus the eventual realization that playing fast is both shunned by all the players much better than yourself, and counterproductive to your results.

Time Management Suggestions

Here are some things you can do to improve your time management:

♟ *Before* each game, estimate how much time you need to average for each move. A good conservative guess is that the game will last 40 moves. So if the time control is 40/2 that means 120 minutes divided by 40 moves, or 3 minutes per move. If you are playing online with a 20 minute game and a 10 second increment, that is 20 minutes for 40 moves = 30 seconds, plus 10 extra seconds per move = 40 seconds per move total. If you are getting the time increment and spend 40 seconds on a move, your clock will only go down by 30 seconds. Of course in the game you should play some moves faster and some slower, but at least you will know the average.

♟ If you wish, you can write down "goalposts" on your scoresheet as to how much time you wish to have left when you reach a certain move number. World champion Mikhail Botvinnik suggested that *in slow games you should use no more than 20% of your time for the first 15 moves*. Of course this assumes that the game was of average complexity. At 40 moves in 2 hours, 20% of 120 minutes is 24 minutes. Subtracting 24 from 120 is 96. Therefore, write "96" next to move 15 – aim to have about 96 minutes left at that point.

♟ Write down your time remaining after *each* move so that you are more aware of your pace. *Compare your progress on the board with the progress on the clock, ask "Am I playing too fast or too slow?" and adjust accordingly.* Time remaining on each move, and time taken per move, is very important information for both you and your chess coach.

♟ Play book and forced moves rather quickly, but not instantly. If you only have one legal move, play it without wasting too much time! In addition, if you are *sure* you have proven a move is best, play it without wasting further time figuring out what is going to happen next. Yet most of the time, be very careful and try to find the best move possible – in many, if not most positions, it takes a bit of time to prove that your intended move is not just good, but best.

♟ Practice the above for many different time controls over many slow games so that you develop a feel on how fast you should be playing at each time limit.

Tip: If you can get a 15 minute to 5 minute advantage in a sudden death time control, that is usually worth about 200 rating points worth of advantage! When you have a time advantage, reinforce your position, waiting until your opponent is short on time to try a decisive breakthrough. Usually the combination of time pressure and board pressure is too much for a defender. Similarly, a common – and bad – mistake is playing quickly when you have sufficient time but your opponent is in time pressure. This only makes sense if you are dead lost and are only continuing because of his time pressure; otherwise it is almost always better to make use of your superior time.

Of course, if your time management is poor, then what you should do to correct it varies tremendously, depending upon whether you are playing too fast or too slow!

Too Slow

Generally, players who are naturally careful and slow do better, but there are extremes to everything. If you play too slow and get into unreasonable time trouble there are many possible causes and solutions. The best source for these is GM Rowson's book *The Seven Deadly Chess Sins*. I will only cover a couple of cases:

- ♟ If you are waiting to make the perfect move and don't want to make a mistake, in some positions you will be waiting forever. So resign yourself (not your game!) to making the best move you can possibly find in a reasonable time and get used to making mistakes! *You are usually making a bigger one by allowing severe time trouble, where mistakes are much more common and catastrophic; realizing this may be half the battle.* Striving for perfection is silly with the clock running.

- ♟ If you have trouble analyzing positions, this is a skill that can be practiced and improved upon. See *Improving Analysis Skills* (2-5).

Too Fast

Weaker players usually play too fast, so let's offer more extensive advice to help the speedsters slow down.

Besides this generic advice, what are the main things you can do if you play too fast for the time control?

- ♟ Learn more about the game so that you will have more to consider each move when you are analyzing and evaluating positions. For example, do you know what a pawn island is? In general, the less pawn islands you have, the better, but how can you take time to consider their effect if you don't know what they are?

- ♟ Make a resolution that you want to get better and playing fast will not serve your cause. Stick with this every move unless you really don't want to improve as much as you think you do. See *Breaking Down Barriers* (4-3).

- ♟ Consistently try to find the best move? Most fast players don't. They just find an idea and, if it looks like it works, go ahead and make the move implementing their idea. If it does work, they are happy. In order to become a master you must at least make an attempt to try and prove your move was the best, and not just a good one ("When you see a good move, look for a better one..."). While the best move usually contains an idea that "works", in each position there may be many ideas that work but are not best, so why settle for one? A common mistake of beginners in the late opening is to take a piece that is developed and try to do more with it. That may be possible, but if you take a piece that is doing *nothing* and make it do *something* the overall effect is better!

- ♟ Take time to evaluate carefully. If you have multiple continuations that lead to positions where the material is the same, how do you really know which one is better? Subtle differences in piece activity, pawn structure, and king safety need to be evaluated for *each* position to see which one is better. Weaker players often give more credence to pawn structure over their total army's activity, but that is usually a mistake. Much more importantly, if you recognize a position is critical, don't play it as fast as you would an average move. If the game can swing in the balance on this move, make sure it swings your way!

♟ Work on utilizing a good and consistent thought process. If you considered a candidate move, did you try to find your opponent's best reply? If you play too fast, you likely don't look for this, and then your opponent may play a move making a threat you cannot meet (See Section 2: Thought Process).

♟ Do the work and make it fun (see *The Fun of Pros and Cons* 2-7). Is it more fun for you to play fast, do much less than your best, and get upset when you lose? If so, then playing slow may not be for you. Yet if you want to reach your potential, you are going to have to settle for less "fun" and more "work" in the short run – but probably more fun in the long run. I don't consider playing slowly and carefully to be work – it is no fun for me to purposely play less than my best.

♟ Burn information into your long-term memory to improve. Playing slow allows you to put more information into your long-term memory, and gives you more time to retrieve it and use it. So after every move, ask yourself, "What are all the things I know about chess which apply to this position, and how can I best use them?" Then if you continue to play slow your experience will add more information to your knowledge base, and the improvement cycle will continue.

Once you pace yourself to use almost all your time in *every* game, you will approach optimum performance and should find a definite improvement in your chess.

3-2) The Two Move Triggers

Never Make a Bad Move Quickly

Author's note: this is possibly my most advanced, and favorite, Novice Nook. Based on feedback from readers, I provided a second, The Room Full of Grandmasters, re-examining and clarifying this material from a slightly different viewpoint.

On the surface, the axiom, "Never Make a Bad Move Quickly" appears to be stating the obvious. What does anyone gain from knowing they should not make a bad move quickly? And what is the sense of warning them? Yet there is much wisdom to be gained by understanding this principle!

Moving too quickly is one of the most common causes of *unnecessary* mistakes. I see this error multiple times *each day*! Stronger players almost never make this mistake, yet weaker ones commonly do, so *there must be some correlation between understanding and eliminating this error and becoming a strong player.*

We can use time management principles to identify the "normal" amount of time one *should* spend on a move, based upon:

- ♟ the time control (the slower the time limit = more time per move);
- ♟ your time remaining (more time remaining = more time per move);
- ♟ how many moves remain in the time control (more moves = less time per move);
- ♟ the criticality of the position (more critical = more time per move).

Critical moves include:

- ♟ Important strategic decisions (see 8-2);
- ♟ Most moves in complicated positions;
- ♟ When the best move may be clearly better than the second best move (excluding trivial recaptures);
- ♟ The first move each game where you are no longer 100% certain you are in your opening "book" (attributed to GMs Alburt and Soltis).

Next, let's define what we mean by moving quickly, or fast: A move is played *fast* if you it play quicker than you should based on the above time management criteria. So, for the purposes of this discussion, "fast" is relative: it means playing too quickly for the circum-

stances, not *moving within a short amount of time.* For example, in time trouble you must make almost every move quickly, but this is not playing *too* fast since in this situation to do otherwise is fatal!

You should spend less than the average time on a non-critical move and more on a critical one. When you begin to run out of budgeted time for a particular move then make the best one you have found so far. If you are sure a move is non-critical, then choosing a second-best alternative may be good enough.

Although this column is generally targeted to players who play *too fast,* it should also be extremely helpful to players who play *too slow,* as *the primary cause of unnecessary time trouble is spending too much time on non-critical moves!*

No one budgets their time precisely. Still, all good players understand the time constraints of the event in which they are participating and don't usually consume more time for non-critical moves than critical moves. There will be obvious occasions for moving quickly, such as when there is only one legal move or when you are playing a book move in the opening. But when you *do* have a decision to make, and assuming you have adequate time, there is no reason to make a quick decision.

Occasionally you can budget almost all your remaining time on the current move if it is critical enough or if there are clearly no further critical moves remaining. For example, if you have 20 minutes remaining and you are sure you will achieve an easily won or drawn position, then using almost all your time is warranted if you deem it necessary, especially if there is a time delay or increment.

If you are playing a slow game and have a large amount of time remaining, why would you make *any* move quicker than necessary? You are trying to make the best move you can, given the time constraints, each and every move (see *The Goal Each Move* 2-2). Sometimes the situation allows you to choose a move that is "good enough" or "the best among equals" but this does not change the logic. Similarly, in this article, "best" can also mean "equally as good". All this allows us to make a powerful statement:

The only time you should use less time than "normal" (i.e. "play fast") is if you can prove you have the found the best move.

But then a corollary is:

If you cannot prove a move is the absolute best one, you should take approximately the normal amount of time to play the best move you have found so far.

Therefore, there are primarily two possibilities to *properly* trigger a move:

- **Trigger 1:** You have *proven* which move is best, so no further time is necessary; or

- **Trigger 2:** You have *not* proven which move is best, but time constraints (good time management) make it efficient for you to play the best move you have found so far.

Trigger 2 includes almost all situations where you are in time trouble and have to move quicker than you otherwise would or else you will lose on time.

Once you understand the time and criticality constraints, move only when you feel that further use of time would yield diminishing returns on your overall time investment. Don't get into unnecessary time trouble and risk playing even worse later on. In simpler terms, *move only when you can prove that a move must be best* or *when your time and position tell you that taking any more time may be unwise*.

Note that Trigger 1 is *not* when you *think* you have found the best move! Anyone can claim that in an attempt to justify unnecessarily quick play, but this excuse makes Trigger 1 meaningless. I reserve Trigger 1 for when you can clearly show your move is best or when no other move can be clearly better. Trivial examples would be book moves, the only legal move, mating with a queen and king against king, or "only-move" recaptures. Of course, it *is* often possible to prove a non-trivial move as best in a reasonable amount of time – this occurs more often as you become better at analyzing. However, for a large percentage of positions, no one can *prove* the best move under normal time constraints – even in slow games; thus the practical need for Trigger 2.

Dr. Adriaan de Groot's thought protocol experiment, where he had subjects find their move "out loud", had no specific time limit, although he did tell subjects they were under normal time controls. Therefore, Dr. de Groot discovered that most of his higher rated subjects used Trigger 1. They completed their thought process by finding the best move, period. Naturally, then, he named the final phase of the thought process "Striving for Proof", meaning that strong players, with no clock running, generally *were* able to continue thinking until they could reasonably prove which move was best.

With today's faster time limits, and with most players not nearly as strong as a typical de Groot subject, it is much more likely that time will be the deciding move trigger (Trigger 2).

There is a subset of Trigger 1 where A) you are a good player, B) you have done the best you possibly can in determining which move is best (with no result), and C) no further thinking will help, even if you have additional time by Trigger 2 criteria. This occasionally happens when there is substantial time remaining in a second time control, but the game is almost decided. In this situation a 20 minute think might yield as much information as possible from the position, but the best move still cannot be proven. In this case you will play the best move you can, even if you could think longer, because there is nothing else to consider (or you are getting diminishing returns on your energy). You will never "prove" the best move; you have proven all you possibly can. This subset rarely occurs among weaker players since they have poorer analysis skills, so they seldom reach a situation where they have thought so long that they have *correctly* derived all they can (but they can get equally tired!).

Trigger 2 is thus a more common reason for making a move, especially for weaker players. Therefore, weaker players should be careful to apply a sufficient amount of thought and then settle for their best guess lest they get into time trouble (and that is no excuse for playing *too* fast!). These players may make sub-optimal moves as a result of "running out of time for a given move", but the alternatives are either A) the greater evil of spending too much time and still making a mistake, while making even *greater* mistakes in time trouble later, or B) the worst evil, playing too fast and making *unnecessary* blunders!

There is also a subset of Trigger 2 that applies only to stronger players. Suppose you are a very strong player who is unlikely to make a big mistake if sufficiently careful. Then it may be possible to quickly find a very strong move without any attempt to prove it is the best move. If you like your move enough, then it may be better to save time for later situations where you feel like you may need it, and that may be enough reason to make the move without waiting for full Trigger 2 time constraints. However, weaker players should understand that their judgment is rarely that good, and they should assume that even a small amount of additional time is likely to be helpful. I believe Capablanca said, "If you see a good move...make it", but few players have Capa's judgment, so instead they should heed Lasker's *If you see a good move, look for a better one*, and the extra Trigger 2 time will be well spent.

The practical consequences of the move triggers are enormous: *One should never make a move faster than is reasonable unless you feel you have shown that it is best*. If you follow this advice, then you would eliminate all errors caused by moving too quickly! The only errors you would make would be those where you did take a reasonable amount of time (Trigger 2), but erred because you are not a perfect player. Players who follow this advice should improve markedly because they not only will become more careful, but also will manage their time better.

Bottom line: In theory, you should not complete your thought process unless you are sure that no other move is better or when taking more time would be counterproductive. To make your move for any other reason is very likely inefficient.

Whenever a student moves too quickly and makes a mistake, I often ask, "Were you sure this was the best move?" You would think the reply would be, "Of course, or else I would not have made it!" Unfortunately, that is not always the case! Often the student simply "forgot" they were looking for the best move and made a move for other reasons. In most cases they admit they should have taken more time.

Let's see how the Two Triggers work in practice during one move for each side in a game. The following position occurred in an online game with a 45 minute time limit and a 45 second increment. Thus, on the average, each side has about 2 minutes to make each move. Critical moves should take more than two minutes (possibly much more) and non-critical moves should take less. For each move we will see if *either* trigger was followed (an * will indicate which trigger *should* have occurred with proper analysis). As we will see, in many cases neither trigger was used, resulting in play that was too fast (not waiting at least for Trigger 2) or too slow (Trigger 2 failed to go off, or was not heeded).

(see following diagram)

Black is about to make his 19th move. White has 40:47 and Black 42:28 remaining on their clocks (over 90% of the initial time). That means both sides have played too quickly, making many suboptimum moves without waiting for Trigger 2. Black normally plays too slowly, but clearly this has not been the case thus far. However, Black is winning and, with a little care, can put the game away in the next few moves. When you see the end is near, that is critical, especially if you have a choice of good continuations, because the best move might lead to a much easier win than the others. Also, when the end is near you don't need to save as much time for later. Black now played the best move **19...Qf2+**, but took 9:27 to do so!

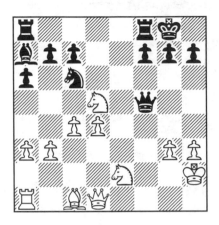

Black to play

Trigger 1*: Trigger 1 was not used, since the extended time taken clearly indicates that a "best move proof in less than normal time" solution was not found. With proper play, Trigger 1 should have gone off much earlier since 19...Qf2+ is best – the extra time is ironic after Black's previously fast play.

Trigger 2: Not necessary since his move was best. However, even if he did not know it was best, 9:27 is too long for a proper Trigger 2 since the best move is not that complicated (the only reasonable check and also an extra attacker on d4). So even though Trigger 1 should have been used, in practice Trigger 2 should have reduced Black's reflection time.

Now White has only one legal move, so he should verify this and play it immediately. Instead, he made the common mistake of unnecessarily trying to figure out what was going to happen next, and played the forced **20 Kh1** using 55 seconds.

Trigger 1*: Not used. This is similar to the comment on Black's 19th move. White had been playing way too fast, and yet ironically now takes 55 seconds to make the only legal move! Remember, *it is not always necessary to predict future moves, especially if you can prove the best move* and can move quickly by Trigger 1.

Trigger 2: Never necessary if you only have one legal move!

A Room Full of Grandmasters

The clock is integral to making chess a fair and interesting game: it elevates chess from just a game to a highly respected mental sport.

I believe that anyone who understands the key role of the chess clock will benefit greatly not only by awareness of time management in general, but also in particular by mastering each time management skill. Let's review The Two Move Triggers:

♟ **Trigger 1:** There can't be a better move than your current best candidate. One test is that you would be willing to stand up in front of a room full of grandmasters and argue that it would not be possible to find a better move. If you are willing to do this (and you have a rational case, of course!), then your work is done and you can make your move, as any further thought is just a waste of time.

♟ **Trigger 2:** Based on the situation (position on the board, time control, time remaining, and – if it is not sudden death – move number) there is a time "t" which is a reasonable length to think for that move.

The instant at the end of "t" is Trigger 2, but I often refer to Trigger 2 as "t" itself since the context is usually clear. The *position* aspect of estimating "t" is called *criticality assessment*.

If "t" has not yet occurred *and* you have not hit Trigger 1, then you should continue to look for a better move (See Lasker's Rule, page 166) up to roughly "t", with the goal of finding the best move you can until that time. On the other hand, the further you exceed "t" without moving, the more you not only likely get diminishing returns for this move, but also the less time you have for all subsequent moves.

Therefore, *Moving Too Fast* on a move can be defined as "*To move in a time less than Trigger 2 without hitting Trigger 1 (best move).*"

Moving before you reach either trigger almost always implies you could have played better if you had taken more time. Inherent in this idea is that "moving fast" implies "moving too fast for the situation" and not moving in a very short period of time.

Consequently, *Moving Too Slow* on a move can be defined as "*Taking noticeably longer than Trigger 2*". In the occasional case where your Trigger 2 gets extended by increasing your perception of the move's criticality, that is not playing too slow – so long as you don't greatly exceed the new Trigger 2!

If you play too slowly in non-critical positions, consider the following: *The more critical a move is, the more it requires careful and specific analysis. The less critical a move is, the more you can make it on general principles.* So once you determine that a move isn't critical, you can relatively quickly gauge whatever principles you think apply and decide which move fits best.

Time management can be segmented into two components:

♟ Macro (game): Pacing yourself to use almost all your time for the game.

♟ Micro (move): Assessing the clock situation plus move criticality (i.e. Finding Trigger 2; the reasonable amount of time that should be taken) and allocating time to each move accordingly.

The Two Move Triggers encompasses the most difficult part of micro time management and has a strong overall effect on macro time management. That's quite a chunk to cover with one idea!

Many internet and tournament players, especially those who previously played fun chess without a clock, think of it as a necessary evil rather than an integral part of the game, and view time management as a virtual non-issue. By ignoring this crucial aspect they are making a bad mistake.

If you play competitive chess, where clocks are not just tolerated but necessary, then using good time management potentially can make a massive contribution to your long-term results.

I now find uses for The Two Triggers *every day* when instructing. Time Management ranks right below "thought process" among off-the-board improvement issues.

A typical use of The Two Triggers occurs when a student makes a middlegame move too fast despite plenty of time on the clock. Even if the move is plausible, it is instructive to ask, "Why did you play this move so quickly?" Not surprisingly, the answer often is "I thought it was the best move."

My answer, however, often comes as a surprise: "Why, of course you did; otherwise why would you have made it? However, your goal is not to take a few seconds and play the best move you have found *so far*; your goal is to play the best move you can find within the time constraints."

There are several factors that should prevent you from moving once you quickly find a reasonable move:

♟ You have plenty of time; there is no great risk in trying to find a better move.

♟ It takes time to show that a move is completely safe, and not doing so – playing Hope Chess – is risking the game each and every time.

♟ One look in the mirror – and at your rating – should tell you that the probability of your finding a move that good that quickly is not high enough to justify a fast move! You don't have to be a genius to have the wisdom to know that even intelligent, experienced adults make errors all the time, especially when they move too fast. So if you want to be a better player, eliminate such quick moves.

Another way of saying this is "Respect Triggers 1 and 2".

Respect Trigger 1 because, unless you are willing to stand in front of that room full of grandmasters and argue that none of them could possibly find a better move, then the excuse "I thought it was the best move" will not hold water – you have not reached Trigger 1! Thinking you found the best move is quite easy; being able to show that no move could be better is much more difficult! If you can't show that your current candidate cannot be bettered, then optimum play (see Lasker's Rule, page 166) would have you continue to look until you reach Trigger 2.

Respect Trigger 2 because since Trigger 1 was not achieved (else you would not reach

Trigger 2), Trigger 2 tells you to hold off moving until you have taken enough time that further thought results in diminishing returns. If you have an hour left on your clock and choose a move among alternatives using only a few seconds, it is rarely getting the most for your time and further thought is most likely beneficial.

In *Chess for Zebras*, GM Rowson suggests that almost all players play better the longer they take for each move, up until about 20 minutes, when most players start to become fatigued and/or confused. Therefore, time taken above 20 minutes, while occasionally beneficial, risks diminishing returns. On the other hand, taking more time when you have used much less than 20 minutes – and not truly hit Trigger 1 – is usually beneficial; no one plays better in 15 seconds than they do in two minutes.

On the other hand, suppose you lose respect for Trigger 2 in the opposite way – you ignore the Trigger 2 "alarm" when it goes off, and consistently take longer than you should to make your moves (see the archived *A Criticality Quiz*). Again the inefficiency of diminishing returns sets in, as further time *might* help you find a better current move, but harms all future moves. If the current move is super-critical, you do need additional time. When that happens, Trigger 2 expands and gives you much more time than the average for your move.

When my students play over-the-board, I recommend they record how much time is remaining after each move. With this information we can figure out their macro and micro time management. For online games it is even easier; servers usually time-stamp each move; when the game is replayed, the exact time remaining is also shown.

Many intermediate level players are unaware of the extent to which bad time management hurts their games. Many play way too fast, and quite a few play way too slow. The reasons that they manage their time badly vary, but the end result is that the effect on their playing strength is dramatic – often a hundred times greater than their perceived weakness of not knowing the Caro-Kann better.

All the above again shows that micro management, *the ability to assess the criticality of the position and, based on the current time factors (time control, move number, remaining time on the clock), properly assess the value of Trigger 2*, is a very important skill to be recognized and nurtured.

A *critical move* is one where the best move gives you a much better chance of winning or drawing than the second best move, *excluding* trivial recaptures where the best move is obvious.

Suppose you are playing in the deep endgame and you have to decide which way you should run your king. Assume this is the final critical move of the game – afterwards the moves are more or less forced and in some lines you will end up with a queen and king against a king (trivial win), while in others there will either be just two kings or perhaps each side will have a queen (trivial draw). In this case Trigger 2 expands to almost your entire remaining time; if there is time delay and you can checkmate with a queen and king against a king with one second left, then Trigger 2 is all your remaining time (minus that needed 1 second).

In this "final critical move" situation your goal is clear: analyze the position until you understand everything and can find the absolute best move, such as one that leads to king and queen vs. king, or gets the draw if you can prove you can't win. This is Trigger 1. Alternatively, if you are not able to analyze it properly or fully, take most of your time trying (Trigger 2). There is no other reasonable possibility. If the position is critical, you think you may be losing no matter what you do, and your opponent is sure to find it, then legitimately trying to find a line that has a chance not to lose until almost all your time is up is reasonable.

Warning! If your situation is trivially lost, or you *can* easily prove that all lines lose, then using up additional time – especially all your time if you have more than just a few minutes – to vainly hope you can find something is not only rude but illegal.

Next, let's consider The Two Move Triggers in the context of two very important concepts:

1. Lasker's Rule: *When you see a good move, look for a better one* (and, if you see a better one, look for an even better one, because you are trying to find the best one you can).

But *how long* should you look? How do you know when you are done? Armed with the Two Triggers, we can now answer this question!

Looking for a long period of time is often not very practical. In many situations your clock may fall before you can prove you have found the very best move. Instead, *you should look for a better move until you have hit either Trigger 1 (the move about which you are willing to argue with GMs) or Trigger 2, the time that is the reasonable amount to spend on that move*.

Learn to recognize critical positions and, when they occur, play carefully. *In a critical position, when you see a good continuation, it is usually quite cost effective time-wise to apply Lasker's Rule and make sure you look for a better one*. Doing so is much more time effective than spending lots of time trying to find slightly better lines on non-critical moves. Conversely, play non-critical moves relatively quickly to save extra time for critical moves, but don't be careless!

2. *Why do I play chess? To challenge and test myself to do the best I can – each and every move!*

But that leaves a very big question: What constitutes "the best I can?"

Again, thanks to The Two Move Triggers, the answer is easy: *if you only move when you hit a trigger, you are playing the best you can*.

Therefore, *the idea of playing "the best I can" is to develop a feel for Trigger 2 and not take less time unless you hit Trigger 1*. If you do that, then you are *both* managing your time as best possible and playing the best move found within a reasonable amount of time. You can't possibly do any better than this!

If you play too fast or too slow use The Two Triggers to improve your play:

If you play too fast, when you find a good move, ask, "Is it possible there can be a clearly better move?" If it is possible, and Trigger 2 has not been reached, then you should usually continue searching. If you understand this and can act upon it correctly and consistently, then you have just become a much better player!

Suppose you move too slowly. This means that you are consistently exceeding Trigger 2. There are four possible reasons:

- ♟ You don't attempt to get a grip on Trigger 2 (have no idea how much time you should take);

- ♟ You consistently think Trigger 2 is higher than it should be;

- ♟ You lose track of time and exceed Trigger 2;

- ♟ You are aware of Trigger 2 and your time taken, but in the time vicinity of Trigger 2 can't bring yourself to pull the trigger, i.e. play the King of the Hill.

If you can figure out which of these applies to you and get a handle on how to overcome them, you are taking a big step toward learning how to play without unnecessary time pressure.

Chapter Four

Skills and Psychology

4-1) Traits of a Good Chess Player

Not all highly intelligent people play chess well, and not everyone who plays chess well is highly intelligent (although if you ask them...!)

A beginner often wonders if he has what it takes to become proficient at the Royal Game. There are many aspects of intelligence and personality that correlate with the potential to become a good player. Almost everyone realizes that a lot of hard work will be necessary to climb the ladder of chess success, and few want to put in many hours of work with little prospects for reward. Knowing that you have some of the requisite talents is always helpful in keeping up your spirits.

I have separated my list of traits into four groups:

- ♟ "IQ" Aspects
- ♟ Physical Traits
- ♟ Personality Traits
- ♟ Emotional Traits

"IQ" Aspects

Memory – The ability to remember things is certainly a "no-brainer", insofar as being helpful for chess. First there is the obvious ability to retain more chess patterns and what you know about them, including opening and endgame knowledge, tactical positions and ideas, positional maneuvers. In addition, there is also everything else you "know" about chess – including guidelines, how to handle a six-hour World Open game, and the information in *Novice Nook*. The better the memory, the better you can store the information and retrieve it quickly and accurately. Memory is not as sharp when you get older, so age does degrade this ability.

Note: "knowledge" is not an ability; it is the information you retain better with a good memory. Knowledge does not correlate one-to-one with your playing strength. For example, a player who reads more books and retains more knowledge is not always better than one who has read much less. As one of my chess friends once said, "Never confuse ignorance with stupidity" – the corollary being "Never confuse knowledge with intelligence".

Spatial Relationships – I call the special vision which enables one to understand what is happening on a chessboard "board vision". But the *general* ability to process spatial relationships is more than just that chess-specific skill; it is the capability to see and/or imagine what is happening in two or three dimensions. An example of how this is measured would be the type of IQ test question where they show you an unfolded cube and you are asked to fold it in your head and select which of four folded cubes could be created from the fold. The ability to visualize geometric patterns is valuable in chess when you are trying to look ahead and imagine a possibly occurring position. An example of an error using this ability would be a "retained image" – when you fail to see that a piece has moved off its square and you visualize it doing something on a later move when, in fact, if that line were actually played that piece would no longer be there!

Deductive Logic – This is the "If A implies B and B implies C, then A implies C" type of logic. In chess you need deductive logic to figure out what is forced and what is not. For example, during analysis of a position you need to be able to look at a move and deduce something like "Because of so-and-so, if my opponent does not stop my killer move, then I can do this, so he must make move A or move B to prevent it or else I win." A common deductive error would be assuming your opponent will make a move that you think is forced when in fact another move is better. Of all the skills in chess, I believe that this one is perhaps the most popularly recognized by the general public. Your deductive logic is another part of the thinking process that slows as you get older.

Concentration – Playing chess correctly requires a lot of thought(!). The better able you are to concentrate and focus your thoughts on the task at hand, the stronger your play. If your mind is wandering – even thinking about a mistake you made earlier in the game – that can only hurt you. Lack of concentration detracts from your ability to perform from the task at hand, which is usually *finding the best move in the current position within the given time available.*

Physical Traits

Stamina – This is the physical ability to sit and play without excessive tiredness or fatigue throughout not just a long game, but possibly even a long series of games in a tournament or match. One of the problems older players have is lack of stamina; they get tired more easily. You can increase your stamina by eating and drinking correctly before and during a long game, getting proper rest, and entering the event in good shape. That is why it is helpful to have an aerobic sport, like tennis, jogging, or swimming, to augment your chess lifestyle – these are beneficial for your non-chess welfare, too!

Nerves – In the course of chess history, it has been stated that several top-level grandmasters were not serious World Champion candidates because they did not have the nerves for top-level play. Playing chess for fun is one thing, but playing for your livelihood is quite another. It requires strong nerves to play chess at the highest level, but having "bad nerves" affects your play negatively at any level.

Personality Traits

Carefulness – Of all the traits that make for a good chess player, one of the most important is the ability to take your time on each move and try to find the best one. And of the personality traits that support this ability, being careful is the key. Interestingly, one can be too careful: you may be afraid to move for fear of making a mistake. This fear inevitably leads to time trouble, requiring fast moves and resulting in even bigger mistakes than the ones you had been avoiding by taking 6 minutes instead of 3. Therefore, the best chess players are the ones that are careful, but not pathologically so. It should be noted that players who are not naturally careful in life can learn to be careful in chess! I have seen several players who were able to overcome their natural tendencies, but to do so one has to feel strongly that it is worth the special effort!

Caring – This trait is different than carefulness, and is actually more closely related to some of the emotional traits below. You want to care about your move, your result, your rating, and your reputation, but not *too* much. If you don't care at all, you won't work to improve it/them, and if you take these too personally then chess becomes too involved with your personal image and you will find it hard to take the necessary risks to play and improve.

Determination – This is one area in which I score well. I will not stop at something until I get it right. My wife thinks I am a little nutty because I once took almost a year on the same tough cryptogram – I would not skip it or take a hint or look up the answer. She is right, but that same determination paid me good dividends when I wanted to become an expert, a master, and get my FIDE rating and Candidate Master title. One should differentiate *game-time* determination to obtain the maximal outcome ("will to win" or "fighting spirit") with the longer-term *career goal* determination to do whatever it takes to become the best player you can.

Note: "Killer-instinct" is not the same as "fighting spirit". Killer-instinct is an intense desire to either beat down the opponent, or at least finish off a won game. Good chess players seem to have one of two special traits: killer instinct or expert problem solvers. Without one of those two traits it is hard to have the determination and perseverance to play hard each move, game after game. I am more the problem solver type – I want to find the best move each and every time – I am not trying to wound my opponent's ego.

Perseverance – This trait is similar to determination, but it represents not the will to do well, but the ability to carry on that will despite whatever roadblocks are presented: lack of time to play and study, unexpected and unnerving losses, the skepticism of others, etc. Again, there is short-term game-time perseverance and the more common long-term career goal perseverance. Surprisingly, I find a lot of students who have the determination (otherwise they would not hire me as their chess coach), but lack the perseverance – they want quicker results than is possible, get discouraged at the inevitable setbacks, and cannot maintain their chess determination for the years that are required to reach their lofty goals. Since extensive chess progress can only be measured in years, it is not surprising that many players cannot persevere in what it takes to maintain improvement over that time period.

Note: I did not forget "Willpower", but it is mostly contained within *determination* and *perseverance*.

Capability to overcome natural shortcomings for the good of your chess play – This is a special type of trait which enables you to not dwell or be held back by any shortcomings you have, but to be able to rise above them due to your strong desire to play well and improve. Everyone has shortcomings in one area or another. No one has a great memory *and* great deductive logic *and* great nerves and everything else – even the Fischers and Kasparovs are not perfect (but they are a lot closer than the rest of us!). However, some players let their concern about these shortcomings hold them back. In some cases, these shortcomings can mostly be overcome by will.

For example, suppose you are naturally impatient or not very careful. It still may be possible, when sitting down at the chessboard, to say to yourself, "OK, I am naturally impatient (or not careful), but if I am going to play good chess I have to take my time on *every* move and be very careful on *every* move or else I can let the game slip away just by that one bad move." If you are able to say this to yourself, you may be able to overcome your natural impatience for the good of your game. Once you get in the habit of consistently practicing correctly, then it becomes easier and easier, despite any natural tendencies otherwise.

Confidence – Like many of these other traits, either extreme is bad: too much confidence is overconfidence, which often leads to carelessness, or lack of respect for the opponent. On the other hand, if you play with lack of confidence your results will surely suffer. *Chess is a mental sport, and one's lack of confidence often becomes a self-fulfilling prophecy*. As a teenager I had a friend who played regularly and studied chess diligently. He learned the English and the Caro-Kann. But in tournaments his low rated opponents did not play into his study lines and he suffered from very poor results, getting an 1100 rating based on several events. He then quit playing. Ten years later he had not played nor picked up a chess book, but asked to play in one of my invitational tournaments, filled with players rated 1300-1500. Despite not having played in a decade and being the lowest rated player, he finished in second place with a performance rating of almost 1700. I asked him how this was possible. He said that maturity made the difference – he no longer worried about what his opponents were doing and just enjoyed playing. Whereas before he doubted his ability and was affected by his opponent's weird play, now he was confident that he could just play well and do the best he can. So the extra 500 points or so of playing strength was almost all due to his new-found confidence and lack of worry.

Awareness – A player who can keep his awareness and be cognizant of what is important has a big advantage. For example, when an experienced player starts to realize that time is running short and time management is becoming a bigger and bigger part of the play, he has an advantage over an opponent who either is not as aware of the importance of this change, or is so but does not change his priorities. Similarly, being aware of possibilities, such as unexpected opponent blunders, or sudden changes in the phase of the game, is a distinct asset.

Flexibility – In a similar manner to awareness, flexibility of plan and action is a big asset. If you are not flexible enough to adapt to the change in state, then being aware of that state is not much use. It is also very important to be flexible in your learning. This flexibility is related to the next trait, open-mindedness.

Open-Mindedness – The ability to listen and to consider new ideas (or realize that the old ones you have are at least somewhat misbegotten), is very important. It is very difficult to learn if you "know" you are right or not open to new ideas, or possibilities of what you are doing wrong. A brilliant, stubborn beginner probably will never get past the beginner stage since it will be very difficult to learn from his mistakes, even (or especially!) if they are pointed out to him.

Emotional Traits

Ability to deal with losses as a learning tool – This is a very important indicator of how good a chess player someone is going to become. Suppose a player take losses so hard and personally that you can't speak to them and they don't want to review or think about the game. Then not only will they not be able to optimally learn from those losses, but eventually the realization that they are going to lose thousands of games in order to become a good player will wear them down. At the other extreme we have someone who doesn't care at all if they lose – they will also not review their games, because "it is just a game" and why should they spend effort to avoid repetition of their cause of defeat if it does not matter? These players are doomed to repeat their mistakes and never get much better. The best outlook is somewhat in between: you cannot take your losses too personally but you have to be the type who vows never to lose the same way twice. A player who takes great interest in their shortcomings and studies them in such a way as to minimize the chance of recurrence will usually be much better than the players who are at each extreme.

Pride in your moves and your reputation – I think this trait is a little underrated. Players who take pride in each move have an advantage over players who are don't care that much about each move. These latter players are often surprised when I ask them about what considerations went into a particular move, often stating "This is just an internet game – why should I try my best?" But almost all strong players share the concern that they put in the proper effort on each move and try to reach the correct decision, or at least do the best they can. Can you imagine Garry Kasparov annotating one of his games and writing, "I made this move without much thought – I really didn't care if it was a good one or not"?!

Ability to deal with setbacks, bad moves – This is different than perseverance, which enables you to maintain your will after setbacks of any type. Perseverance is therefore part of this trait, but not the only part. For example, the ability to maintain equanimity – not lose your cool – when things have gone wrong, is important. Players who get upset and let previous moves affect their judgment of the current move, or even think about the previous move instead the current move, are almost always making a big mistake.

Playing chess is fun – This is the most common trait shared by chess players. Humans who lack this trait may become good scientists, doctors, lawyers, or businessmen, but they won't become good chess players.

Studying chess is fun – Hand someone *Capablanca's Best Games* and ask them to read it. The ones that quickly and gladly accept find that *doing chess work is fun*. For more on these last two traits, see the next Novice Nook: *Chess, Learning, and Fun* (4-2).

Coachability – No one becomes really good at chess in isolation. Many factors, including some of the above, can contribute to this trait. A player might have many reasons they are less coachable: bad listening skills, stubbornness, know-it-all, doesn't care enough, lack of maturity, or just believes that books alone can make him a great player. In any case, coachable players obviously have an advantage in the long run.

Conclusion

Next time you run into someone who says, "So-and-so is really smart – he would make a good chess player", consider how well that person fits some of the above, "non-IQ" criteria. How well did you score? If you were above average on most of the critical traits, that may mean that you have a promising career ahead – assuming you are not damagingly low on a couple of others! A player is usually only as good as his weakest link.

4-2) Chess, Learning, and Fun

The top line of a sign on the wall of my den where I teach chess: "If you are not having fun, you are in the wrong place!"

I don't think nearly enough is made about the fun factor in chess. I am not referring to the fact that people play chess for fun, as they surely do, but rather the important effect fun has on how easily you can improve, how good you are likely to become, what openings you should play, what style to adopt, and even what moves to play.

For most of us, chess is just a hobby – but that's the key. If you are practicing your *profession* and your boss says, "You have to do X" and you don't like it, and it happens too often, you either have the wrong profession or a poor boss – or possibly both. Nevertheless, you have to put up with the unpleasantness whether you like those aspects of your job or not.

But suppose you are practicing your *hobby* and part of your hobby is not fun; then you likely will minimize or possibly omit that part altogether! There are many aspects to playing and learning chess; some you undoubtedly find more fun than others. Yet, most likely you will de-emphasize those parts of chess you do not enjoy. Understanding which aspects of chess you do and don't enjoy and how that enjoyment affects your decisions can help you immensely if you strive to be a good player.

For example, suppose you don't like over-the-board play for any number of reasons, then you might just play on the internet or with computers. Or suppose you don't like to look at the games you lost, then you might only study the games you won. You might like to play but don't like to study: not by yourself, not with an instructor, nor read the books which are appropriate for your improvement. For every aspect you omit because it is not fun, you may be omitting a key part of what you need to improve. This is not necessarily fatal to your improvement plans, but it is helpful to make these decisions consciously so you are more aware of the trade-offs.

I once had a potential student who was eager to take lessons. Knowing that good practice goes along with good theory, I asked him if he wanted to visit Philadelphia and play in the World Open. He thought about it for a couple of days and decided that *actually playing chess was no fun for him* – he just liked the idea of becoming a good chess player!!

Take the following "fun-determination" quiz. It will estimate how *you* rate on the chess fun scale; it should also help you understand your present and future chess-learning capability. Rate your enjoyment from each of the following activities from 1 (Agony) to 5 (Great Fun):

1. After you play 20 speed games with a friend you research each game – using opening books, databases, or a chess program – to figure out where you would improve if a future opponent played the same opening moves again.

2. Someone hands you *Capablanca's Best Games* and you read it.

3. You go over your game with a really strong player and he shows you all the mistakes you made, and what you could have done instead.

4. You travel to Philadelphia to play in the World Open, where you play nine 6-hour over-the-board rated games. First prize in your section is $10,000.

5. You get into a position that contains a complicated set of captures. You have to work through each capturing sequence carefully to make sure that you are not losing material, and that takes 10 minutes of analysis consisting of "If I take there first, then which capture would he make, how good is that for me, and what should I do about it...?" You need to do all this analysis in order to find the best move.

6. You are a strong scholastic player, but to win the local scholastic championship you have to play five weaker players, and drawing with even one of them will cause you to lose rating points for the tournament.

7. You go to a local chess club for the first time and you are a stranger. After the club manager says hello, he does not help you find a game and afterwards no one approaches you to play for a while. Finally a player offers you a game and beats you easily.

8. You log on to the internet to attempt to find some slow games to play, but it is difficult finding opponents who want to play seriously. This causes you to wait around at least ten minutes, whereas if you wanted to play a speed game you would find hundreds of willing opponents within a minute or two.

9. After losing a tough game you go home and feed the game to your chess program to help show you all the mistakes you made and how you might have won (or drawn) the game.

10. You go through 1,000 basic tactic problems, all easy, over and over, until you can do 85%+ of them within 10-15 seconds, quickly recognizing the position and thinking something like "Oh, yeah! In this one I sacrifice the exchange and then get a double attack to win a piece, ending up two pieces for a rook."

We are not going to state something silly like "Players who score 45-50 will become grandmasters and players who score less than 10 are hopeless"; after all, it is a test to measure chess fun, not ability. But obviously a "high" score – say over 40, is a very good sign and a low score – under 20, is not. Yes, some of the situations were basically unpleasant, but your perseverance to make potential work into fun is an issue. For example, in #7 if you keep going to the club, attempt to make friends, and discuss the activities you would like to participate in, you probably won't remain a stranger for long. On the other hand, if ... cide the club is unfriendly, don't do something about it, and never return; you ... ly are not creating the kind of fun that could be available if you worked at it a little bit. The player who proactively works to make his chess environment more fun is likely to become a much better player than the one who immediately gives up or only makes a half-hearted attempt.

Given the same overall levels of experience, players who score higher in the above quiz should have, on the average, a higher playing strength than similarly experienced and skilled players who score distinctly lower on the fun scale. You should also be able to consider your result from the "future potential" aspect. If you are an inexperienced player who scores high on this quiz, your "chess upside" is likely much higher than someone else who is similarly inexperienced and who scores distinctly lower.

While most chess players have fun *playing* chess, there is a definite dichotomy between those who find *studying* chess fun and those who do not, and those that enjoy doing the "work" it takes to find a good move. In fact, if you take two otherwise identical chess students who are about the same in *Traits of a Good Chess Player* (4-1) and if one of them really loves studying chess and the other one does not, this crucial difference alone *could* be enough to make the difference between one of them possibly becoming a grandmaster and the other dabbling in a few meaningful events and then giving up serious chess, or at least only hanging on as a talented but mid-level player.

Let's take each of the 10 "fun quiz" issues and see what can happen when it is not fun:

1. If you don't like to review your opening moves, then it is much more likely you will repeatedly make the same opening mistakes. Even though looking up any single game does not mean that much, the habit of doing so consistently will have a large cumulative effect on your opening knowledge and eventually should make a big difference over your chess career.

2. Much of your "board vision" is derived from watching good players play. One way this can be accomplished is by reading instructively annotated games. Learning how good players properly apply guidelines to specific positions is much more helpful than just reading the guidelines. When masters have to make decisions in critical games you can benefit from seeing these ideas and patterns. If playing over annotated games is drudgery, then it will be very difficult get a good feel as to how all these types of positions should be handled.

3. There is nothing as helpful as finding out specifically what you did wrong. If you don't like strong players to look at your play because you are embarrassed, it is unlikely that reading a book will pinpoint those mistakes for you. Even chess software is usually insufficient, in that these programs are best at identifying tactical mistakes

4. If you don't like playing in slow, serious over-the-board play, your learning is greatly curtailed. When playing slow games you should ask yourself on each move, "What do I know about such positions and how can I apply this knowledge?" During slow games you not only have time to apply what you

have learned before (including figuring out the similarities and differences and their effect), but also you have time to "burn" new information into your long-term memory for future use. So playing many slow games has a positive "snowball" effect that does not exist with fast time controls.

5. If you do not find the analysis work of a complicated position fun, then obviously you won't consistently do it – after all, chess is a hobby, and why would you do part of the hobby that is "optional" and not fun? But just as obviously, players who do this work every time the position gets complicated are going to have much better results than the ones that just do some superficial analysis and try something to see what happens.

6. If you consistently avoid all weaker players, this has many bad side effects:

♟ You don't develop sufficient technique on how to consistently win won games;

♟ Psychologically you create a barrier where you don't do as well against players who "may take your rating points";

♟ You don't do as well in open championship events because when Swiss pairings are used you must beat the weaker players to finish among the top places;

♟ You end up playing too few games overall because instead of playing for fun and learning, you only play when the "rating" situation is right;

♟ You play fewer and fewer games as you get to be a strong player because it is tougher and tougher to get the competition you wish, and you decelerate your learning when you exclude more and more players (and events) from your playing agenda. Yes, it is better to play stronger players most of the time, but going out of your way to do so *all* of the time can be quite harmful.

7. Most times, you are only a stranger so long as you choose to remain one. If you don't take the time to help yourself feel at home (yes, others should be helping as well), then you are not giving yourself the chance to enjoy a life-long hobby. (For the benefits of slow, over-the-board play, see *An Improvement Plan: Practice* 1-2.1.)

8. If you are so anxious to play that you will settle for the less-helpful fast game, it is likely that this lack of patience will affect your ongoing improvement. Yes, fast games are good for your chess – but slow games are better per unit time. If you are impatient at this aspect of chess then that may carry over to other areas where patience is required, like carefulness, time management, etc.

9. Losing tough games – or even losing games through "basic blunders" are good learning experiences so long as you *consistently know how to identify*

the mistakes and avoid repeating them. If you cannot bear to look at these games, you probably are doomed to repeat the mistakes. Interestingly, many students do not wish to show me games that include their biggest mistakes, but in fact *identifying why you left that piece en prise every fourth game or so, will probably do more to help your game than fixing any five small mistakes.* After all, if you make a big mistake periodically, that will much more likely result in a loss than a small mistake – and even though many students think they know why they left the piece en prise ("I did not see his bishop over there") the real sources of the problem (bad thought process, need for board vision exercises) often surprise them.

10. Going through lots of simple tactical problems can be tedious, but there are ways to make it fun. Intersperse other activities, keep statistics and records to beat, have an ever-decreasing time limit, etc. If you don't learn these chess ABC's so that you can do them fast and accurately, you will likely end up like a student who wants to be a mathematician, but thinks he doesn't need to know his multiplication tables "cold" – he can get by with his calculator...

The bottom line is that if these typical chess events are fun – or you can make them fun – then in the long run you have a big advantage over those that can't, or won't, find the fun in the work.

One of the criteria for making many of your chess decisions rests on your reason for playing a particular game or event. You might be playing for lots of reasons, but most of them boil down to one of the following three: playing for fun, improvement, or money/prizes. Of course, you can be playing for a combination of two or more. In general, if you are playing for:

♟ *Money*: You play your best moves and openings, no questions asked. Experimenting is kept to a minimum. In big tournaments like the World Open or US Open you play in your "normal" rating section.

♟ *Improvement*: You play mostly players better than yourself (e.g. "up" a section or two in a big open event). If, when analyzing, you see an unclear line versus a solid equal one, you choose the unclear one so that you learn something about that kind of position and next time it won't be so unclear. You play openings that help you work on your weaknesses, or to learn new positions and build the foundation for better play in the future. You review all your games religiously and work on your tactics, etc. You play mostly slow games to build up your long-term memory with positions and how to play them. You hire the best chess coach you can find and afford.

♟ *Fun*: You do whatever gives you the most enjoyment. Suppose you are a poor tactician but love sacrifices, then go play that next classical bishop sac! Like the adrenaline of a time trouble rush? Then likely you play primarily fast games. If you hate fast games, play slow ones. Any interesting line of analysis is fair game, win or lose. You should not take losing too badly since you are choosing your moves on the fun factor, rather than on the "best move" criteria.

Let's summarize the fun issue by taking what can be called the Big Three of Chess Fun, with their corresponding quiz items in parentheses: *It's Fun to Play* (#4,6,7,8) *It's Fun to Study* (#1,2,3,9,10), and *It's Fun to Take Your Time and do Complicated Analysis when Required* (#5). If you don't like to play, then all bets are off – but you could become a problemist, a tournament director, or an organizer. If you like all three, you probably will do well. However, if you like to play and only enjoy only one of the other two, then you are likely just muddling along.

Of course it is possible that someone finds each of the Big Three fun and is still not a good player. A player could love playing, analyzing, and studying but, because of one reason or another, repeatedly make the same mistakes and remain a weak player. Of course we all have our limits. Even if chess is your full-time profession and you love it, it is unlikely you have the kind of talent Fischer or Kasparov has, and your upside potential is not likely 2800.

The fun factor is a large one that is often overlooked in deciding many things about a chess player. Hopefully this article has helped you learn a little more about yourself and will make your chess a little bit more enjoyable in the future.

4-3) Breaking Down Barriers

Email: "Your new Novice Nook is one of the absolute best articles I have ever read concerning the subject of chess improvement. It deals successfully with the subject of what it psychologically takes to improve at life and chess. Outstanding. You have my vote for Cramer 2007. I reread your recent novice nook and will say that long after you are dead and doing radio shows from the beyond you will be remembered for the info contained in this article."

One way of differentiating the chess population is into divide it into:

- ♟ Players that are frozen by (or erect) barriers to improvement; vs.
- ♟ Players that do whatever it takes to eliminate barriers to improvement.

Most of us have barriers to improvement we can't eliminate: school, work, family, etc. However, other barriers are either removable or are just false perceptions. Nevertheless, many players find these barriers daunting for a variety of psychological reasons.

I have found that almost all good players have – or have developed – the mentality to break down most barriers. Very successful players tear at barriers, rip at them, and want to destroy them with any weapon available. Nothing gets in their way!

When a young Kasparov sought support from the Soviet government for a run at the World Championship, he was told by one high-ranking official "Why do we need another young Soviet World Champion? We already have one in Karpov!" Even though this was about as formidable a barrier as anyone can face, Kasparov did not shrink away! You know how that story played out.

Weaker players often have the same "mental capacity" as stronger players, but display less fortitude in overcoming barriers, real or imagined. Not only are these players "stopped" by these barriers, they often dwell on them, complain about them, and come up with every possible excuse as to why these barriers cannot be surmounted.

How one handles barriers is very important in determining who is going to be a good chess player. This distinction is not limited to chess; in John Molloy's interesting book *Live for Success* he cites this "breakdown barrier mentality" as the reason why a chosen set of Harvard graduates was able to achieve success, while an otherwise similar set was not. Another book, *How I Found Freedom in an Unfree World* by Harry Browne, is dedicated entirely to recognizing and overcoming barriers people erect due to their perceptions.

If you are one who tears barriers, then changing your mentality may be difficult. However, many successful people have done it. They recognize the limitations of self-imposed barriers and the harm they are doing, and resolve to overcome, ignore, or break down their barriers.

Take my first game against a master. I was a teenager who had been playing serious chess for only 18 months. When the pairings went up and my friends saw who I was paired against, they said "Boy, are you unlucky! You got paired against the only master in the tournament. He is going to kill you!" But instead of bowing to the *"I-can't"* barrier, I determined to do the best I could on each move and see what happens. I reasoned that "if he plays better than I – and that is likely – then he will win. But I can't worry about that – I can only do my best." So I did my best *and I won!* I was nervous and at one point my chances looked slim, but I never once thought "Oh no! I am going to lose!" Six months later I was again paired against that same master, who was surely not taking me lightly and looking for revenge and...*I won again!*

That doesn't mean that sheer will can beat a master, but it does mean that a defeatist attitude can be a self-fulfilling prophecy! Chess is a mental sport, and one's mental state has an enormous effect on your ability to play well. *All you can do is apply 100% of your energy on each move to finding the best move possible in the given circumstances. Anything else is counterproductive.* Many players, even those aware of the benefits of not letting other issues get in the way, often get unnecessarily distracted for any number of reasons.

Consider the book *Pawn Power in Chess* by Hans Kmoch. When I ask a strong player what he thinks of this classic, the answer is often "Great book; lots of good, basic ideas that everyone should know." But when I ask weaker players about it, the two dominant answers are:

- ♟ "I can't read it; it is in descriptive notation" (horrors!); and/or
- ♟ "I couldn't finish it; I couldn't remember (or tolerate) the strange terminology."

I sympathize with those who find descriptive notation frustrating, but overcoming the "Kmoch" barriers is not asking all that much. The point isn't that we need to remember that he calls weak light squares *leucopenia*; it is that we can learn quite a bit about the concepts of weak squares!

It is not a coincidence that several of my students and acquaintances took the time to notify me about an article in *Scientific American* about achieving chess expertise (see http://www.scientificamerican.com/article.cfm?id=the-expert-mind). This article touches on many of the factors that have been discussed in Novice Nook. The two Novice Nooks which were most similar to this article are *Traits of a Good Chess Player* (4-1) and the archived *Every Good Chess Player*, which discussed the shared abilities and experiences, respectively, of strong players.

One of the key conclusions of the *Scientific American* article was that "motivation appears to be a more important factor than innate ability in the development of expertise." This conclusion reflects the one reached in the *Chess, Learning, and Fun* (4-2). I believe there are multiple components of motivation. Besides the catalyst of "fun", determination and perseverance are the dominant ones. It is relatively easy to be determined, but it is much harder to maintain perseverance. The tortoise usually beats the hare, especially in a complex field like chess, which presents a variety of social and competitive barriers. If I had to choose the two biggest aspects of improvement, I would select the fun/perseverance combination coupled with an excellent feedback loop to identify mistakes and minimize their repetition.

The trait that allows one to break down (or prevent the creation of) barriers can be considered a type of determination, and the ability to do it over a long period of time a type of perseverance. Let's consider some common barriers and how one can attempt to overcome each:

1. Finding Good Practice and Feedback at a Club

Suppose setting up your improvement "feedback loop" involves playing slow games, preferably against stronger players, and having strong players review your games. However, you travel to your local chess club and find that the players are standoffish to new members and only play fast games. This sets up multiple barriers, none of your making. However, with some determination and perseverance club barriers can usually be overcome.

In this circumstance, a typical reaction is to give up immediately: the players are "unsociable" and "No one wants to play a slow game". However, you must try to knock down those barriers. If you are to achieve your objectives, you have to be proactive and explore the possibilities.

Some clubs are much better than others at making newcomers welcome. There are those with welcoming committees that try to help newcomers feel comfortable and those that let the newcomer sink or swim on his own volition. But no matter where your club lies, it is incumbent upon a determined newcomer to persevere – that stranger in the corner may someday be a lifelong friend if you give him half a chance.

Start by finding a club officer and, in the friendliest manner possible, ask pertinent questions:

- ♟ "Do you ever play slow games here?"
- ♟ "Who is near or just above my playing strength that might play me a slow game?"
- ♟ "If there are no slow games here, can I help organize a slow event?"

You get the idea! If you offer a little help, you might be surprised how much that is appreciated. I have been a member of clubs for over 40 years and the number of members who volunteer to help is low. No wonder they are greeted with open arms! Don't know how to run an event? No problem. These days the internet is full of helpful pages – start with the U.S. Chess Federation.

2. Worrying About Your Rating

It is human nature to worry about your rating, especially since the chess community is so "class" conscious. But the biggest way to overcome this barrier is simply to realize that in the long run your rating simply reflects your playing strength.

Therefore *anything you do to increase your playing strength will eventually help your rating, and anything you do that does not increase your playing strength will not help (and may hurt) your rating*. For example, avoiding an event with weaker players because you may lose rating points is far inferior to playing and learning, even if you lose games and ratings points. Paradoxically, if you lose to a weaker player and learn from the experience, it is not only better for you than not playing, but also better than beating them and learning nothing!

3. Competition Too Good at Tournaments

Quite a few players fear playing in their first (or second) over-the-board (OTB) tournament (or local club) because "the players are too good and I will get killed." Not only is this perception often false but, even if it were true, then with a little initiative you can turn this into a golden learning opportunity! Consider all those strong players from whom you can play and learn. Who knows, you might even win more than you think! Bottom line: if you are not the worst player on an online server, you are also undoubtedly not going to be the worst player in any large gathering of over-the-board players either.

4. Some Players Unfriendly on the Internet

Unfriendly people are everywhere. Are you going to go without food just because someone scowls at you in a supermarket? Unfortunately, the percentage of poor behavior is higher on the internet than over-the-board, because of the impersonal and anonymous nature of the medium. However, some comments can also be perceived incorrectly because you cannot hear the intonation of a person's voice or see their body language.

Suppose you are losing a game, but your opponent makes a terrible blunder, and you go on to win. In person, if he says "I had you beat!" you can see that he is despondent and angry with himself. But have the same events happen on the internet and you think, "That arrogant, sour grapes so-and-so!" Similar events: different perceptions.

5. Players Only Want to Play Fast on the Internet

This is not true! There are many slow games and there are leagues for individuals and teams who want to play them. The reasons for this misconception are that:

- ♟ Many slow players only play one game per session on the internet, so unlike fast players, once they are done they do not seek another game,

- ♟ Slow games take a much longer time, so the "seek" turnover is much lower and it seems there are less games being sought;

- ♟ Many slow games are played with friends or are prearranged as part of leagues or tournaments, so there are fewer "public" challenges.

The Internet Chess Club has a *Team 4545 League* (and others) devoted to slow play. You can also network and compile your own list of willing opponents, which will grow as you find new friends on your server.

6. Homework is Not Fun

This is a tougher one. If some aspect of your hobby is not fun, you should not do it. Yet if you want to improve at chess, you have to work hard at it. So what do you do? Here are a few suggestions:

Using different media – material that seems dry in a book may come across as lively on a DVD. Make it into a contest by timing your problems, keeping track of your percentages, and trying to beat your personal solving records.

Consider an annotated game collection equivalent to a good mystery book. How will the game turn out? Will that queenside majority get shepherded home, or will the outcome have nothing to do with that. If the author is attacking on the queenside, how will he avoid being mated on the kingside first? How could the author's opponent not draw such a "simple" endgame?

Working with a friend is generally more fun than going it alone.

7. Finding Patience to Play Slower

Some players are naturally careless and others are naturally quick-triggered. Neither is good for your slow chess play or your eventual improvement. But just because you do things outside of chess quickly, does not mean that you have to do chess things quickly. Case-in-point: I once had a 13-year-old student who had Attention Deficit Disorder (ADD). His mother was a psychologist and we were watching him play. He was wiggling in his seat, but was using his entire two hours to play 40 moves! His mother turned to me and said "You don't realize what a miracle this is. We couldn't get him to pay this much attention to anything! But he wants so badly to do well at chess that he is willing to take his time despite his nature to do otherwise." It would be great if all my readers could even come close to emulating the self-discipline of that fine young gentleman.

See *Real Chess, Time Management, and Care* (2-3), *The Goal Each Move* (2-2), and *The Case for Time Management* (3-1).

8. Don't Have the Time to Study or Play Enough

As noted earlier, this is true for some players. But for others there are two possibilities: 1) You use "lack of time" as a convenient excuse, perhaps because you fear that you won't be as good as you think you are if you do spend the time, or 2) You tried to improve but spent your time unwisely, so you no longer make the time.

In the former case, all I have to say is "If you want something badly enough, eventually you will make time for it." For the latter, if you have used your chess improvement time unwisely, now *you are reading this book* to help you make better use of it!

9. Not that Talented

Sometimes students confuse knowledge and intelligence. They think that because they don't know something that they are less talented. Or they confuse talent with current ability. They think that because they can't visualize well now, they won't get better with practice. This is nonsense, of course; everyone can get better if they practice.

A great example is that I could not play blindfold chess until I had practiced visualizing my moves in dozens of tournament games. So I always had the ability, it just needed to be developed. Everyone starts with poor "board vision", tactical vision, etc. How well you develop these skills will likely determine your ultimate level, not when you hit your *"I can't get any better"* barrier.

Yes, Fischer and Kasparov are talented geniuses. But you might be surprised to know that one study I read revealed that the average grandmaster, while above average in IQ, was not the super-genius of lore. Instead, the researchers found results similar to the *Scientific American* article: it was not the innate raw talent that set them apart, it was other factors – ones that you may have, too. Attitude counts for much in chess. Always play with confidence and try to find aggressive moves. Have respect but not fear for your opponent.

10. Find Competitive Chess Daunting

OK, it's possible that this barrier may be a show-stopper. Still, chess is one sport that is as competitive as you want to make it. Some players enjoy the aesthetic aspects rather than the competition, and there is certainly lots of room in between. On the other hand, you can always become a club or tournament organizer, TD, scholastic coach, or problemist! There are more positions available in the chess world than just "player".

Summary

If you are someone who is accustomed to putting up barriers, you may need a long look in the mirror. Changing yourself from a *barrier-maker* to a *barrier-breaker* may be the best thing that ever happened to your game.

4-4) The Three Types of Chess Vision

You can't play what you don't see.

From my experience with students who feel they have trouble "seeing" things on a chessboard, these difficulties almost always fall into one of three types, which I have categorized as:

- ♟ *Visualization* – the ability to keep track of where all the pieces are (and "see" them as a position) as you move the pieces in your head, analyzing future possibilities.

- ♟ *Board Vision* – the ability to quickly and accurately recognize where all the pieces are and assess what they are doing in the present chess position.

- ♟ *Tactical Vision* – the ability to quickly and accurately recognize known tactical patterns and their likely consequences. Tactics include more than just winning material and checkmate, but also the defensive side: preventing material loss and checkmate.

It is possible to be very good at one type of vision and quite weak at another. I have students who are good at visualization but poor at tactical vision, while another may be good at board vision and poor at visualization (because he can see everything on the present board, but has trouble imagining moves or keeping track of where a piece moved during analysis), etc.

Let's consider each in more detail:

Visualization

Visualization is the most well known of the three. Much more than the other two, it requires imagination and keeping track of where all pieces will reside as each branch of analysis is attempted. In his interesting book *Chess Psychology*, GM Nicolai Krogius defined various types of visualization errors. One of the most prominent was the *retained image error*. In the following exercise, many of my students made the same visualization error:

(see following diagram)

In this position I asked the question "Is 1 Nxe5 safe?" Ignoring the question for a moment, many students analyzed the following line: 1 Nxe5 Qe7 2 Bf4 Bd6 "attacking the pinned knight again". What is wrong with this analysis?

White to play

Aside from the fact that none of these moves are forced, the key issue is that 2...Bd6 is illegal! The students who made this error all retained the black queen on d8, and "seeing" the clear path for the bishop to get to d6 and attack e5, made it without hesitation. This type of visualization error is very common.

Another common visualization error, but of a different type, occurred when analyzing "Position A", from Dr. Adriaan de Groot's seminal *Thought and Choice in Chess*.

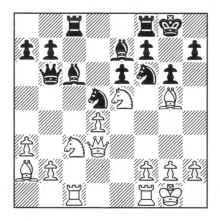

White to play

I have had about 500 players analyze this position, and others, for me "out loud". This was the subject of my book *The Improving Chess Thinker*. Many in this position stated: "I can play 1 Nxd5. Then recapturing 1...Nxd5 is not good because I win a piece with 2 Bxe7."

In this visualization error, the players are "removing the guard" on e7 by capturing the knight on d5, but they don't "see" that the recapturing knight is just as able to guard e7 as the original one, so that 2 Bxe7 is easily met by 2...Nxe7. Of additional interest, most players, whether they make this visualization error or not, stop at 2 Bxe7. They don't consider further removal of the guard with 2 Bxd5, so that recapture on d5 would indeed remove the guard on e7 and allow the win of the piece with 3 Bxe7. Therefore after 2 Bxd5 Bxg5 is forced. Almost no one rated under 1900 realized this and thus made no attempt to further analyze this critical line.

When testing students on their ability to look ahead, I sometimes observe a visualization error where at some point they lose track of whose move it is and give one player two moves in a row.

One way to minimize visualization errors is to go back to the current position and carefully replay the moves of the sequence. This is slower than, say, only going back to the previous branch to make a different move, but it does reinforce where the pieces have moved.

Board Vision & Tactical Vision

Board vision – your brain's capability to interpret a chess position and see what is *legal and/or possible* on the chessboard. Board vision tells you what is possible, but does not differentiate what is good or bad. For example, quickly seeing that a bishop in one corner of the board attacks squares at the other corner is good board vision (even if the possible moves to those squares are unsafe or the attack is inconsequential). Both board vision and tactical vision are related – but board vision usually comes first.

Tactical vision shows you when there are short-term safety issues that might win or lose material or involve checkmate.

The following two examples show the difference between board vision and tactical vision.

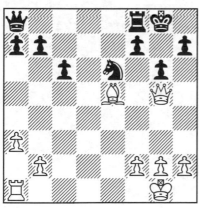

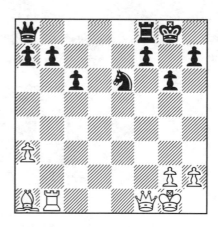

White to play and win   **White to play and win**

In both diagrams the tactic is the same: White plays **1 Qf6** and mate on h8 is unstoppable. But in the second diagram the board vision aspects are more difficult because both the queen and bishop are further away from the target h8-square. So in these cases the tactical vision is similar but the board vision is not.

We can make the first problem easier to spot the tactic by removing all extraneous pieces:

White to play and win

With only the relevant pieces, the tactic is even easier to spot. The best way to improve your tactical vision is to do lots (probably there are about 2,000 different ideas) of easy problems repeatedly like drilling the multiplication tables (see *A Different Approach to Studying Tactics* 5-1 and *An Improvement Plan: Theory* 1-2.2).

A board vision puzzle is one where you are not trying to find good moves, but just moves that serve a certain function, like a knight tour, or even just legal moves. Bruce Albertson does this in his ChessCafe column *Chess Mazes* (http://www.chesscafe.com/archives/archives.htm#Chess Mazes) and I have several in my archived *Chess Exercises*.

In the interesting book *Genius in Chess*, English GM Jonathan Levitt reveals that the accuracy and speed of solving even simple board vision puzzles can differentiate players of all levels.

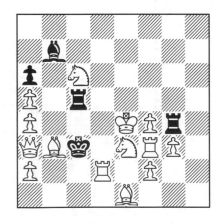

White to play – how many legal moves and how many checkmates?

The diagram above is one of Levitt's board vision exercises. Time yourself to find as quickly as possible:

1.   How many legal moves does White have; and
2.   How many checkmates in one move does White have?

The answer would be two numbers, e.g. "40 legal moves and 7 of these are checkmate" along with the time it took to generate these numbers.

The answer is that there are 29 moves, and all 29 checkmate:

♟   4 queen moves
♟   7 moves with the bishop on b3
♟   10 moves with the rook on d2
♟   8 moves with the knight on e3.

No other white piece can move. If you got both parts of the answer right in under 1 minute, you are probably already a very good player! If you did not get the answer right, you might check your board vision:

♟   Did you miss that most of the checkmates were discovered checks?
♟   Did you miss that the pinned knight on c6 can't move?
♟   Did you miss that the rook on d2 can move in four directions?

All of these errors represent deficiencies in types of board vision that can be improved by either lots of very slow play or more board vision exercises. An important point: *Your chess memory improves when your board vision is better, so improving board vision improves most other studies!*

For example, if I show an opening sequence to players of differing board vision abilities, the ones with the best board vision will remember the sequence more quickly and accurately.

One of my students sent me the following puzzle, which involves both tactical vision and board vision:

(see following diagram)

I solved this puzzle in one second! My board vision told me that the knight and bishop are covering b8, c8, d8, and e8. So I immediately asked if it would do any good to cover f8, g8, and h8 with 1 Kg7. The answer was yes, that puts Black in *zugzwang*, and no matter where he puts the queen it gets captured and it is not stalemate, so White wins.

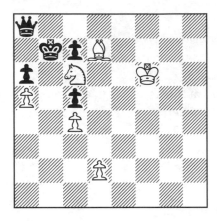

White to play

How far can you visualize? Hopefully as far as you need to. Here is a problem by C.S. Kipping.

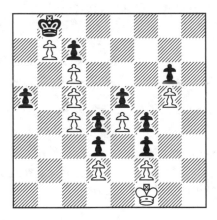

White to play – if both sides play perfectly, can either side win?

The answer is that Black is stuck guarding the b8-square, so White can win with the following steps, primarily king marches:

1.   Capture the pawn on a5;
2.   Capture the pawn on f3 via g4;
3.   *Zugzwang* the black king by going to a6 to force Black to play ...f4-f3;
4.   Go back and capture the pawn on f3; and
5.   Break through with f2-f4 and then promote and mate.

This takes about 40 moves of "easy" visualization. Did you see it?

Chapter Five

Tactics and Safety

5-1) A Different Approach to Studying Tactics

The science of chess piece safety is called tactics.

Tactics is almost undoubtedly the most productive single area that beginners and intermediates can study to improve their game – the more practice, the better.

I had a student who was performing less well than expected. He was missing very basic tactical ideas in almost all his games, both for him and for his opponent. Here my student played Black:

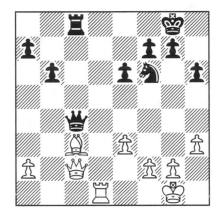

Black to play

He is up a pawn, it is his move, and has a pin on the c-file. But, instead of studying all the tactical possibilities and thinking, "Hmm. If I win a piece, then the rest of the game should be relatively easy, so I should make sure I am really winning it", he immediately plays 1...Qxc3? allowing the basic removal-of-the-guard reply 2 Rd8+, winning the queen (which White also failed to play, thus bringing to mind the guideline: "Try to play stronger opponents – they will punish you for your mistakes, so you will learn to identify them and be less likely to make them"). Instead, he should have played 1...Nd5, which does win the piece.

After watching a whole bunch of his games with incidents like this, I reminded him to keep up his tactical studies. He said that he was, but it was apparent to me that he wasn't doing as much as he should to be effective. He went on to say that the reason he was no longer studying the kind of basic problems he was missing was that he was getting a high percentage of the answers in his book (Bain's excellent *Chess Tactics for Student*), so that additional study at that level did not seem worthwhile. However, in his games he was still missing those same simple tactics, such as basic "removal of the guard" motifs.

I thought about this apparent contradiction and came to the following conclusion: *Just because you can solve a tactical problem does not necessarily mean that you will spot this tactic in a game.* While this is obvious, the reasons for this and the remedy are not quite so clear. In a problem, you know 1) it is a problem; 2) there is a specific solution; and 3) you are just looking for a tactic to solve it. However, during a game, you have to do much more than look for tactics – in fact, you may not know that the tactic even exists, so you may not spend much energy looking for it (this led to the archived *The Seeds of Tactical Destruction*).

Therefore, in a game relatively little time is used to spot tactics. If you cannot find it quickly, you might not find it at all. So it is not just the ability to find the tactic that is important, it is also important to be able to do it quickly and efficiently, as well as consistently asking "Is it safe?" (see 5-3) about *both* players' moves. So I told my student, "Go back and do the problems again until you can get most of the simple problems within a few seconds. It may be a little boring, but if you can recognize most of the basic tactical motifs: removal of the guard, double attack, effects of pins, etc much faster, then you will start seeing a much higher percentage of them in your games."

Since then I have been giving this advice frequently, because it works. When I give it, many of my students ask, "What good is doing the same problem again and again? I will just learn to memorize the answer! I want to learn something, not memorize."

Good question. My answer is: "Do you know your name or do you have it memorized? How about 1+1=?".

Problem 1: White to play and mate

Do you know Philidor's Legacy (solution at the bottom of this article) as well as 1+1=?. Although almost anyone understands, and can intellectually explain *why* 1+1 =2, you don't have to go through that process each time you need to make that addition. Similarly, it is important to quickly recognize the most basic forms of common tactical motifs – *both* the problem and the solution – in game situations, not just be able to solve it when presented in problem form. There is a strong link between "knowing" and "memorizing" simple ideas (in long-term memory). Some would say the difference is only semantics.

Here is another familiar tactical motif:

(see following diagram)

Did you already know this common pattern, or did you have to figure it out? The solution is at the bottom of this article (page 198).

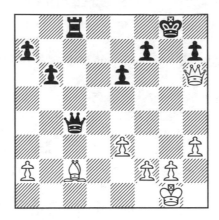

Problem 2: White to play and mate

I would conjecture that the more basic the tactic, the more beneficial it is to do it multiple times until you can do it quickly, while the more difficult the problem, the relatively less benefit it is to do it repeatedly. Complex combinations often consist of multiple basic tactics, but not vice versa. You see basic tactics in most games, while difficult ideas are more complex, and so occur much more rarely – in the future you may only see something similar. Therefore, the capability to figure out complex problems is more important than their rote recognition. Players who know basic tactics very well can more easily figure out difficult tactics.

There is an analogy to multiplication – you spend lots of time learning single digit patterns like 6x8=? but relatively little time multiplying numbers like 568 x 46,753 = ?. Once you know single digit multiplications and how to process multiple digits, you can much more easily calculate any N digit x M digit multiplication.

For example, I saw a tactical problem where the final four moves of the solution were almost identical to the previous diagram. So when I got that far, I just said, "That's it! White now mates." I did not have to *figure out* the rest of the problem because I recognized that "basic" part.

So my conclusion is worth rephrasing:

The most important goal of studying tactics is to be able to spot the elementary motifs very quickly, so studying the most basic tactics over and over until you can recognize them almost instantly is likely the single best thing you can do when you begin studying chess!

The good news is that my student figured out a way to make his basic tactics study more interesting: he cut the problems out of the book to randomize them and remove them from their "tactical motif" identification. He then reviewed them several more times until he could get almost all within a short period. Next he is graduating to a more difficult level of problem (although doing additional basic problems first is likely more helpful). Now his rating is starting to rise pretty steadily...

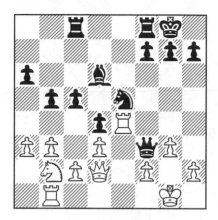

Black to play

In this position, this same student had Black and it was his move. After some thought, he recognized the line clearance and his opponent – already down a piece – resigned after 1...Qxg3+ 2 hxg3 Nf3+ 3 Kg2 Nxd2. He was very proud of this and emailed me, requesting that I look at this position. I did. Ever the diligent instructor, I replied, "Might not 1...Qxe4 have be better?" There is always room for improvement...

The Five Levels of Tactics

Here is another simple idea involving tactics that I never seen written anywhere: There are five "levels" of piece safety, from most basic to most complex:

1. *En Prise* – a piece is attacked but not guarded.
2. *Counting* – can any sequence of exchanges win material?
3. *Tactical Motifs* – individual motifs for winning material or mating; e.g. pins, double attacks, removal of the guard, back-rank mates, skewers, promotion, etc.
4. *Combinations* – combinations of tactical motifs; for example, a pin that sets up a double attack, or an interference move that allows a back-rank mate, etc.
5. *Sacrificial Combinations* – combinations which include the sacrifice of material in order to force either win of material or checkmate.

This idea, while simplistic, helps make it easier for instructors to teach tactics and for students to understand how to study them.

Beginners often have trouble recognizing not only when they are putting a piece *en prise*, but also when their opponent is leaving one *en prise*, since they concentrate more on their possibilities than their opponent's. At a slightly more advanced level, near-beginners still have trouble determining when a discovered attack causes a piece to be in danger.

Counting takes place when a piece is both attacked and defended on a square. The question is whether the piece is safe, i.e. is there *any* forcible sequence of captures on that square that would leave you behind in material? Usually Counting is fairly straightforward, but when extended to multiple squares at once it can be extremely tricky (see *The Two Types of Counting Problems* 5-5).

A couple of years ago I got an email from a 1600 player who had purchased my book *Back to Basics: Tactics*. Upon seeing that the first chapter was "Introduction to Safety and Counting" he decided such basics were beneath him and skipped the text. However, to his chagrin, he found that he got the first six problems at the end of the chapter wrong! This opened his eyes and he implored me to *let intermediate players know how overlooked and important Counting was*. This is my chance, dear reader...!

Single-motif tactics are the pure tactical maneuvers that enable a player to win material, achieve a mate, or possibly a forced draw from an inferior-looking position (not strictly "safety", but classified this way because checkmate is really the ultimate king safety tactic). Examples of tactical motifs are double attacks/forks, discovered attacks and checks, pins, skewers, removal of the guard, and back-rank mates. I believe combinations are so named because they combine tactical motifs. A combination might start with a pin and, if the opponent tries to save material, that allows a back-rank mate. Or a combination can use a skewer followed by a double attack and removal of the guard.

Many famous combinations involve sacrifice of material for eventual greater gain, so some theoreticians have deemed that a combination requires a sacrifice. However, the idea of "combining" motifs, or elements, seems to make more sense. There is no doubt, however, that a high percentage of combinations, including most of the beautiful ones, involve sacrifices. So a reasonable compromise would be to say that there are five levels of tactics, with the highest level, combinations, divided into "basic" combinations, which involve multiple motifs without sacrifice, while "advanced" combinations include sacrifice.

Players should study and learn tactics in increasing order of complexity. *The ability to play combinations in a timed game is highly dependent upon the player's ability to recognize the basic, underlying motifs accurately and extremely quickly.* This has led myself and others to conclude that, rather than studying individual motifs "once-over" and then proceeding to more difficult combinations, it is more efficient to learn individual motifs extremely well by repetition (as noted above) so that the player has the possibility of recognizing *both the possibility and the solution* to as many tactics as possible. The archived *The Seeds of Tactical Destruction* discusses the bases for recognizing the existence of combination *possibilities*, and many combination books discuss how to analyze tactical positions. The big differences between doing problems and finding tactics in a game are:

- ♟ the time element;
- ♟ the need to prevent tactics for the opponent and not just play them yourself;
- ♟ the possibility that the combination may not exist.

Solutions
Problem 1 (Philidor's Legacy): 1 Qb3+ Kh8 (interpositions delay, but do not alter the solution; if 1...Kf8 2 Qf7 mate) 2 Nf7+ Kg8 3 Nh6+ Kh8 4 Qg8+ Rxg8 5 Nf7 mate.
Problem 2 (Mate in Four): 1 Bxh7+ Kh8 2 Bg6+ Kg8 3 Qh7+ Kf8 4 Qxf7 mate.

5-2) When is a King Safe?

Pushing pawns in front of your king can be safe!

The two most important evaluation criteria are king safety and material. The latter is easy to improve through puzzles (see *A Different Approach to Studying Tactics* 5-1), but weaker players have a much more difficult time deciding when a king is safe.

I asked several players about king safety and the most common answers were:

- A king is not safe if there are weak squares around it.
- A king is not safe if there are lines of attack to it.
- A king is safe if it's castled and its surrounding pawns have not moved.
- A king is not safe if the pawns around it are compromised.
- A king is not safe if it is not castled, etc.

While all of these answers are somewhat correct, they all quite miss the point!

Consider the following analogy: Who is safer, a person locked in a house with a shotgun or one sleeping unarmed outdoors? While *on average* the answer might be the person in the house, you might consider whether it makes a big difference whether there is a SWAT team outside the house desperate to get to our gunman, or whether the person sleeping outside is in the middle of nowhere, with no animals or humans within 100 miles.

Using this analogy, it is easy to construct positions contrary to the above answers. Consider the following:

If we re-examine the answers using this position as a measure, all would result in the conclusion that Black's king is safer. After all, Black has a better pawn covering, no weak squares, and less open lines to his king. Yet, the "exposed" white king, with his supporting

SWAT team, is clearly safer!

So the proper perspective is: *A king is safe if the opponent's pieces cannot successfully attack it.* Or *a king's safety is inversely proportional to the opponent's ability to forcibly attack it.* This supposes that the attack is successful despite the best defense. Of course, in almost any position a bad defense can succumb to an attack!

It is *still* important whether you weaken squares or open lines to your king! In many positions such weaknesses, especially if unnecessary, *are* foolish and dangerous. However, in many other positions, pushing the pawns around your king is not only meaningless with regards to your king's safety, but actually necessary to achieve your own attack.

In the following position which king is safer?

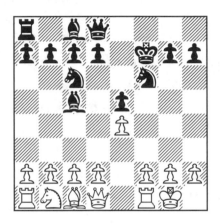

White to play

Almost all beginners and quite a few intermediates think: "White's king is safer. White's kingside pawn integrity is intact and not only has Black lost the sheltering f-pawn but – horrors! – the black king is on the "precarious" f7-square instead of the safe g8-square.

But that is not correct. While both kings are relatively safe, it is actually Black's king which is somewhat safer! Why? Because Black is better developed, and therefore the black minor pieces are not only closer to White's king, but Black's material advantage, semi-open f-file, and ability to mobilize a kingside attack are far superior to White's.

Let's consider a more complex example from a very instructive game. There are some excellent lessons here besides king safety! One of my students had Black:

1 d4 Nf6 2 c4 e6 3 Nc3 Bb4

The characteristic of the solid Nimzo-Indian Defense.

4 a3 Bxc3+ 5 bxc3 c5 6 e3 d6 7 Nf3 0-0 8 Bd3 Nbd7(?)

Up to here my student has played excellently, but now he starts to lose the thread. The correct idea, and the one consistent with the blockade 5...c5, is to play 8...Nc6 and, later, possibly ...b7-b6, ...Na5, and ...Ba6 attacking the weak white c4-pawn.

9 0-0 e5 10 e4 b6 11 Bg5 h6 12 Bd2

12 Bh4 is more consistent.

12...Bb7 13 Qe2 Qc7(?) 14 Ne1 Rfe8 15 d5

The closed center is normally good for the side with the knights, despite White's superior space.

15...Nf8 16 f4

White plays his only reasonable break move.

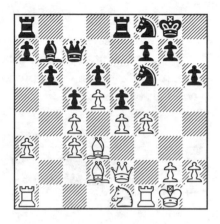

Black to play

Consider the pros and cons of capturing the pawn:

In Black's favor to capture 16...exf4:

- ♟ The e4-pawn becomes backward;
- ♟ White doesn't have the option to push the f-pawn or capture (less flexibility);
- ♟ The black rook will be more menacing (with the queen on the e-file);
- ♟ The e5-square becomes weak and a knight can reside there.

In White's favor if Black captures 16...exf4:

- ♟ White has the bishop pair and thus would rather have a more open game;
- ♟ The knight on f6 becomes vulnerable to an exchange sacrifice along the semi-open f-file;
- ♟ White gets more open lines for his rooks and bishops.

Assume that you add up Black's pros and cons for capturing on f4 (but not the pros and cons for not capturing) and decide that the cons outweigh the pros. Is this sufficient reason not to capture? To illustrate the proper logic, consider an analogous question: suppose you have to decide between choices A and B, and A is somewhat bad for you (e.g. you lose $5). Does that mean you should automatically choose "B"? Of course not! What if B means you lose $1,000,000? So the real question is *not* whether A is good for you; it is whether A is *better* for you than B. In this case capturing may, on balance, help White, but that is not sufficient reason for Black to refrain from capturing, as not capturing may help White more!

As it turns out, Black should capture. In the actual game Black played:

16...Kh7?

That allows White to play:

17 f5

17 fxe5 is also good since 17...Rxe5 18 Bf4 and, if the rook moves, then 19 e5+ wins the knight. The black king should not have gone onto the same diagonal as the light-squared white bishop. And if 17...dxe5 then White has the very promising exchange sacrifice 18 Rxf6! gxf6 19 Qh5 and the h-pawn falls with a violent attack.

17...Qe7

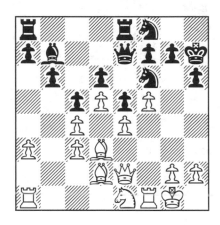

White to play

One principle to try to apply is *an attack on the flank is best met by a counterattack in the center*. But here the center is locked so a counterattack is impossible! We can conclude: *If the center is completely locked, then an attack on the flank can not only be good, but it is mandatory – if possible!*

The most pertinent fact in that *White is now free to attack the kingside, while Black hardly has any counterplay since he has no advantage on either flank!* Any time you can get a position where you can attack but your opponent cannot, then, with some care, you are likely going to win, and here White has such a position. Thus Black is not only worse despite the "advantage of the knights", and instead should have taken any steps necessary to avoid this situation. As one local FIDE Master immediately stated about Black's choices when he saw the move 16 f4, "You've gotta take!"

We have reached a crucial king safety question: White is much better, but *how* should White attack? Should White...

♟ Bring his pieces in front of his g- and h- pawns and attack the king; or

♟ Play 18 g4 and bring his pieces behind his g- and h-pawns and try a pawn storm? Does this unnecessarily expose the white king?

This question is slightly harder than the first one since both plans have some chances for success. However, as that same FM stated, "Well, here I would play 18 g4."

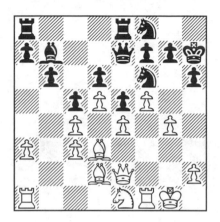

Black to play after 18 g4 (analysis)

All the advanced players understood this idea correctly, but many intermediate players failed. These intermediate players were reluctant to push their g- and h-pawns and expose the white king so dramatically. Yet, based on our earlier definition of king safety, it should be relatively easy to see that *White can push his kingside pawns without any real danger to his king at all!*

As noted earlier, if White plays very poorly Black can later take advantage of the weakened king, *but that would be true in almost any position.* You shouldn't think, "I won't make this good move because if I play poorly later I can lose!" I often see weak players make a good move like 18 g4, then play terribly and lose, only to conclude, "I shouldn't have pushed my kingside pawns." This is bad logic and leads to future poor play. In that case, while the loss may have been prevented if 18 g4 was not played, the correct conclusion is that later moves were the real culprit, and instead the player should learn how to better handle the attack. The destructive conclusion: "I should avoid good kingside play with (powerful) moves like 18 g4 in similar positions" is throwing out the baby with the bathwater.

Try playing this position against a friend, with both players twice taking White after 18 g4. When playing White, place most of your pieces behind the g- and h-pawns (at some point you usually should play h2-h4) and then break through appropriately with g4-g5, keeping in mind each move to *open lines for your attack* – don't close them. In other words, White would almost never play g4-g5 and then g5-g6, allowing Black to lock up the kingside with ...f7-f6. Often beginners think that terrible moves like g5-g6?? for White gives them more "space", but in reality it just closes off your attack forever, and your "space" is worthless. After you play both sides twice you should soon find that White's king, even without his kingside pawns nearby, is much the safer of the two!

In this game, White decided to take the less aggressive and "safer" (and probably not completely unreasonable) course of attacking first with his pieces. I can't say that the decision was bad since White's game is so good that any reasonable plan will leave him better. However, the attack is far more likely to succeed in similar positions if you lead with your pawns. *Too many players try to play chess with their pieces in front of their pawns when often the pieces are much more effective with the pawns used as a battering ram.*

18 Rf3 Ng8 19 Rh3 f6?

It is not necessary to weaken the light squares until White threatens an otherwise unstoppable g5.

20 Qh5 Red8 21 Be2 Qe8

Black offers to trade queens. Should White decline just because Black wants to trade?

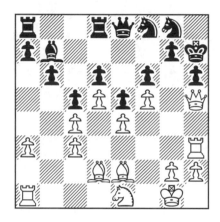

White to play

Of course not. Your decision to trade should be based solely on whether it is the best move for you, and not whether your opponent offered it or not! In this position White is conducting a mating attack on the flank, so it would be a serious error to trade queens. He should avoid the trade for that reason alone – not because Black offered it!

22 Qh4 Ba6

Black decides to counterattack, but it is so late that White probably does not even need to defend; the attack can continue.

23 Nc2

Why does White play this move?

White wants to play Ne3 (where else?!) and then Ng4, putting a fourth attacker on h6. That would enable him to sacrifice a piece on h6 for two pawns, opening the g-and h-files for his queen and rook. When is the correct time for Black to realize this potential threat and prepare a defense? Now, of course! Mentally "place" the knight on g4 *now* and ask: "How can I stop him from sacrificing on h6?"

The answer is "If I wait that long, I can't!" So you need to prevent it *now*. If you don't think this way and instead wait until the threat is unstoppable, that would be Hope Chess. The proper time to ask yourself about whether a threat can be stopped is *before* you allow the threat, because in chess *it is often possible to make threats which cannot be stopped.* Therefore, the only way to defense these threats is to prevent them from being made. Unfortunately here Black played...

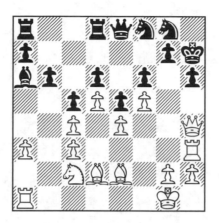

Black to play

23...Qa4!?

"Attacking" the knight, so White naturally "made it safe" with:

24 Ne3

OK, now Black may think the knight went to e3 to save itself *and* to guard c4, which are both true. But it would be wrong to stop your reasoning here, as moves are allowed to do more than two things. Black continued blissfully with:

24...b5?

Losing. 24...Kh8 or 24...Qd7 were necessary. So White played the natural...

25 Ng4

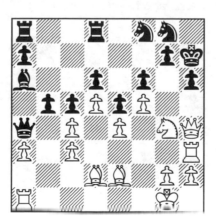

Black to play

The threat to sacrifice on h6 cannot be defended, e.g. 25...g5 26 Nxf6+ (removing the guard) 26...Kg7 (if 26...Nxf6 27 Qxh6+ will win; if 26...Kh8 then 27 Bxg5 is one way to win easily) 27 Bxg5 (not necessary, but thematic) 27...hxg5 28 Qxg5+ and White has many ways to finish off Black. So Black tries the desperate...

25...Qc2 26 Bxh6 gxh6

If 26...Nxh6 27 Nxf6+.

27 Nxh6

Winning, but the computer likes 27 Nxf6+ with a forced mate even better. After 27 Nxh6 if you are playing a computer you could resign, but against a human what is Black's best practical chance?

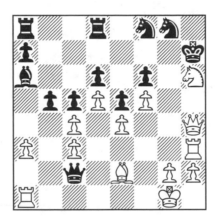

Black to play

Here a little logic suggests you *must* play 27...Qxe2!?. The reason is simple: White has a devastating attack, but the material is still close to equal. If you don't take some extra material then there is no pressure for White to find the correct line – *anything* positive White finds is sufficient (see *The Principle of Symmetry* 8-6). At least after the bishop capture Black is ahead two pieces for two pawns, and thus the onus is on White to find the win:

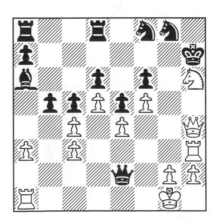

White to play and win after 27...Qxe2 (analysis)

Winning the exchange with 28 Nf7+ Kg7 29 Nxd8 Rxd8 is excellent if White finds 30 Re1; otherwise there is still work to do. The best win is 28 Nxg8+! Kxg8 29 Qxf6 threatening the mating pattern 30 Rh8. This wins on the spot, e.g. 29...Nh7 30 Rg3+ mates. But this line requires White to see 29 Qxf6 *before* playing 28 Nxg8+, and even intermediate level players can easily miss this, so Black has some hope that White can misplay this position.

Instead, from the previous diagram Black played "automatically" to get out of the discovered check with:

27...Kg7?

And, after the simple and strong:

28 Rg3+

Black resigned. Games such as this one, with the proper notes, can be more instructive than some books!

Compare White's excellent kingside pawn thrust possibility in the previous game (after the excellent possibility 18 g4) with the following position, from another student's game played at the 2005 World Open:

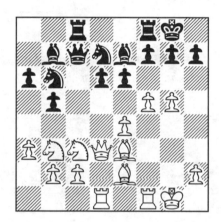

Black to play after 1 f5

White has launched a kingside pawn attack. However, unlike the previous game, not only is the center unstable and fluid, but Black has several ways to perform a central counterattack. Therefore just the opposite conclusion can be made: White has implemented a faulty plan, because the kingside pawn push should fail against proper play. The game continued:

1...exf5!

Black opens lines to the white king, e.g. the a8-h1 diagonal.

2 exf5 Ne5!

Placing the knight on the weak e5-square where it both defends the black king and attacks White's. With the attack on White's queen there is no time for the thematic f5-f6, so the kingside attack is already crumbling.

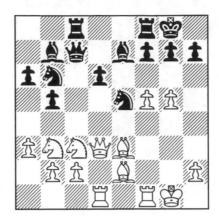

White to play

Black is taking over the center and White's king is beginning to feel the heat.

3 Qd4 Qc6

Black continued nicely: since White cannot play Bf3, the long diagonal is fatally weak.

4 Kf2 Nbc4 5 Bxc4 bxc4

Not 5...Qxc4?? – *Don't trade queens when you are attacking unless it either wins material or you are already ahead enough material to win easily!*

6 Nd2 Qg2+ 7 Ke1 Bxg5

and White's position was crumbling into the dust. A nice example of how to counterattack in the center!

It was not just White's lack of pawn protection that was his fatal flaw. In both games the white kingside pawns could be pushed and doing so could eventually open lines and create weak squares, but only in the second did Black's pieces have forced access to the white monarch.

The conclusion is worth repeating: *A king is only unsafe if the opponent is able to forcibly attack it.* If making weak squares and open lines to the king allows the opponent's pieces deadly access, then these weaknesses should be avoided if possible. But if such weaknesses cannot be exploited and, instead, grant *you* attacking opportunities, then such pawn storms can – and sometimes *must* – be played. In relatively even (or worse!) positions it is almost always better to play aggressively than passively.

5-3) Is it Safe?

Safety is the #1 issue on a chessboard.

The "it" in "Is it Safe?" includes the entire position; *not only the piece that was moved, but anything affected by that move* (see *The Safety Table*, page 219).

After an opponent's move, many of my students incorrectly ask "What does it do?" which often leads to big oversights. *The first thing you should do after your opponent's move is ask "Is it safe?"* and later "What are *all* the things that move does?"

Many players remain weak because their thought process is incorrect or because they think that just by acquiring knowledge they can get better. However, they will never get stronger if they don't prioritize their thought process regarding all-important safety issues. Each time I see a move, I first consider:

♟ Can the piece that moved be captured?

♟ Is it adequately guarded?

♟ Can it be trapped by a piece of lesser value?

♟ Is it no longer guarding something else?

These basic safety issues should be addressed *before* investigating what the move threatens. After all, if I can safely capture the piece, then it often can't pose any threat. (But watch out for discoveries!)

Preserving the safety of your pieces and *recognizing the vulnerabilities of your opponent's pieces are among the single most important concepts on the chessboard.* This also includes king safety. Strategic and positional ideas almost always take a back seat to safety – see *The Principle of Tactical Dominance* (2-6).

Whenever a move is made, the safety of various pieces and squares is affected. *The recognition of this effect (for both players) in terms of new attacks, indirect attacks, former attacks, discovered attacks, etc is the paramount initial issue that must be addressed when you continue to think about your move.* In other words, "Is it safe?"

A safety check should not only be performed immediately after your opponent makes a move, *it also must be performed early in your thought process for all* your *initial candidate moves to see if they are safe.* If safe, they may become *final candidate moves* (see *Initial and Final Candidate Moves* in *Making Chess Simple* 2-1).

Our first example occurs after **1 e4 d6 2 f4 Nf6 3 Nc3 g6 4 Nf3 Bg7 5 Bc4 0-0 6 d4 c5** (the center fork trick 6...Nxe4 7 Nxe4 d5 regaining the piece was good – a good maneuver to know!) **7 e5** (attacking the knight) **7...Be6** (counterattacking the bishop). Is it safe?

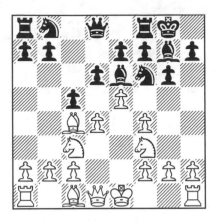

White to play

No. Although the bishop is guarded, White has several ways to win a piece here, such as 8 Bxe6 fxe6 9 exf6 or 8 exf6 Bxc4 9 fxg7 or even 8 d5. *If Black had seen just one of them, that would have been enough to eliminate 7...Be6 from consideration.* Black *has to assume the opponent will make the best move*, even though human opponents don't always do so. Never make a bad move and assume your opponent will make a worse one! *This is also a great example of making chess too difficult; Black should simply have moved his attacked knight.* When you first start playing chess, counterattacks are tempting but often dangerous; it is often much simpler just to move your attacked piece to safety.

In the next position, White has just played **1 d4 d5 2 Nc3 Nf6 3 Qd3?! Nc6 4 e4**. Is it safe?

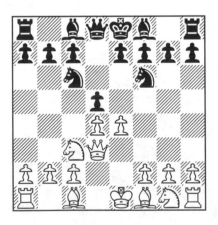

Black to play

No, 4 e4 allows the simple discovered attack **4...dxe4 5 Nxe4 Nxe4 6 Qxe4 Qxd4** winning the d-pawn. All too often, weaker players do not recognize this pattern, while intermediate players almost always do. Importantly, *6...Qxd4 is better than 6...Nxd4, because it develops* a piece and forces White to choose between trading queens (when down in material) or moving his queen again to avoid the trade.

In the following position, Black has just captured **1...Nxe5**. How should White recapture?

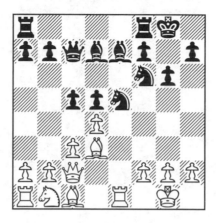

White to play

2 dxe5 is forced. The "active" 2 Rxe5?, as played in the game, is not safe because it allows the skewer 2...Bd6, winning the h2-pawn. Black could also play the more complex double attack 2...Ng4!?, e.g. 3 Rxe7? Qxh2+ 4 Kf1 Rae8 with an winning attack.

The next example is **1 e4 e5 2 Nf3 Nc6 3 Bb5 a6 4 Ba4 b5?!** (this rush to push the bishop away is common at lower levels) **5 Bb3 Na5?! 6 Nxe5** (reasonable, but theory holds that 6 0-0 is even stronger). Black now plays **6...Nc4**. Is it safe?

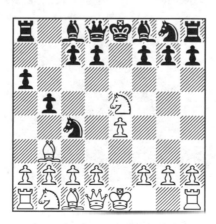

White to play after 6...Nc4

This is easy: of course not. The knight is attacked twice and guarded only once, so

Counting reveals that 7 Nxc4 bxc4 8 Bxc4 wins a pawn, as does 7 Bxc4 bxc4 8 Nxc4. Even trickier lines like 7 Nxf7 are possible. However, White played **7 Qh5** because he wanted "to put more pressure on f7". This is yet another example of weaker players making chess more difficult than it is. Just win the pawn! Is 7 Qh5 safe?

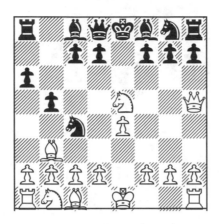

Black to play after 7 Qh5

No. Although threatening checkmate, 7 Qh5? allows the removal of the guard tactic **7...g6**, when the queen can no longer guard the attacked knight on e5. *If you don't look for forcing replies like this* before *you make your move, you are playing Hope Chess!* Then White's best move is the desperate **8 Nxf7**, when Black has **8...gxh5** (but not the disastrous 8...Kxf7?? 9 Qd5+ winning the rook – you always have to be careful and calculate each line!) **9 Nxd8 Kxd8** and Black is better.

In the following position, Black has just attacked White's knight on h4 with his bishop. *List all the ways the knight can be saved, from most safe to least.*

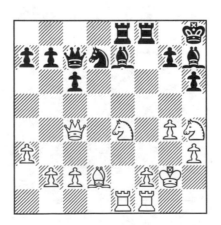

White to play

The correct order is 1 Nf5, 1 g5, and 1 Nf3. Why is 1 Nf3 least safe?

The answer is that the *only* "new" capture, 1...Rxf3!, leaves White down a piece, as 2 Kxf3 is met by the simple fork 2...Ne5+ picking up the queen. Did you see that when listing the safety of the moves? If you did not, you are not alone. About 85% of intermediate students failed to see this basic tactic.

This result illustrates a great divide between improving players' theory and practice. Although most intermediates missed 1 Nf3 Rxf3! they all agreed it was no more difficult than the problems in John Bain's basic *Chess Tactics for Students*. This illustrates two very important points:

- ♟ Seeing a tactic in a "non-problem" setting by posing the question as an open, practical safety issue is much more difficult than posing it as a problem with an assured solution.

- ♟ Most intermediate players could greatly benefit from the study of basic tactics. Learning to *recognize* (or at least quickly solve) 90%+ of the basic tactical patterns that occur during a game is far superior to the goal of being able to correctly *calculate* 100% of those same tactics – only after you know there is a tactic in the position. Repetitive study of easy tactics results in a much bigger "bang for the buck" than most believe!

In order to further understand the amateur's mind, I gave my students a choice of three reasons for why they missed 1...Rxf3:

- ♟ They did not consider all checks, captures, and threats, and thus did not analyze 1...Rxf3;

- ♟ They considered 1...Rxf3, but thought that White just wins the exchange, and so dismissed it as bad for Black and did not look any further (see the archived *Quiescence Errors*);

- ♟ They considered 1...Rxf3 and looked for any further checks, captures, and threats following 2 Kxf3, but missed 2...Ne5+ (tactical vision error).

Of these three possible causes, #3 is most tolerable because it indicates a good thought process but inadequate vision. See *The Three Types of Chess Vision* (4-4).

However, the other two reasons are more cause for concern. If you didn't see that 1 Nf3 was not safe because of a quiescence error (bad) or not considering all checks, captures, and threats (worse!), then you need to seriously consider revamping your thought process to make it more efficient.

Consider how much easier this problem is when stated differently. Suppose I show you 1 Nf3 and *tell* you it is not safe:

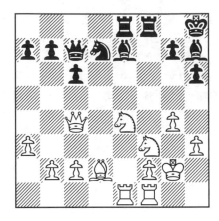

Black to play and win

Knowing there is a win, hopefully you would find **1...Rxf3!**.
Or we can go to the easiest level and show only the final dénouement:

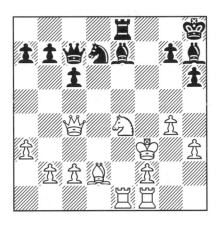

Black to play and win

Everyone should find **1...Ne5+** here!

Here is another example showing that a tactic missed on offense (you failed to win material) is a completely different problem than if that same pattern is missed on defense (you failed to stop your opponent from winning material)! Let's consider two "matching" positions:

(see following diagram)

In Position 1 many players are distracted by the Seed of Tactical Destruction (see the archived *The Seeds of Tactical Destruction*), the easy-to-spot pin 1...Qe7, and therefore miss the much more forcing 1...Qa5+ winning the knight. If you are Black, play 1...Qe7? and later give this position to a chess engine, it will of course tell you that you should have played 1...Qa5+. Unfortunately the engine will not explain *why* you missed this check, or how to improve your thought process so you are less likely to miss a future tactic shot. Many students are satisfied to just know that 1...Qa5+ was the correct move, as if this information is enough to ensure that next time they won't miss a similar chance. However, it makes a lot more sense to figure out why 1...Qa5+ was missed:

Position #1: Black to play after 1 Nxe5

♟ Believing 1...Qe7 wins and not finding it necessary to look for another winning move;

♟ An inefficient thought process, in that you consider threats before examining more forcing checks;

♟ A lack of board vision, in that you did not see 1...Qa5+ as a candidate;

♟ Not following Lasker's Rule and, after seeing that 1...Qe7 is OK, not looking for a better move; and/or

♟ Playing too fast; not taking the time necessary to find the best move possible in a more reasonable length of time.

In each case the "cure" might be something different. For example, changing your thought process to look at checks first is not the same as getting better board vision to see that 1...Qa5+ is possible, or learning to play slow consistently to find better moves.

Now suppose we take the same problem, but from White's point of view *before* capturing the e-pawn:

(see following diagram)

This illustrates a different aspect of the thought process, the issue of safety for the player contemplating the capture. There may be several possibilities why White might erroneously play 1 Nxe5:

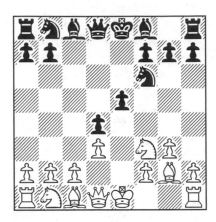

Position #2: White to play – is 1 Nxe5 safe?

- White doesn't consider any Black possibilities and just waits to see what happens and how Black will respond (Hope Chess);

- White plays 1 Nxe5 too fast, not doing the required analysis to see if the move is safe;

- White plays Real Chess and considers Black's replies, but does not start with checks and overlooks 1...Qa5+;

- White lacks the board vision and/or tactical vision to see 1...Qa5+;

- White played 1 Nxe5 and only considered 1...Qe7, being distracted by the Seed of Tactical Destruction. He found that 1...Qe7 can be safely met by 2 Qe2, 2 f4, or even 2 0-0! (2...Qxe5? 3 Re1 wins a queen and pawn for a rook and knight). However, the plausible 2 Bf4 is not safe:

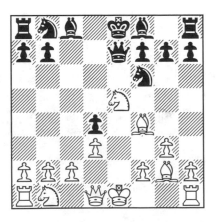

Position #3: Black to play and win a piece

2...g5! is a standard removal of the guard tactic – this type is deflection. If you have trouble quickly and accurately finding and resolving these safety issues, repetitive study of basic tactics will probably yield big returns (see *An Improvement Plan: Theory* 1-2.2).

Positions 1 and 2 again show *it is one thing to be able to see an easy combination when it is "White to play and win"; it is quite another to be able to see that your candidate moves are unsafe because your opponent has that same combination*. In the above example, routinely seeing (a) 1 Nxe5 is not safe when White is much more difficult than (b) finding a win after 1 Nxe5 as Black, which in turn is much more difficult than (c) solving a "Black to play and win" problem given 1 Nxe5?. I have estimated the difference is about 700-800 rating points between the rating level of players who solve (a) vs. (c).

The following is a more advanced example. White is considering 1 R1xa5.

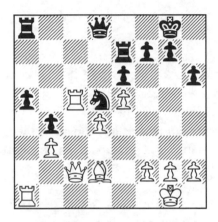

White to play – is 1 R1xa5 safe?

The answer is "No", but requires some serious analysis.

After **1 R1xa5?** basic Counting shows that 1...Qxa5 2 Rxa5 3 Rxa5 trades a queen and a pawn for two rooks, roughly even (and therefore safe). But when you see a good move, look for a better one. Instead, Black should refute White's play with **1...Rxa5! 2 Rc8**. At first glance this looks like it yields the same "safe" result: a queen and a pawn for two rooks. But looking a little further Black finds **2...Ra1+** (missing this check would be a quiescence error!) **3 Bc1** (this pin will prove fatal) **3...Qxc8+! 4 Qxc8+ Kh7**. Now the threat of 5...Rc7 forces **5 Qc2+ g6**, when Black still threatens 6...Rc7, but there is no defense! For example, if **6 Qb2**, then **6...R7a7!** threatens 7...R7a2 and eventually Black will win the bishop.

I made this analysis and correctly concluded that Black was winning, but I suspect that most players rated under 1900 USCF – and a great majority under 1800 – would not see this far, missing at least the sting in the tail (6...R7a7!).

However, in the game Black settled for the "quieter" **1...Rc7**. Was this safe?

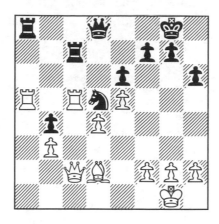

White to play after 1...Rc7

No, again. This time it is easier, but one still must count carefully. First, consider the capture of the piece that moved: 2 Rxc7 Rxa5?? 3 Rc8 does work this time because Black has one less rook than he did in the previous combination. Black's second capture (after 2 Rxc7) 2...Qxc7??, fails to 3 Rxa8+. That leaves only 2...Nxc7 3 Rxa8 (not 3...Qxa8?? 4 Qxc7 Qa1+ – don't forget to look for these potentially deadly moves at the end of combinations! – 5 Qc1 winning a piece) 3...Nxa8, when White remains ahead at least a pawn by eventually capturing on b4. But *just because a candidate move is safe does not mean it is best!* Before playing 2 Rxc7, look for a better move.

Try **2 Rxa8**. This multi-square Counting issue takes advantage of the overworked black queen. Now 2...Rxc5?? fails to 3 Rxd8 mate. So, **2...Qxa8 3 Rxc7 Nxc7 4 Qxc7 Qa1+ 5 Qc1** and White is ahead a piece. Therefore, the correct move is 2 Rxa8. I suspect that most (but not all!) players over 1600 would get this correct.

In the game, White made the *same mistake* that Black did on the previous move – instead of carefully calculating a winning trading sequence, he settled for a "quiet" move that missed the win, 2 Qa2?. Ironically, this game was played at a slow time limit of 40 moves in two hours. White had plenty of time, yet he chose to move rather quickly and threw away the win. We can conclude:

If there are capturing sequences, then playing quiet moves is often a mistake. Instead, it is usually correct to capture first and see if your opponent can capture last and stay even. But don't let him capture first and then leave you wondering if you can capture last to remain even!

Correctly and consistently performing the two safety checks mentioned in this article may do more to increase your rating than reading 100 chess books!

The Safety Table

There are many ways safety can be affected by a move:

- ♟ The moving piece's safety on the square where it lands.

- ♟ A capture made by the moving piece.

- ♟ Any new squares attacked and/or guarded by the moving piece.

- ♟ Any squares no longer attacked and/or guarded by the moving piece.

- ♟ Any discoveries (for both sides!) made by the moving piece – this would include any squares cleared for movement. For example, 1 Nf3 clears g1 for the possibility of 2 Rg1, but at this point the safety of other pieces is not yet affected since no black pieces are attacking the white first rank.

- ♟ Any squares blocked (for both sides) by the moving piece – this would be the opposite effect of a discovery.

- ♟ The allowance or prevention of castling or *en passant*.

- ♟ Indirectly: squares that the moving piece can affect next move (or in future moves) that have to be attended to this move, e.g. the threat to make an unstoppable threat next move.

A player also must consider safety issues left over from the previous move, such as those ignored by a *zwischenzug* (in-between move) or missed by a weaker player.

Strong players maintain a "feel" for which squares are safe. As each move is played, they quickly calculate how that move affects the safety of each affected square. You can consider this a mental safety database or subconscious "safety table", where each entry represents an attacked square and the content is the safety issues for that square.

I mentioned this "safety table" to one of my students, and he asked me to use a well-known opening as an example. Here is an edited transcript of our conversation:

Dan: Give me an opening.
Student: French, Tarrasch.
Dan: Let's do the safety table from White's point of view. That means the table will be updated primarily after Black's move.
Student: OK.

1 e4
   Dan: No pieces are attacked by either side.
1...e6
   Dan: No pieces attacked by either side, but now White cannot safely put pieces on the a3-f8 diagonal. For example, 2 b4 is no longer safe.
2 d4 d5
   Dan: The pawn on e4 attacked once, guarded zero: Attention! Pawn *en prise*!

White to play after 2...d5

3 Nd2

Dan: Defends e4. Which Black line do you want to choose?

Student: 3...Nf6.

    3...Nf6

White to play after 3...Nf6

    Dan: e4 is again attacked more than defended and not safe: threats are ...dxe4 and ...Nxe4. Also, d5 is attacked once and defended three times – safe for Black, but White can safely capture on d5. Also, Black's ...dxe4 discovers an attack on d4, so d4 is also in the table. So the three squares in the table at this point are e4 (not safe), d5 (safe for Black) and d4 (may be unsafe if a capture is made on e4 if White cannot retake with the knight, discovering a guard on d4 with the queen).

4 e5

    Dan: The table is cleared except for f6!

4...Nd7

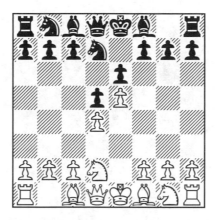

White to play after 4...Nd7

Dan: Now e5 is attacked once with a knight and guarded by a pawn, so e5 is very safe.
5 Bd3 c5

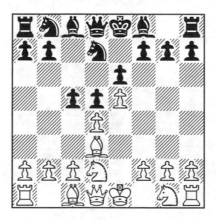

White to play after 5...c5

Dan: The bishop on d3 attacks h7, which is adequately guarded and safe. The pawn at c5 is attacked, but adequately guarded. Now e5 looks the same as it was before ...c5, except the d4 defender is in danger; therefore, indirectly so also may be the pawn on e5. However, the main issue of 5...c5 is that it attacks d4; the pawn on d4 is now clearly not safe (one attacker and no defenders), so...
6 c3 Nc6
Dan: e5 is attacked twice and defended only once, but it is safe for now because the defender is a pawn and both attackers are knights. However, d4 is now attacked twice and defended once, so it is unsafe.
7 Ne2 Qb6

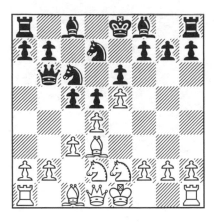

White to play after 7...Qb6

Dan: e5 is still safe, d4 is now defended twice, but attacked three times and not safe; b2 is now attacked, but also guarded, so safe. Also, c5 is attacked by the white pawn, but guarded three times, so safe. Number of squares in table: e5, d4, c5, b2, and h7, for a total of five.

8 Nf3 cxd4

White to play after 8...cxd4

Dan: Capture! White is temporarily down a pawn. d4 will be safe with a recapture, but it has to be with the pawn because a capture with the knight will leave e5 unsafe! b2 and h7: no change (safe), c5 no longer attacked.

9 cxd4 f6

Dan: d4 now attacked twice and defended twice (safe), b2 and h7 unchanged (safe), but e5 attacked three times and defended only twice, so unsafe. Therefore...

10 exf6 Nxf6

Dan: Move 11: d4 still safe, h7 and b2 safe, so finally White has time to castle!
11 0-0 Bd6

White to play after 11...Bd6

Dan: d4 and b2 still safe as is h7, but now h2 is attacked by a bishop. However, it is also guarded twice, so h2 is safe for now.

Dan: After each move (for both sides) the table is changed by the effect of the moved pieces, and the table contains the safety on each attacked square. This "table" only covers Counting and tactics, such as double attack, removal of the guard, etc. Yet it can be very helpful in identifying which of those tactics can cause problems on what squares. Is this the kind of thing you wanted?

Student: Yes. So I need to get in the habit of updating the complete table after every move.

Dan: You keep track of which squares should need attention. If you forget and remove a defender or miss a new attacker (by a discovery, for example), that can be enough to lose the game. Strong players do this subconsciously. They just look for the changes and assume things are safe otherwise.

Student: At least for now, I need to gain discipline by doing it consciously.

Weaker players unfortunately sometimes "cancel out" crucial parts of their table, especially if the issue is left over from the previous move. The temporarily saving of material by a *zwischenzug* sometimes causes them to forget that the ongoing safety issue has not been resolved.

In games by strong players, the leftover issues occur almost exclusively with *zwischenzugs*. Here is an example:

Strauch-Heisman
1st Valley Forge Open 1967

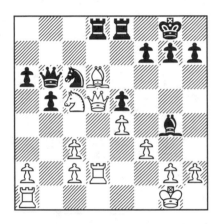

Black to play after 1 f3

The safety table notes that the bishop on g4 is unsafe, but I left it that way and played the *zwischenzug* **1...Re6!** (the simple 1...Be6 is good, too, but in a different way). Now the bishop on d6 is guarded twice and attacked twice, but it is unsafe because the white queen is the lead guard. Notice how the order of the recapturing pieces can determine the safety of the guarded piece (in this case the bishop on d6).

Moreover, the rook on e6 is safe, since the knight on c5 is pinned to the king. Unfortunately for White, he cannot easily move the bishop, as it is also pinned, e.g. 2 Bc7 (best, but not enough) 2...Qxc7 3 Nxe6 Qa7+ (now the White queen and rook are effectively skewered) 4 Qc5 (else the queen is lost) 4...Rxd2 wins material.

White tried **2 Rad1**, but only after **2...Rexd6 3 Qxd6 Rxd6 4 Rxd6 Qxc5+ 5 Kh1** did Black have to finally resolve the safety issue on g4.

(see following diagram)

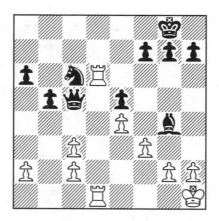

Black to play after 5 Kh1

...which I did not "forget", but still handled it horribly with **5...Be6?** (better is 5...Kf8 or 5...f5 with an easy win).

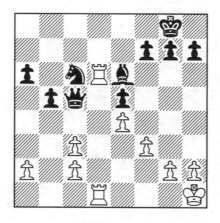

White to play after 5...Be6?

White should play 6 Rxc6! and the safety table shows 6...Qxc6?? no longer allows safe interposition on f8 and thus allows mate via 7 Rd8+. Best after 6 Rxc6! is 6...Qe7, when the win is not trivial. Instead, White blundered with **6 Rd8+?** and after **6...Nxd8 7 Rxd8+ Qf8**, Black won easily with his extra bishop.

Here's a beginner *zwischenzug* where the player forgets the original concern: **1 e4 e5 2 Nf3 Nc6 3 d4 Nf6 4 Bg5 d6 5 dxe5 dxe5 6 Qxd8+ Nxd8 7 Nxe5 Nxe4**. Now the bishop on g5 is not safe:

(see following diagram)

225

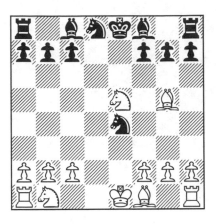

White to play after 7...Nxe4

But instead of simply and properly saving the attacked bishop with a sequence like 8 Bxd8, where Black must be careful to avoid the obvious 8...Kxd8 9 Nxf7+, but instead must play a complicated line with 8...Bb4+, White tries the "aggressive" *zwischenzug* **8 Bb5+** and after **8...c6** finds both bishops attacked:

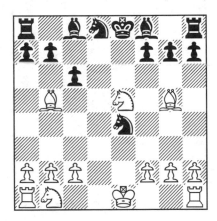

White to play after 8...c6

Now White must successfully resolve the safety issues on both b5 and g5 (see *The Two Types of Counting Problems* 5-5) by first capturing 9 Bxd8. Instead, White either fails to re-member the carry-over danger on g5 or fails to solve the problem, and after **9 Bd3??** Black, in saving the knight, is virtually forced to win a piece with **9...Nxg5**.

Reminder: You don't have check the safety of every square, or even every attacked square each move, but you do need to check at least all squares affected by the opponent's previous move. If you can eliminate common Counting mistakes by keeping track of the status of key squares and properly resolving all safety issues, it will go a long way toward making you a better player.

The Five Ways to Make a Piece Safe

The following are the five ways to make an unsafe piece safe. After each is an oversimplified two-word description of its effectiveness; we will elaborate below.

1. *Move the piece* – simple and clear;
2. *Guard the piece* – passive and binding;
3. *Capture the attacking piece* – desirable and aggressive;
4. *Block the attack* – pinning or counterattacking;
5. *Counterattack* – dangerous and complicated.

In any given situation one method may be best or more than one about equally effective. However, we can make some strong generalizations about each that should prove helpful *if analysis fails to reveal which is best in a given situation*. Listing *all* the moves that can make the piece safe is usually a good first step. Only three of the five ways apply to getting out of check.

1. Move the piece to a safe square

Moving a piece to a safe square is the "default" way to make something safe and, in many cases, the best. Moving often presents the opportunity to relocate that piece to a better square.

A common example occurs after **1 e4 e5 2 Nf3 Nc6 3 Bc4 Bc5 4 0-0 Nf6 5 Ng5? 0-0 6 Nc3 h6**:

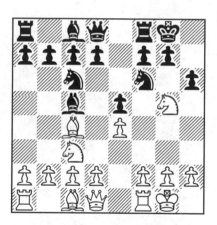

White to play after 6...h6

White's knight is not safe. Some players might think "I can't *retreat* to f3 because I came from there and that loses tempi. I can't go to h3 because *a knight on the rim is dim*. Therefore, I won't retreat, but will boldly attack with 7 Nxf7."

The problem with this logic is that, when faced with three choices of A, B, and C, deciding by process of elimination that C is best because you don't like A or B may fail because C can be worse! Here the sensible move 7 Nf3 is best – the loss of tempi was caused by 5 Ng5? not 7 Nf3. Making this best, safe move is not a retreat in any way except direction!

Here is a more advanced example from a student's game:

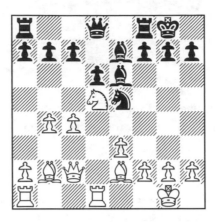

Black to play after 1 Rfd1

White has an indirect d-file pin and threatens 2 Bxe5 dxe5 3 Nf6+, winning the queen for a rook and a knight, or possibly 3 Nb6. Black's easiest defense is to just move the attacked knight, say, 3...Ng6. Instead, he missed White's threat and played **1...Re8?**. After **2 Bxe5**, he finally realized what he had missed, but instead compounded the mistake – as often happens – with the Counting error **2...Bxd5?**. After **3 Rxd5**, the d-pawn was pinned to the queen and since 3...dxe5 4 Rxd8 Raxd8 would leave him down a queen for a rook, Black resigned.

This example also shows the rewards for following the strong principle *develop your rooks to the same file where your opponent has his queen*. As a corollary, if your opponent develops his rook to your queen's file, you should consider moving your queen.

The following occurred during an online 2+12 game (two minutes with a twelve second increment). White has built up time and now has over five minutes remaining.

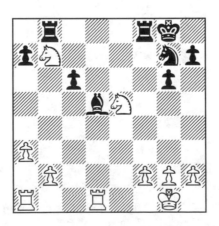

White to play after 1...Rb8

White is ahead a pawn, but his b7-knight is skewered to the b2-pawn. The best way to make the knight safe is just to move it, e.g. 2 Nc5 Rxb2 3 Ncd3 (or 3 f3) with roughly equal chances. Instead, White sees a fork and "counterattacks" with **2 Nd7(?)**. White is not winning the exchange, but rather giving up two pieces for a rook, a loss of about a pawn and a half. However, when compared to the better 2 Nc5, which gives back the pawn, it is "only" a Counting error of approximately half a pawn. Black, who was short on time, fails to play the simple 2...Rxb7, when after 3 Nxf8 Kxf8, Black has two pieces for a rook and a pawn with good winning chances. Instead, he also blundered with **2...Rfd8??** and after **3 Nxd8 Rxd8** was behind the exchange and a pawn. However, despite his winning position and huge time advantage, White continued to play extremely rapidly and lost anyway; at the end of the game he had seven minutes left.

White's hasty play brings up the important question: "When given the choice (such as before a fun internet game), why choose a time limit if you don't want to use all the given time?" *To choose to play a slower time limit than you feel like playing is like giving your opponent a handicap.*

Except under special circumstances, you are never trying your best if you don't attempt to use your given time – see *The Room Full of Grandmasters* (3-2).

2. Guard the attacked piece

Guarding is the idea most closely associated with "making a piece safe", but, ironically, it is often one of the worst! When I ask a student what they should do with an unsafe piece, they often respond:

"I need to *guard* (or protect) my piece" rather than the correct "I need to find a way to make the piece safe." This mislabeling of the problem often results in an incorrect solution. *In general, using the correct terminology – and asking the correct questions – can often help lead to better answers!*

Guarding has the following disadvantages:

- ♟ It ties down the guarding pieces.
- ♟ It may allow the attacker to pile on more attacking pieces.
- ♟ It may allow the removal of the guard tactic (see the archived *The Underrated Removal of the Guard*).

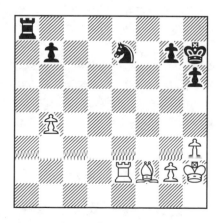

Black to play after 1 Re2

In this equal position the knight is attacked and Black should simply move it. Instead, guarding it with 1...Re8? is not safe because it creates a pin; after 2 Bc5 the knight is lost. Counterattacking with 1...Rf8? loses the exchange after 2 Bc5 (much better than winning the b-pawn with the simple 2 Rxe7 Rxf2 3 Rxb7 – *when you see a good move look for a better one!*) 2...Ng6 3 Bxf8 Nxf8. If in the diagram the bishop were on c4 instead of f2, then the counterattack 1...Rc8 would lose a pawn to 2 Rxe7, while the guarding 1...Re8 loses to the removal of the guard 2 Bb5. Once again the common theme: guarding bad, moving good.

Of course, sometimes guarding – or any other way to make something safe – is clearly correct because it is the only logical method, or at least the options are limited. After the common **1 e4 e5 2 Nf3**

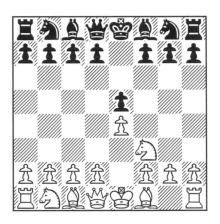

Black to play after 2 Nf3

...the most common move is the guarding **2...Nc6**, although counterattack by 2...Nf6 (Petroff's Defense) is very popular among strong players, and pawn counterattacks with 2...f5 (Latvian Gambit) or 2...d5 (Elephant Gambit) have their devotees.

Echoing Nimzowitsch, GM Andrew Soltis mentions in his helpful new book *The Wisest Things Ever Said About Chess*, "The stronger the piece, the worse protector it is." Strong pieces have better things to do! Therefore, pawns are usually the best guarders and kings are good protectors until the endgame, when they must activate.

3. Capture the attacking piece

Just as weaker players may think "My piece is unsafe – I have to guard it", rather than "My piece is unsafe – How can I best make it safe?", those players, when checked, may think "I have to move my king", instead of "I have to find the best way out of check." I have seen the following situation more than once in youngsters' games:

(see following diagram)

This kind of mindset leads to the "safest" king move: 1...Kd8??, instead of the simple capture 1...Kxf7.

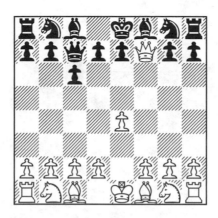

Black to play after 1 Qxf7+

This type of error may seem farfetched, but I notice that adults often make a similar mistake. They choose a clearly inferior defense because they don't list all the ways to make the piece safe and choose either the first move they see or one that looks good, but the safety is superficial. The following is from a Team 4545 game involving players rated over 1500 ICC standard. Both players had over 30 minutes left, but the following moves were blitzed:

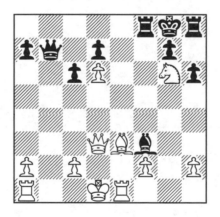

White to play after 1...Bf3+

White is ahead a piece and has the rooks forked. However, he played the hasty:

2 Kd2??

2 Kc1! is the safe square and even 2 Re2 wins easily.

2...Qb4+

What else did White expect? If White were playing slowly, he might see that his once easily won game is now a fight.

3 c3

If White tries 3 Qc3!? Qxd6+ (this double attack on the knight is key) 4 Kc1?! (better is 4 Qd3, which guards the knight and allows 4...Qb4+ to repeat, or 4 Bd4!?) 4...Qxg6, Black is now somewhat better.

3...Qb2+ 4 Qc2 Qxc2+ 5 Kxc2 Be4+

The other key double attack.

6 Kd2 Bxg6 7 Bxa7 Rxf2+??

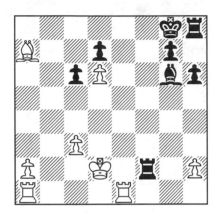

White to play after 7...Rxf2+

8 Re2??

Despite having more than 30 minutes remaining, White made this move in *two seconds*. He probably thought this interposition was the best way to save the h-pawn. Later the game was drawn. Once again the best way to save the piece (in this case the king *and* the h-pawn) was to capture the rook with 8 Bxf2. Psychologists say that the hardest chess moves to see are retreats and long distance moves on diagonals, and 8 Bxf2 is both.

4. Block the attack

Blocking, also known as *interposition*, can only occur against a distant attack by a queen, rook, or bishop. Blocking has pros and cons. The pro is that if the blocking piece moves in the same direction as the attacking piece, it may be counterattacking that piece. The bad is that if the blocking piece is not counterattacking, then blocking usually creates a pin.

Here are some simple examples:

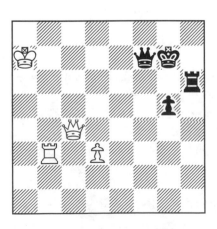

White to play after 1...Qf7+

White can move the king to the eighth rank, but then 2...Rh8+ might become trouble-some. And 2 Qxf7+ leads to a roughly equal ending. But best of all is to interpose with **2 Rb7**, pinning the queen and winning it for the rook.

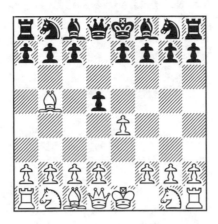

Black to play after 1 e4 d5 2 Bb5+(?)

Instead of saving the e-pawn with 2 exd5, White has "counterattacked" with the silly 2 Bb5+. Some beginners consider meeting similar checks as great opportunities to develop a knight with 2...Nc6(?), but that misses an opportunity to play the much better **2...c6**, attacking the bishop and giving Black the initiative.

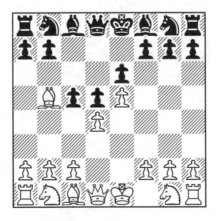

Black to play after 1 e4 e6 2 d4 d5 3 e5 c5 4 Bb5+(?)

A move commonly found in the games of weaker players. Black has no choice but to block as 4 Ke7 is rather senseless. Black has no problems after 4...Nc6, even though the knight is pinned. If White continues with the poor 5 Bxc6? bxc6, the doubled pawns are very strong, as, after a later ...c5xd4 c3xd4, Black can break again with ...c6-c5! when the white center crumbles and Black gains the bishop pair. But even more logical is **4...Bd7**, blocking the check without the pin and attacking the white bishop. If 5 Bxd7+ Qxd7, Black has rid himself of his bad bishop, his only problem piece in the Advance French.

Let's consider an opening position where blocking is bad, but weaker players often do it anyway. Such a position occurs quite often in the French Defense, say after **1 e4 e6 2 d4 d5 3 Nd2 Nf6 4 e5 Nfd7 5 f4 c5 6 c3 Nc6 7 Ndf3 Qb6 8 g3 cxd4 9 cxd4 Bb4+**.

White to play after 9...Bb4+

In this and similar French positions weaker players often play the "forced" 9 Bd2, which loses the d-pawn because it blocks the queen's ability to guard d4. Instead of interposing and losing a pawn, it is much better to play the book 9 Kf2, forfeiting castling rights and retaining material equality. Many weaker players weigh the right to castle so heavily that they will voluntarily and unnecessarily fall behind in material to retain that right. But in general *if you fall behind in material you are just losing, so retaining equal material, even at the cost of the right to castle, is usually the correct decision.*

5. Counterattack

Counterattack takes many forms, but most of them are "I won't make the unsafe piece safe; instead, I will attack one of my opponent's pieces so that he can't – or won't – capture my piece." This is a very powerful weapon, but, unfortunately, it introduces complications and many weaker players are often victimized by their own cleverness.

The most common failure of counterattack is that if your opponent uses his piece A to attack your B and you reply by using your C to attack his D, then often he can answer saving D by attacking your E. Then A is still attacking B and now D is attacking E and both your B and E cannot be saved.

After **1 e4 e6 2 d4 d5 3 Bd3 Nf6 4 e5**, Black might think "Yes, I can just move my knight, but I see a chance to develop a piece with check first" and play **4...Bb4+??**.

(see following diagram)

After **5 c3**, two black pieces are attacked and one of them must fall.

White to play after 4...Bb4+??

Disaster is common when a counterattack is made without careful analysis. For example, consider the play after 1 d4 in diagram on page 244 in *The Two Types of Counting Problems* (5-5), where one of my intermediate students fell for a similar misplayed counterattack.

In the following position from an internet game, Black is in some danger and must make the correct decision:

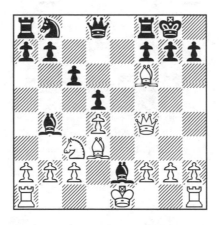

Black to play after 1 Bxf6

Black's best move is simply to capture the piece attacking his queen with 1...Qxf6. Although weak pawns are usually weakest in the endgame, this position follows another guideline, which is *if you have to weaken your king position, much better to do it with queens off the board*. So after 1...Qxf6 2 Qxf6 gxf6 3 Kxe2 or 3 Bxe2, White has somewhat the better position, but there is a lot of game left to be played. However, Black did not like that possibility and instead found a much worse counterattack with **1...Bd6??**.

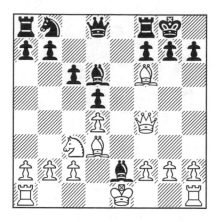

White to play and win after 1...Bd6??

White correctly found **2 Qh4!** threatening both mate on h7 and the white queen and Black resigned.

Finally, a completely different type of counterattack:

White to play after 1...Qe5+

White saves his loose bishop on g5 with **2 Qe2**, pinning the black queen to the king.

A good general principle is *counterattack is very dangerous! Use it very carefully, when it is the only defense* (such as in the previous diagram, where it is the only way to save material), *or when you are losing, or if you are a pretty good player. Further, when you are way ahead avoid counterattack if at all possible because it introduces complications, which usually greatly favor the losing side.*

While principles or assumptions may be helpful, analysis is usually required to determine which of the above methods may be the best way to make something safe – take your time and try to find the best move.

5-4) Is it Safe? Quiz

If a move is not safe, the strategy probably doesn't matter.

A move is **safe** if the opponent has no forcing moves in reply that win material or checkmate. The ability to determine if a candidate move is safe and to reject it if not safe is more important than the ability to recognize a chance to win material, because the chance to lose material may occur almost every move. Let's test your ability to find safe moves.

Read the directions for each diagram carefully because they are not all the same.

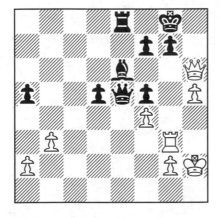

1. Black to play – list all of Black's safe moves.

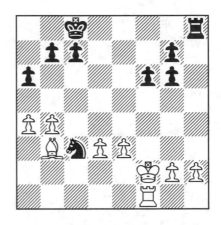

3. Black to play – list all of Black's safe moves.

2. White to play – is 1 Bxc6 safe?

4. White to play – what is the best way to defend c2?

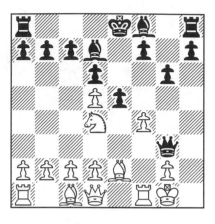

5. Black to play – is the *zwischenzug* 1...Bh3 helpful, harmful, or neutral?

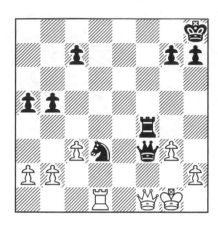

8. White to play – can he regain material equality?

6. White to play – what's the easiest win?

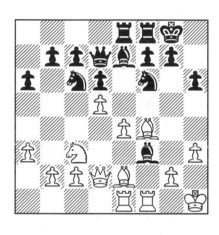

9. White to play after 1...Bxf3 – can he win a piece?

7. White to play – can he avoid losing the exchange?

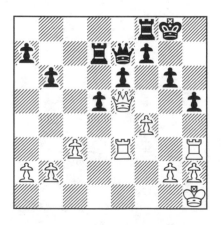

10. White to play – is 1 Rxh5 safe?

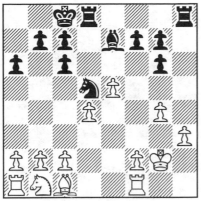

11. White to play – is 1 Nc3 safe?

14. White to play – what is his best move?

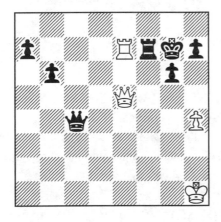

12. Black to play – what is his best move?

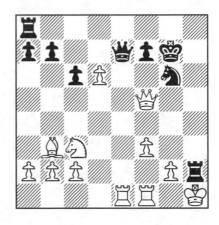

15. White to play – list all of White's safe moves.

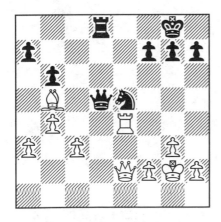

13. Black to play – what is his best move?

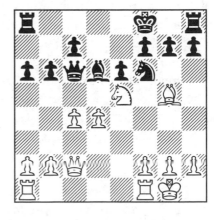

16. Black to play – is 1...Qe4 safe?

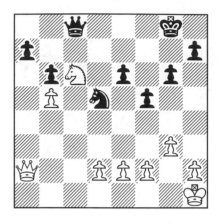

17. Black to play – is 1...a5 safe?

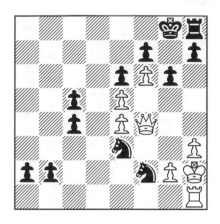

Bonus puzzle:
18. White to play – would you rather be
White or Black?

Answers

1. Only 1...Qd4, 1...Qc3, 1...Qb2 and 1...Qa1 are safe. 1...Qc3 is safe because 2 Rxc3 gxh6 leaves Black ahead a piece. 1...Kf8?? as played in the game, is not safe due to 2 Qh8+ (in the game White played 2 Rxg7?? which is also not safe) 2...Ke7 3 Qxe8+ Kxe8 4 fxe5.

2. No. 1 Bxc6 is not safe, as Black can play 1...bxc6 attacking the queen and the knight, winning a piece. If Black plays 1...Qxc6? then White has 2 Nxe7 and Black does not win a piece, e.g. 2...Bxe2 3 Nxc6 Bb5 4 Na5.

3. White threatens 2 Rc1 trapping the knight – you have to take the time to calculate this to figure out what is safe. So Black can play 1...Rd8, 1...Rh5, or 1...b5. 1...c6 fails to 2 Rc1 Nd5 3 Bxd5.

4. While the passive 1 Na3 does the trick, the best way to "defend" c2 is to win the knight, and thus remove an attacker, with 1 Qa4+. Too many weaker players think "defend" and then just play a move which guards instead of asking "How do I make that safe?" and looking for other possibilities that may be better.

5. It is harmful, as after 1...Bh3? 2 Bf3! Black has to regain his piece with 2...exd4, allowing the removal of the guard 3 Qe1+! Qxe1 4 Rxe1+ winning the bishop on h3. In the game White played correctly until the third move, but then completely missed the idea with 3 Re1+?.

6. This is a little more like a normal problem. White has multiple ways to win. 1 Rxe7+ Kxe7 2 Nxa8 wins the easiest. 1 Rxd6+ Kxc7 "only" wins the exchange, although after 2 Nxb5+ White wins fairly easily, too.

7. Yes. An easy "defensive" tactical problem: 1 R4d7 and if 1...Nxd8 2 Rxe7. But not 1 R8d7? when 1...Nxd4 2 Rxe7? Nf5+ wins for Black.

8. Process of elimination helps here: White is down a knight so he has to do something to regain it. 1 Rxd3?? Qxf1 mate is obviously bad. Or 1 Qxf3 Rxf3 2 Kg2 (trying to remove the guard) 2...Re3 and White remains down a piece. So 1 Qxd3 Qf2+ 2 Kh1 is forced, when White is equal with careful play. If you reject moves like 1 Qxd3 because 1...Qf2+ is too scary, that is a form of *quiescence error*.

9. The hope is that, instead of recapturing on f3, 1 dxc6 hits the queen and the bishop to win a piece. Unfortunately Black has the adequate defense 1 dxc6 Qxh3+! 2 Kg1 Qxg2 mate so you have to be careful. Your opponent is trying to play his best move, not help you!

10. It seems like after 1 Rxh5 gxh5 2 Rg3+ leads to mate, but what about the *zwischenzug* 1...f6 spoiling everything? Instead, 1 Qxh5! does the trick as 1...gxh5 2 Reg3+ again leads to mate, and 1...f6 (or 1...f5) loses to 2 Qh8+ Kf7 3 Rh7+ Ke8 4 Rxe7+.

11. A typical mundane move which is not safe. 1 Nc3? Nb4 and the threats to d4 and c2 cannot both be met so White loses his extra pawn.

12. Black can go for a draw with 1...Kh6 2 Qg5+ Kg7 but does he have better. In the game Black played 1...Kf8 but was not happy after 2 Re8 mate. That leaves 1...Kg8, when 2 Re8+ Rf8 looks scary after 3 Rxf8+ Kxf8, but after 4 Qh8+ or 4 Qb8+ Black is ahead two pawns in the endgame so that is clearly the best try.

13. Black wanted to play 1...f5 to attack the pinned rook with something worth less, and correctly visualized that 2 Bc4 was dangerous. While it is true that 2...Qxc4 3 Rxc4 is now legal and 2...Nxc4 3 Re8+ Rxe8 4 Qxe8 is mate, Black failed to visualize that 3 Re8+ is not legal! After 1...f5 2 Bc4 Nxc4 3 Qxc4 Qxe4+ is illegal, but Black still has 3...fxe4 winning. So 1...f5 works after all.

14. Here White has to be very careful as his exposed king could easily lead to disaster. Normally you would *think defense first* and this is no exception, but here the best defense is to take away all quiet moves with the threat 1 d7!. Then if Black plays 1...Rxg3+ White has a single safe square 2 Kf2 attacking the rook, when the double threat of 3 d8Q+ and 3 Kxg3 is enough to win, e.g. 2...Qxh3 3 d8Q+ Kh7 4 Qe4+. All other first moves lose; e.g. 1 Kg2 Qe2+ 2 Kh1 Rxg3 with the double threat of 3...Qg2 mate and 3...Rxh3+, or 1 Qg4 Qe3+ 2 Kh1 d2.

15. White only has two legal moves, so that limits the choices. In the game White decided that since he was a piece ahead, exposing his king unnecessarily with 1 Kxh2! was unnecessary and played 1 Kg1?? and had to resign after 1...Qh4 2 Qh3 (the intended 2 Qxf7+ Kh6 does not help) 2...Rxh3 3 gxh3 Qg3+ 4 Kh1 Rh8. After 1 Kxh2 White is ahead a rook and a bishop and survives easily after 2...Rh8+ 3 Kg1 Qh4 4 Qxf7+ Kh6, or 2...Qh4+ 3 Kg1 Qd4+ (3...Rh8 4 Qxf7+ transposes to the previous line) 4 Rf2, or 2...Qxd6+ 3 Kg1 Qd4+ 4 Rf2. If you played 1 Kg1 "on general principles" then you are guilty of *hand-waving*, or using general principles in analytical positions when only analysis will do.

16. No. Black probably only calculated the mundane 1...Qe4 2 Qxe4 Nxe4 or the more dangerous 1...Qe4 2 Bxf6? (attempting to remove the guard) 2...Qxc2. However, after 1...Qe4 White threw in the *zwischenzug* 2 Nd7+!. Then 2...Kg8 or 2...Ke8 3 Nxf6+ removes the guard with check and does win the queen after 4 Qxe4. If Black tries 2...Nxd7, that self-removes the guard and 3 Qxc4 again wins the queen. Finally, If Black tries 2...Ke7 that self-pins the knight and once again 3 Qxe4 wins the queen.

17. Yes – it is also the best move! If White tries to win a piece with 1...a5 2 Qxd5?, then Black wins after 2...exd5 3 Ne7+ Kf7 (other moves are possible) 4 Nxc8 a4 and the pawn promotes. To stop your analysis after 4 Nxc8 would be a major quiescence error. Also bad for White is 2 bxa6? Qxc6 3 a7 Nf4+ or 3...Ne3+ mates!

If you got all these problems correct quickly, you are a much better player than I am...

Bonus puzzle:

18. 1 Qh6 N(any)g4+ 2 hxg4+ Nxg4+ wins the queen, so the clever 1 Rd1!? looks interesting, as if either knight captures, then 2 Qh6 works. However, 1 Rd1 only draws: 1...N(any)g4+ 2 hxg4 Nxg4+ 3 Qxg4 h5 4 Rd8+ Kh7 5 Qd1 b1Q 6 Rxh8+ Kxh8 7 Qd8+ Kh7 8 Qf8 Qh1+! 9 Kg3 (9 Kxh1?? a1Q+ 10 Kh2 Qxe5+ and 11...Qxf6 wins for Black) 9...Qe1+ 10 Kh3 draws (but not 10 Kh2?? Qh4+ 11 Kg1 a1Q+ and wins). Nevertheless, White does win with 1 Qh6! N(any)g4+ 2 hxg4+ Nxg4+ 3 Kh3! (3 Kg3?? Nxh6 4 Rd1 Nf5+ 5 exf5 h6 wins for Black) 3...Nxh6 4 Rd1 and White mates! Most of my students really enjoyed analyzing this problem!

5-5) The Two Types of Counting Problems

It's the little things that count.

In previous Novice Nooks (see *A Different Approach to Studying Tactics 5-1*) we defined Counting as the basic tactic that determines if any sequence of captures on a square might lose material. However, it is very likely in practice for counting issues to arise simultaneously on multiple squares on the same move. Therefore, we can define two types of Counting *problems*:

♟ Those that only involve capturing sequences on one square;

♟ Those that involve capturing sequences on multiple squares.

Counting sequences on one square can sometimes be tricky, but Counting problems involving capturing sequences on multiple squares can be fiendishly difficult.

White to play – is the d7-pawn safe?

In this position White is attacking the d7-pawn twice – the second time indirectly with the bishop – and thus the pawn is not safe after 1 exd7. Easy enough.

Next, let's consider a slightly trickier counting problem involving one square:

(see following diagram)

White has two possible captures on d7. He can play 1 Qxd7??, but, after 1...Rbxd7, no matter how White captures on the second move, Black no longer has to recapture and has won a queen for a rook and pawn. Instead, 1 Bxd7? might seem better, but, after 1...Rbxd7, Black is temporarily up a bishop for a pawn, and if White continues 2 Qxd7 then, after 2...Rxd7 3 Rxd7, Black has won a bishop and queen for two rooks and a pawn. This is better for Black by approximately two pawns worth of material, *although strong players rarely need to calculate pawn equivalents to decide whether a sequence is good!*

White to play – is the d7-pawn safe?

So we can conclude that in the initial position, White does not have any favorable capturing sequence – assuming Black makes the best replies – and therefore the d7-pawn is safe.

When I ask a student, "What type of tactical mistake is 1 Bxd7?" they often answer, "It is a blunder." That answer is inaccurate, as "blunder" is simply a synonym for a mistake – it does not pinpoint a *type* of mistake, much less a specific kind of tactic. Years ago, I designated this type of tactical calculation as "Counting", because there was a gap in the chess literature with regard to categorizing this type of tactic.

The above example shows that single-square Counting can be tricky, and many players, especially rated below 1800 USCF, fall prey to this error more often then they would wish.

Let's begin our overview of multi-square Counting mistakes with a simple error, as played in an internet game between two intermediate players:

Black to play after 1 d4

First, determine if the d4-pawn is safe: it is guarded twice, but it is also only attacked twice, as the knight on c6 is pinned. Since the capturing and defending units are of the same value (pawn-pawn; piece-piece), the pawn is safe.

An important Counting rule: *If the respective attackers and defenders are not of the same value, then simply counting the number of attackers and defenders is insufficient to determine the safety of the attacked piece.* For example, if a pawn attacks a queen, then the number of defenders is irrelevant: the queen is not safe, excluding non-Counting issues such as checkmate threats on other squares.

In this diagram, Black tried to activate his knight, counterattacking the pinning bishop by...

1...a6??

This Counting error involves four squares: b5 (not safe), c6 (safe), c5 (not safe), and d4 (safe).

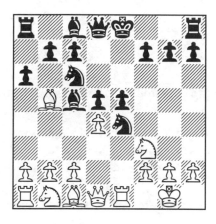

White to play and win (Counting problem)

2 Bxc6+

By capturing the knight first (the check does not matter much *in this case*), White simply trades off his unsafe bishop for the safe knight. Fair trade so far, but after...

2...bxc6

...Black cannot do anything about saving the bishop that was attacked on move 1, so...

3 dxc5

...and White wins a piece.

This was an easy problem, but quite a few intermediate players could not find the correct idea in a reasonable amount of time. This surprising lack of "tactical vision" once again shows that, even for intermediate players, it greatly pays to improve your tactical vision by studying simple Counting problems – along with "single motif" problems such as removal of the guard, double attack, pins, etc.

While the above position involved a sequence of captures on multiple squares, the key to designating this a Counting problem was the lack of "removal of the guard" or any other type of tactical motif that *affects* multiple squares; it was simply a set of captures that allowed a winning sequence.

Contrast the previous example to a simple removal-of-the-guard tactic:

Although the position is similar to the previous one, the principal difference here is that the knight on c6 is guarding d4, so the bishop's safety depends on it. Therefore, it is no longer *just* a matter of being able to calculate a proper capturing sequence, although the sequence of captures still matters.

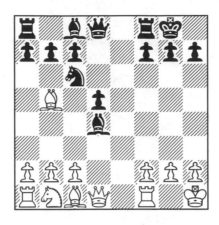

White to play and win (Removal of the guard)

White cannot capture on d4 first, since 1 Qxd4?? Nxd4 wins the queen. So to win material White must first play **1 Bxc6**, removing the guard on d4. If Black plays 1...bxc6, then White will play 2 Qxd4, while if Black tries to save the bishop; for example, by 1...Bf6, then 2 Bxd5 leaves White ahead.

We can combine the two ideas presented above to create a combination with Counting and removal of the guard:

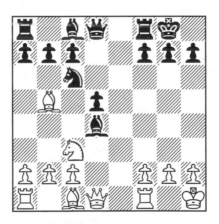

White to play – can White win a piece?

Here, with a white knight on c3, the question could also be posed in tactical defensive terms: "What should Black play after 1 Bxc6 to not lose a piece?"

The answer is that **1 Bxc6** is not as powerful as in the previous example, because Black does not have to recapture on c6 (1...bxc6?? 2 Qxd4). Instead, he can capture a piece on *any* square. Therefore, you should carefully analyze the counting sequences on both the c6- and c3-squares to find the best sequence for Black. Black should use his desperado bishop to play **1...Bxc3!**, trying to maintain the balance, although White can win back his pawn (but not a *piece*) by **2 Bxd5**.

In the above problem, the more encompassing Counting aspects include the well-defined issues of both "desperado" – since, after 1 Bxc6, the bishop on d4 is hanging and about to be lost – and *"zwischenzug"* (in-between move), since the capture 1...Bxc3 is made before a possible recapture on c6.

Let's add another layer of complexity:

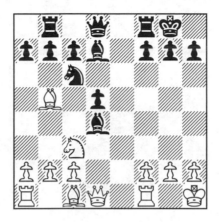

White to play and win

In this example, after the capture **1 Bxc6**, White will also have a desperado that can make a second piece capture, so a combination removal of the guard and Counting tactic is possible. For example, 1...Bxc6 2 Qxd4 is a simple removal of the guard. If Black tries the intermezzo **1...Bxc3**, then White has **2 Bxd7**. Thereafter, if Black saves his bishop (by, say, 2...Bf6), then so does White, while if Black captures **2...Qxd7**, then **3 bxc3** again leaves White ahead a piece.

If you understand the difference between the above examples, and can routinely recognize these situations during a game, you are on your way to becoming a good player!

Here's another easy multi-square problem:

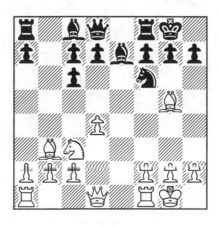

Black to play after 1 Bg5

Black played **1...Ng4??** This would work fine if White's only capturing option were 2 Qxg4?? Bxg5 winning the bishop pair, but the other capturing sequence 2 Bxe7 Qxe7 (or 2...Nxf2 3 Rxf2) 3 Qxg4 just wins a piece for White. I categorize the 1...Ng4?? blunder as a Counting error. I see them all the time.

Here are a few more examples from a recent internet game:

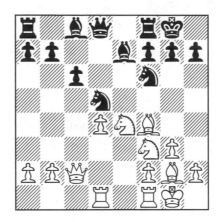

White to play after 1...Nbd5

Black is threatening to capture the bishop on f4 and White should just move it to a safer square. But instead he "counterattacks" with **2 Ne5?**.

Black gladly takes the bishop with **2...Nxf4** and now White should just recapture with the simple 3 gxf4. The simple moves are often best, but weaker players tend to "outsmart" themselves, by making things more complex than they need to be. Accordingly, White decides to play the seemingly harmless *zwischenzug* **3 Nxf6+??**.

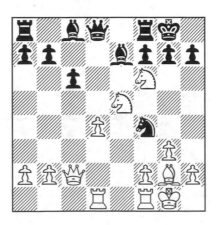

Black to play after 3 Nxf6+??

At this point Black, normally a very deliberate player, quickly played the "obvious" **3...Bxf6??**. This failure to seriously consider the alternative capture demonstrates a very common time management problem among intermediate players: *making recaptures very quickly despite multiple choices*, as if they know which capture is best, when the issue is often unclear.

Here, however, those issues *are* clear. Since White is temporarily down a piece, Black should take the opportunity to play 3...gxf6 to attack the knight on e5, when Counting reveals that if White saves the knight on e5, then Black will save his on f4. If White instead captures 4 gxf4, then 4...fxe5 will still win a piece. Of course, Black played 3...Bxf6?? because 3...gxf6! would expose his king. However, strong players understand that winning a piece is usually more important than king safety in most positions (see *The Principle of Tactical Dominance* 2-6).

Unless your opponent has purposely sacrificed a piece to demolish your kingside, then it is much more likely that *your extra piece will make your king safer, because of your superiority of forces*!

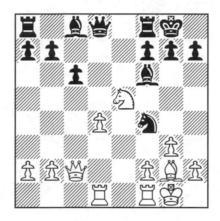

White to play after 3...Bxf6??

The last two Counting errors negated each other, and here White should regain approximate material equality with the simple 4 gxf4. Instead, White uncorked the "aggressive" **4 Be4??**. The third Counting error in a row! Black could just play *any* move that saves the knight, say, 4...Nd5 and, after 5 Bxh7+ Kh8, all White has is a check and a pawn for his bishop, with a completely lost game. 4 Be4?? represents a common type of mental mistake: *overrating a check*. Instead of the mundane 4...Nd5, Black played the superior **4...Ng6** (4...Nh3+ is even slightly better, but unnecessary) and White did not even get the check *or* the pawn for his bishop! With the extra piece, Black went on to win.

I know I can "count" on the reader to be more aware of this common tactic in the future!

Chapter Six

Openings

6-1) Learning Opening Lines and Ideas

The importance of a chess concept is directly related to how often it occurs.

When a player first starts out to learn the openings, he gets the most efficient use of his time by learning:

- ♟ General opening goals and principles;
- ♟ A few main opening sequences (tabiyas);
- ♟ How to avoid making the same mistakes over and over.

Teaching you how to do these instead of just showing you a set of acceptable opening sequences is definitely a case of "Give a man a fish and he eats one meal; teach a man to fish and he eats forever."

Learning General Goals and Guidelines

There is a big difference between trying to memorize lots of lines and variations from an opening book and learning how to play opening moves wisely. I have two theories:

- ♟ The weaker the player, the more he should learn about general ideas; the stronger the player, the more he needs to know how to play specific positions, for example those that occur in his openings.
- ♟ The weaker the player, the more important it is for him to follow general opening principles; only stronger players who understand these principles well should think about exceptions.

Suppose you learn that in the Closed Ruy Lopez, after **1 e4 e5 2 Nf3 Nc6 3 Bb5 a6 4 Ba4 Nf6 5 0-0 Be7 6 Re1 b5 7 Bb3 d6 8 c3 0-0**, playing **9 h3** (the tabiya) to prevent 9...Bg4 is more accurate than 9 d4, which allows 9...Bg4 with pressure on d4. This particular idea is well known among stronger players; however, the difference between the two moves is so small that *Fritz*'s evaluation function rates 9 d4 as slightly *superior* (!) to 9 h3 on a 14-ply search (+0.14 to 0), so if 9 h3 is superior the difference is not great!

How useful is it to know that, in the Ruy Lopez sequence, 9 h3 is preferred? That greatly depends on your rating level, assuming you usually play opponents around your rating:

♟ **600**: You probably don't have the board vision to remember the nine-move sequence! But that is OK because, even if you did, your opponents would never stumble across this sequence anyway.

♟ **900**: Even if you do remember the sequence, almost none of your opponents will play it. And on that rare occasion when they do, it will not make any difference since the player who plays the best tactically will win in any case – usually someone at this rating level drops a piece or more in the middlegame.

♟ **1200**: You may run across this sequence occasionally but, again, the player who plays better tactically will prevail. Your winning percentage would hardly be affected by playing 9 d4 or 9 h3.

♟ **1500**: At this level of play knowing the sequence idea starts to make a small difference. You might get a slightly more comfortable game with 9 h3, but, on the other hand, your opponents who do know the book will probably have only studied 9 h3, and may not even know why 9 d4 is supposed to be inferior. So by playing 9 d4, you may wind up benefiting by taking them out of their "main line book", especially if you know something about the 9 d4 lines or even just follow *Fritz* 9 d4 analysis (which is *not* the main line!).

♟ **1800**: At this rating most of the players are aware of the difference and why it is supposed to be a difference. It may not greatly affect the probability of victory if you choose one line or the other, but at least the Black players will have some idea as to what to do, theoretically, if you play the rarer 9 d4.

♟ **2100**: At this level almost all the Black players will know what to do and probably have some experience in slow and speed games playing against 9 d4. Any surprise value is mostly lost, and if there is a weakness to 9 d4 (or whatever sideline you choose) it may well affect the outcome of the game.

From this perspective, we can quickly conclude that studying lots of opening sequences that go as deep as 9 h3 likely gets diminishing returns on your study time until you are at least an intermediate player.

This leads us back to the supposition that first one must study general principles that apply in most/all opening positions before it is helpful to learn specific moves that only apply to unique positions. What are some of these general guidelines that should be used in the opening? One way to study these guidelines is to classify them according to goal. The major goals of the opening include:

♟ Activate all your pieces. (One can state that: the main goal of the opening is to safely and efficiently activate all your pieces. This is similar to: the main goal of the opening is to reach a playable middlegame.) While "pieces" in this context does not mean pawns, a certain number of pawns will be moved to both gain/control space and open lines for pieces.

- Try to get some control (not necessarily occupation) of the center.
- Get your king into safety (which can be considered a special aspect of #1).

The overall goals of the *game* (keep your king safe; keep your pieces safe, and if you can win material safely, strongly consider doing so) include the opening, but *usually take precedence over phase-dependent goals and guidelines.* In other words, if it comes down to clearly losing/winning material or development, 85% or more of the time material is more important so long as the material had been even.

With these goals in mind, we can list some of the more important opening principles:

Piece Activation Guidelines

- Move every piece once before you move any piece twice unless there is a tactic.

- Put your bishops and rooks onto open lines, or at least where you can create open lines via break moves.

- Use break moves to weaken your opponent's pawn structure and open files for rooks and queens.

- Develop knights before bishops (this often means the knight on each side before the corresponding bishop, rather than both knights before both bishops).

- Develop the pieces on the side you are going to castle before developing pieces on the other side.

- The player who uses his rooks best usually wins the opening.

- Don't put your knight in front of your c-pawn in double d-pawn openings. In general, don't put your pieces in front of your break moves (see the *Break Moves: Opening Lines to Increase Mobility* 8-4). Even more generally, pieces are often better placed behind pawns than in front of them, but this has many exceptions! Absolute beginners usually move out too many pawns, but then more advanced beginners and even lower intermediates usually move out too few!

- Don't make trades that help develop your opponent's pieces.

- Don't give up the bishop pair unless you get at least ½ pawn compensation for it.

- Move more than two pawns, but six is probably too many! In general, smooth pawn development, with at least two pawns side by side on the fourth rank, is preferable to putting most of your pawns on the same color, leaving the opposite color squares as a weak square complex. This guideline also affects center control (see the next set of guidelines).

♟ Moving a pawn to h3 (or h6) to allow your bishop to develop to e3 (or e6) without harassment by a knight on g4 (or g5) is *usually* more justified than playing h2-h3 (or ...h7-h6) to prevent a bishop pin or a knight attack on f2 (or f7).

♟ Don't move your queen out too early if it can easily be attacked and forced to move again. In general, don't move any piece out that can be attacked by a piece of lower value and forced to move again (unless your opponent's attack on your piece results in a weakening for him).

♟ Don't pin the opponent's king's knight to the queen before your opponent has castled (a Lasker rule), especially in double e-pawn openings.

♟ Move a piece where you know it must go before you move another piece where you think it may go. The extra information of your opponent's move may help you decide where the latter is better placed.

Control of the Center Guidelines

♟ Develop your pieces to point (have future moves) toward the center.

♟ Knight on the rim, your future is dim/grim (but later it can reactivate!).

♟ At least one center pawn should be moved. Corollary: If your opponent lets you safely move both center pawns up two squares (to e4 and d4 for White especially), this is often the correct idea. For example, in openings like the French, Caro-Kann, or Pirc, Black just lets White play 1 e4 and 2 d4, and those are the main lines! For White to play 2 Nf3 is usually considered at best inaccurate in those openings.

♟ A piece does not have to occupy the center to control it – for example, a fianchettoed bishop on g2 or g7 attacks two central squares (even if your knight is on f3, since that temporary blockage should be under your control).

King Safety Guidelines

♟ Castle early and often. Humorous, but you get the idea!

♟ Castling is not a "waste of time" – in fact it is the only opening move that allows you to get two pieces toward where you want them to go, so in that sense it is the only opening move that *gains* time!

♟ Don't castle "into an attack".

♟ Don't push too many pawns needlessly in front of your king – but keep in mind that with the pawn structure that results from some openings you may need to do so in the *middlegame*!

♟ Castle on opposite sides (with queens on the board) only if you think that your attack will get there before your opponent's. *If you have already gotten a very good position, it is often right to castle on the same side* since the extra wildness of opposite side castling games often cancels out other advantages – even small material ones!

Very strong players understand these guidelines and when to break them, so it is common to see a grandmaster move a piece several times in the opening, but one must learn to walk before one can run. Until you know, understand, and are able to follow the principles, it makes sense to abide by them (at least the major ones) consistently and as best possible. Don't try to "be like GM Mike" and in doing so end up making a bad mistake trying to figure out and play exceptions. For example, more than 80% of the time weaker players who move pieces twice in the opening do so erroneously (that is, they do so when they are not in book, those pieces are not threatened, and there is no forced tactic). With this high percentage of error, it makes sense for those players to not to waste their time figuring out exceptions at all! Most errors I see like this are the result of players trying to make chess a lot harder than it is: unless there is a forced tactic (not just an easily met threat), get the next piece out!

Learning Opening Tabiyas

Often a student wants an instructor to give them a "pill" so that they can learn a new opening! Sure, it is more *helpful* per unit time for you to pay an instructor to teach you openings, and I have several prepared lessons on the tabiyas for several common openings wherein I explain the reasoning behind the move sequence. An instructor can – and should – give the student a good "kick start" in the form of an overview, including the understanding of the reasons behind the tabiya and where in general the pieces and pawns tend to be placed in the early middlegame. However, it is neither *cost* nor *time effective* for you to pay an instructor to do this for *every* opening idea that you run across. An occasional lesson on an opening sequence is helpful, but does not make a big dent into what lower intermediate players eventually need to know to become strong intermediates.

Therefore, it is much better if a student learns how to study opening lines. Sure, if you look up opening sequences and don't understand them, head for the nearest strong player/instructor to ask why, but at least attempt to do it yourself first.

Books that are compendiums of tabiyas include *Winning Chess Openings* by Seirawan, *Chess Openings Essentials* from New in Chess, and *Mastering the Chess Openings* by Watson. These books are meant to be more "talky" than encyclopedias, but still attempt to cover many common opening lines, and are thus not nearly as detailed as books specifically tailored to one opening – a good compromise. Alternatively, you can get a software program like *Chess Openings Wizard*, purchase one of its electronic "books", and go through lines. Finally, you can purchase a book that just focuses on a specific opening.

When learning new sequences, it helps to play over the tabiya a couple of times with the book open and then try to remember and replay the sequence with the book closed.

Tip: It is easier to remember a line if, after each move, you ask yourself, "What are the opponent's threats from the previous move?" If there are some, they usually need to be met by a logical reply. If there are none, then ask yourself, "Which piece needs to be developed next?" and that usually helps you find a logical candidate move, hopefully the one you are trying to remember. Another great tip is to study the tabiya with a friend, and then take turns playing each side. Afterwards, you might even play a speed game or two (or ten!) with those moves required. In no time you will know the sequence! It generally takes me about 20 minutes to put a tabiya into my long-term memory.

Avoiding Continual Repetition of Mistakes

If you asked me which advice I give to students is second least followed (see *Getting the Edge* 1-5), I would say it was the guideline mentioned above, *Move every piece once in the opening before you move any piece twice, unless there is a tactic*. But if that is second least, which advice is followed even less? It would have to be:

After each game look up your opening in a book (or database) and answer the question "If I had to play this opening sequence again, where would I deviate?"

In this way you slowly but surely learn opening lines and avoid all major traps. In his practical, excellent, but somewhat advanced book *Grandmaster Secrets: Openings* Soltis states "How much book do I need to know?...The bare minimum is: You need to know the traps that come up in your openings"!

Regular readers of this column know that I strongly discourage lower rated players from memorizing of tons of opening lines in favor of rigorous tactical study along with patient learning, understanding – and following! – of opening principles. However, as you get stronger you are going to have to learn specific opening lines, so everyone should know at least one reasonable way this can be accomplished. Of course stronger players desire more specific information on their favorite openings than they can get in a single-volume opening encyclopedia, so they purchase books that provide this not only in more (often gory) detail, but also have the satisfying explanations that the general reference books cannot contain. This *Novice Nook* assumes you are at the level where you don't want to keep repeating basic opening mistakes (such as falling into standard traps or playing clearly inferior lines), and for this purpose *MCO-15* is usually perfectly adequate.

In his book *Rapid Chess Improvement* de la Maza gives exactly the same advice about religiously looking up your games to avoid making the same mistake. Interestingly, I had been giving this advice for years before its publication, but I don't think Michael had ever seen my suggestion. Hopefully, this coincidence shows that my suggested method is very effective and logical – it prevents you from making the same mistake twice, which is a key to continual (and not necessary rapid!) improvement. It is truly a case of *a long journey starts with a single step*.

Why is this advice rarely followed? The reasons given to me vary:

1. "I don't know how to use the book."
2. "It is too tedious."
3. "I can't remember what I see after I look it up."

4. "I will never play that sequence again."
5. "The lines my opponents (or I) play are never in the reference books."

Let us consider each in turn:

I don't know how to use the book. Learning to use the encyclopedic and table-oriented *MCO* is pretty easy with about 10-15 minutes of practice. *MCO* runs its moves down a column and has six variations across the page. This helps explain the meaning of all the blank spaces in the tables. In *MCO* when a space is blank it means that that move is the same as the first one you can find to the *left* of it. *MCO* has a table of contents in the front with names *and* moves to help you find each opening, and throughout the book has brief discussions of the variations before giving the tables for each opening.

It is too tedious. If you are eventually going to become a strong player you indeed will have to learn a lot of opening ideas and sequences. This is time consuming, but, if it is enjoyable and profitable, you will not have much problem doing it; hopefully you will be playing chess for a long time, so your learning period will be spread out over several years. If you are looking for shortcuts, sure you can play a non-booky opening, and that is plenty sufficient for 97% of us. But today even the most 'non-book' openings have a fair amount of opening theory, so today 'non-book' opening is almost an oxymoron. Also, if you learn one main sequence at a time and then practice it, that is a lot less tedious than taking an opening book and trying to pour through hundreds of lines in an afternoon. If you do the latter, you likely will never see most of those lines, even if you could remember them all. The moves from your games are often the most likely ones you will see again.

I can't remember what I see after I look it up. It is true that if you understand what you see, you will remember it better. Some of the tips in the previous section on learning tabiyas should help. Try not to just look it up, say "Oh!" and forget it forever.

I will never play that sequence again. This depends on whether you were experimenting or not. If you were trying to play your best and fell into an opening trap, then surely you might play that sequence again up until the point of the trap, and you should make sure you understand what you should do instead, because that sequence (up to the trap) will surely occur again.

The lines my opponents (or I) play are never in the reference books. This is a common complaint; of course "never" is a strong word; more likely your weak opponent played a silly moves like an unnecessary ...h7-h6, and that kind of wasteful move is not covered since it basically loses a tempo (but just in case, see *It's Not Really Winning a Tempo!* 8-5). There are several possibilities:

a)   The move played was so terrible that it instantly loses material, and the author of the book/database did not want to waste space including moves that are obviously bad and need no mention of how to refute. To check to see if this is the case, put the game on any reasonable chess engine and let it tell you what to do. If there is such a sequence, the engine will show that the side to move has an immediate tactic and provide the Principal Variation (PV). One way to determine this is if the evaluation of the PV jumps from that of a reasonable opening sequence (where White usually has a small edge of about +0.1 to

+0.3) to a large edge, say one pawn or more advantage for either side.

b)   The line played is innocuous for White, such as playing h2-h3 or a2-a3. White is always striving to get an advantage out of the opening. Moves that make no attempt to do so may not be included in a standard text or database. If that is the case, then Black should continue making reasonable moves and should get a reasonable game; often the recommended Black move against the normal White move can be played with even more effect against the innocuous one (but not always, so be careful!). If White makes such an innocuous move, often Black gets near equality or better; but don't be upset because you can't "win" or "instantly punish" White's innocuous move.

c)   The move is a reasonable sideline that cannot be addressed in a single-volume encyclopedia. In this case the software databases may address the line, or it may be addressed in detail in a book on that opening. Of course it is always possible to see what a chess engine suggests even if you do not have a specific book on that opening!

The good news is that if your opponent played a terrible move, then you were not falling into a trap, but rather the reverse: you want to make sure that if a future opponent plays the same move, you are ready to take advantage of it!

The tabiya process in the previous section offers a great foundation that can be extended via the process in this section. Think of your opening knowledge as an upside-down "tree" of moves with the first move at the top of the main trunk. Then the tabiyas form the main trunk(s) and the new moves from each game are a branch. Use the two processes to steadily extend your current mental opening "tree". Be patient: if you attempt to learn too much at one time you will not remember it anyway.

Conclusion: If you learn about good opening principles, follow them, learn a few tabiyas, and start adding sequences – even if one move at a time – then you will soon be well ahead of other players with similar experience. You will be able to avoid repetitious mistakes and that is a key to improvement: *there are so many possible mistakes in chess that players who make the same ones many times are inevitably much weaker than those who only make them once or twice, almost without regard to their other talents*!

Example Tabiya: Closed Ruy Lopez

A tabiya (also spelled 'tabia') is a standard, popular position, usually reached by a specific (or transposing) move order. Since this is the *Closed* Ruy Lopez, it must start with the Ruy Lopez!

1 e4 e5 2 Nf3 Nc6 3 Bb5

(see following diagram)

The idea behind the Ruy Lopez is twofold:

1. Put pressure on e5;
2. Try to set up the "little center" e4-d4 by playing c2-c3 and d2-d4.

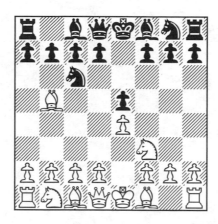

Black to play

c2-c3 is played so that if Black plays ...e5xd4, White can recapture c3xd4.

In the immediate position, is White threatening the removal of the guard tactic Bxc6 followed by Nxe5 winning a pawn? Let us test this with 3...a6:

3...a6 4 Bxc6 dxc6

Normally one recaptures toward the center with bxc6, but in this case it is better to capture toward the outside for tactical reasons.

5 Nxe5

Now Black has three ways of winning back his pawn, but only one is really good. Can you find which way is best for Black?

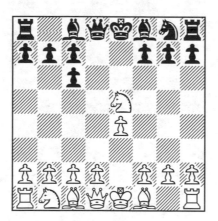

Black to play

It is 5...Qd4 with the double attack on e5 and e4. For example, after the knight retreat 6 Nf3 Qxe4+ 7 Qe2 Black is better *not* because after 7...Qxe2+ White cannot castle. White's king might even be better in the center with queens off, but Black has the bishop pair, which is worth about ½ pawn. Therefore 4 Bxc6 is *not* a threat and "Morphy's move" 3...a6 is possible.

Returning to the position after 1 e4 e5 2 Nf3 Nc6 3 Bb5:

3...a6

This is a good idea since later (say after White guards e4) White may eventually threaten Bxc6 and Nxe5, so Black can guard the pawn simply by later playing ...b7-b5.

3...d6 is the Steinitz Variation.

3...Nd4 is the Bird Variation.

3...Nf6 is the currently popular Berlin Variation.

3...Bc5 is the rarer Classical Variation.

4 Ba4

Many beginners play 4...b5 here, but that is not always the best move order. After 5 Bb3 this is similar to an Italian Game 3 Bc4 except:

1. The bishop is guarded on b3;

2. The bishop is not vulnerable to ...d5 counterattacks;

3. Black has weakened his queenside with pawn pushes.

In modern theory, this is why 3 Bc4 is considered only OK, but 3 Bb5 a6 4 Ba4 b5 5 Bb3 is considered good for White! For example, after 5...Nf6 even 6 Ng5!? is possible as in the Two Knights Defense.

Back to the main line:

4...Nf6

Black follows the advice, knights before bishops and attacks the e-pawn.

4...d6 is the Modern Steinitz Variation (or "Steinitz Deferred").

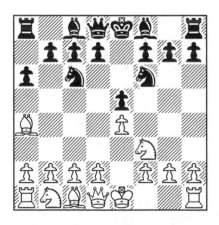

White to play

How should White defend the e-pawn? Not 5 Nc3 or 5 d3, which go against the plan of c2-c3 and d2-d4, but:

5 0-0

White guards the pawn indirectly.

5...Be7

Black closes the e-file to threaten ...Nxe4 when there are no pins. Other moves:

5...Nxe4 is the *Open Variation*. What do almost all Grandmasters play here?

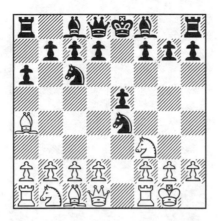

White to play (Open Variation)

No, not the natural 6 Re1, which is not bad but does not promise much after 6...Nc5.
6 d4 is the main line. The tabiya of the Open Variation continues 6...b5 7 Bb3 d5 8 dxe5 Be6.
5...d6 leads to the Steinitz Deferred Variation.
5...b5 leads to the Archangel Variation.
Continuing with the main line of the Closed Variation:

6 Re1

Now White guards the e-pawn and creates a threat. What is it?
It is the "removal of the guard" 7 Bxc6 followed by 8 Nxe5 winning a pawn.
How does Black normally protect against this?

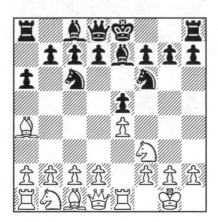

Black to play

6...b5

He makes the remover move! Now the knight can continue to protect the pawn.
6...d6 can again lead to the Steinitz Deferred Variation.

7 Bb3

No credit for other White moves!

Black to play

Here Black can castle or play 7...d6. Many Closed Ruy Lopez players play 7...d6 because 7...0-0 is the signal for the Marshall Attack on the following move: *8 c3 d5!?*. So those who do not wish to play the Marshall for Black or face anti-Marshall lines just play...

7...d6

Now that the black e-pawn is "overprotected", what is Black's threat?

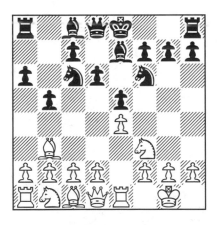

White to play

He threatens to "win" the bishop pair with ...Na5 and ...Nxb3, worth ½ pawn.

White's next move is clear since he wants to save his bishop *and* play d2-d4:

8 c3

No credit for other moves!

Now Black can play ...Bg4, but that is not so good! The general rule is to *not play ...Bg4 until White has committed himself with d2-d4.*

For example, if Black tries the inaccurate move *8...Bg4*, then *9 h3 Bh5* (else the pin is for naught or Black just gives up the bishop pair with 9...Bxf3?!) *10 d3!*, avoiding d2-d4 and planning Nbd2-f1-g3. (Instead 10 d4 is rare; if 10...Bxf3 and either d4 is lost or the king is opened up, although 11 Qxf3 exd4 12 Qg3!? is an interesting computer suggestion.)

Play after *10 d3!* might continue: *10...0-0 11 Nbd2 Na5 12 Bc2 c5 13 Nf1 Re8 14 Ng3 Bg6 15 Nh4 Bf8*, and now not 16 Nxg6, but put a knight on f5! White is much better with good kingside attacking prospects and Black's bad bishop. This occurred in Kolker-G.Kramer, New Jersey Open 1968, and GM Arthur Bisguier, watching the game, told me "Now Black has a terrible game – he does not resign, but it is pretty bad!"

Back to the main line; instead of 8...Bg4 Black plays...

8...0-0

What should White do here?

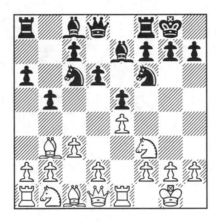

White to play

Not 9 d4 because 9...Bg4 is effective once d2-d4 has been played. That's considered a rare line. Instead...

9 h3

Normally, moves like 9 h3 are a waste since the bishop has other squares, but in this case 10 d4 cannot be stopped, so it justifies White's entire play!

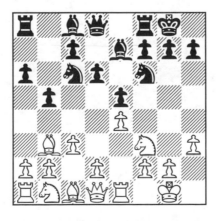

Black to play

This position is the "tabiya" of the Closed Ruy Lopez! All its main variations start here. For example:

9...*Bb7* is the popular Zaitsev Variation.

9...*Na5* is the Chigorin Variation.

9...*h6* is the Smyslov Variation.

9...*Nb8* is the Breyer Variation.

9...*Nd7* is the (rare) Karpov Variation.

I hope you learned a lot and can practice these opening ideas in your games!

Chapter Seven

Endgames and Technique

7-1) Trading Pawns When Ahead

You can't win without material to checkmate.

Which of the following is 100% correct?

- ♟ When ahead material, trade.
- ♟ When ahead material, trade pieces.
- ♟ When ahead material, trade pieces, but not pawns.

None of the above! The problem with the third statement is the ambiguity of the word "not". It could mean "never", as in "never trade pawns when ahead material", or it could mean "not the same as the previous subject", as in "unlike pieces, you don't necessarily trade pawns". In the case of trading pawns, "...but not pawns" means "not necessarily", and *not* "never trade pawns". Therefore, a more accurate way to phrase this principle is *when you are ahead material then, everything else being equal, make fair or advantageous trades of pieces, but don't necessarily trade pawns.*

It follows that in some positions, when you are ahead you actually *want* to trade pawns. This is encountered most often when both sides have many pawns and the defender has the possibility of locking the position. Here are some examples:

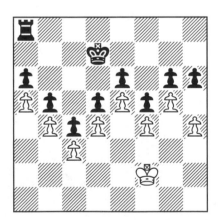

Position #1: Black to play

In this position, avoiding the trade of pawns by 1...h5?? is a monstrous mistake, because the position is completely locked and Black's extra rook is meaningless. Instead, opening a line with **1...hxg5** wins:

a) **2 hxg5 Rh8 3 Kg2** (if 3 Kg3, then 3...Rh1 penetrates and wins) **3...Rh4 4 Kg3 Rh1** wins.

b) **2 fxg5 Rh8** (2...Rf8 followed by pushing the f-pawn also wins easily) **3 Kg3 f4+** (Black offers a pawn to deflect the king) **4 Kxf4** (4 Kh3 f3 eventually forces the same deflection, as White must abandon the h-pawn to stop the f-pawn) **4...Rxh4+** and Black again penetrates and wins; e.g. **5 Kg3 Rh1** and the c3-pawn will soon fall.

Position #2: Black to play

Again, locking the position with 1...g4?? would make the extra bishop meaningless and only draw. Therefore, the side ahead in material should trade pawns:

1...gxf4 2 gxf4 Bc6 (White could draw were it not for the bishop, as after 2...Kh5, White could just shuttle his king back and forth on h3 and g3 and keep the black king out) **3 Kh3 Be8 4 Kh4 Bh5 5 Kg3 Be2 6 Kh4** (if 6 Kf2, then 6...Kh5 and if 7 Kxe2 Kg4 8 Ke3 Kg3 wins) **6...Bf1** (White is getting into *zugzwang* and must let the black king in!) **7 Kg3 Kh5 8 Kf3** (or 8 Kf2 Kg4, similar to the previous note) **8...Kh4 9 Kf2 Kg4 10 Ke3** (again, 10 Kxf1 Kxf4 wins) **10...Bh3** and Black wins easily.

Even the "jumpy" knight often needs the king to help:

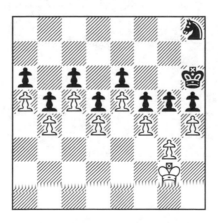

Position #3: Black to play

Once again 1...g4? is bad, as White can try to position his king to defend against knight sacrifices. For example, if the knight maneuvers to the queenside (f7-d8-b7), then White can also move his king to stop ...Nxa5 or ...Nxc5 from breaking through. In other words, White can shuffle his king to whichever side the knight goes to prevent a winning break-through. If there is a win after 1...g4, it is difficult to find!

But after the simple **1...gxf4**, Black wins easily by opening lines and bringing his knight to g6. For instance, after **2 gxf4 Ng6 3 Kg3 Kg7**, White is in *zugzwang*. The white king must give way and Black wins easily: **4 Kf3 Nxh4+ 5 Kg3 Ng6 6 Kf3 h4 7 Ke3 Kh6 8 Kf3 Kh5** (*zugzwang* again) **9 Kf2 Kg4** etc.

So from the above we can formulate a principle about when to trade pawns:

If you are ahead in material and there are so many pawns that your opponent may have the ability to lock up the position and make it difficult – or impossible – to win, then trade pawns to open lines for your extra power to be effective.

We have thus determined when it is clearly good to trade. At the other end of the spectrum – with very few pawns – we can just as easily find positions where it is clearly terrible to trade. Why? Because you need mating material to win.

Position #4: White to play

This is clear. If one "trades when ahead", then 1 exd7?? Nxd7 leads to a draw, as White cannot force a checkmate with two knights vs. a king and one knight, barring exceptional circumstances. Even if White had a knight on e5, instead of h2, then 1 exd7?? Nxd7 2 Nxd7 would still be a draw. Therefore, White must keep his pawn, so the only winning move is **1 e7** and White will promote. As can be shown with many endgame positions, we can extend this idea "back" in time to show that trading in a similar position with more pawns is often a bad mistake.

(see following diagram)

Again, White would be making a big mistake to trade when ahead, as after 1 fxe6? dxe6, White is helpless to stop 2...Nd7 and 3...Nxe5. White cannot force checkmate with just two knights. (Yes, I know two knights against one pawn can sometimes win, but that's making the concept too advanced!) Instead, the easy **1 f6** preserves the passed pawn and wins.

Position #5: White to play

From the above examples we now know where the maxim "When ahead in material, trade pieces but not pawns" applies, but this is only clearly true if there is a danger that you might run out of mating material, so we can postulate:

When ahead in material do not exchange pawns if there is any danger that you might not be able to checkmate because of a lack of mating material.

For example, let's change the position from the previous one by putting a bishop on h2.

Position #6: White to play

Now 1 fxe6 dxe6 is, theoretically, not as bad, as after 2...Nd7 and 3...Nxe5 White can play 4 Bxe5 and eventually snap up the e6-pawn and win with bishop and knight vs. king. But that is much harder than just playing **1 f6** and going for a queen. The reply 1...d6, to allow ...Nd7, is hopeless. So, from a practical standpoint, 1 fxe6 has to deserve a question mark for making the win more difficult.

Another corollary of the pawn trade principle is:

If you are ahead a rook or more (mating material by itself), then preserving the pawns on the board by avoiding trades is not as necessary as it would be if the material imbalance was not so great.

This makes sense because, even without the pawns, the player ahead by that much can usually win by trading into a simplified position and checkmating with the remaining material.

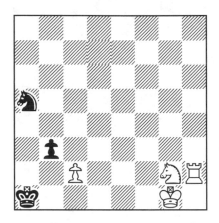

Position #7: White to play

Here, it is logical for White to trade off Black's dangerous passed pawn by **1 cxb3 Nxb3**, because White is ahead a rook and should win easily. Note that even if White were only ahead by a knight instead of a rook, it might be still necessary to trade off this pawn to avoid losing! Getting rid of your opponent's most dangerous piece is usually a good idea!

Finally, let's take a practical example, a recent club game where Black has rook and four pawns vs. rook and two pawns. Thus, neither of the previously stated guidelines for very few or very many pawns may apply.

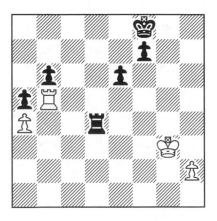

Position #8: Black to play

After the game, Black stated that at this point he remembered the principle: "When ahead, trade pieces but not pawns", and misinterpreted this as "don't trade pawns"! Therefore, he avoided any trades with the passive 1...Rd6?. However, this allowed White to hold up two queenside pawns with only one of his own, making the win more difficult. Trading pawns with 1...Rxa4 2 Rxb6 is much better, as Black then has a third passed pawn. Moreover, immediately after the game, club member Will Moyer pointed out that best of all is **1...Rb4!**, when White cannot play 2 Rxb4 axb4 because the passed b-pawn is "outside the square" of the white king and promotes easily. Moreover, after **1...Rb4**, Black threatens to win easily by *making an even trade of pieces when ahead*. If White avoids the trade by 2 Rg5, then 2...Rxa4 wins yet another pawn for nothing.

The conclusion of this endgame is instructive:

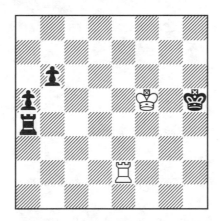

Position #9: Black to play

Black has a very awkward king, but can try 1...b5 (not 1...Ra1?? 2 Rh2 mate). White can attempt to hold with 2 Rb2 Rg4 (2...b4?? 3 Rh2 mate) 3 Rh2+ (3 Rxb5? Rg5+) 3...Rh4 4 Rb2. However, Black can play for a win with 4...b4 or 4...Kh6; e.g. 4...b4 5 Ra2 Kh6. At this point, 6 Rxa5? again fails to the skewer 6...Rg5+, but, instead of 6 Rxa5?, White should play 6 Kf6 and now 6...Rh5 holds the pawn. Yet the win is still not trivial. This idea was much too difficult for me to find while observing the rapid pace of the game in progress!

In the game, Black played **1...Rc4?** and White missed an easier draw by 2 Rh2+ Rh4 3 Rb2 when, if Black tries to avoid repetition of position with 3...a4, then 4 Rxb6 draws. This draw I did see! If 3...Rb4 4 Rh2+ can repeat, and 4 Rxb4 axb4 5 Ke4 draws, too. Instead, White ended up losing after **2 Rb2? Rc5+ 3 Ke6(?) b5 4 Ra2 a4** etc.

So Black avoided trading pawns when ahead – incorrectly – got a more difficult game, but eventually won because White did not play the best defense. The meta-principle of this game is:

If you are going to make a move on general principles, make sure that either your un-derstanding of the principle is correct or your position is not an exception!

7-2) The Endgame Bind

The hardest thing to win is a won game.

The following position occurred in a recent game between two promising juniors at our local Main Line Chess Club. Black had eleven minutes remaining, and White, who was slightly higher rated, had three. They were playing with a five second time delay.

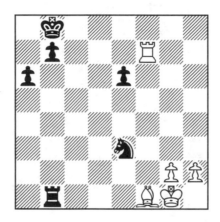

Black to play – how many plans are reasonable?

White's situation is called a *bind* because he cannot easily extricate his pieces. For example, if it were White's turn he can't play 1 Kf2? because 1...Rxf1+ wins the rook via a skewer. His bishop is pinned and his rook is stuck guarding the bishop. However, this position is not *zugzwang*, as White can readily push his kingside pawns. Nonetheless, his choices are limited.

Whenever you have your opponent in a bind, think carefully about how to fully exploit it. There are usually several possibilities:

- ♟ release the bind if that allows a forced win of material;
- ♟ force a favorable simplification;
- ♟ make use of the tempi that your opponent needs to break the bind.

In the above position Black's three major plans are:

A. Trade off all the non-pawns via exchanges on f1 and try to win the king and pawn endgame with an extra pawn;

B. Push the a-pawn one square and then trade on f1. At that point the white king will be outside the promotion square of the pawn (See the archived *King + Pawn vs. King*), or

    C.   Continue to push the a-pawn and try to promote (without releasing the bind – don't trade on f1).

Take a few minutes to answer the following:

- ♟   Which of these three plans win?
- ♟   Which plan is the easiest for Black to play?
- ♟   Which plan gives White the least counterplay?

Let's consider each.

Plan A: Trade off all the non-pawns via exchanges on f1 and try to win the king and pawn endgame with an extra pawn.

This brings up the key and instructive question, which Black did not consider in the game: "Which initial capture is best and most forcing, taking with the knight or taking with the rook?"

Most players correctly understand that taking with the rook is forcing because it double attacks the rook on f7 and thus forces off the rooks, but that is not the only concern.

The answer is that it depends: in positions such as these, sometimes capturing first with the rook is best and sometimes capturing first with the knight is correct, and often it makes no difference. We will see why shortly. In Plan A it makes no difference, since either way the capture is made on f1 virtually forces all the pieces off the board, so we will return to this question when we analyze Plan B.

So let's assume Black trades off all the pieces by capturing with the knight first:

1...Nxf1 2 Rxf1 Rxf1+ 3 Kxf1

How should Black proceed?

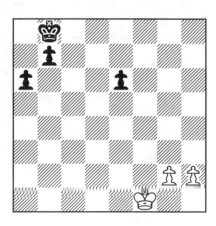

Black to play

While it is not the only idea, Black gets a couple of free tempi to tie down White's king because White must first stop the a-pawn and cannot race yet with the h-pawn:

3...a5 4 Ke2 a4 5 Kd3

At this point Black has several possibilities, but only one wins "easily". What should Black do?

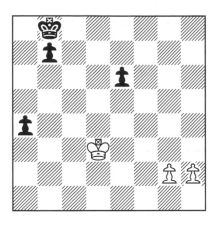

Black to play

The easiest win is **5...Kc7!**. This move places the black king inside the square of the white h-pawn. Once this is accomplished, White has absolutely no chance.

The plan of racing alternately with the a- and e-pawns is trickier, but it wins, too. It is of interest that when I gave this position to *Rybka*, it immediately saw that the pawn race won. However, the clearer "inside the square" idea requires much more ply and it took *Rybka* quite a while to see that it was as good as the pawn race. I guess this is one of the few remaining areas where a master's "vision" is still faster than a computer's!

Play might proceed **6 h4** (a move like 6 Kc3 will likely transpose) **6...Kd7 7 h5 Ke7 8 g4 Kf6 9 h6 Kg6 10 g5 b5 11 Kc3 a3 12 Kb3 b4 13 Kc2** (13 Ka2 makes no difference)

Black to play

Now, finally, the extra pawn wins easily: **13...e5** and White is helpless against the combined advances of the black pawns. If you don't think this kind of easy win is inevitable after **5...Kc7!** you are welcome to try other moves for White. Black can win without this idea, but putting the king inside the square is both clear and simple.

Verdict: Plan A wins.

Plan B: Push the a-pawn one square and then trade on f1 when the white king will be outside the square of the pawn.

This is the plan Black chose in the game, and is perhaps the most instructive.

1...a5 2 h4

What else? White can't easily stop the a-pawn, as any rook move is met by exchanges on f1, and then White is not only losing the race, but also his king is outside the square of the a-pawn.

Now, in order to implement Plan B, how should Black capture on f1?

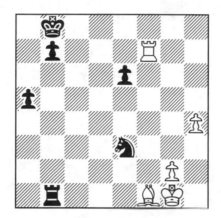

Black to play

Although capturing first on f1 with the rook forces the trade of rooks, *White nevertheless has the option of not capturing whenever Black takes with the knight*. Further, any trade-off into a king and pawn endgame is clearly dead lost for White, since he is not only behind in the promotion race, but Black can promote with check. Therefore, another way of determining the move order of capturing on f1 is to ask "Assuming White does *not* capture the knight, is it more advantageous for Black to take with the knight first or after capturing with the rook?"

In this case capturing first with the knight with 2...Nxf1 is more forcing, since Black has little problems winning if White does not capture the knight: after 3 h5 Ng3+ Black wins the h-pawn, or 3 g4 Ne3+ wins the g-pawn. However, as we shall see from the game continuation, capturing first with the rook is a different matter.

In the game Black played **2...Rxf1+** and after the forced **3 Rxf1 Nxf1**

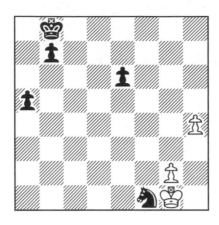

White to play

White *immediately* captured **4 Kxf1**. After Black replied **4...a4**, White just stared at the board for most of his remaining time, as he can neither get inside the square, nor stop the pawn with the king, nor race: 5 h5 a3 6 h6 a2 7 h7 a1Q+ is check and also covers the h8 square, when either will suffice. White played a few meaningless moves and then resigned.

After the game I asked Black "What would you have done if White had played 4 h5!? instead of 4 Kxf1? Did you consider that move?" Black admitted that he had not looked at 4 h5!?. White also admitted that he never considered playing this potentially winning idea.

Making big assumptions and moving quickly is sometimes dangerous to your chess health! I suggested to White that he could take an improvement step if he would not assume such recaptures are always forced – especially in a deep endgame. This advice was most applicable here, since the recapture 4 Kxf1 led to such an obviously hopeless position. In this sense *playing 4 Kxf1 immediately is a time management error* – White thought long and hard *after* this move, but not before it, when possibly something could have been done.

Returning to **4 h5!?**, I asked both players if they could find a way for Black to stop the pawn:

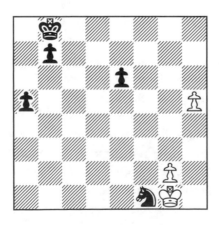

Black to play

Both players said they could not, but I believe that if this continuation had actually occurred, Black would have sunk into serious thought, and might have found **4...Ng3 5 h6 Ne2+!**. *Sometimes going "backwards" with knights is the fastest way to go forwards!* If you can't easily find this type of move, try some "knight path" exercises (see the archived *Chess Exercises*). **6 Kf2 Nf4** and then **7...Ng6** will save the day. Therefore, it turns out that with best play Black is not only winning in Plan B with 2...Nxf1, but also with the move played, 2...Rxf1+.

Plan C: Continue to push the a-pawn and try to promote.
With Plan C Black has no intention of trading on f1 and releasing the bind until White forces him to do so. He simply wants to win the race and promote first, while White's options are limited. Indeed, White is hard-pressed to stop the plan:
1...a5 2 h4

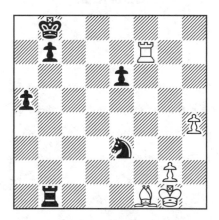

Black to play

As noted in Plan B, White cannot play otherwise, as then Black can trade on f1 and reach a superior form of Plan B, e.g. 2 Rf3 Rxf1+ will transpose into Plan B an entire tempo ahead. Thus, White is forced to race.
2...a4 3 h5
Again by the same logic, this is almost forced unless White just wants to move the rook off the f-file and play a piece down, e.g. 3 Rd7 Rxf1+, which is rather hopeless.
3...a3 4 h6 a2 5 h7 a1Q

(see following diagram)

6 Rf8+
Without this move Plan C would clearly win for Black, as his queen attacks the h8-square.

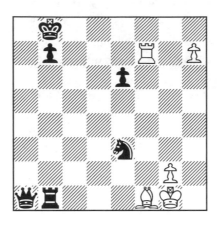

White to play

6...Ka7 7 h8Q

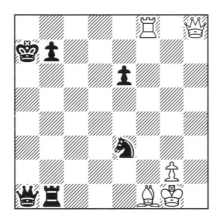

Black to play

For all his heroics, White is still lost.

7...Rxf1+

And now White has his choice of poisons:

a) **8 Rxf1** allows **8...Qxf1+** (also 8...Qxh8) **9 Kh2 Qxg2** mate.

b) **8 Kh2** allows **8...Rh1+** picking up the queen.

So Black is winning with Plan A, Plan B, and Plan C. It is also good to know that without the e-pawn, Plan A would not work. Which one is easiest and allows the least counterplay? That's a matter of opinion, and depends on who you are and what you know!

Similar endgame binds are not uncommon. Therefore, it is important to be open to many possibilities; playing the first one you see is not a good idea unless you are 100% sure it wins easily. Analyze each carefully to find out which continuations are forced and/or plausible, and choose the one that best ensures the desired result.

7-3) When You're Winning...

"When you have more to lose, you should be more careful."

One of the most common problems beginning players have is that they do not know how to win with a large material advantage. This means they are ahead at least the exchange (rook for bishop or knight) or more, and their opponent has no compensation. Even when they are ahead a full piece (bishop or knight), they often still do not understand how to capitalize on such a large advantage and give it all away.

Very few chess books contain much information on how to win in these situations. That is because it is supposed to be "easy" and "common sense", but unfortunately many players have never been taught this common sense, and therefore draw or even lose what should be easily won positions. When strong players fall clearly way behind against other strong players, they almost always resign since they know their opponents inevitable will win. However, weaker players spend a fairly high percentage of their games trying to win won positions, so knowing the "technique" of how to play such positions is important.

Here are five things you should do when way ahead, in descending order of importance:

1. Think Defense First!

This does *not* mean play passively or not to attack. "Think Defense First" has to do with the *order* of your priorities, and does not mean "play defensively".

"Think Defense First" means that the more you are ahead, the more likely any reasonable plan will win *so long as you do not let your opponent win back material or generate an enormous attack*. Therefore, *his* moves become *more important* than yours!

The further ahead you are, the less important your attack is and the more important your opponent's threats become. Looking for which checks, captures, and threats *he has* is more critical than looking for the ones you have. So long as you do anything reasonable you can always win later with your superior force, but if you give that force away carelessly, you no longer have the superiority with which to win. Therefore, immediately after your opponent moves, take the time to ask yourself those questions *you should always ask anyway*:

♟ Is his move safe? (See *Is it Safe?* 5-3.)

♟ What are *all* the things he can do to me now that he could not do to me before? And what can he not do? For example, his moved piece may no longer be guarding something.

♟ What checks, captures, and threats does he have *next* move if I don't stop them? In other words, "Suppose I pass and make no move. If I were he, after that pass what move would I make next?"

Any candidate move you select which does not meet your opponent's threats, or *allows forcing moves on your opponent's next move which cannot be met* should likely be discarded.

This also includes avoiding *The Seeds of Tactical Destruction* (see the archived Novice Nook column of that name). The Seeds of Tactical Destruction are patterns that lend themselves to a tactic for the opponent, such as:

a)   Loose, unguarded pieces (LPDO: Loose Pieces Drop Off);
b)   Pieces on the same file, rank, and diagonal that are pinnable or skewerable;
c)   A weak back rank or weak squares around the king with the queens on the board;
d)   Pieces that can be forked by pawns or knights;
e)   Under-protected pieces;
f)   Overworked pieces that can be subject to the "removal of the guard" tactic, etc.

2. Keep it Simple (KISS principle)

Don't do anything fancy or clever. Avoid complications! You almost undoubtedly don't need complications to win.

When Steinitz wrote, "If you have the advantage, you must attack" he was *not* referring to positions where you are up a piece or more! He was trying to say that if you have an advantage in space or time, you must use that advantage to keep the initiative by being aggressive. But if you are way ahead in material, then your extra material will eventually guarantee that you can apply superior force to an opponent's position, so being overly aggressive can backfire.

Complications make it more likely for a human to make a mistake. Who has more to lose, the player who is winning, or the player who is losing? Of course, the player who is winning has more to lose from mistakes (or time trouble or whatever), so the player with a large advantage should be striving for simple positions where big mistakes are harder to make. Contrarily, a player down considerable material is likely lost anyway, so he has nothing to lose and a lot to gain by creating complications where a big mistake is likely.

As an example, suppose you are up a piece and your opponent attacks an unguarded bishop with a knight. Then the *worst* thing you can do is counterattack one of his pieces, thus creating complications. Your opponent might be able to move his attacked piece and attack another one of yours and then you would have two pieces attacked, and might lose all of your advantage! But if you just move the attacked piece to a safe square (preferably one where it is also guarded), that is usually much simpler and less likely to lead to the loss of your advantage.

3. Make fair trades of pieces, not necessarily pawns

Suppose (for simplicity) we use the old 'Reinfeld' values to count the total value of all your material: queen=9 pawns, rook=5, bishop=3, knight=3, pawn=1. Further, assume you have on the board a queen, rook, rook, bishop, knight, and 5 pawns (total = 30) versus your opponent's queen, rook, bishop, and 3 pawns (20). Usually it is most helpful to just think in terms of material differential: you are 'up a rook, knight, and two pawns'.

Now suppose you have a chance to trade rooks. Is it almost always better for you to have a 25-15 material advantage after a rook trade than a 30-20 lead before the trade? It sure is! Make fair trades of pieces when ahead!

The reasons:

a) A larger percentage advantage of forces (30-20 is 50% more; 25 to 15 is 67%).
b) Fewer enemy pieces left which your opponent can use to narrow the advantage.
c) Closer to the endgame where extra pieces can more easily be used to promote pawns.
d) Fewer pieces on the board, so less chances for complications and error; likely shortens the game.

Think of being ahead a piece like a basketball team having a 60-30 lead. Before a rook trade you may be ahead 60-30 in the second quarter, but after the trade you have the same lead, but in the third quarter. Moving ahead a quarter with that big lead increases your chances of victory quite a bit.

Trading pieces is not the same as trading pawns. The player *behind* in pieces should trade pawns because it is a draw if you are ahead a piece or two knights without any pawns; see *Trading Pawns When Ahead* (7-1).

4. Make sure you are using *all* your pieces all of the time: get *every* piece into the game fast!

What good is being up a piece if your material superiority is not being used?

Think of being ahead material like coaching a hockey team on a power play. Would your correct strategy be to sit some of your players on the ice until the other team is back to full strength? That is how silly you look if you are up material but don't use all of your superior force. So just get all your pieces into the game every time and don't hesitate or fool around before doing so.

For example, if you win a queen for a piece early in the game, don't use your queen to go around winning a pawn here or there! That is penny wise and pound foolish. You are already ahead enough material to win easily, and winning more material is not only unnecessary, but often loses tempi that enable your opponent to generate an attack. Instead, get all the other pieces helping the queen and your material superiority should soon prove decisive.

It is especially noteworthy to include: *In the endgame, use your king*. The king has infinite trading value, but it is not so well known that the king has about 4+ pawns of fighting value. That means if you are up a piece and a pawn, but your opponent is using his king and you are not, then the fighting forces are about equal and you likely will not make progress! One of my students was playing in a large local event and got into an endgame up a bishop and a pawn. From that point on, I counted 20 king moves for his opponent to none for my student. He was essentially giving "king" odds, worth roughly 4 pawns – about the same value as a bishop plus a pawn! He lost.

5. Don't worry about the little things

De-emphasize guidelines that primarily apply to "close-to-even" positions. For example, consider the following two positions:

White to play

White is ahead a bishop for a pawn and has the bishop pair. Normally you would not give up the bishop pair for nothing, but here you are so far ahead that trading down is more important, so White wins with the simple **1 Bxe8 Kxe8**, e.g. **2 Ke4 Kf7 3 Ke5 Kg7** (or 3...Ke8 4 Kf6 Kd8 5 Kf7 Kc8 6 Ke7 Kb7 7 Kxd7 Ka8 8 Kxc6) **4 Be7 Kf7 5 Kd6 Ke8 6 Bh4**, when Black is in *zugzwang* so both pawns fall.

Two Bonus Items:

♟ Don't get into unnecessary time trouble

When you are winning easily, playing the absolute best move on each move is usually not required – you usually just need a series of reasonable ones that avoid big blunders. Therefore, if you are sure that your move is not a big mistake that lets your opponent back into the game, then taking lots of time to find the perfect move is often counterproductive as you may get into time trouble. Once in time trouble, then moving fast will often result in that big blunder that throws away the win – or even losing on time, which is the last thing you want to happen to you when you are winning easily.

♟ Don't get overconfident

You have the most to lose. Would you feel more on guard with a million dollars in your pocket or twenty? Similarly, when you are winning you have to be the most careful.

One more reminder – only because most students get this wrong!

Think Defense First is *Not* Think Defensively!

One of the most common misconceptions about items I write involves my #1 advice to "Think Defense First" when you are way ahead. This is often misread as "Play Defensively" or worse: "Play Passively". Nothing could be further from the truth. *Attack all you want, but first make sure your opponent cannot get back in the game via a tactic.*

Suppose you want to think 10% defense and 90% offense when ahead a rook. In many situations that ratio is perfectly fine *so long as you chronologically order your thinking 10%-90% and not 90%-10%!* In other words, if you *first* check and see that your opponent has no tactic that can possibly get him back in the game, then if you want to spend 90% of your time seeing what you can do to him, that is OK. Give priority to seeing that your opponent can't get back in the game. Making sure a losing opponent has no "swindles" is *not* playing defensively or passively. In any case you still can – and eventually should – either end up attacking like crazy with your large material advantage or, even more commonly, just winning easily by attrition.

Don't Allow the Floobly!

Telling someone to avoid getting checkmated is like telling them not to make bad moves – how does that help?

Suppose an American Football team is leading 70-0 in the fourth quarter. What would the proper strategy be? The answer is that it does not matter much – professional football teams can't score ten touchdowns in a quarter, so the team that is ahead can pretty much do anything it pleases to run out the clock.

That strategy is solid, but what happens if we change the rules by adding a new offensive scoring possibility called a *floobly*, which is worth 1,000 points? (A floobly is a lot like catching the snitch in Harry Potter's Quidditch, but that's a different story...) Let's assume the floobly is a very difficult and rare play that requires the cooperation of the defense, such as five players each from the offensive *and* defense simultaneously singing *Oklahoma!* while standing on their heads.

What would be the offense's strategy then, given the same 70-0 lead? Why, don't allow the floobly, of course. Don't let your players stand on their heads, and certainly don't teach them the words to *Oklahoma!*

This may all sound silly – and what does it have to do with chess? Everything, if you are a weaker player and often lose or draw games after you were winning easily.

That's because chess has at least one floobly, and that's checkmate. That's right – you can be ahead three queens, but if you allow checkmate, then you lose no matter how much material or other advantages you possess.

In a sense, flooblies are the *opposite* of the items listed above in *When You're Winning, It's a Whole Different Game*: flooblies are the gigantic mistakes that can cause you to lose a game, even though you are either far ahead in material or otherwise winning easily.

Go out of your way to prevent common checkmate patterns. For example, avoid back-rank mates by providing *luft* (air) for your king:

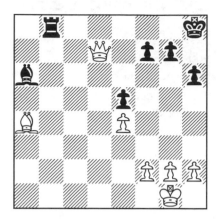

Floobly #1: White to play

In a position like this, the greedy 1 Qxf7?? loses to 1...Rb1+ 2 Bd1 Rxd1 mate.

Instead, White should *think defense first* and stop most easy checkmate patterns forever with a move such as **1 h4!**, creating a *luft* square on h2 (the opposite color of the opponent's bishop). In terms of our football analogy, this preventative measure stops your players from ever standing on their heads, thus eliminating the possibility of the disastrous floobly when the band strikes up Rogers and Hammerstein.

1 h4! is slightly better than the mundane 1 h3 because the pawn is on the opposite color of the black bishop and later may even help hem in the black king. Less good is **1 g3**, which creates a *luft* square the same color as the black bishop. After 1 g3, White should visualize that it is still possible to lose by playing poorly:

1...Bc8 2 Qxf7 Bh3

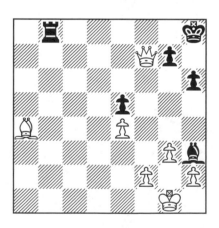

White to play

3 Qc7??

This "offensive" move double attacks the rook and the e-pawn, but **3...Rb1+** and Black mates.

In order to prevent fiascos such as the above, whenever you are way ahead in material, start by asking: *"How could I lose?"* and *"If I were him, what would I do to get back in the game?"*, visualizing as many possibilities as you can for throwing away your advantage, and then ask: *"How could I (permanently) prevent such situations from occurring during the remainder of this game?"*, and then giving the appropriate actions top priority.

By taking these key steps, you are following the #1 suggestion for what to do when way ahead: "Think Defense First".

Think Defense First suggests you should begin your thought process by not only seeing what your opponent is threatening, but also what he might threaten in the near future. Such defensive queries should be done *before* you spend time contemplating "offensive" maneuvers. After all, there are a myriad of ways to win games like the above – any decent strategy will do – but there are only a few ways your opponent can get back in the game, so concentrate on stopping those first (see Example #3, "Letting the One-Trick Pony Win", in *A Fistful of Lessons* 9-1).

If you first take steps that ensure you can't lose, eventually you will almost always stumble your way into a win, even with a bad plan, so long as you continue to avoid any big mistakes.

Allowing checkmate is clearly the ultimate floobly. However, since losing on time is equally disastrous, *allowing your time to expire unnecessarily* is another big one. There are other flooblies:

- ♟ stalemating your opponent;
- ♟ getting your queen trapped (or allowing other trivial queen-winning tactics);
- ♟ allowing your opponent to promote a pawn when you otherwise have a big material advantage;
- ♟ playing overconfidently and too quickly, allowing something disastrous to happen when almost any small amount of care would have sufficed.

Below are examples:

Floobly #2: White to play

Here the correct procedure is to move the queen a "big knight's move" (3&1 squares) away from the corner with 1 Qg5. This is a good pattern to remember:

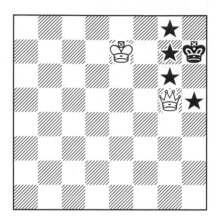

After the correct 1 Qg5 – Black to play

Here, so long as the white king is outside the g5-h5-h8-g8 rectangle that traps the black king, there is no stalemate possibility. Black is reduced to moving his king back and forth from h7-h8, while the white king approaches f7 to support the checkmate.

Instead, White players often mistakenly reason, "I can't mate without the king, so it must move closer" and, instead of 1 Qg5, quickly play 1 Kf7?? stalemate.

After the incorrect 1 Kf7?? Stalemate

In the following position,

(see following diagram)

Black is ahead a queen for a knight and can save his attacked queen with several moves, including the clearly safe 1...Qe8. Instead, he might notice that White's kingside is weak, which is *not* much of an issue when ahead by this much material, and play the "attacking" 1...Qh4??.

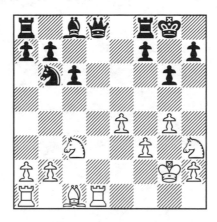

Floobly #3: Black to play

This is a good example of "Hope Chess" because Black is clearly not asking himself whether he can safely meet all checks, captures, and threats in reply – for 2 Bg5 traps the queen! Notice that compounding Black's problems with 2...Bxg4?? (hoping for 3 fxg4?? Qxg4+) loses an entire queen after 3 Bxh4, and leaves Black behind a knight for a pawn. Instead, Black could at least salvage a bishop for the queen with the simple 2...Qxg5, resulting in even material. I often see weaker players making silly desperation moves such as 2...Bxg4??. They are not only illogical (making a very bad move and hoping the opponent will make an even worse one is not Hope Chess – it is bad chess!), but not even necessary since Black would not be losing until after that move.

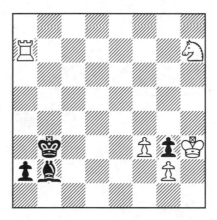

Floobly #4: White to play

White is winning fairly easily but needs to see that Black has a dangerous threat. If White hastily plays 1 Kxg3??, then the clever promotion tactic 1...Ba3! turns the tables and allows Black to promote. Much worse would be to answer 1 Kxg3?? with the hasty 1...a1Q?? 2 Rxa1, when the double blunder again leaves White with an easy win. Instead, White should just take the pawn before Black blocks with 1 Rxa2 Kxa2 2 Kxg3 with a technical win.

Floobly #5: Black to play

Black has reached a clearly winning position. With a little thought – and perhaps some help from *The Principle of Symmetry* (8-6) – Black should find an easy win with the mundane 1...gxf5!. Then no matter whether White plays 2 Kxa5 fxg4 or 2 gxf5 Kxa4 the game is over.

But if Black is hasty and erroneously concludes that "the first person to capture an a-pawn wins", then 1...Kxa4?? loses to 2 fxg6! (or 2 g5!) 2...hxg6 3 h5!, when White has created asymmetry with the outside passed pawn and is the first to promote.

In endgames there are many possible flooblies, so keep your wits about you until the last:

Floobly #6: White to play

In this final example, from an online "45+45" game (45 minutes with a 45 second time increment) the floobly was a combination of poor time management and overconfidence.

White may be behind in material, but he has aggressively sacrificed to blast open black's king and can force resignation within a move or two; for example, 1 Re3 and the threat to check on h3 is deadly. On top of that, White has been playing quickly – much too quickly – and now had over 50 minutes left on his clock to finish the game.

But instead of taking his time to find a proper finish, White decided to show how smart he was by moving quickly. He played **1 Qg7+??** almost instantly, obviously thinking it was checkmate. The problem was that the only defense was forced, and from the opposite corner duly came **1...Bxg7** and White resigned.

White probably felt "unlucky", but *playing so fast when you are winning is not bad luck; it is an enormous time management mistake.* If you really believe you have a checkmate, what is the benefit of being so "clever" and moving quickly? No one with any sense will feel you are any less intelligent if you take your time to check to see if your move is really a win; in fact, they may think it rather wise of you! If it is a win, you have lost nothing by being a little extra careful (for a world champion's view on this, see Tale #11 in the archived *Time Management Tales*); if it is not, then you would be very happy you found out beforehand.

As GM Lev Alburt and Al Lawrence wrote in their handy book *Chess Rules of Thumb* (pun intended), if you see a move which you think is winning, then that is a critical move and *a critical move is one about which you should think long and hard.*

Always remember...

When you are winning you have the most to lose.

...so playing quickly and overconfidently is not a sign of brilliance. A better sign of intelligence is consistently recognizing positions where you must be careful and taking appropriate action!

Two Favorite Problems

Doing problems, even ones unlikely to ever occur in a game of yours, can help you improve. Although you may well know how the pieces *move*, problems help you better understand what the pieces can *do*, especially in coordination with one another.

The following problem is from Irving Chernev's fun book *The Bright Side of Chess*:

White to play and mate in 3

There are many possible mate in *four* moves. For example, the straightforward 1 Rg8 is defended by 1...Bd4 when 2 Rg1+ Bxg1 3 Bg7+ Bd4 4 Bxd4 mate takes one move too many. 1 Nf7 Bxh8 2 Nxh8 threatens an "unstoppable" 3 Bg7 mate, but unfortunately is stalemate.

So what is the key to doing it in three? Answer after the next problem.

The following is a *Helpmate in 2*. A helpmate is where Black moves first and purposely aids White in mating in a specified number of moves. In the next diagram White must mate on his second move. This type of cooperation may not be *directly* related to playing better regular chess, but doing problems like these (where the pieces move normally but the goals might be different) can definitely help you learn how the pieces can work together and enhance board vision:

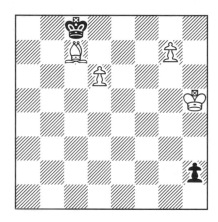

Black to play and help White mate in 2

If you want a hint: The first thing you should notice is the pawn on h2. Since in problems every piece is supposed to be there for a reason, what can it be doing? It is likely that the black pawn needs to promote and help White to mate in some way...

Answer to the first problem: **1 Nf5! Bxh8 2 Ng7!** (*zugzwang!*) **2...Bxg7 3 Bxg7** mate. If **1...Be1** then **2 Nd4 "any move" 3 Nb3** is a cute mate. Not 2 Rh1?? stalemate. After 1 Nf5! Be1 2 Bg7+ also mates in three.

Answer to the second problem: **1...h1B! 2 g8B! Bb7 3 Be6** mate.

7-4) The Margin for Error

It's not what you trade that matters, but what's left on the board.

Let's introduce a very useful concept, "The Margin for Error". This will help address the definition of being "way ahead" and consequently improve the reader's "technique" – the ability to win a won game.

"Early in a game, about how far ahead does one side have to be before we would consider that side winning?" When I was working at the second Kasparov-Deep Blue match in New York in 1997, I asked several chess programmers this question (not the Deep Blue ones – they were busy!). They unanimously agreed the cut-off was roughly one pawn. In other words, if the program's evaluation indicated that it *was ahead by one pawn or more, they expected to win*; otherwise they did not consider the position to be winning.

Does that mean whenever you win a pawn (not a gambit one) in the opening you are winning? No, because in most cases it costs you something to win the pawn. Either:

♟ You had to spend up to three tempi to capture the pawn and return the capturing piece to a good square (one tempo is roughly worth a third of a pawn early in the game);

♟ The opponent foresaw the loss of a pawn and played the line that cost the least, for example sacrificing it to mess up your pawn structure or get a similar benefit; and/or

♟ When the opponent loses a pawn he automatically gains an extra semi-open file for his rooks. *This is especially helpful if it is the only semi-open (or open) file on the board*, since that likely makes his rooks stronger than yours.

This means that when one player wins a pawn, the evaluation is often something a little less than a pawn ahead and, by the above definition, you are not quite winning yet.

But suppose you can win a pawn and your opponent has absolutely no compensation; even better, your extra pawn may cover key squares, so that you judge yourself ahead by slightly more than a pawn. *If a proper evaluation of an early game position shows you are ahead by the equivalent of a pawn or more, then you are winning.*

Technically, the correct definition of winning is when, if both sides play perfectly, one side would win. However, the "one pawn or more" statement shows approximately *how much ahead* one needs to be for that theoretical win.

This definition only applies early in the game, because late in the game the concept of minimum mating material (plus the changing value of pieces to pawns) becomes paramount. In the deep endgame you could be ahead an entire piece and not be winning; alternatively, you might be up only a pawn and be easily winning. The possibilities of promotion, plus the fact that you can't win with only a knight, a bishop, or two knights left on the board skews what it takes to win in the late endgame. So the phrase "early in the game" has a wide scope, meaning before the late endgame.

Now that we have a value for "winning" we can define "margin of error".

In general, a player who is winning has a margin for error equivalent to how much evaluation he can lose (or the value of any mistakes he can make) and still be winning. Translating this into a formula, the margin for error to *win* is:

Margin for error (win) = A player's evaluated advantage (in pawns) − 1

Example: Early in a game a computer evaluates your position as better by 3.5 pawns. In this situation you have a 2.5 pawn margin for error to win. If you thereafter lose a pawn for no compensation, then you are still ahead 2.5 pawns, and your 1.5 pawn margin for error means you are still likely winning easily.

Similarly, we can make a definition for the margin for error for drawing, since *your opponent* needs to be a pawn or more ahead early in the game to win:

Margin for error (draw) = A player's evaluated advantage (in pawns) + 1

Example: You feel you have a slight advantage, about half a pawn. However, your position is lifeless and, if played correctly, is likely to only draw. Therefore, you want to take a risk in order to win. How much leeway do you have in making a move that could harm your position, but which is tricky and might allow your opponent to go wrong? The answer is 0.5 + 1 = 1.5 pawns. So long as the evaluation stays above minus one (-1) you are likely still drawing.

OK, we have made definitions, but how can this theory help you become a better player? The answer is: Quite a bit! If you know your margin of error, this tells you how much leeway you have in:

- ♟ Finding the best move;
- ♟ Forcing trades;
- ♟ Trading to simplify into an even easier winning position.

I have used positions such as the following as an example of simplification:

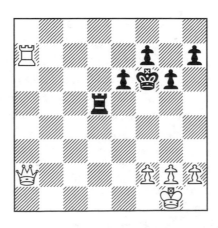

White to play

White has many ways of stopping the threatened mate (1 Kf1, 1 f4, and 1 h4 come to mind), but the enormous margin for error suggests eliminating most threats with **1 Qxd5!?**. After 1...exd5, the only way Black could ever form another threat would be to try to promote the d-pawn. Realizing this, White should activate his last piece with 2 Kf1! and, after establishing the king on the d-file, White cannot help but win easily. 1 Qxd5!? is not a move a computer would play nor "best", but it is an easy way to permanently eliminate the possibility of further error, and results in a trivial win.

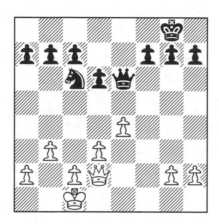

Black to play

In this position Black is ahead a knight, so his margin for error is equivalent to a little more than two pawns. Therefore, it is prudent to force the trade of queens with **1...Qh6!**, when the resulting doubled and isolated pawns after **2 Qxh6 gxh6** represent only a small fraction of his margin for error. However, the reduced material and diminished possibility for active play by White make the win much easier than if the queens had remained on the board.

The position after the queen trade is still an easy win for Black, assuming he remembers to activate his most powerful piece – the king! *The king is worth about four pawns of fighting power*, so if Black refuses to use his king for the remainder of the game, then instead of being ahead about two pawns, Black is down about two and White should win! Don't believe me? Make the queen trade and then play the game out with the condition that Black cannot make any king moves.

In the above two examples, there is enormous margin for error. Therefore, if we apply one of the principles on how to play when way ahead, "Don't worry about the little things" (see *When You're Winning, It's a Whole Different Game* 7-3), we can define "little" as "a small percentage of the margin for error". In the second example, Black's margin for error was more than two, so to isolate the f-pawn and double and isolate the h-pawns is relatively minor compared to trading off the queens. But suppose Black was only ahead a pawn instead of a piece:

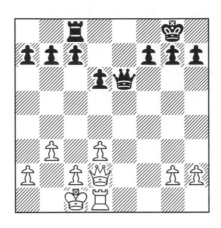

Black to play

In this position Black is only ahead one pawn, and thus has no margin for error. There-fore, to pay the enormous price of wrecking his pawn majority with 1...Qh6? 2 Qxh6 gxh6 just to trade queens would seriously jeopardize Black's winning chances. Instead, Black should retain control of the only open file with 1...Re8, and perhaps soon thereafter create *luft* with a move such as ...f7-f5, activating the potential passed pawn, and retaining excel-lent winning chances. But *remove White's rook on d1*; then Black is ahead a rook, so 1...Qh6 would be excellent as the wrecked pawn structure means comparatively nothing.

Understanding the difference between the previous two diagrams – and thus the prin-ciples involved with margin for error – means you have gone a long way toward developing good technique, or the ability to win a won game.

The larger your margin for error, the more you are willing to sacrifice. In the first exam-ple, White was ahead a queen, so the sacrifice of the queen for the rook was well within the margin for error tolerance for preserving an easy win.

Since ahead one pawn constitutes no margin for error, we can postulate a corollary to our principles for how to play when way ahead:

If you are ahead exactly one pawn (early in the game), then to "sacrifice" little
positional edges in order to trade pieces is usually incorrect.

For example, one would not give up control of a file just to trade rooks when ahead a pawn:

(see following diagram)

In this position Black is only ahead a pawn, so, although Black may conclude that 1...Rxe1? both trades rooks and removes the attacker for f7, giving up the file without being able to contest it is very dangerous.

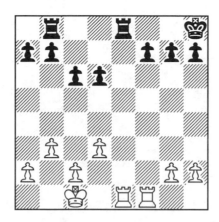

Black to play

After 2 Rxe1, White's rook can penetrate to the seventh rank and make Black's life miserable. Stating that Black's move jeopardizes his winning chances is an understatement, yet I see this misconception quite frequently. Instead, Black should activate his king by 1...Kg8, or play 1...f6 with solid chances to play for the win.

On the other hand, suppose we replace the extra pawn on f7 with a knight on g6:

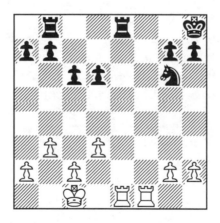

Black to play

Here, while 1...Rxe1 may not be the best move, since Black cannot quickly contest the file with ...Re8, the magnitude of the mistake is of no real consequence, as the much larger margin for error allows for such relatively minor inconveniences.

Below is another example of a sufficient margin for error to allow a "sacrifice" to simplify:

(see following diagram)

Black to play

In this position Black has several ways to win, but a very easy way is the "sacrifice" **1...Rxd1+ 2 Kxd1 Kf3** with a quick and easy tic-tac-toe win (see the archived *King + Pawn vs. King*), e.g. **3 Ke1** (if 3 Kd2 Kf2; instead, White needs to allow Black to go wrong) **3...Ke3!** (it is not too late to get sloppy and play 3...e3?? 4 Kf1 with a draw) **4 Kd1 Kf2** and Black shepherds in the pawn to promote. Black should never play a move like 1...Rxd1+ unless he understands all of the above analysis! Otherwise, he should just play safe and win with the extra exchange.

This again illustrates the principle: *when trading it is not so important to evaluate what is traded as what is left on the board*. In the endgame if your trade leaves you with a position that is easier to win, then you should do it no matter what the value of the traded pieces. The following position occurred in a practice game at our club:

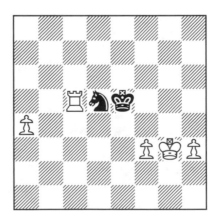

White to play

White wanted to follow the principle: *rooks belong behind passed pawns*, and played 1 Rc1. However, I kibitzed that White would have made life much easier with the simple 1

Rxd5+, eliminating the last enemy defender and possibilities of leaving the rook *en prise* or future knight forks. Any time you can simplify into an easily won king and pawn endgame you should probably do so. Suppose the initial position was:

White to play

The easiest idea is to pin the knight and take it off: **1 Rc5 Kd6 2 Rxd5+**. On the other hand, if your trade/sacrifice makes the win harder, I call that a *Delen Sacrifice*. I named it after my son, who performed this dubious feat on several occasions. Here is an invented example:

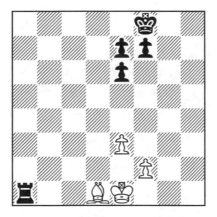

Black to play

Unlike the previous examples, sacrificing the exchange here does *not* make the position quicker or easier to win. Therefore the Delen Sacrifice **1...Rxd1+?!** is dubious at best. It is much better to just activate the black king and then push the black pawns to create a more favorable situation. The opportunity should arise later to sacrifice into an easily winning king and pawn endgame, so you should be on the alert for that possibility. But to do it now is unnecessarily – and dangerously – premature.

"The more you are winning, the more you can play differently" has been discussed in several Novice Nooks: *The Six Common Chess States* (8-3); *When You're Winning, It's a Whole Different Game/Don't Allow the Floobly* (7-3); and *Trading Pawns When Ahead* (7-1). This principle can now be rephrased more precisely:

When you are winning, the larger your margin for error, *the more you can – and should – alter your normal play accordingly to make the win as easy and risk-free as possible.*

Finally, let's use The Margin for Error to show how much better it is to win a piece (bishop or knight) than the exchange (rook for bishop or knight). A rook is worth about 5 pawns and a piece about 3.25 pawns. Then the exchange is worth about 1.75 pawns. So if it takes one extra pawn to win, then the margin for error in winning a piece is 3.25-1 = 2.25, while the margin for error in winning the exchange is only 1.75-1 = 0.75. That means the margin for error in winning is about three (!) times as much if you win a piece than if you win the exchange.

Chapter Eight

Strategy and Positional Play

8-1) Strong Principles vs. Important Principles

One of the most difficult – and important – concepts for a player to learn is how to re-solve conflicting principles.

Principles are short "sayings" or rules of thumb that are designed to help one make deci-sions, be it identifying possible moves or plans, when to play for a draw, or how to perform time management. *Principles exist primarily to help one decide what to do when there is no "book" knowledge, the position is very quiet with little or no analysis required, analysis fails to reveal a clearly best move, or lack of time precludes the ability to find a good move via analysis. In that sense principles are used to tiebreak equally safe moves or identify candi-dates from an otherwise innocuous selection of moves.*

Principles can be contrasted with *goals*. A goal identifies *what* you are trying to achieve, while a principle usually gives a "tip" on *how* to best do something. For example, a goal is to make your king as safe as possible, while a corresponding principle might be to castle at the first opportunity.

Players of all levels have difficulty deciding which principles apply in a given position, especially when the principles conflict. I found the existing "tools" for addressing this con-cern inadequate, so I created the following definitions to clarify these difficulties:

- ♟ **Strength** – a principle is *strong* if there are relatively few exceptions, i.e. it applies to a high percentage of potentially applicable positions. Similarly, a principle is *weak* if the percentage of exceptions is relatively high. If the ad-vice always applies, it is not a principle, but a **rule** (see below).

- ♟ **Importance** – a principle is *important* if the consequences are often disas-trous when violated. Thus a guideline is less important if the consequences of breaking it are not as severe. Similarly, a principle is also important if its application occurs frequently in practical play and, therefore, consistent fail-ure to follow it can accumulate considerable harm in a short period.

A guideline can be both important and strong, but there is little correlation between strength and importance!

In Soltis' *Grandmaster Secrets: Openings* he notes that all opening principles have many exceptions (are weaker), except one: *develop a rook to the same file that your opponent de-velops the queen*. Soltis states that this principle has very few exceptions (and thus is very strong).

Now consider the principle *when behind in material don't make even ("fair") trades of pieces*. This is one of the stronger principles, but it is certainly not a rule, as one could con-struct some counterexamples. The avoidance of trades when behind is extremely impor-tant; when violated the consequences are usually disastrous.

Soltis' rook-onto-queen's-file principle is roughly as strong, but not nearly as important as don't-trade-when-behind. If you don't develop a rook to the same file as your opponent's queen, then the rook may be less effective, but failure to do so is hardly as harmful as helping your opponent win a game by unnecessarily trading down into an easier-to-win position.

One of the most important principles, but not the strongest, is *in the opening move every piece once before you move any piece twice, unless there is a tactic*. The exceptions are numerous, but, as any beginner eventually learns, violating this principle is often disastrous. Therefore, weaker players should treat this principle as very strong until they become proficient enough to consistently and correctly identify exceptions.

A principle that is weak and not so important is *avoid doubled pawns*, because the net result of doubled pawns is often positive (see the archived *A Positional Primer*) and, even when doubled pawns are weak, they rarely are the primary reason that a beginner – or even an intermediate – loses a game.

An opening principle that is fairly strong and important is *don't move a piece to a square where the opponent can develop by attacking it (usually with a piece of lesser value), and force its retreat*. For example, after **1 Nf3 e6 2 g3** a move like **2...Bc5(?)** does not make sense.

White to play after 2...Bc5(?)

This encourages **3 d4**, which not only forces the bishop to move again, but is additionally a very useful move for White (see *It's Not Really Winning a Tempo!* 8-5).

Another strong – and very helpful – guideline is *whenever a player makes a break move with a center (d- or e-) pawn and cannot capture back with a pawn, it is usually correct to capture the break pawn*. If the player making the break move can capture back with a pawn, then the capture is not necessarily correct. Here is an example:

(see following diagram)

Black to play after 1 e4 c5 2 Nf3 Nc6 3 d4

Although 3 d4 is not strictly a break move (since the black c-pawn is not fixed), it has the power of one, since Black cannot pass the d-pawn with 3...c4?. Here White cannot capture back with a pawn, so Black's best move is to trade the c-pawn for the central pawn with **3...cxd4**. Instead, the beginner move 3...e6? is strongly met with 4 d5.

Contrast this with the following:

White to play after 1 c4 c6 2 g3 d5

Again 3 c5 is not a good move, so 2...d5 has the effect of a break move. However, this time the capture 3 cxd5 is not necessarily indicated, because the black d-pawn, the central break, can be replaced with another pawn. White has options other than 3 cxd5, such as 3 Nf3 or 3 Bg2, when Black's capture 3...dxc4 is OK, but the extra pawn is difficult to hold. Thus 3...dxc4 is not usually played by grandmasters. Not 3 b3? because of 3...dxc4 4 bxc4 Qd4, with a double attack on a1 and c4.

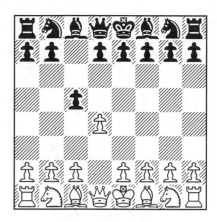

White to play after 1 d4 c5

In the Benoni, we have just the opposite – the pawn attack is not by a central pawn. Furthermore, it does not have the effect of a break, since pushing past is an option. Therefore, the main line is just to grab space with 2 d5.

Resolving Conflicts

The capability to prioritize principles in a given position is a very difficult and learned skill. The strength, importance, and overall applicability of principles vary *greatly* depending upon which "game state" you are in (see *The Six Common Chess States* 8-3).

Let's consider some simple examples:

Move every piece once before you move any piece twice, unless there is a tactic.
The bishop pair is worth about ½-pawn; don't give it up unless you get something for it.

Suppose your opponent threatens to trade a knight for a bishop in the opening and win the bishop pair. The only way to retain the bishop is to move it again and lose a tempo. Which principle should you obey?

In many opening positions the answer is relatively easy – if everything else is equal, you should move the bishop again and preserve the bishop pair. There are several reasons for this:

- ♟ Preserving the bishop pair is a tactic – if the bishop pair is worth ½ pawn that is a material cost, and winning material and mating are the primary aspects of tactics, so keep the bishop;

- ♟ At the start of the game a pawn is worth roughly three tempi, so a tempo is worth about a pawn and that is less than the ½-pawn you lose if you give up the bishop pair, so move the bishop;

🌢 Permanent liabilities are usually more important than transient ones – you might be able to gain back the tempo, but winning back the bishop pair requires a more concrete achievement.

En passant, *don't give up the bishop pair unless you get something for it* is an instance of the more general *never give up something positive for nothing*! If you sacrifice your queen for a rook to go into a winning king and pawn endgame you are giving up material for simplification into an easier endgame. That would not be violating the principle.

The decision to give up the bishop pair often goes the other way. Consider a typical position from the Advance Variation of the French Defense:

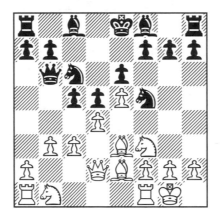

Black to play

In this type of fixed-center position, it is often incorrect for Black to play 1...Nxe3. Moreover, in support of *doubled pawns aren't always that bad*, if Black does capture on e3, it is usually incorrect for White to keep his pawn structure intact by playing 2 Qxe3, but instead to purposely double pawns with 2 fxe3.

Let's consider why White would voluntarily do this:

🌢 White's bad bishop is the one on e3 – it is blocked from its maximum mobility by the white center pawns. One more readily gives up a bad bishop than a good one.

🌢 There are no semi-open files on the board, but if Black captures on e3, White will already control the only semi-open file, the f-file, with his rook on f1. This is especially good since the pawn on e5 causes the black pawn on f7 to show signs of backwardness, and thus is more vulnerable than normal.

🌢 Black's entire play depends upon his break move ...c7-c5 and pressure on d4. If White can recapture on e3 with a pawn, then that frees his other pieces, since the d4-pawn would be overprotected via the pawns on e3 and c3, and Black could never break down that square nor generate strong central counterplay.

How can an improving player learn to properly apply principles? I suggest a several step process:

1.　Learn as many principles as you can. I have a Principles/Guidelines page at my website, and any book written for instruction contains many principles. Moreover, two books, Alburt and Lawrence's *Chess Rules of Thumb* and Soltis' *The Wisest Things Ever Said About Chess*, are devoted entirely to principles. Every annotated game collection is full of principles, so reading these books not only helps with planning, but also the applicability of principles. Make your own list if you think that will be helpful.

2.　Once you reach a position where you are "out-of-book", ask yourself "which principles should apply to this position?" You many not get them all, or get them right, or apply them correctly, but you will learn to do so more effectively. If you don't ask yourself applicable questions about the position, you may forget about something important that would guide you toward the right idea.

3.　Learn when specific principles apply. For example, some types of positions call for using (or ignoring) specific principles. This issue is discussed at length in *The Six Common Chess States* (8-3).

4.　Play many slow games and go over them with strong players – tell them when you are using a principle and get their opinion on whether you are applying it properly.

5.　Don't purposely ignore principles. If you think they apply in a particular position, then you should probably follow it. But, as you get stronger, in slow games always question a principle. Ask "Does it make sense in this position? Are there other guidelines that might have higher priority?" Some principles, even when most applicable, have a very minor impact, while others can be major. It is your job to try and figure out whether a minor one should be ignored, or whether it becomes major in the given situation. *This sometimes takes time, so not only does it pay to play slow to try to get the correct answer, but doing so helps you learn. Therefore, you can apply the same ideas more quickly and accurately to future similar situations.*

6.　Use common sense. For example, if a principle tells you to develop your pieces unless there is a tactic, you should do so, and not just ignore your development because weak opponents allow successful premature attacks. To help make these decisions use the meta-principle *principles that involve the result (win, draw, or loss) and/or tactics are more important than principles that involve other issues, such as piece activity* (see *The Principle of Tactical Dominance* 2-6).

You should never trade down into a king and pawn endgame unless you are sure of getting what you want. If you are ahead in material, then you want to be sure of winning. And, if you are behind in material, you usually want to be sure of at least drawing. This guideline is, of course, the extreme case of the principle *when behind in material don't make even ("fair") trades of pieces*. The ultimate simplification is into a king and pawn endgame! That makes the king and pawn version a very strong and important principle – essentially a rule!

Here is a great example from a game recently played at our chess club:

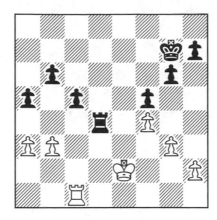

White to play

In this position, White decided (without much calculation!) that if he trades rooks, he can penetrate with the king on the queenside and cause problems. So against all principle (down a pawn) he played **1 Rd1??**, offering the trade of rooks into a king and pawn endgame.

This brings up an interesting meta-principle: *in non-analytical positions you can often play quickly by following principles; however, if you want to break a principle, then you usually need to analyze the situation carefully to make sure you really have an exception.* It is important to emphasize that one almost never plays an analytical position by following a guideline; I call this mistake *hand-waving* – roll up your sleeves and do the analysis!

By this meta-principle, White should not play 1 Rd1 without analyzing whether his idea actually works. Assuming it is an exception without analysis is not a good idea, because you should assume general principles work unless you carefully calculate otherwise. *If there are several pawns on the board in a king and pawn endgame, then, unless something unusual is happening, the player with one extra pawn almost always wins.* In the game, Black could not believe his good fortune and correctly replied **1...Rxd1 2 Kxd1**.

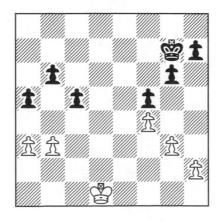

Black to play

Black must decide whether it is more important to advance his king first with 2...Kf6 or play 2...b5 to prevent White from creating a backward pawn with 3 a4. While this type of decision sometimes makes the difference between winning and losing, in this case it turns out the choice "only" determines how easily Black can win, as either is possible. Here are the main ideas:

a) 2...b5 3 Kd2

The position after the tricky 3 a4!? can transpose: 3...bxa4 4 bxa4 Kf6 5 Kd2 Ke6 6 Kd3 Kd5 wins, as in the main line 3 Kd2.

3...Kf6 4 Kd3 Ke6 5 Kc3

White can mix ideas with 5 a4 bxa4 6 bxa4 Kd5, but it transposes to the 3 a4!? line above. Instead, 5 b4 cxb4 6 axb4 loses to both 6...a4, when the a-pawn can be sacrificed to allow the black king to penetrate, and 6...axb4, when White has to spend time gathering the queenside pawns and Black mops up on the kingside.

5...Kd5 6 Kd3

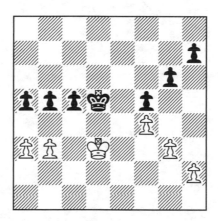

Black to play

This is a good position to know how to win ("good technique"), as similar positions occur frequently. Black can win in more than one way, but the most straightforward is:

6...c4+ 7 bxc4 bxc4+ 8 Kc3 Kc5 9 h3 h5 10 a4 Kd5 11 h4 Kc5

White must inevitably give way and Black now has several ways to win.

12 Kc2 Kd4 13 Kd2 c3+ 14 Kc2 Kc4 15 Kc1 Kd3 16 Kd1 c2+ 17 Kc1 Kc3 18 g4 hxg4 19 h5 g3

19...gxh5?? stalemate.

20 h6 g2 21 h7 g1R mate.

b) 2...Kf6

This makes the win more difficult than 2...b5, but not much more so for an experienced player.

3 a4

White hurries to make the black queenside pawns backward.

3...Ke6 4 Kd2 Kd5 5 Kd3

Now it is easiest to first run White out of kingside pawn moves.

5...h6 6 h3 h5 7 h4

If 7 Ke3, 7...c4 wins. If 7 Kc3!? Ke4 and – have to count! – Black wins the race after 8 Kc4 h4!. More difficult is 8...Kf3 9 Kb5 Kxg3 10 Kxb6 Kxf4 11 Kxa5 g5! (not 11...Ke3 12 Kb6 f4 13 a5 f3 14 a6 f2 15 a7 f1Q 16 a8Q) 12 Kb6 g4 13 hxg4 h4 and Black wins.

7...Kc6

Threatening 8...b5.

8 Kc4

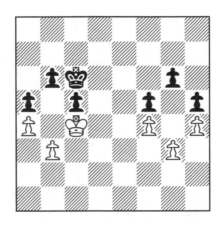

Black to play

8...b5!

Anyway! A good trick to know.

9 axb5+ Kb6

Zugzwang!

10 Kd3 Kxb5 11 Kc3 c4!

Another trick to get the outside passed pawn.

12 bxc4+ Kc5 13 Kb3 a4+ 14 Kxa4 Kxc4

and Black's king is closer to the pawns and wins – a good reason to fix the pawns first. With all the tricks involved, you can see why Black should play 2...b5 and not allow a3-a4, making the b-pawn backward.

The granddaddy of all principles is attributed to World Champion Emanuel Lasker: *when you see a good move, look for a better one.* You are trying to find the best move you can, given the circumstances, especially the time. This principle is both important – because it can be applied on almost every move – and strong, because most of the exceptions are trivial, like forced checkmates or book moves.

Another important principle is *having more pawns in the center is good* and its corollary: *when you have a choice of pawn captures, capture toward the center.* Notable exceptions toward the outside include the Exchange Variation of the Ruy Lopez: 1 e4 e5 2 Nf3 Nc6 3

Bb5 a6 4 Bxc6 dxc6 and the topical Nc3 variation of the Petroff: 1 e4 e5 2 Nf3 Nf6 3 Nxe5 d6 4 Nf3 Nxe4 5 Nc3 Nxc3 6 dxc3. *The nearer to the edge, the stronger the principle to capture toward the middle!*

In contrast to a principle, a **rule** has either no exceptions or the exceptions are easily enumerated.

Either side to play (opposition rule)

Here the rule is *if there is only one non-rook's pawn on the board, the offensive king is immediately in front of his pawn, and the opponent's king is on the same file separated by one square/rank, then whoever is not on move has the opposition and with correct play gets the desired result* (White to play draws; Black to play loses).

White to play wins (opposition rule exception)

Exception: once the offensive king reaches the sixth rank, then opposition no longer matters and the side with the pawn wins no matter who is to move. I have dubbed this the Tic-Tac-Toe rule; see the archived *King + Pawn vs. King*.

In *Chess for Zebras*, GM Rowson notes that giving an intermediate player more chess knowledge (such as specific opening or endgame sequences) does not make them a better player. I completely agree. However, some knowledge, especially in the form of general principles, is not only helpful, but somewhat necessary in becoming a better analyst and evaluator, the key skills for improvement.

8-2) The Most Important Strategic Decisions

Tactics dominate positional concepts and strategy. Nevertheless, a bad strategic decision can prove disastrous.

What are the most important strategic decisions? Let's exclude the short-term strategic decisions that should be made *on every move*:

- ♟ Which piece do I want to move?
- ♟ What am I trying to accomplish – what are the reasonable plans?
- ♟ Where does this piece want to go?
- ♟ Given this pawn structure, where should I place my pieces?
- ♟ How do I want to arrange my pawns?

We will also exclude decisions that are tactical (Can I save material? Does this combination work?), time management (Am I playing too fast?), and anything else "non-strategic".

That leaves the strategic decisions that can make or break your game, which only occur a few times during each game. I believe that these eight are most consequential:

1. Keep the position closed or open?
2. Trade queens or not?
3. Trade into a king and pawn endgame?
4. When to attack?
5. Where to attack?
6. Where to put the king?
7. How should I adjust my strategy for material?
8. Do I get enough compensation for an uneven trade/sacrifice?

Honorable Mention: Do I play passively and defend or give up material and counterattack?

For each, let's examine why these decisions are important, which criteria can help you make the decision, and what disasters can befall if you arrive at the wrong conclusion.

1. Keep the position closed or open?

In many positions a player must decide whether to use pawns (or, less commonly, sacrifice material) to keep the position closed or open. There are several factors which point one way or the other:

- ♟ Ahead in development? Open it.

- ♟ Behind in development? Close it.

- ♟ Want to attack on that side? Open it.

- ♟ Want to defend? Close it.

- ♟ Your king in that area? Close it.

- ♟ Opponent's king? Open it.

In the archived *Chess Master vs. Chess Amateur* I played White in each game and was always ahead in development, so I was looking to open the position. Conversely, in the game below, the human playing Black was trying to trick the computer (notoriously good in open positions) into closing the center. By clever play – and with help from his "unsuspecting" opponent – he was able to do so:

COMP Shredder-C.Garcia Palermo
Mercosur Cup, Vicente Lopez 2005

1 d4 d6 2 e4 g6 3 Nf3 Bg7 4 Nc3 a6 5 a4 b6 6 Bc4 e6 7 0-0 Ne7 8 Re1 Bb7

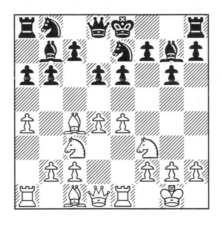

White to play

Ask yourself, *where is White developing all its pieces?* or *What part of the board are White's pieces attacking?* The answer is the center. So White should try to pry open the center and Black should try to lock it (also because he is playing a computer). That is why Black has placed his two center pawns side by side on the sixth rank, opposing White's two pawns on the fourth: with this "Modern Hippopotamus" setup if White plays d4-d5, Black can respond ...e6-e5, and if White plays e4-e5, Black can play ...d6-d5. If the black knight had been on the f6-square instead of e7, this anti-computer "close-it-up" strategy would not work, as Black could not respond ...d6-d5 to e4-e5 because of e5xf6.

9 d5?

This move threatens e6 and blocks in the bishop on b7. Is it a good move? No! It is terrible! Black naturally plays:

9...e5

With the center closed, Black has time to redeploy his light-squared bishop onto the c8-h3 diagonal and support the strong pawn break ...f7-f5. Meanwhile White's indicated pawn break, c4-c5, is almost nonexistent. Black got a good game, later won material and... eventually lost when the game got complicated – tactics dominate! The instructive game finished:

10 Qd2 h6 11 Qd3 Nd7 12 Nh4 0-0 13 b4 Bc8 14 Qe3 Nf6 15 Nf3 Nh7 16 Nd2 f5 17 f3 f4 18 Qd3 g5 19 Bb2 h5 20 b5 a5 21 Kf2 g4 22 Rh1 Ng6 23 Raf1 Bf6 24 Ke1 Kg7 25 Kd1 Ng5 26 Kc1 Qe7 27 Nd1 Bd7 28 Rhg1 Rf7 29 Nf2 g3 30 hxg3 fxg3 31 Nd1 Nf4 32 Qe3 h4 33 Re1 h3 34 Bf1 h2 35 Rh1 Nh7 36 Qc3 Rc8 37 Ne3 Bg5 38 Bc4 Ng6 39 Ndf1 Bf4 40 Kb1 Nh4 41 Bc1 Qg5 42 Rd1 Rcf8 43 Be2 Bc8 44 Ng4 Bxc1 45 Rxc1 Nxf3! 46 gxf3 g2 47 Nfxh2 gxh1Q 48 Rxh1 Rh8? 49 f4! Qxf4 50 Rf1 Qg5 51 Rxf7+ Kxf7 52 Qxc7+ Qe7 53 Nh6+ Kf6 54 N2g4+ Bxg4 55 Nxg4+ Kf7 56 Nh6+ Kf6 57 Qc6 Rd8 58 Nf5 Qd7 59 Qxb6 Ng5 60 Bd3 Nh3 61 c4 Nf4 62 c5 Nxd3 63 c6 Qe8 64 c7 Ra8 65 Qxd6+ 1-0

2. Trade queens or not?

Whenever there is a potential trade it can be a crucial decision, but two types of trades stand out as almost always critical: a trade of queens and trading off the final pieces into a king and pawn endgame.

When a queen trade is offered a player always has to ask himself, "Am I better off with the queens on the board or off?" This is crucial because there are many types of positions where one has a dynamic advantage (ahead in tempo, better king safety, attacking chances) and can be better with the queens on the board, but immediately worse (static weaknesses) if queens are traded!

Here are some of the considerations with the general tendency:

- ♟ If you are attacking – likely leave the queens *On the board*
- ♟ If you have the better endgame – Off
- ♟ If you are ahead in material – Off
- ♟ If you are behind in material – On
- ♟ If your king is safer – On
- ♟ If your opponent's king is exposed – On
- ♟ If you have structural weaknesses – On
- ♟ If the only other piece besides your queen is a knight and your opponent only has a queen and a bishop – On
- ♟ If your opponent's queen is more active or will be – Off

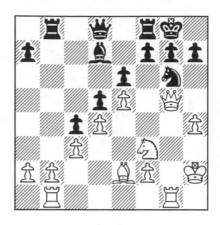

White to play

White has a strong attack along the g-file with a threat of h5 – therefore he should decline Black's offer to trade queens and play 1 Qg3.

Strangely enough, White understood that 1 Qxd8 was bad, but "kept the queens on" with **1 h5?**. This *still allows the trade of queens*, so it amounts to the same bad result. Of course, Black does not have to move the knight but, instead, traded queens himself with **1...Qxg5**, when after **2 Rxg5 Ne7 3 R1g1 g6** Black had pressure along the b-file and eventually won the endgame, although Black is probably not winning yet.

If instead White had avoided the trade of queens by playing the correct 1 Qg3!, threatening 2 h5 Ne7? 3 Qxg7 mate, then after 1...h5 2 Ng5 threatens the unstoppable 3 Bxh5 with a big attack. Notice that 1 Qg4 is not as accurate as 1 Qg3! because 1...f5 is a good defense. This last line is a good example of how proper analysis must back up proper strategy or the strategy may fail.

3. Trade into a king and pawn endgame?

King and pawn endgames are deterministic. Detailed analysis is required before entering a closely contested endgame of this type, and the evaluation should be either "win, lose, or draw". No shades of advantage are useful. It is critical to make sure you don't enter a king and pawn endgame where you are not getting what you want.

For example, if you have a rook and pawn against a rook, you should never trade rooks if the resulting king and pawn endgame is trivially drawn. Similarly, if you have the rook against the rook and pawn, you should never trade rooks if the king and pawn endgame is trivially won. In the following position, is 1...Rd7 a good move?

(see following diagram)

No, it is not, as after 2 Rxd7! Kxd7 3 Kd5! White has the opposition and wins (see the archived *King + Pawn vs. King*). Instead, Black could try 1...Rh5, when White cannot play 2

Rd5? since 2...Rxd5 leads to a draw; e.g. 3 Kxd5 Kd7!, or 3 exd5 Kd6 and Black draws the king and pawn endgame. Black's goal is to get his king in front of the pawn.

Black to play

The computer program *Fritz* prefers the straightforward 1...Re7!, when it is difficult for White to guard the pawn and prevent the black king from getting in front; e.g. 2 Rc3 Kd6 (but not 2...Rxe4+?? 3 Kd5+ winning – tactics!) or 2 Kd4 Rd7+ 3 Ke3 Rxd3 with a draw.

In the following position White has to decide whether to trade queens or allow 1...Qh1+.

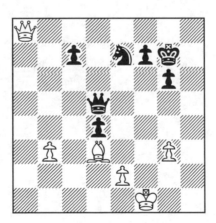

White to play

White was afraid of 1...Qh1+, and so played **1 Qxd5**, but that is dubious. However, he compounded the error after **1 Nxd5** with **2 Bc4?** (disastrous) **2...Nc3! 3 Kf2 Nxd4+** with a winning king and pawn endgame and White soon resigned!

So any idea was better for White than trading off the queen *and* the bishop! *Often it is better to allow an attack or even a loss of material than to trade into a king and pawn end-game that is easily won for your opponent.* The king and pawn endgame is the greater of two evils.

4. When to attack?

Of the questions, "who, what, where, when, how, and why?" the three that most apply to attack are "when, where, and how". But "how" is a difficult question, worthy of many entire books. So "how" is not a "one-time" strategic question, but a matter of technique, knowledge, and skill.

On the other hand, "when to attack" is legitimate. Everyone should know the famous dictum: *a premature attack is doomed to failure*, but many fail to heed that advice. Applying the adages *don't attack unless you have an advantage* and *don't start a fight until your army is ready* will help prevent you from attacking too soon. Finally, if you have an advantage in time, you must act to use it, because delaying action is, almost by definition, counterproductive.

It requires experience and good guidance to learn the nuances of when to attack but, in general, if you avoid premature attacks you are 80% of the way there.

5. Where to attack?

This is another pertinent attack question. Assuming material is equal, the answer is usually either:

1.   Where the opponent has an *exploitable* weakness;
2.   Where you have the predominance of forces;
3.   Where you have a pawn majority;
4.   Where your opponent's king resides (assuming it can be attacked);
5.   (In a locked center) Toward where your *locked* d- and e-pawns point; and/or
6.   (In other locked pawn positions) Where the base of your opponent's pawn chain lies.

Learn these simple principles. These can often provide powerful results by correctly indicating where you want the action to be. For example, if you castle on opposite sides, then #4 says to play where his king is, not yours!

If you are in a typical locked center (King's Indian or French pawn formations), then use #5 to find your pawn break. For example, in the main line of the King's Indian after **1 d4 Nf6 2 c4 g6 3 Nc3 Bg7 4 e4 d6 5 Be2 0-0 6 Nf3 e5 7 0-0 Nc6 8 d5 Ne7**

(see following diagram)

White's locked d- and e-pawns point to the queenside, so his break move is c4-c5 and White wants to play on the queenside. Black's locked d- and e-pawns point toward the kingside, so his most useful break move is ...f7-f5 and he wants to play on the kingside.

Note that both answers are also consistent with #6, attacking toward the base of a pawn chain. In the "Bayonet Attack" both sides strive for their goals with **9 b4 Nh5** and a later **...f7-f5**.

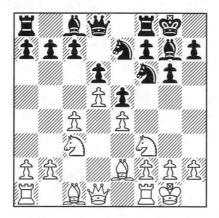

White to play

6. Where to put the king?

The five possibilities are:

1. Kingside
2. Queenside
3. In the center
4. The same side as the opponent's king
5. The opposite side to the opponent's king

For example, suppose you win a pawn in the opening, and your opponent has no compensation. Then, assuming that neither side has castled and everything else is equal, where should you castle?

Easy! The *same side* as the opponent's king. Because if you castle first, your opponent should follow the strategy of what to do when behind and complicate (see *When You're Winning, It's a Whole Different Game* 7-3). Therefore, he should castle on the opposite side and start a complex game where his pawn deficit is not nearly as important. You, on the other hand, should do all you can to avoid such a situation (within reason), and try to make the game as simple and calm as possible by castling on the same side, when you are just up a pawn with pleasant prospects.

This "common sense" strategic decision-making will make your job much easier!

What is the most common reason why you would *not* have to make a strategic decision as to where to place your king?

Answer: When it is a book move! For example, suppose you have chosen to play the Ruy Lopez as White and your opponent plays the main line of the Closed Variation. Then, assuming you have studied that line and wish to play it, you answer 4...Nf6 with 5 0-0 not because you are "deciding" to castle kingside, but because that is the recommended move. The strategic decision was not *where to put your king during the game*, but instead *what opening you would study before the game!*

7. How should I adjust my strategy for material?

This is another important strategic consideration that only occurs when one side is playing with a material advantage. For example, when you are ahead, that same *When You're Winning, It's a Whole Different Game* (7-3) tells how you should adjust your strategy.

Many players make a big mistake by playing uneven positions using the same principles as in even positions, yet this is often a big mistake. To make a football analogy, field position is important in a tie game, but not if it is 70-0!

8. Do I get enough play for an uneven trade/sacrifice?

The decision to give up material "long-term" is usually an interesting one. For example, the material sacrificed might be small – you might give up the bishop pair to create a pawn weakness or get an outpost square for a knight. More dramatically, you may be making a large investment – for example, sacrificing a piece for a long-term, unclear attack. In any case, such a big strategic decision is usually critical, so take some time and use your experience and judgment to decide if the risk is worth it.

Your evaluation of how good the position would be if you do *not* make the sacrifice is important. For example, suppose you can sacrifice a bishop for what looks like an unclear attack. If you are otherwise equal if you *don't* sacrifice, then the sacrifice is likely a reasonable or at least instructive idea. But if you are winning easily or at least much better without the sacrifice, then why go into an unclear position?

The strategic consideration about real material sacrifices does not include *pseudo-sacrifices*, where you temporarily give up material to forcibly win it back shortly thereafter. Such "sacrifices" entail no risk nor judgment, as proper analysis will simply reveal these as good tactics.

Honorable Mention: Do I play passively and defend or give up material and counterattack?

This is almost the opposite of #8. In this case your opponent is threatening to win material. You have to decide whether to passively place your pieces to defend or to jettison some small amount of material – usually a pawn, but sometimes the exchange or more – to keep your army active.

For example, in rook and pawn endgames it is often better to sacrifice a pawn and play a pawn down with an active rook than it is to passively guard all your pawns and tie down both your rook and king. One way to decide is to ask: "If I passively defend can I do anything at all? If not, *and* my opponent gets many tempi to bring up his king and add pressure, will I be able to do nothing and draw?" If your opponent gets such a free position *and* can make progress, then passive defense is useless and active defense, which likely may require a pawn sacrifice, is required.

8-3) The Six Common Chess States

Not California, New York...

In his great book, *Secrets of Grandmaster Endings*, Soltis correctly notes that many weaker players don't play endgames well because they are not fully aware that in the endgame the principles have changed; they continue to follow principles that make sense in the middlegame but not in the endgame. Examples include activation of the king (necessary in endgames but usually disastrous earlier), use of tempi (crucial not to waste them earlier but often useful to be patient in the endgame), or space (useful in the middlegame and often meaningless in the endgame), etc. In this sense the middlegame and the endgame can be thought of as different game "states". Those chess states are also chronological "stages" of the game, but not all game states have to be chronological stages.

I would like to extend Andy's idea to not just those two game states, but the entire game. There are many guidelines that are only used in a very specific game state, such as "play a minority pawn attack with the following pawn formation" or "in the following situations a knight is often better than a bishop". However, it seems to me that there are primarily six commonly occurring game states, each with their own set of guidelines:

1. The Opening
2. The Endgame
3. Castling on opposite sides with queens still on the board
4. Middlegames with a closed, fixed center
5. Positions where one player is winning easily (this is usually the dominant state even if another state exists)
6. Most other positions, especially other middlegames with an open center

If a player learns to recognize these states, understands why each state has special considerations, and learns specific methods of conducting a game when in a state, he is well on his way toward achieving better planning and making more logical moves. While there are some guidelines that are more or less true at all times, such as "don't give up the material for no compensation" or "if you see a good move, look for a better one", many guidelines change dramatically from one state to another.

There are other (primarily more specific) states, but being aware of these six should suffice to cover most general situations. Let us consider each, providing it's the key principles:

1. The Opening

From the start of the game until all your pieces are mobilized for middlegame action.

While most students know what the opening guidelines are supposed to be, many weaker players wish to play the opening like State #6: Other middlegames with an open center (they may also treat any of the other five states this way, sometimes with disastrous consequences – hence this article). Under certain conditions this works, but most of the time they end up with a "premature attack" and/or behind in development. The key aspects of the opening are:

a)   Efficient development – while many GMs often move pieces twice or delay castling, they understand these exceptions very well. Beginners and intermediates would be better off just mobilizing their entire armies as quickly as possible, using "Move every piece once before you move any piece twice, unless it wins material or prevents losing material." Even some intermediate players would be a lot better in this phase if they learned to mobilize their rooks before starting "action".

b)   Castle your king into safety – it is the only move that "gains" a tempo by developing two pieces at once, as opposed to beginners that think castling "loses" a tempo for the (non-existent) attack.

c)   Use your pieces to try to control (or neutralize your opponent's control of) the center.

d)   Often consider developing slow pieces (knights) before fast pieces.

e)   Make moves that you must play before moves which leave you choices – it is more flexible.

f)   Don't take inordinate amounts of time to play opening moves – save your time for later positions that are much more critical (but never play quickly "just to see what happens").

2. The Endgame

The part of the game where material is diminished and the king can take an active part.

a)   Often trying to do something too fast is wrong – repeating the position or outright loss of tempo may even be beneficial.

b)   The king must go out and fight – king safety is still important, but the king is more often safe in the fight!

c)   The concept of space is often useless, except possibly for pawns threatening to promote. It is usually easy for an opponent's forces to get "behind" advanced pawns and therefore the space advantage in the middlegame may turn into vulnerability in the endgame.

d)   Pawn structure can be thought of differently in the deep endgame. That weak isolated pawn in the middlegame may be the passed winner in the endgame.

e)   Centralization is important sometimes, but "uncentralized" concepts, such as having the "outside" passed pawn, may the key to victory. A centralized pawn formation can be inferior to the "outside" pawn formation that causes a king to go out of its way to stop.

f)   Faster pieces gain more power as the board is cleared, so unless all the pieces are in one area, knights may become relatively weaker.

g)   For the player who is ahead, keeping mating material (such as a final pawn) may become important. So in many cases the bishop and knight, which are worth more than 3 pawns in the opening, may become worth much less if few pawns remain on the board.

3. Castling on opposite sides with queens still on

This is the most violent type of middlegame. The rules of engagement change; in some cases they are similar to the rarer state where the enemy king is exposed in the opening (not discussed in this article):

a)   You throw the kitchen sink (often led by pawns, but not always) at the enemy king. Whoever gets there first usually wins.

b)   Material is less important here than in any other state (endgames are second because of the changing concept of material – see '2g' above). Often it is helpful to lose a pawn in front of the enemy king, opening files for rooks and queens. And piece sacrifices to get to the enemy king are much more likely to be effective.

c)   Keeping queens on the board is a big help to the one whose attack is faster.

d)   Pawn moves in front of your king that do not blockade the pawn structure can be disastrous; pawn moves that blockade the pawn structure in front of your king are often wonderful.

4. Middlegames with a closed, fixed center

(or at least very stable, such as possibly a Stonewall)

a)   If all four center pawns are locked, use the famous guideline, "See how your center (d- and e-pawns) are pointing. If they point toward the kingside, you should expand and attack there; similarly, if they point to the queenside, then queenside action is required.

b)   Often in games like this you can "lose" one side of the board and win another. If you win the side of the board with the enemy king, that is usually enough! For example, in the famous Spassky-Geller match in 1968, Spassky played the Closed Sicilian and attacked on the kingside; Geller on the queenside. Geller "won" the queenside, usually first, but still lost when Spassky won the kingside, where Geller had castled. The story goes that Geller said afterwards, "I did what I was supposed to – I attacked queenside" and a kibitzer replied, "Yes, but the king is more important!"

c)   In closed positions tempi are less crucial. This allows action like extensive knight maneuvers. Due to the closed structure, the knights may be relatively more effective than the bishops.

d)   Opening files via pawn "break" moves are often crucial to provide mobility for rooks. The player who can get his rooks into the action first usually has a big advantage.

5. Positions where one player is winning easily

(a condition overriding all other states; for example, an opening where one player is winning easily needs to incorporate the principles below, possibly even in priority to normal opening principles)

"Winning easily" varies according to the strength of the players. For intermediate tournament players this may mean being up the exchange or more (> +1.75 pawn advantage) with no compensation for his opponent, while weaker players may have to be up at least a piece (> +3.25). This situation is not covered in most books because good players often resign when playing other good players who know how to win, but many beginning and intermediate players are often baffled as to the correct strategy because they don't read about it very much! Principles and more are provided in *When You're Winning, It's a Whole Different Game* (7-3).

6. Most other positions, especially other middlegames with an open center

This is the "plurality" of positions – the ones that occur the most often. Most of the guidelines you know and read about usually apply best to these wide-ranging positions, so my "special" notes below are few:

    a)   Weak pawn structures are often more of a liability, since they can be easily accessed by the enemy and can become vulnerable.

    b)   Piece values are more towards the norm.

    c)   Trades or pawn maneuvers can change the state from this state to one of the others, so you have to be mentally ready to shift gears, *à la* Soltis, etc.

Conclusion

Recognizing these states and understanding the underlying principles and guidelines can help put you on the correct path towards better planning and candidate move selection. I believe World Champion Alexander Alekhine said something like: "The idea is not to find the correct move, but to find the correct plan and then the move which best implements it."

8-4) Opening Lines to Create Mobility

Anything which discourages you from playing (e.g. worrying about your rating) is likely unproductive; anything which encourages you to play (e.g. incentives, titles, prizes, camaraderie, a stronger mind) is likely productive.

"I get all my pieces out and then I don't know what to do" is a common complaint. Sometimes students do need advice on "planning", but often the source of their problem is that they don't understand the concept of *break moves* and how to give their pieces – especially rooks – more mobility in the middlegame.

A "break" move is a pawn move that "breaks up" an opponent's (fixed) pawn chain by attacking the opponent's pawns with that pawn. In his classic work *Pawn Power in Chess*, Kmoch calls this move a *liberation lever*.

Let's start with a common example:

1 d4 d5

This is a "double d-pawn opening", defined by pawns initially fixed on d4 and d5. The solidity of this pattern and its tendencies to lead to dense pawn structures is why it is commonly called a "closed opening".

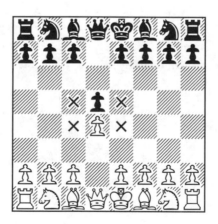

White to play

White's two break moves are c4 and e4. Note that Black's pawn is "fixed" on d5 and thus has no choice to avoid exchange if White plays these breaks. This lack of flexibility gives White the opportunity to force semi-open the c or e-files. Correspondingly, Black's two break moves are ...c5 and ...e5.

2 c4

This is the easier – and tactically justified – classic break that defines the *Queen's Gambit*. The other break move, 2 e4, leaves the e-pawn unguarded and thus is the rarer (but fun!) *Blackmar-Diemer Gambit.*

Break moves are important:

1. You need a pawn to best attack any pawn that can easily be guarded by other pawns – piece attacks against pawns are usually ineffective if the attacked pawn can be guarded by another pawn.

2. You can open files for rooks when either side exchanges after a break move. The adage is *the player who uses his rooks best in an opening usually "wins" the opening.*

3. It can enable you to trade a lesser pawn for a more valuable one, such as a flank pawn for a center pawn or an isolated pawn for a non-isolated one. A pawn attack that is *not* against a fixed pawn does not necessarily invoke a trade – it might simply be bypassed by the opponent advancing his pawn – so those type of break moves are often less effective because of the opponent's flexibility.

In double d-pawn positions it is much more difficult to break with the e-pawns because they are not as easily supported by bishops, and the opponent's knights easily protect the e4- and e5-squares from break possibilities when naturally developed at f3 and f6.

Breaking with the c-pawns sometimes enables one to trade a flank pawn for a center pawn. Also, the break c2-c4 allows White to put his knight *behind* the c-pawn where it is not only more effective, but gives White some needed space for his other pieces. This leads to the guideline: *Don't put your knight in front of your c-pawn in double d-pawn openings.*

The Queen's Gambit is not really a gambit. If Black takes the c-pawn with 2...dxc4, then White could always recover it with 3 Qa4+, although 3 Nf3 is much more common.

Suppose after **1 d4 d5**, instead of 2 c4, White plays **2 Nf3**. Then it is less flexible for Black to play the natural-looking **2...Nc6(?)** because this knight blocks his best break move ...c5. [Yes, I know masters have occasionally played this move, but it's not for beginners for the reasons stated...]

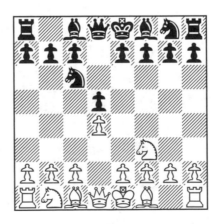

White to play

Black is somewhat cramped and already (!) it will be difficult for his rooks to find open lines. For example, the c-file will likely remain closed for him for quite a while. But White can still play his break move **3 c4**.

At this point if Black plays 3...e6 to reinforce d5 he has a cramped position, and after that his only remaining break move, ...e6-e5, is hard to achieve and wastes time. However, playing 3...e5 is not a strong possibility (then 4 Nxe5 leads to an even better game for White), while after **3...e6 4 Nc3** White has more than his normal opening advantage. The game might continue **4...Nf6 5 Bg5 Be7 6 e3 0-0 7 Bd3 Bd7** (passive, but consistent with Black's previous play) **8 0-0 Rc8 9 Rc1**

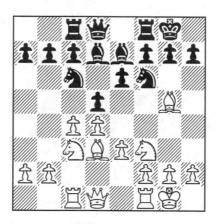

Black to play

White has a very nice advantage due to his extra space and mobility. For example, compare the two queenside rooks on c1 and c8:

- ♟ White's rook has more mobility and he can make the c-file semi-open for him.

- ♟ Black's rook has moved "toward the center" but is not really doing anything, primarily because White's break move was achieved and Black's was blocked.

No wonder Black players here might complain "they have nothing to do"!

In the normal move order with **1 d4 d5 2 c4** Black has three main replies, all pawn moves:

a) 2...c6 (Slav)

b) 2...e6 (Queen's Gambit Declined)

c) 2...dxc4 (Queen's Gambit Accepted)

Other moves are rarer and may lead to a cramped game. For example 2...Nf6(?) is a common beginner's inaccuracy:

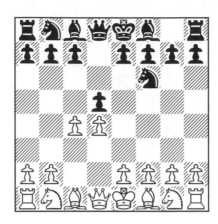

White to play

After **3 cxd4 Nxd5 4 Nf3!** (*Rybka* thinks the common 4 e4!? Nf6 5 Nc3 e5! is also good for White but is much more tricky) White has a very pleasant game; after most normal Black replies, **5 e4** will be annoying. This not a trap, but does give White more than his normal opening advantage.

Another reason that break moves are important is tactical in basis. Suppose after **1 d4 d5 2 Nf3 e6** White decides to attack the d-pawn with pieces, starting with **3 Nc3?!**:

Black to play

This move again violates the guideline *don't put your knight in front of your c-pawn in double d-pawn openings*. In accordance with the first reason for playing break moves (and a basic idea of counting material exchanges explained in the archived *A Counting Primer*), *no matter how many pieces (non-pawns) White uses to attack d5, the single defending pawn on e6 always suffices.*

Suppose we ignore Black's moves but additionally attack the d5-pawn with g2-g3, Bg2, Nd2-f1-e3:

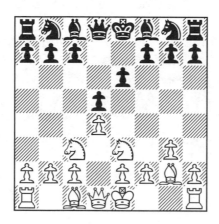

Black to play

From the standpoint of the d5-pawn's safety, these extra non-pawn attackers are not effective since the pawn will always be adequately guarded. *But once White attacks the d-pawn with even one pawn, such as after the better 3 c4, then the future possibility of inadequate defense arises and the black pawn is no longer so safe.* This possibility arises quite often, since at the start of the game every pawn attack can potentially be countered with a pawn defense! Later, if the pawn structures become asymmetric, then the possibility of consistent, equal pawn defense for each attack diminishes and the play may become sharper. This is a big reason why symmetric positions are more drawish.

Break moves occur in many positions, but especially in positions with locked centers, as occurs in many lines of the French Defense. For instance, **1 e4 e6 2 d4 d5 3 e5** is the "Advance Variation", marked by White's 3 e5, locking the center. The Advance Variation is popular among beginners but less so masters, because beginners are attracted by the slight gain in "space" via 3 e5. Here Black's break moves are ...c7-c5 and ...f7-f6. As a general guideline, *break moves are best played against the* base *of the pawn chain*, just like it is better to chop down a tree from the base – with both pawns and trees, chopping the base also weakens the top!

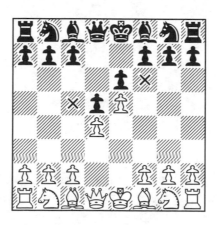

Black to play

So here the more effective break move for Black is **3...c5**, attacking the base at d4. 3...c5 is usually the only move recommended for Black here! Consistently, White usually keeps his pawn chain intact with **4 c3** and Black continues the pressure on d4 with **4...Nc6**.

Now suppose White errs and plays **5 Bb5(?)**. This is not much of a pin since the knight is happily guarded by b7 and easily unpinned. If Black plays the normal queen move **5...Qb6** and White captures **6 Bxc6** how should Black recapture?

The answer is that 6...Qxc6 keeps the pawns undoubled, but 6...bxc6 allows Black a *second* break move on d4 after the first capture, so **6...bxc6** is even better! White's center will fall after **7 Nf3 cxd4 8 cxd4 c5**. With this second break move White can no longer maintain a pawn on d4. So Black has a good game because e5 is also weak and his bishop pair is worth about an extra ½ pawn.

Another well-known break move position occurs in the main line of the King's Indian Defense:

1 d4 Nf6 2 c4 g6 3 Nc3 Bg7 4 e4 d6 5 Be2 0-0 6 Nf3 e5 7 0-0 (7 dxe5 dxe5 8 Qxd8 Rxd8 9 Nxe5 does not win a pawn because of 9...Nxe4 and if 10 Nxf7?? then 10...Bxc3+ wins a piece) **7...Nc6 8 d5 Ne7**

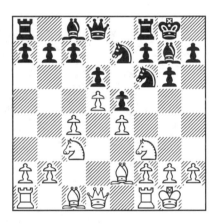

White to play

What is Black's best break move (hint: it is not legal – yet)?

The answer is to *break at the base with ...f7-f5 as soon as possible after ...Nd7, ...Ne8, or ...Nh5*. Notice that the "other" White pawn base, c4, is not only not fixed (and thus a break ...b7-b5 could in some lines be answered by c4-c5, but also not in the center and on the "wrong" side of the board. Using the principle *When all four central pawns are fixed, attack on the side where your center (d- and e-) pawns point*, then White wishes to attack queenside and Black wishes to attack kingside.

Some weaker players want to break first here with ...c7-c6, but that break is both on the wrong side of the board and less effective against the top of White's pawn chain.

The ...f7-f5 break is also why it is often incorrect to play ...Re8 too early in these type of pawn structures, those that commonly occur in King's Indians, Pirc Defenses, and others. If

White is going to commit himself to locking the center with d4-d5, then blindly "developing the rook into the middle" with ...Re8 is just bad. Instead, the rook is much more well positioned on f8, where it is behind and supports the break move, and far more effective than stuck behind two locked e-pawns! Sometimes even if it looks like you might need the rook to support ...e5 it is still the wrong idea! Of course, in some lines if Black captures ...e5xd4 instead of allowing d4-d5, then *the center is not locked, the ...f7-f5 break is probably wrong, and ...Re8 is usually justified.*

These eight moves have been the main line tabiya in the King's Indian for 60 years and a favorite for Black of great attacking players like Kasparov, Fischer, Korchnoi, and Radjabov.

The above discussion forms a basis as to why I suggest that players looking to improve learn and play the French and King's Indian Defenses for at least a few months each. The pawn structures in these two openings are often reached in other openings, so a basic understanding of how to play both is usually a good sign that one understands pawn structures in general and can survive many irregular (and some regular) openings. I have never had a student who has followed this advice tell me later that they regretted it; while many do not stick with the French or King's Indian, their experience while playing these proved both transferable and valuable.

Break moves do not have to be played against fixed pawns, but they are most effective against them because the opponent's pawn does not have a chance to advance. However, break moves against non-fixed pawns can still be effective. For example, you might consider the "Open" variation of the Sicilian as having a break move:

1 e4 c5 2 Nf3 Nc6

Or 2...d6 or 2...e6. Now White wants to "break" Black's control of d4, so he plays:

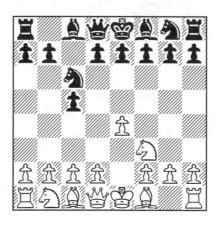

White to play

3 d4

Although his c-pawn is not fixed, it cannot safely advance, so 3 d4 has the power of a break move. Black is forced to capture because White threatens 4 d5, driving the knight out of the center with a nice advantage. Note that playing d2-d4 not only contests Black's pawn control of d4, it also enables the white queen to attack it as well, but the fight is not yet over...

3...cxd4 4 Nxd4

This is the most popular Open variation of the Sicilian (as would also be the case by substituting 2...e6 or 2...d6).

For each opening you play, you should try to understand where your break moves are, the most effective times to play them, and where your pieces go before and after the break. Armed with this knowledge, you will have a much smoother development and more to do in the middlegame!

Break moves are just as important in the middlegame – and sometimes in the endgame – as they are in the opening. This topic could easily fill an additional column or three, but one example will have to suffice. Evaluate the position from the practice game D.Heisman-H.Schwartz, 1997:

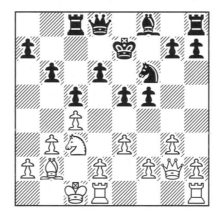

White to play

White has the better of it with Black's pieces uncoordinated and his king safety questionable, but how to take advantage of this? Given sufficient time, Black can overcome his problem, so the right answer is to break open the position at once:

1 d4!

Now Black cannot prevent White from making big progress in the center. Notice that the fixed pawn on c5 means that Black cannot avoid letting White have at least one semi-open file.

The game concluded nicely:

1...Qc7?

Better is 1...cxd4 2 exd4 e4, attempting to keep the position closed. However, White has the advantage since he will – you guessed it – break open the kingside with either 3 d5 and then a further break move f2-f3, or even the immediate 3 f3. But after 1...Qc7? White crashes through and it is all over:

2 dxe5 dxe5 3 Nd5+ Nxd5 4 Rxd5

Black has no way to guard the fifth rank and prevent large material loss.

4...Kf7 5 Rxe5 Rd8 6 Rxf5+ Kg8 7 Qe4 h6 8 Qe6+ Kh7 9 Rf7 1-0

Next time you do not know what to do with your rooks in the opening (and you *do* want to develop your rooks in the opening!), take a "break" and watch your mobility – and results – rise.

8-5) It's Not Really Winning a Tempo!

Not all threats are helpful.

Why is the sequence **1 e4 d5 2 exd5 Qxd5 3 Nc3** supposed to be good for White?

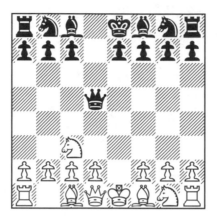

Black to play

Because White is supposedly winning a "tempo" – that is, he gains a move because he gets to bring his knight out while Black "wastes time", forced to use his turn to move the queen a second time. But White is not really winning a tempo by attacking the queen – that is just what we call the result in this particular case. We can prove that this type of attack, in general, does not always win a tempo. For this purpose, suppose that Black plays the bad move **3...Qc5**.

"Wow!" thinks White, "If every time I move my knight and attack the queen I win another tempo, then if I won one with 3 Nc3, then I can win another the same way with **4 Na4**.

Black to play

See something wrong with this logic? You should. The key is that "winning a tempo" has little to do with attacking a piece with a weaker piece so that the stronger piece has to move (!), although that could indeed be a very good idea.

The correct way to look at it is, "Suppose I make a threat. Now unless that threat is unstoppable or ignorable, I have to assume that my opponent will meet the threat, so the execution of the threat is not going to happen, and I can pretty much ignore that possibility. Instead, I will suppose that my opponent will meet the threat in the best way he can. As a result the position is altered, where I have made the threatening move and he has made his response. Who has gained more from this pair of moves?"

If the answer is you gained more, then your threat is a viable candidate move (but don't forget, "If you see a good move, look for a better one!") and you may have indeed "gained a tempo" because you have used your tempo more effectively making the threat than your opponent has meeting it. On the other hand, if your opponent gains more from this same sequence, then making the threat is just a bad idea – it may even "lose a tempo"! With this in mind, let's re-examine the prior two cases:

1.   After 2...Qxd5 3 Nc3 White is moving his knight from a fairly immobile square (b1) to a much more active one (c3). On the other hand, Black has to move his queen from an active (though vulnerable) square d5, to a possibly equally active one. So White gains by spending his tempo activating his knight, while Black gains safety, but not positional value, by moving off d5.

2.   On the other hand, after 3...Qc5 4 Na4 Qa5, just the opposite has happened: Black is using the tempo to move from one OK square to another, while White is moving his knight from a good square, c3, to a weaker one, a4 ("knight on the rim, your future is dim/grim"). Therefore, Black is doing more with his tempo and White's move is bad, even if he is "making the queen move".

Therefore, the key theme is: *you should not make a threat with the expectation that your opponent might not see it, but rather because you believe the tempo will do more for you than it will for your opponent.* In other words, there are primarily two situations when you should make a threat: 1) if your threat can't be met, or 2) if it can be met, but when that happens you "gain" relatively more from your threatening move than your opponent does meeting the threat.

One of the most difficult transitions from beginner to intermediate is to understand that *chess is not a game where each side makes threats and the one who misses the most or the final threat loses.* In order to progress, you should recognize that, even at the intermediate level, almost all the basic tactical threats will be recognized and defended (in slow chess!), so the "percentage" of missed threats should not be a consideration in the decision whether to make a threat.

However, in beginner's games, missed threats are so common that players get used to making simple threats just to see if they will defended, and this habit is hard to break. That is one reason why *players who seek out stronger opponents improve more rapidly: their opponents will almost always defend well against simple threats, teaching you that many threats are counterproductive.* On the other hand, a weaker opponent might not see your threat, and that reinforces your psychology that such threats are "good", and so you likely will keep making them, even if they are not good moves.

The following is another very common example of "not winning a tempo". After **1 d4 d5 2 Nf3 Nf6 3 e3 e6 4 Bd3 c5 5 c3**, Black decides to "win a tempo" with **5...c4(?)**

White to play

The reason 5...c4 does not win a tempo is because it takes one tempo for Black to make the move and one tempo for White to respond. So in order to really gain a tempo the pawn on c4 has to either:

1.   Be going to a square that it is better than on c5, while forcing the bishop in a spot that is no better;
2.   Be going to a square that is about equal to c5, while forcing the bishop to an inferior square; or
3.   Trap the bishop.

...in each case gaining more for Black than for White. But here White responds **6 Bc2** and all Black has done is to take the pressure off of d4 and thus strengthened White's up-coming "break" move e3-e4 (see *Break Moves: Opening Lines to Create Mobility* 8-4).

Another argument that 5...c4 is "good" is that it "gains space", but this is also some-what nebulous. Which space did it gain? It did not gain the vacated c5 since White's d-pawn now controls that square. It did not really gain d3 because although White does have to vacate that square, Black has no access to it either. 5...c4 did block White from playing c3-c4, but I would not describe this as gaining space.

Understanding Threats

Most of my students, when asked to define "threat", are at a loss for a reasonable answer. *A "threat" is a move which, if not stopped by the opponent's reply (or, similarly, ignoring any possible reply), can do something harmful to the opponent and/or useful for you next move:* create a passed pawn, make the opponent's king unsafe, win material, mate, ruin the opponent's pawn structure, etc. It is important to note that *not all threats are good moves nor are all threats necessarily very harmful.*

A trivial example of a threat that is not a very good move is **1 e4 e5 2 Nf3 Qh4??**. Black threatens the e-pawn, but while this is a "good" threat it is not a good move because the threat can obviously be stopped by **3 Nxh4**.

Threats that are not harmful are also common. Suppose you are ahead a queen and your opponent makes a move to "threaten" to win a pawn. It may be correct to ignore the threat and continue to develop your pieces, or just let him take the pawn if in doing so he has to trade off a few pieces. In the latter case the move is not a threat because, although he wins material, the net result (trading off pieces when down a queen) is not good for him.

Consider the following after **1...Ke6**:

White to play

Black "threatens" to win the d-pawn, but actually it is not much of a threat since White would be very happy if he ignores it, say with **2 Ke2**, and allows **2...Rxd6 3 Rxd6+ Rxd6 4 Rxd6+ Kxd6** trading off all the rooks and leaving White with an easy win.

Don't Miss Threats That Also Have Other Functions

In *Everyone's 2nd Chess Book* I have a chapter "Just Because It Is Forced". I examine the common problem where a player makes a forcing threat and the opponent replies as expected. The first player then thinks, "Every time my opponent moves, I need to make sure I understand why he made that move and what it does. Therefore, I deduce that he made that move because it is the only move that meets my threat. OK. Now what can I do next?"

Do you see the possible error in this logic?

The problem is that a forced move may still contain threats. So while it is true that the opponent made that move because it is forced, that does not mean it cannot contain new threats that are "incidental" to meeting your threat. If you don't search for those new threats, you may be in for some nasty surprises. Suppose White has just played **1 Rh1** threatening the black queen:

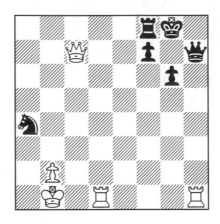

Black to play

Black replies **1...Qg7**. White may reason that this was the only way to save the queen and forget to look that Black is now threatening **2...Qxb2** mate! So he may play another "threatening" move like 2 Qc4 and lose instantly. This type of error is more common than you might suppose.

It is a good idea to always consider all of your, and your opponent's, checks, captures, and threats. Some threats can be even more forcing than a capture or even a check. For example, any time your opponent has a possible reply to your candidate move that threatens a forced mate, this sequence must be examined with high priority. The forcing nature of the threat, plus the finality of the possibility you might not be able to stop it, makes it extremely likely that the sequence may be critical. Any candidate move of yours that allows an *unstoppable* mate-in-one threat reply must be discarded unless that candidate move also contains a threat to mate first which is not simultaneously stoppable by the opponent's mate-in-one threat reply (got that?). The following two examples are easy to understand:

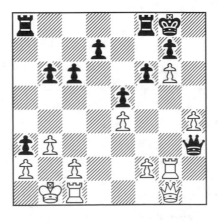

White to play

In this position 1 Rh2 is not a good candidate move since Black can play 1...Qc3 threatening an unstoppable mate on b2 next move.

But remove the pawn on white pawn on h4 and it is a completely different story:

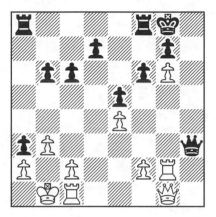

White to play

Now **1 Rh2 Qc3** is met by the common motif: **2 Rh8+!** (clearance for the queen) **2...Kxh8 3 Qh1+** (or 3 Qh2+) **3...Qh3** (just delaying the inevitable) **4 Qxh3+ Kg8 5 Qh7** mate.

So 1 Rh2 is winning, as the Rh8+ threat can only be met by 1...Qxh2 or 1...Qh6 and Black loses his queen. Coincidentally, these two positions are also good examples of why, when castling on opposite sides with queens on the board, it is often not a bad idea to sacrifice pawns in front of your opponent's king to open files for your rooks and queen!

Exceptions

There is a third reason you might make a threat besides "threats that can't be met" and "threats where you gain more than your opponent meeting them". If you are losing badly, you might make a difficult-to-see threat that, if your opponent does counter correctly, may "weaken" your position (from dead lost to dead-dead lost!) but, if he misplays, lets you back into the game. In this case you have a lot to gain and very little to lose, so the risk is worth it.

Another exception occurs when, even if your opponent correctly reacts to your threat (which was not your best move), your position does not degrade from won to drawn or drawn to lost. For example, a subtle threat that, if parried, takes you from the better side of the draw to dead even or to the worse side, might be tolerable if you need to win and can likely draw anyway if your opponent finds the best reply. An example from one of my games:

(see following diagram)

As a young expert, I had White, was paired down against a younger "A" player, and had possessed the initiative the entire game. At this point the natural culmination of my play would be 1 Qxe6+ with a microscopic endgame advantage.

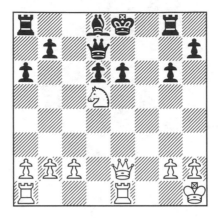

White to play

The problem is that in this line my opponent has a fairly easy defense and I would have almost no chance of winning. I thought for over half an hour, quite a rarity for me. Finally I decided to play the speculative **1 Qc4?!**. 30+ years later, even at 14 ply, *Fritz* did not rate 1 Qc4 as good as 1 Qxe6+.

But 1 Qc4 does have subtle threats that set some problems for my opponent. For example, as a good player he would soon find that the "obvious" 1...Rc8? ("winning a tempo"!) loses instantly to 2 Rxe6+!. Then 2...Qxe6 loses the queen to the double check 3 Nc7+!, as all king moves can be met by a capture on e6 with check. But not capturing the rook is no good either: after 2...Kf8 simply 3 Rf1+ wins, while 2...Kf7 3 Rf1+ wins easily, as 3...Kxe6 4 Qe4 is mate.

Would you miss this and play 1...Rc8? - ? Seeing this is not really very difficult since the lines are forced and not too long, and I did not expect my talented young opponent to fall for this trap. But it would get him thinking that this line is one reason why I took so much time for my move and, once he found it, he may relax and not realize that the hard part is to come.

Sure enough, he saw the trap and figured out that he had to move his king to stop the threat of 2 Rxe6+. But what he did not correctly calculate was that one king move leads toward equality and the other one loses instantly! So I was gambling my tiny endgame advantage (not enough to win, for sure) for a chance to win. However, since the downside was a draw anyway, although my move was not "best" I was not really risking anything.

The game continued **1...Kf8?** (the saving move was 1...Kf7, when 2 Nf4 leads to a fairly even game – likely a very small Black advantage – with White's activity offsetting Black's extra pawn; Black can continue 2...Re8 3 Qb3 Qb5 or possibly 2...d5), but after the incorrect king move I had **2 Nf4** and my threats are unstoppable. The game concluded **2...Kg7 3 Nxe6+ Kh6 4 Re3** ("rook lift") **4...g5 5 Rh3+** and Black resigned as White has a forced mate.

The Three Types of Reasonable Threats

It is understandable that players are sometimes confused about the difference between tactics and threats. Indeed, the line is sometimes fuzzy and differentiated by semantics. I like to use the terms consistently, so let's define these:

♟ A **tactic** is *a forced sequence of moves that leads to material gain or check-mate.* We can extend the definition of tactics to include defensive tactics, which are moves that prevent material loss or checkmate.

♟ **Threats** are *moves that allow a player to do something positive next move, unless it is prevented.* A check threatens the king, so technically qualifies as a type of threat. Unlike other threats, by rule a check *must* be met.

It is important to understand that *threats are not tactics unless there is no defense.*

Let's make these definitions clearer with three simple examples:

Example #1: White to play and win with a tactic

1 Rd8 mate is a tactic.

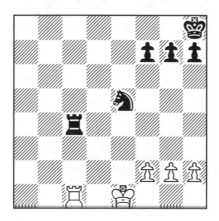

Example #2: White to play and make a threat that is not a tactic

1 Rd1 (or 1 Ra1 or 1 Rb1) is a dangerous threat to mate on the back rank, but is easily parried by *luft* moves like 1...g6, so it is not a tactic.

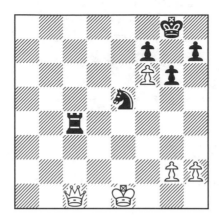

Example #3: White to play and win via a threat that cannot be met

1 Qh6 is a threat (2 Qg7 mate) that cannot be met. Black has a couple of checks, but, if White parries the checks correctly, the mate will be executed; e.g. 1...Re4+ 2 Kd2 (2 Kf2?? Ng4+ wins the queen and the game – it is never too late to be vigilant: *on most moves it is possible to throw away your gains with quick and/or inattentive play!*) 2...Rd4+ 3 Kc3 Rd3+ 4 Kc2 and then mate. Therefore, 1 Qh6 is a threat that initiates a tactic in the form of an un-stoppable mating sequence.

A fourth example provides insight into the more subtle area of the definitions:

1 e4 e5 2 Bb5 a6

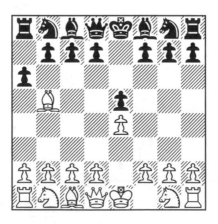

Example #4: White to play and avoid loss of material

Black's second move is clearly a threat, but is it a tactic? It is not an offensive tactic, since 2...a6 is clearly not a forced sequence leading to a material win or checkmate. However, the fact that there is no forced material win is from Black's point of view!

Let's consider this from *White's* point of view. Moving the bishop is clearly forced or else White *will* lose material. Therefore, White's third move, say **3 Be2**, can be considered a defensive tactic!

Why is this semantic issue even worth considering? Because it helps explain why White's third move does not violate the principle "Move every piece once before you move any piece twice, unless there is a tactic" – he had to move the bishop or lose material.

The above discussion is preparation for the key question, "When is it reasonable to make a threat?" This important consideration is touched upon in *It's Not Really Winning A Tempo!* (8-5) and in my book *Looking for Trouble*.

Earlier we listed the only three circumstances, *with relation to the possible outcome of the threat*, where a threat may be justified:

1.   When the threat cannot be met;
2.   When the threat can be met, but the tempo the opponent uses to meet the threat is less (or equally) useful to the opponent as was the tempo spent making the threat; or
3.   When the threat can be met, even though the opponent's tempo meeting the threat will be more useful than the tempo spent making it. Normally you would *not* make this kind of threat because, with best play, your position will get worse. So what is the only situation where making this "bad threat" is correct? The answer is *when the position is dead lost and resistance by good play is futile*. In this "desperate" case it makes sense to complicate the game and hope to swindle your way back into the game.

An important point: *just because a threat is justified or even unstoppable does not mean it is the best move*. For example, suppose we have an unstoppable threat to win a pawn on the queenside, which satisfies #1. That does not mean winning the pawn is best; there could be a win of bigger material somewhere else, or the tempi spent winning the pawn might be better spent elsewhere. So a threat that meets any of the above criteria may be worthy of consideration, but should not be played just for that reason.

1. Threats that cannot be met

Example #3 above, with 1 Qh6 threatening unstoppable mate, is an excellent example.

2. Threats that can be met but the threatening tempo does more

1 e4 e5 2 d4 exd4 3 Qxd4

(see following diagram)

Here **3...Nc6** is a threat where Black, the maker of the threat, gets more out of the tempo than White gets from defending. White would love to leave his queen on the dominant d4-square, but it must be vacated, thereby "losing a tempo".

Black to play

3. Threats that can be met but the threatening player is desperate

Reasonable threat #3 is easy to understand. Although the threat can be met – and is even "detrimental" – *the fact that the game is theoretically lost anyway makes any move equally good* (because they all should lead to a loss), so one may as well make a move that allows the opponent to go wrong, no matter what its optimal evaluation.

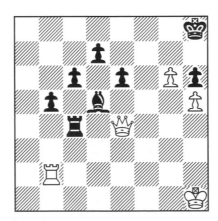

White to play

In this position, White is dead lost and is searching for a way to get back in the game. The theoretically best move is 1 Qxd5, leading to a completely lost endgame. However, the best practical try is 1 g7+!?. Strictly speaking, after 1...Kg8!, the endgame is an even easier win for Black, since the g-pawn will easily fall, too. Yet, since White is lost anyway, 1 g7+!? is a better practical try, because the apparently reasonable 1...Kxg7?? allows 2 Rg2+ unpinning the queen. If Black allows that swindle, then White is better! For example, 2...Kf6 3

Qg6+ Ke7 4 Kg1 Bxg2 5 Kxg2 and the h6-pawn falls, leaving White a dangerous pawn on the h-file. Since there are few ways for White to cause problems, it makes sense to try 1 g7+!?, even though the threat is easily met and the tempo 1...Kg8 helps Black more than 1 g7+!? helps White.

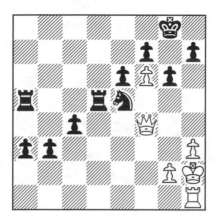

White to play

Here again White is in desperate straits. So he may as well try **1 Qh6!?**, threatening mate on g7. Even if White sees that this fails to **1...Ng4+! 2 hxg4 Rh5+ 3 gxh5 Rxh5+ 4 Kg3** (or 4 Qxh5 gxh5 5 Rd1 h6) **4...Rxh6 5 Rd1** (or 5 Rxh6 a2 6 Rh1 b2) **5...Rh3+! 6 gxh3 h5**, when Black's passed pawns beat the rook. If Black does not take the time to find that defense, then he is *Acquiescing* (see the archived Novice Nook).

Finally, an amusing example:

Black to play after 1 Kg3

In this endgame situation White has allowed Black to promote, but has an unstoppable mating threat. Therefore, Black is desperate and may as well try **1...Qf3!?+** since he has nothing to lose. Of course, if White plays too quickly, he may fall for 2 Qxf3?? stalemate! By playing carefully, White should find 2 Kxf3 winning.

Unreasonable threats: those that should not be made

The above categories include only reasonable threats. It follows that you should not make threats that do not meet any of the three criteria – we could call these unreasonable threats.

Why do beginners constantly make unreasonable threats that are easily met or clearly detrimental? One answer is that other beginners often ignore even the most obvious threats. So a beginner gets *positive reinforcement* from the fact that their opponents miss their threat entirely and thus deduce that the more threats they make, the more likely the opponent is to miss them. Plus, at that level, the likelihood of the opponent properly punishing the error is not very great. So these beginners make as many threats as possible, good and bad, in the hopes of scoring that common, gratifying – and immediate – win.

As beginners progress, hopefully they begin to notice that, when their opponent properly answers a frivolous threat, it is often to their detriment. So as the level of their opposition rises, the percentage of frivolous threats decreases. If their progress is great enough, they may arrive at the understanding that threats should only be made if it meets one of the three criteria.

The following is a terrific example of an "unreasonable threat" from a young student who, as typical of many youngsters, wants to threaten mate as much as possible, hoping his opponent will not see it. While this "big reward" strategy may work against the rawest beginners, the idea of making a bad move and hoping your opponent does not see the threat is a terrible habit. Here it is at its worst. No, I don't call this Hope Chess. How about Hopeful Chess?

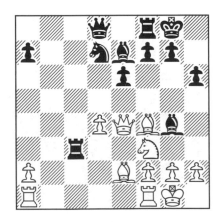

White to play

White sees he can threaten mate and, although he has 54 minutes remaining, takes only *18 seconds* to play the suicidal **1 Bd3**. How should Black meet this threat?

Black played the adequate **1...Nf6**, not only stopping mate but attacking the queen and getting ready to remove the guard of d3 and fork f4; i.e. if 2 Qe3? Nd5. But simpler and strong is 1...Bf5!, skewering the queen and the bishop, winning the latter.

In this perfect example Black has two good replies to the threat and either one should have been enough to dissuade White from playing 1 Bd3??. However, White was not looking to see how Black could stop the mate; he was trying to play quickly and win the game immediately. That's not how to play if you want to become a good player.

For an example of a very common "unreasonable threat" in a beginner's opening, see White's 5th move of Position #3 in *Evaluation Criteria* (in 2-4).

A practical example: a threat easily met but with some value

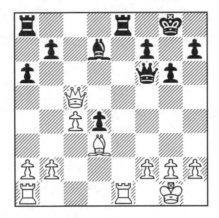

White to play

White played **1 Qc7**, threatening the pawn on b7 and the bishop. But Black has the simple and obvious **1...Bc6**, which he played, not only meeting both threats, but activating the bishop on the long diagonal. Clearly Black's move to meet the threats makes the bishop a better piece, so 1 Qc7 can't be a good move in terms of the threats it created – *it can only be justified if White is using c7 as a jumping point to return to the kingside* with, say, 2 Qg3. *Rybka* calculates that 1 Qc7 is a decent move just for that reason, although that was not my student's intention.

Conclusion

The next time you consider making a threat, make sure that your opponent does not benefit more in meeting the threat than you do in making it. If he can, then the threat is probably not such a good idea and you should look for a better move.

8-6) The Principle of Symmetry

In a chess fight, it is best to eliminate your opponent's advantages in order to eradicate his counterplay.

[This, along with *The Two Move Triggers* (3-2), is one of the two most advanced Novice Nooks and a favorite of the author's.]

What do the following twelve criteria have in common?

1. When you are winning, keep the position simple.
2. If you are going to win material, it is usually better to win a pawn than to win the exchange for a pawn; similarly, it is better to win a piece than to win a queen for two pieces.
3. When you are winning an endgame, you should generally avoid pawn promotion races, unless you are 100% positive you will win.
4. If you win a pawn (not "accept a gambit"!) before either side has castled, it is usually better to castle on the same side as your opponent. If you lose material in the opening, try to castle on the opposite side.
5. If you are ahead a pawn in the endgame with pawns on both sides of the board, in general it is better to move your king to the same side as your opponent's king.
6. If you are ahead an exchange in the endgame, it is better to have a position where no pawns are passed, than it is to have a position where most or all are passed pawns.
7. If you are way ahead in material, you can often "sacrifice" material to simplify. For example, if you have a queen and rook for just a rook, it is usually a good idea to exchange your queen for your opponent's rook.
8. If you can win a pawn in a bad position where the material is even, then take the pawn, even when winning that pawn costs you some time.
9. When you are winning, general symmetry (a balance in the position) is better than asymmetry.
10. If the game is even and you want to win, create asymmetry and imbalance.
11. As an answer to 1 e4, the Sicilian Defense is more popular among grandmasters, especially those playing for a win.
12. If you play a stronger player, you have more chances if you play someone with a style dissimilar to yours.

Answer: All of these can be derived from what I call the *Principle of Symmetry*. In general:

It is better to have everything your opponent has and more, than an imbalance where you have more in some areas but less in others.

For example, if your opponent has X, but you have X as well as Y, then that is better than you having more X and him having more Y even if the net advantage is roughly the same. So the opposite of the *Principle of Symmetry* is the *Principle of Imbalance*:

If you are worse (for example, are behind in material), it is better to have something that your opponent does not – something on which you can "hang your hat".

Let's examine #2 from the above list: you have the option of either winning a pawn or winning the exchange (bishop or knight for rook) for a pawn. Although the latter is generally considered to be somewhat inferior in terms of material advantage (about ¾ pawn as opposed to 1), you should usually shun this for a different reason. If you win the exchange and also give up a pawn, your opponent will have one more piece on the board (e.g. a knight and pawn versus your rook) and can create potential problems by locking the position (where the knight is comparatively strong) or creating an extra passed pawn. Instead, all things being equal, it is much better to just be ahead a pawn, where you have the only advantage and your opponent has no theoretical counterplay. This principle would apply even more so, if you had the choice between winning a piece or winning a queen for two pieces. The former should be an easy win; the latter can sometimes be tricky.

Let's show how item #1 is derived from this principle. Complications are a form of compensation for your opponent. If the losing player misplays the complications they are risking very little, because they were losing anyway. But if the player who is winning misplays the position, they might actually lose or only draw. Let's take that one step further: from the inferior side's perspective, it is usually better to be losing by the equivalent of two pawns with a very complicated game, than it is to be down one pawn with no play at all. We can apply this logic to both sides: since action is good for one player and bad for the other, it follows that when you are losing you want to play aggressively, complicate, and/or attack.

Black to play

In this position, White will win easily, if he is experienced enough to realize that all he needs to do is to attack the f-pawn twice. He can do this by forcing the black king away, and then sacrificing the exchange for a pawn. But, in the next diagram, let's mirror Black's pieces over to the queenside. Then we get quite a different story:

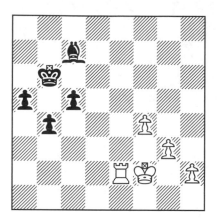

Black to play

This is a race where the advanced black pawns, which were formerly blockaded on the kingside, are now extremely dangerous. A race favors the player who is behind in material! The fact that Black is still down the exchange is much less meaningful, and Black has more than enough compensation. *Even if we move the black pawns back a tempo or two to make the race more even*, the position is dynamic and complicated – in practice someone is likely to win – and it could be Black, especially if White misplays it!

White to play

Here White is ahead a queen for a knight and three pawns – about a piece worth of material. But the win will take plenty of care because of the great imbalance in the position.

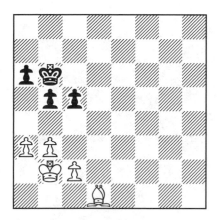

White to play

In contrast, this position has the same black pawn structure, but opposed by symmetric pawns. White's extra material, *although similar in scope to the previous example*, combines with the symmetric nature of the position (and thus lack of Black potential threats) to make this an easy win.

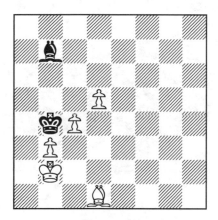

White to play

This position, with White ahead three pawns, is a fairly easy win. But unbalance the position by giving Black an opposite-colored bishop instead, and things are not so easy!

(see following diagram)

If White brings his king to the kingside (e.g. Kf5), Black can – carefully – move his king to d6.

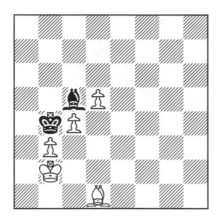

White to play

Even in asymmetric positions, the player ahead often wants to balance matters as much as he can to win as easily as possible, *if he can win without extreme imbalances.*

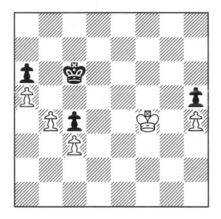

White to play

In this position, White is winning, but has to decide which side to move his king. Of course, *since this decision is critical, only calculation should decide*, but suppose you were in a speed game and had to move quickly using just principles? In that case, the theory of imbalance would apply. Black wants a race (imbalance) and White does not, so the white king, in these types of positions, generally wants to go to the same side of the board as the black king.

In the game White chose the race, and the game continued **1 Kg5 Kb5 2 Kxh5 Ka4 3 Kg4 Kb3 4 b5 axb5 5 a6 Kxc3 6 a7 b4 7 a8Q b3**, and now White had to figure out how to stop the connected passed pawns with his queen, which he did, and won.

But White could have made things *much* easier for himself by following the Principle of Symmetry and avoiding imbalance. White should keep his king on the same side as the black king. After **1 Ke5** (or 1 Ke4) **1...Kb5 2 Kd5**, he would be winning the c-pawn and have two extra pawns on the queenside – no race, no complications, no problem!

Another derivative of the Principle of Symmetry is that the side ahead is always seeking symmetry (where the "ahead" part is clearly the difference in the symmetry), while the side behind is seeking imbalance, where both sides have pros and cons. In a king and pawn endgame, if you have three pawns to your opponent's two, it is better to have three pawns against two on one side of the board, than it is to have all the pawns on opposite sides of the board (a race!). Consider the following position, which occurred in a student's game:

White to play

Since White has an extra pawn on the kingside, he wants all the play to be there, and so should seek symmetry on the queenside. Therefore, the proper move is 1 a3!. No matter what Black plays, the queenside will remain symmetrical and White can win on the king-side. Play might continue: 1...bxa3 2 bxa3 Ke7 3 Kf5 Kf7 4 e6+ Ke7 5 Ke5 Ke8 6 Kxd5 and White wins.

Instead, White thought that he could win by *zugzwang*, so he just waited for Black to abandon e6 by playing **1 Kf4??**. Black followed the Principle of Imbalance and played **1...a3!,** ensuring a win despite his pawn deficit; e.g. **2 bxa3 b3!** (but not 2...bxc3?? 3 Ke3) or **2 b3 cxb3 3 axb3 a2**. So White, by allowing imbalance, turned a win into a loss in one move!

The famous three-pawn problem requires the winner to create asymmetry – symmetry is good for Black because the black king is closer. Therefore, all things being equal, Black wants the pawns in balance until the king can come to the rescue:

(see following diagram)

White needs asymmetry to win, so moves like 1 h6? g6 2 fxg6 fxg6 (symmetry) don't work – in fact *Black* wins by approaching with his king to capture the white pawns.

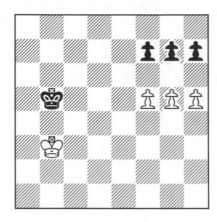

White to play

Instead, White wins with **1 g6 hxg6 2 f6! gxf6 3 h6** or **1...fxg6 2 h6! gxh6 3 f6**. If 1...hxg6 2 fxg6? Black creates symmetry and holds with 2...fxg6.

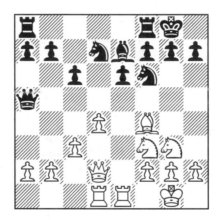

Black to play

In this position, Black is behind in development and space, and so chose 1...Rad8. But this was a major mistake; instead he should play the bold **1...Qxa2!**. It is true that when you are behind in development you generally should not waste more time snatching pawns – *and* this move also jeopardizes his queen – but here the position is relatively closed and the queen can escape. By winning a pawn, Black sends a major psychological message to White: "You may be ahead in some areas, but I am ahead material! Therefore, if you want to win, you have to act, or I will eventually trade off and win the endgame." Since White is better, Black wants an imbalance to apply some counterpressure. In the main example in *When is a King Safe?* (5-2), similar logic supported the capture of the bishop with 27...Qxe2 (see page 206).

Of course, if everything is balanced, then *you have no advantages*, and you want to create imbalances, so you can take advantage of your strengths and your opponent's weaknesses. That is quite different from the previous examples, where *you already had an advantage and wanted to avoid further imbalance in your opponent's favor.*

Take the following common position after **1 e4 e5 2 Nf3 Nc6 3 Bc4 Bc5 4 Nc3 Nf6 5 d3 d6 6 0-0 0-0**. Suppose White plays **7 Be3**. Should Black capture the bishop?

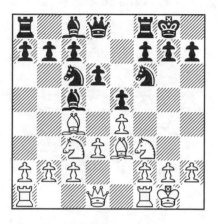

Black to play

7...Bxe3

Not necessarily; more common is 7...Bb6.

8 fxe3

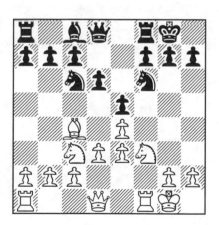

Black to play

Beginners consistently allow this position as Black, happy that they are "ahead" because White has "bad" doubled pawns. But that is an incorrect evaluation. White not only has an extra pawn in the center to cover the key squares d4 and f4, but, more importantly, the only semi-open file on the board to provide activity for his rooks. The imbalances are much more in White's favor! In one game between an intermediate player (Black) and an expert, the game continued something like:

8...Be6 9 Bb3

White does not give Black the extra central pawn!

9...Bxb3 10 axb3

More "bad" doubled pawns!

10...Qe7 11 Qe1 a6 12 Qg3 Rfe8 13 Rf2 Rad8 14 Raf1 b5 15 Nh4

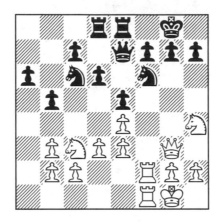

Black to play

White has a knight on the rim and two sets of doubled pawns, but all the important imbalances – including much superior rook activity and the bunched pawns controlling the center – are in his favor. He threatens 16 Rxf6 and has a massive kingside attack. White won easily. After the game, Black, thinking about his "perfect" pawn structure, said to me, "I don't understand. I did everything right, and he did everything wrong, and I lost!"

Chapter Nine

Shorter, Lesson Material

9-1) A Fistful of Lessons

All the chess knowledge in the world won't help you if, each time you move, you don't take your time and use the information that is applicable to your current position.

Sometimes the best lessons are the ones that hurt, like the ones from games where you are winning easily and then lose through a series of seemingly incomprehensible moves. If that often happens to you, then you should learn quite a bit from the Reversals of Fortune shown below. The following four examples are pretty rough, so if you have a weak heart I suggest you take your pills before continuing. We could call them The Good, The Bad, and The Ugly, but then I would need a name for the fourth...

1. Justice is Not Served

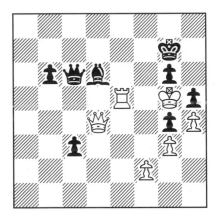

White to play

This position occurred in a game at our local chess club. White was a new student, an adult who had not been playing seriously very long. Black is a much higher rated player who is more experienced, but has also made a very bad mistake by taking his inexperienced opponent extremely lightly. So, despite his superior playing strength, Black has crashed from a winning position into a completely lost game.

White has many ways to win, but the most powerful is to checkmate in two moves with 1 Re7+ Kf8 (1...Kg8 is the only other legal move since Black is in *double check*, but in either case the next move for White would be the same) 2 Qg7 mate. White can also win the queen with 1 Rc5+. My coach IM Donald Byrne once told me "Unless you are 100% sure about the mate, take the queen first and mate him later; most players will resign and the ones that don't you can beat easily." Here the mate is so easy that Byrne's Rule does not apply, but either move will do!

Instead, White played **1 Re6+**, which is comprehensible, if not anywhere near best. It turns out (I asked White after the game) that White rejected moves like 1 Re7+ and 1 Rc5+ because "Black could just take the rook", ignoring the fact that Black is in a discovered check after those moves and capturing the rook is illegal!

You may chuckle, but even players who have been playing for years make similar mistakes by not considering moves that at first blush seem silly. Moves that at first glance seem terrible may possibly be worth a second look whenever discovered checks, pins, pseudo-sacrifices, and other tactical motifs are present. It is ironic that most tactic books are full of problems that start with "pseudo-sacrifices" – temporary sacrifices of material that are not real sacrifices because the sacrificing player can win all that back and more, and yet often players do not even consider these same moves in real games. Cutting off your analysis just because the initial capture loses material without continuing to see if you can end up ahead eventually is a *quiescence error* since you mistakenly assume the position is "quiet" (no more checks, captures, and threats) and stop analyzing.

Anyway, the good news is that White is still winning easily. He has a choice of either winning the bishop or possibly mating, and either should be quite good enough. After 1 Re6+ the game continued:

1...Kf7 2 Qf6+ Kg8 3 Qxg6+

So far, so good. Looks as if White has decided to play for mate and not just the win of the bishop, and that's OK so long as the mate is there and he pulls it off!

3...Kf8

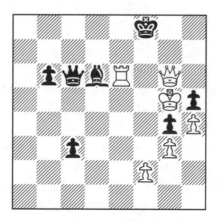

White to play

Now White has four safe checks: 4 Rf6+, 4 Qf6+, 4 Qf5+, and 4 Qh6+. Which one of these is best? – or should White settle for winning the bishop with 4 Rxd6, or even possibly a non-check move that closes the noose around the black king?

4 Kf6??

This quiet move violates a fundamental guideline of attack, which is *Don't stop kicking a man when he is down* or, to put it more politely, *When both kings are exposed and the heavy pieces are still on the board, the initiative (or attack) is often worth everything – so you*

usually should keep checking (or capturing) if you can. The best check was the "retreat" 4
Qf5+!. This fifth rank check allows the rook to check on the sixth rank, forcing the black
king into the corner, where his pieces cannot help him: 4...Kg7 5 Rg6+ Kh7 (5...Kh8 6 Qf6+
Kh7 7 Qg7 mate) 6 Qf7+ Kh8 7 Qg7 mate.

Now Black gets a chance to start an attack. At this point Black has about 20 minutes left
and White has about 5; they were playing with a time delay clock.

4...Qf3+

Black misses the trickier but better 4...Be7+!. But it is not Black's errors that are the most
instructive.

5 Kg5 Qd5+ 6 Kf6?

6 Kh6 would spoil the fun.

6...Qf3+ 7 Kg5 Qd5+ 8 Kf6? Qf3+

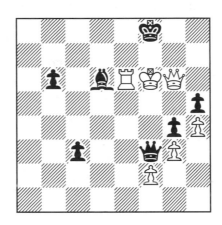

White to play

Up to now White has been very content to repeat moves, and indeed Black could even
have claimed a draw before his last move by writing the move on his scoresheet, stopping
the clock, and claiming that 8...Qf3+ would lead to threefold repetition. But instead Black
now said "If you move to g5 again that will be a draw by threefold repetition." In response
to this comment, what should White, a relative novice, do?

The first answer is, "Don't believe your opponent!" *Even the most well-meaning opponent likely does not know the rules,* so White should have stopped the clock and asked the
Tournament Director (TD) about the threefold repetition rule, which White did not know.
The second thing White should have done is to ask himself if the only alternative to drawing, 9 Qf5, was good or not. *If 9 Qf5 is not good,* then taking a draw against a higher rated
player, especially when you have much less time on the clock, would be the prudent course
of action. White did neither of these things. Instead, he thought to himself, "Well, *of course*
we can't have a draw" and, without any more logic than that, proceeded to play:

9 Qf5??

Black did not overlook the gift horse this time.

9...Qxf5+ 10 Kxf5 Bc5

The simple 10...c2 won immediately, but it does not matter – Black's game is too good.

11 f4?

11 Re2 was certainly called for, when White can at least make Black do some work.

11...gxf3 *e.p.*

At this point White was again surprised. He was not sure of the *en passant* rule. He asked his opponent something like "Can you do that?" and Black replied "Yes, you can take a pawn that way" and White was satisfied. I think in their current mindsets Black could have taken White's king (!) and if Black told White it was legal White would have accepted it! After the game I again suggested to White that he not be so quick to believe his opponents, but to stop the clock and request the appropriate rule(s) from the TD. The rest is not pretty:

12 Rf6+ Kg7 13 Rg6+ Kh7 14 Kg5 Be3+ 15 Kxh5 c2 16 Rh6+ Bxh6 0-1

Still, I have to give White a lot of credit. Despite going from an easy win into a loss, he still took the whole thing remarkably well and graciously accepted all the lessons learned. After I went over what happened, he just said "Thanks, Dan! I learned a lot!" and smiled a genuine smile.

2. Forcing the Opponent to Win!

White to play

Although the position doesn't look nearly as good for White as it did in the previous game, it is nonetheless a win. The key is that White's king can both block Black's king from getting out, while simultaneously getting a passed pawn via a sacrifice: 1 c4! dxc4 2 d5 c3 3 Ke3 (White's king can stop the black pawn, but Black cannot promote either the c-pawn or the h-pawn) 5 Kg3 4 d6 h4 7 d7 h3 6 d8Q h2 7 Qg5+ Kf4 8 Qg3 h1N (8...h1Q 9 Qf3 mate) 9 Qh2 c2 10 Qxh1 mate.

1 b6?

Now the game is a draw – Black has time to promote the h-pawn, too.

1...h4 2 c4

Here it is a case of "Better late than never", because 2 Kf2? Kg4 can even win for Black since he has the dreaded "outside passed pawn" to deflect the white king while the black king goes to the queenside.

2...dxc4 3 d5 c3 4 d6?

White completely forgot his king could catch the c-pawn and stop it from promoting!

4...c2 5 d7 c1Q 6 d8Q Qf1+ 7 Ke3 Qg1+ 8 Ke2 Qg2+ 9 Ke1 Qg1+ 10 Ke2 Qg6

Not the best way to stop checking, but irrelevant for our story.

11 Qd7+??

Now Black can trade queens and win with 11...Qg4+; this is the kind of transition point that White must not allow.

11...Kh2??

Returning the favor.

12 Qc7+ Kh3 13 Qd7+

13 Qxb7 is probably a draw.

13...Kg2?

Again missing 13...Qg4+.

14 Qd5+ Kg1 15 Ke3??

Making a similar mistake as made by the player in the first game: halting offense maneuvers with a "negative" quiet king move. 15 Qd4+ would be drawing.

15...Kf1??

Missing the win starting with 15...Qxb6+. Now it is White to play the worst possible "safe" check:

White to play

16 Qh1+???

This is one of the best examples of "Hope Chess" I have ever seen! White literally forces Black to win. If White had made any attempt to see what would happen next (he gives Black no choice, so seeing what must happen does not take any special effort), there is no way this move would be played. Black is forced to trade queens into an easily won king and pawn endgame. Besides the easily drawing16 Qxb7, correct was 16 Qf3+ Kg1 17 Qf2+ Kh1 18 Qxh4+ Kg1 19 Qf2+ Kh1 20 Qf3+ Kg1 21 Qxb7 with a theoretical draw, but good practical winning chances.

16...Qg1+

Hmm. What did White think would happen?

17 Qxg1 Kxg1 0-1

White cannot stop the h-pawn from promoting.

3. Letting the One-Trick Pony Win

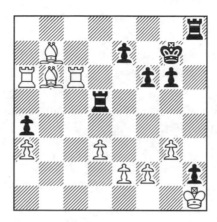

White to play

Black, a 1400 player, has lost two pieces as a result of the all-too-common but rarely discussed problem of *miscounting* on two capturing sequences (see the archived *A Counting Primer*). Therefore, Black's only remaining game plan is a one-trick pony: if the rook on d5 can eventually check on the first rank, then ...h1Q+ would follow with a win. But if Black *cannot* find a way to check on the first rank, then there is little to be done. So long as White follows the principles in *When You're Winning, It's a Whole Different Game* (7-3) and *thinks defense first*, he should come up with the obvious idea 1 Rc1! (or its cousin 1 Rc8!). Then White could figuratively laugh at Black as the one-trick pony is gone forever and his extra two bishops win easily. Sure, many other moves win, but that is not the point!

Unfortunately White did not have my advice in mind and instead played:

1 Rxf6?!

This tricky discovered attack on the rook is completely unnecessary, flouting the second principle of *When You're Winning*: Keep it Simple – don't play tricky. 1 Rxf6 is tricky. From a practical sense I could give this move two question marks since it causes all of White's future problems but, theoretically, that would not be correct since White is still winning.

1...Rb5

was the immediate reply. So, with one tricky and unnecessary move, White goes from up two pieces and completely winning to figuring out how to save the game! Black admitted after the game that he would have resigned if White had just stopped any back-rank check.

2 Rxg6+!

Great move by White, who is also a 1400 player. It is a shame that such a great move is required just to keep winning, when a move ago almost any non-tricky move would have won. Now Black is faced with only bad choices.

2...Kxg6?!

Not the best. Black should try to stay off of the sixth rank by playing 2...Kf7. White would still be winning easily, but it would only be so after the difficult-to-find 3 Bd5+! Would you have found this move for White if Black had played 2...Kf7 - ?

3 Be4+?

Definitely not best. *When you see a good move, look for a better one!* Much better is 3 Bd4+!, when White wins back the entire rook with interest: 3...Kh7 4 Be4+! removes the guard (and is much better than 4 Bxh8?) and is winning easily. 3 Be4+? is a direct check and 3 Bd4+ is a discovered check, but they are both checks – make sure to consider all of them!

3...Kf7

White has lost a rook from the original position! White is still winning, but *The Margin for Error* (7-4) has decreased dramatically.

4 d4

This was White's idea from 3 Be4+, to guard the b1-square. It all would have been much easier if White had followed the *think defense first* idea and played 1 Rc1, preventing these problems forever.

4...Rb2

Black continues to ride the one-trick pony, searching for places along the second rank that will allow the rook to get to the first rank safely.

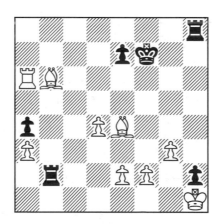

White to play

5 Bd3??

This is Hope Chess. If White had looked to see that nothing could be done about the threat created by Black's obvious reply, then this move would have been rejected as not playable. White should not be worried about the e-pawn, but instead focused on preventing Black's infiltration points onto the first rank. After the game I suggested 5 Ba5, which wins. 5 Bc7 is also an option, allowing Bg6+ with the idea of trading rooks with Ra8+ after the black king is forced to the back rank.

5...Rd2!

What did White expect? Black threatens the unstoppable 6...Rd1+.

Now White began to think hard, but it is too late – the hard thinking should have been done last move to prevent this from happening! You must plan to meet your opponent's upcoming checks, captures, and threats before they make them, not after. 5...Rd2 is a good example of a threat that cannot be met, so it should never have been allowed. On the previous move White should have thought: "Suppose I play 5 Bd3, then what will Black do? Black wants to get on to the first rank, so the rook will move somewhere safe along the second rank to where the first rank is not guarded. Since 5...Ra2?? allows 6 Bc4+, suppose Black tries 5...Rd2 - ? Then there is no defense to 6...Rd1+, so I can't play 5 Bd3..."

6 Bg6+

Too late, but worth a try. Maybe Black will blunder big time and capture!

6...Kg7

Oh well. Good for Black. The rest needs no comment:

7 Bc2 Rxc2 8 f4 Rc1+ 9 Kg2 h1Q+ 10 Kf2 Qh2+ 11 Ke3 Qxg3+ 12 Kd2 Qxf4+ 13 e3 0-1

4. I've Seen Enough – I Win the Queen – Whoops!

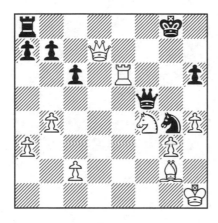

White to play

In this position, what could be easier? White is to move, is up a piece and a pawn, has a mating attack, a discovered attack on Black's queen, and Black has no threats! Do you think it could be possible for White to get a losing position just by making a couple of superficially reasonable moves? We have to cut White considerable slack here because this was a fairly quick game. Even so, watch and learn:

1 Re8!?

Not a terrible move, but the prelude to a disaster. Better is 1 Rg6+, when the discovered attack on the queen forces Black to give up his queen with 1...Qxg6 2 Nxg6 and the game is about over.

1...Rxe8

Forced.

2 Qxf5??

Looks good – superficially. This was White's idea, to win the queen. Instead of this capture, 2 Qxe8+ is still winning easily. Once again this example shows that if you don't look to see what might happen next, anything that happens to you is deserved!

2...Re1+

Believe it or not, Black missed this move in the game despite having lots more time than White. But the win for Black was "this close"! Instead, Black played 2...Nf2+?? and resigned a couple of moves later. He made the common mistake of assuming his game was hopeless and not even taking time to look for the gift White had handed him on a silver platter. *You should start by looking at your checks, captures, and threats.* In this case Black only has two checks and one of them wins. *When you see a good move, look for a better one!*

3 Bf1

The only legal move.

3...Rxf1+

Not hard to spot.

4 Kg2

The only legal move again.

4...Ne3+

Ouch! Not only does this move fork the king and queen, it also guards the rook to boot! So, instead of being down all that material, Black is going to end up ahead a rook after he captures the queen! This is a great example of how superficially reasonable moves in a won position can still lose. You always need to be careful...

9-2) Examples of Chess Logic

Just because a move is good does not mean it is best.

Chess requires the use of deductive logic in many situations. The most common occur each move, during a player's analysis, when you determine which move is best or which replies are forced. For example, to determine if a move is forced, you might ask yourself: "If I move there, does he *have* to answer *that*, since then he cannot win, or perhaps cannot draw?" However, logic plays a substantial part in other aspects of the game.

Recognizing as many of these situations as possible, and knowing what you should typically do when they occur, puts important tools in your chess toolbox. Therefore, let's list five principles that apply to such situations and then examine each in more detail:

1. Don't capture a promoting piece until after it promotes.
2. Don't capture a pinned piece until the opponent attempts to unpin it.
3. Don't capture one of two forked pieces of equal value until one of them moves.
4. Consider winning a tempo for a trapped piece, rather than capturing a pawn or ruining the pawn structure.
5. Doing nothing is sometimes a great policy – it can be the only way to save or even win a game!

As with other principles, the above do not hold in every case. Be especially aware of the important unwritten caveat: "...unless there is a tactic!" If there is a tactic, then all bets are off!

1. Don't capture a promoting piece until after it promotes

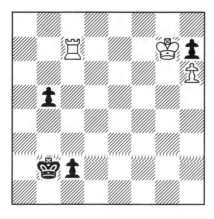

White to play

I once had a student who, in a similar position, played 1 Rxc2??. After the game I asked him why he made the capture immediately, instead of waiting until after the pawn promoted and, with the air of someone puzzled as to why I would ask a question with such an obvious answer, he replied: "Because I could not stop him from queening, so I had to do it!"

His is the correct answer as to why one must *eventually* capture the pawn, not why one should do it *this move*! 1 Rxc2?? throws away the win, as after 1...Kxc2 2 Kxh7 b4 3 Kg7 b3 4 h7 b2 both players promote with a draw. Whereas after the correct **1 Kxh7** White wins, e.g. **1...c1Q 2 Rxc1 Kxc1 3 Kg7 b4 4 h7 b3 5 h8Q** and White is a tempo ahead of the 1 Rxc2?? line, and can win with a queen against a knight pawn on the seventh rank.

This "premature" capture can even cost you the game, much less a draw:

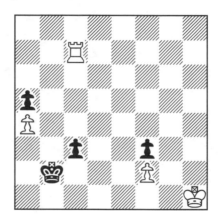

White to play

White can win by waiting before capturing the pawn: **1 Kh2 c2** (or 1...Kb3 2 Kg3 Kxa4 3 Rxc3 etc) **2 Kg3 c1Q+ 3 Rxc1 Kxc1 4 Kxf3 Kb2 5 Ke4 Kb3 6 f4 Kxa4 7 f5 Kb3 8 f6 a4 9 f7 a3 10 f8Q a2** (no better is 10...Kb2 11 Qb4+ Ka2 12 Kd4 – *zugzwang*! – 12...Ka1 13 Qxa3+) **11 Qf6!** (or 11 Qh8) and then **12 Qa1**.

For more on this type of easy win, refer to the archived *Going to Sleep in the Endgame*. However, White *loses* with 1 Rxc3?? Kxc3 2 Kh2 Kb4 and *Black* then wins the race.

Of course, do *not* wait until the pawn promotes if the opponent is threatening to block your capture (a tactic!). Consider the following position, with Black to play:

(see following diagram)

Here Black's best chance is to give up the rook right away with **1...Rxa7!**. Instead, if Black gets greedy and waits with 1...Kg4?? then 2 Ra6 will block Black's rook and White will get a queen instead!

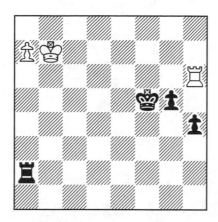

Black to play

2. Don't capture a pinned piece until the opponent attempts to unpin it

If an enemy piece is pinned, it cannot move. So, unless there is a looming tactic to interfere, why would you trade a piece that can move for one that cannot? In addition, if your opponent takes a tempo to get out of the pin, or threatens to do so in some favorable way, then you can capture afterwards and gain that tempo since the pinned piece will still be there for one move!

White to play

In this example we isolate the pin (other pieces are not shown). All things being equal, White should play some constructive move other than 1 Bxf7+. After **1 *any constructive move for White* 1...Kg7 2 Bxf7 Kxf7** it is White's move with the extra constructive move, while after 1 Bxf7+ Kxf7 the resulting position is identical, but it is White's move without the constructive move.

We can combine this idea with a promotion theme similar to the one shown earlier:

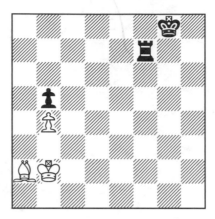

White to play

Just as in #1 (waiting to capture after promotion), the extra tempo makes the difference: **1 Kc3 Kf8 2 Bxf7+ Kxf7 3 Kd4 Ke6 4 Kc5 Kd7 5 Kxb5 Kc7 6 Ka6** wins, but 1 Bxf7+?? Kxf7 2 Kc3 Ke6 3 Kd4 Kd6 draws.

This guideline is not just for endgames; it might be applied at any point in the game. As a reminder, if the opponent is threatening a maneuver that will render the pin worthless, such as moving the pinned or pinned-to piece with check, then of course you must make the capture right away.

3. Don't capture one of two forked pieces of equal value until one of them moves

The logic with forked pieces is almost identical to the previous pinned-piece situation. Why not wait until your opponent has wasted a tempo to save one of the pieces?

White to play

Assume both rooks are doing approximately the same amount of work and they are the only pieces guarding each other. As in the previous situation White should try to play some constructive move other than 1 Nxa8 or 1 Nxe8. After **1 *Any constructive move for White* 1...rook moves 2 knight takes other rook 2...rook takes knight**, it is White's move with the extra constructive move included, while after **1 knight takes either rook 1...rook takes knight**, White's is down a tempo (lacks the constructive move) compared to the previous line.

This waiting scheme can often turn into a game of "chicken" where Black refuses to move a rook and thus waste a tempo, and White refuses to capture a rook until one of them moves! Usually Black wins the battle, but loses the war as White is eventually forced to capture a rook before one of them makes a larger threat (a tactic) and saves both.

If both forked rooks are not of equal worth and you *cannot* delay capturing one, you should capture the *less* valuable one! If instead you capture the rook doing *more*, the lesser one recaptures and takes its place as a valuable rook. If you take the one doing less, then the one doing more has to recapture, relieving it from its more important duty!

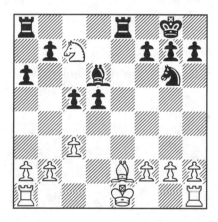

White to play

In this position White cannot delay capturing a rook, so *the knight should take the one which is doing nothing on a8* with **1 Nxa8**. That way if Black decides to recapture the knight with 1...Rxa8, the rook is no longer pinning the bishop on the e-file, nor threatening ...Nf4.

4. Consider winning a tempo for a trapped piece, rather than capturing a pawn or ruining the pawn structure

This situation often occurs when a knight is trapped in the corner after capturing a rook. The knight cannot escape, so when it is attacked many weaker players *automatically* move it, capturing a pawn or ruining the opponent's pawn structure.

In the first diagram below, weak players usually play 1 Nb6 so that after 1...axb6 Black doubles his b-pawns.

In the second they play 1 Nxb6 to get a pawn for the knight. But while these knight moves are *sometimes* correct, often it is much more important to leave the knight on a8 to force Black to waste a tempo and also to move his king further from the center. It is even more likely the tempo is worth more than just doubling the pawns.

White to play

White to play

As with the above situations, I tried to create a simple endgame example to show why this is so, but I accidentally created a beautiful problem which players of all levels will enjoy:

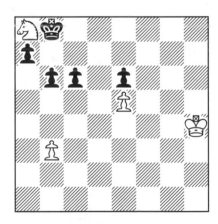

Dan Heisman, 2004
White to play and win

As intended, sacrificing the doomed knight on b6, as well as Black capturing it on a8 are bad. 1 Nxb6?? just goes into a bad endgame, as after 1...axb6 2 Kg5 Kc7 3 Kf6 (3 Kf4 c5 is no better) 3...Kd7 will win for Black. So **1 Kg5** and then:

a) 1...Kxa8? (the failure of this move shows the thematic idea that capturing is clearly too slow) 2 Kf6 c5 (2...Kb7 is even slower) 3 Kxe6 b5 4 Kd7 c4 5 e6 c3 (5...cxb3 is no better) 6 e7 c2 7 e8Q+ wins easily.

b) 1...Kc8 2 Kf6 Kd7 3 Nc7! with the threat of 4 Nxe6 wins, as 3...Kxc7 4 Kxe6 wins for White.

c) **1...c5** (the most resilient defense) **2 Kf6 b5 3 Kxe6 c4 4 Kd7**

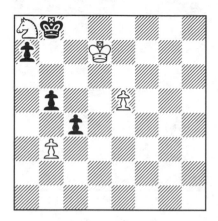

Black to play

c1) 4...Kxa8? (this transposes into line 'a') 5 e6 c3 6 e7 c2 7 e8Q+ wins easily.

c2) 4...cxb3 (plausible, but Black's loss of coverage on the c8-square will prove fatal, in a pretty way) 5 e6 b2 6 e7 b1Q 7 e8Q+ Kb7 8 Qc8 mate.

c3) **4...c3** (to guard the c8-square after promoting and prevent the mate that occurs in line 'c2'). This is the critical line. Now the extremely tempting 5 e6 c2 6 e7 c1Q 7 e8Q+ Kb7 is not correct. Black can hold the draw since the knight cannot escape. Try it and see! Yet how else to proceed?

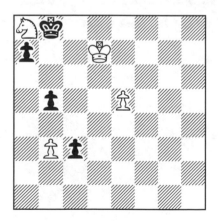

White to play

5 Nc7!! c2

5...Kb7 6 Ne6! c2 (or 7 Nd4 wins) 7 Nc5+ Kb6 8 Nd3 stops the pawn and the e-pawn decides.
6 Na6+ Ka8

6...Kb7 7 Nc5+ Kb6 8 Nd3 again allows the formerly cornered knight to catch the c-pawn. But after 6...Ka8 how does White win?

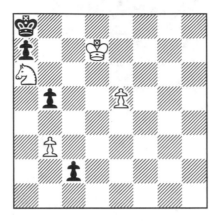

White to play

7 Kc8!!

Paradoxically, the king moves onto the promotion file and allows check!

7...c1Q+ 8 Nc7+ Qxc7

The new queen cannot last more than one move.

9 Kxc7 a5 10 e6 wins.

My most beautiful problem! (To be complete, before 4 Kd7 White could also win by inserting 4 bxc4 bxc4 with the same solution.)

5. Doing nothing is sometimes a great policy – it can be the only way to save or even win a game!

Endgame books are full of positions where the weaker side can draw by setting up a "fortress" and just move back and forth. The most famous might be:

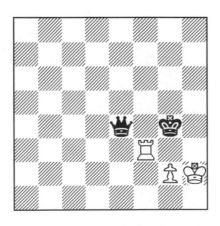

White to play

White just plays **Rf3-Rh3** and occasionally moves out of check. Black cannot get "inside" White's fortress on the lower right nine squares. Attempts to do something more "active" for White can be disastrous!

There are many examples of locked positions where the weaker side can draw since the stronger side cannot break through, but if the *weaker* side decides to play actively, that loses instantly (see *Trading Pawns When Ahead* 7-1). *In some cases your best move is to shuffle a piece other than a pawn back and forth and not destroy your position!*

More interesting are positions were you wait until your opponent runs out of time and commits hara-kiri: he gets into *zugzwang* and must make a losing move:

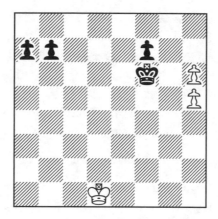

Either side to play

Here it does not matter whose move it is. Black dare not move the king lesl White promote. Yet after Black runs out of pawn moves, the king must move and White wins, so White can just put the king on the a- and b-files and let Black's game self-destruct.

Next time you encounter one of these five situations, you will have a better "toolbox" on which to rely!

9-3) Odds and Ends

It's not whether you make a mistake that matters. It's how many times you make the same mistake. Players who repeatedly make the same mistakes never get to be very good.

Not as Simple as ABC

"If A implies B, and B implies C, then A implies C."

True in logic and chess, but does this *also* mean that if you calculate, "If I play move A and he plays B, then I can play C", then you should quickly play move C following moves A and B?

No!!

Except in special situations, like severe time trouble, *playing a move quickly just because you calculated it on the previous move is almost always a big mistake*. Here are three reasons:

1. Visualization. No one can visualize a position that is yet to occur as well as they can visualize the position on the board. Good players are almost always perfect, but not quite.

2. When you thought about playing move C earlier, it was just hypothetical. The entire game did not depend on how good C was, only A, since that was the move actually played. If A was a good move but C is bad, then there is no harm done if you have not played C yet. But if you quickly play C just "because I was planning to do it", then it can cost you the game.

3. The most important reason is that when you have a candidate move (A) and you are trying to prove that it is better than any other move, one good way to do this is to find your opponent's best (or most dangerous) reply (B), and then see if you can find a move (C) that results in a better position than any other sequence.

For example, suppose in a position you have candidate moves A, A1, A2, A3... you have evaluated every move other than A, and you decide that A3 is the best option so far, leading to a position that is evaluated as +0.2 pawns (using computer evaluation values). Then, to prove that A is better than A3, you first find your opponent's best reply, "B". Then search for a reply you can make next move to B, "C", which results in a position you evaluate as better than +0.2 pawns. If you find such a C, then you are done and you can play move A with confidence!

But that does not prove that C is the best move on your next turn! It only establishes C as a promising candidate move. There may be other moves C1, C2, C3... that could be better – possibly *much* better! So to play C right away would be an enormous mistake!

The correct thought process after you play A and your opponent does follow with B is to re-analyze C and come to a fresh conclusion as to how good you feel it is. If your analysis and evaluation still stand up, then put C "in your pocket" as your King of the Hill (best move you found so far) and see if you can find a better one. If you can't, only then play C.

Spend Some Time on the Move Actually Played

When testing the thought process of weaker players, I am constantly amazed at the small amount of time they spend, out of their total thinking time, on what will happen after the move they actually choose to play!

For example, if they spend 10 minutes on a move, possibly only 1 minute is spent on the move actually played, and possibly less than 20 seconds on what might happen afterwards. If they spend only 1 minute on a move, maybe 20 seconds may be spent on that move with no thought as to what might happen afterwards.

Yet one should never think 10 minutes on a complicated move and only spend a small percentage of their time on what will happen afterwards! Ask yourself the following question: "If I spend 10 minutes on a move and then my opponent spends the same 10 minutes in reply, how much of his time will be spent trying to see what he can do about defeating my move?" The answer is 10 minutes! Because *all* of his effort will be spent on the position you gave to him. So for you to only spend 20 seconds of those ten minutes considering his reply is quite dangerous. Stronger players always spend a much higher percentage of their thinking time on the ramifications of their candidate moves – it would be too dangerous for them to spend so little time that their opponent might find a refutation!

Moral of the story: *Spend at least a decent percentage of your time examining what your opponent can do to you after your proposed move – if you don't, your opponent surely will!*

Learn Tactics To Prevent Loss of Material – Even More than for Offense!

One of the things I have learned from being a full-time instructor is that the most common use for basic tactics – and the most commonly overlooked use – is to prevent material loss. When you study a tactics book, you are almost always put in the position of offense: White to play and win, White to play and mate in two, etc.

However, as you improve and you face stronger opposition, the opportunities to use these basic ideas on offense diminish considerably, as your opponent does not allow simple tactics to win material. Nevertheless, that does not mean that you rarely get to use those skills! Instead, a higher and higher percentage of tactical skills are used to determine if your candidate moves are tactically feasible (see *Initial and Final Candidate Moves* in 2-1). In other words, you are using these same tactics defensively to see if your opponent can do anything to you that would refute your candidate moves. In this manner, these same tactics occur *quite frequently*, for while your opponent may rarely give you easy tactics, there are plenty of opportunities for you to give them to him, and it is one of your main duties to make sure you do not!

A simple example will suffice. First let's look at a problem as "Play and win"; then we'll examine the same issue from the White "Is it safe?" perspective:

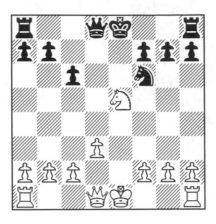

Black to play and win

The answer is easy: **1...Qa5+** is a double attack, picking up the knight on the next move. If you analyze the pin 1...Qe7 first because of the Seed of Tactical Destruction (the loose knight on the same file as the king), that is a mistake; just put 1...Qe7 on your candidate list. You should always look at the most forceful moves first, and those are checks. Only after analyzing checks should you spend time on captures and threats like the pin. If you analyze 1...Qe7 first and see that White has defenses such 2 Qe2 or even the "trick" 2 0-0, so that 2...Qxe5? 3 Re1 wins the queen, then you are just wasting time on your clock. Of course, if the check fails, then to consider the pin would be absolutely required.

Now let's consider the same tactic from a defensive standpoint. Go back one move and ask the question that was featured in *Is it Safe?* (5-3). Can White safely take the e-pawn with the knight?

White to play

Obviously, you say, the answer is "No!" Because doing so would lead to the previous position. That's correct and too easy!

But when I give players *the second position first*, the percentage of correct answers drops dramatically! There is more than one reason for this. The most prevalent is that almost all weaker players give more weight to their own tactics than they do to their opponent's: "It's more fun to win material than to work to avoid losing material."

If you ask someone, "At the start of a game, if you assume the position is about even, is it more important for you to win a piece, or for your opponent to win a piece?" Amazingly, you often get the answer that it is more important for the player to win a piece. However, to a neutral observer, both answers carry equal weight! If both sides are even, then clearly whoever wins a piece is ahead a piece and it is equally important for them whether they started as White or Black or him or you! If you don't believe me, then just switch chairs!

This leads to several important conclusions. One of the main reasons why one studies basic tactics is *not* just so that if your opponent makes a basic mistake you can take advantage of it – it is also so that you will not make moves that allow your opponent to use a basic tactic to beat *you*. For more on this subject, see the archived *The Most Common and Important Use of Tactics*.

Two Ideas in One

Suppose a game starts **1 d4 d5 2 Nf3 b6 3 Nc3 c5**. Is 3...c5 safe?

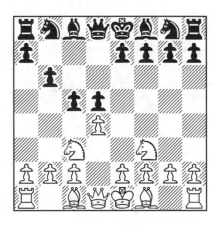

White to play

The answer is "No". White has the discovered attack **4 dxc5 bxc5 5 Qxd5**.

The added bonus is that *you want to capture with the queen*: it develops an unmoved piece and, most of all, puts Black between a rock and a hard place. Black either has to trade queens when down material or find some way to avoid trading his strongest piece while saving the attacked rook on a8. Many weaker players automatically play 5 Nxd5, which is not intrinsically bad; but capturing this way often moves into a pin and, even worse, later may allow Black's now-surviving queen to champion a counterattack. *It is embarrassing to lose material to a piece you could have – and should have – forcefully traded off when ahead!* Some students say they always "take with the lowest valued piece", but there is no such rule! However, in a similar position...

1 d4 d5 2 Nf3 Nf6 3 e3 Bd7 4 Be2 b6 5 Nc3 c5

White to play

Now after **6 dxc5 bxc5**, 7 Qxd5?? loses the queen, so it is not at all the same. With a lesser piece guarding the pawn, the only reasonable capture is with the lowest valued piece: **7 Nxd5**. See the difference?

Another "two-ideas-for-one" safety problem: White has just played **1 Nf3-e5**. Is it safe?

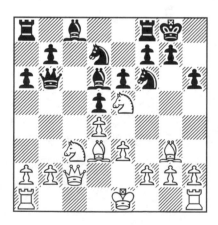

Black to play after 1 Ne5

Black cannot play 1...Nxe5?? 2 dxe5, forking the bishop and knight. But **1...Bxe5 2 dxe5 Ng4** or **2 Bxe5 Nxe5 3 dxe5 Ng4** snares the pawn on e5, since f2-f4 allows ...Nxe3 or ...Qxe3+. So 1 Ne5? is not safe.

The white player in this game was not a bad player, but if one make moves that are not safe, it's tough to save the game! As is often the case, instead of moving 1 Nf3-e5, White should just move *every piece once before he moves any piece twice* and play 1 0-0, followed by putting a rook on the open file with 2 Rc1. White was afraid of 1 0-0 Bxg3, doubling his g-pawns. *But the pawn structure after 2 hxg3 is actually good for White*, as he creates a "normal" knight pawn that attacks two squares for a weak rook's pawn.

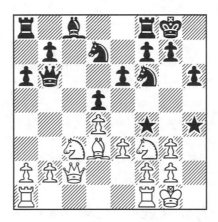

Black to play after 1 0-0 Bxg3 2 hxg3

The semi-open h-file is of little use to Black, as it is almost impossible to get two major pieces on the h-file. *In similar positions White rarely ruins his pawn structure by playing 2 fxg3(?) to get a semi-open file for the rook on f1*, as White would have to have a very strong attack to justify such decentralization of his pawns.

As always, if you did not see that 1 Ne5 was not safe in the second diagram previously, try to identify the reason – didn't look (Hope Chess); can't see (board vision); didn't look far enough (quiescence error) – and take the appropriate steps to improve your all-important analysis skills (see *Improving Analysis Skills* 2-5).

I gave this situation to about 15 intermediate players and, despite their understanding that I had picked out the situation for some reason, *none* of them saw that 1 Ne5 lost a pawn! I would bet most 1800+ players would get this relatively simple counting question correct, and almost all players rated over 2000. Moral of the story: if you want to become a stronger player, *make sure you are analyzing all the little safety issues correctly or all your other improvement efforts may go for naught!*

Look Wide First, Not Deep

The old saying is, "If you see a good move, look for a better one." But a similar saying could be, "Check out all your likely candidates before spending too much time on one." When testing thought processes, I find that many students become transfixed with a single idea – often the first one they see – and then spend time trying to convince themselves it is a good one. Unfortunately, this means they often overlook quite obvious – and much better

– choices. So you can save yourself plenty of time by first surveying all the moves that accomplish something positive, rather than focusing too much on the first one that catches your eye. If one then still stands out, commencing deeper analysis with that candidate certainly makes sense. If it checks out, then it is your King of the Hill and... then you look for a better one anyway.

When You're Ahead...

When you are way ahead, you need to *think defense first* (but don't play defensively!), *keep it simple*, trade pieces (not necessarily pawns; see *When You're Winning, It's a Whole Different Game* 7-3). *When ahead in material but down in tempi, you want to catch up in tempi, not win more pawns at the cost of tempi* (see *The Principle of Symmetry* 8-6). The following is one of the best examples I have seen of *not* doing the latter!

Opponent-Student
World Open 2005

1 d4 Nf6 2 Nc3 g6 3 e4 d6 4 f4 Bg7 5 e5 Nfd7 6 Nf3 0-0 7 Bd3 c5 8 Be3 cxd4 9 Bxd4 Nc6 10 Be3 dxe5

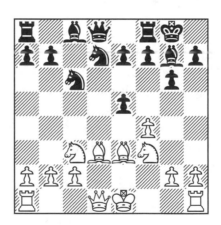

White to play

Black, at the time an elementary school player, has played superbly: he has destroyed White's center, and is ahead a pawn. However, *White is slightly ahead in development, so Black should do his best to catch up, or "consolidate".* Instead, Black decides winning more pawns might be nice...

11 0-0 exf4 12 Bxf4 Qb6+ 13 Kh1 Qxb2!?

The computer's top move, but it is very tricky for a human. Simpler is 13...Nc5, continuing smooth development.

14 Bd2 Bxc3 15 Rb1 Qxa2 16 Bxc3

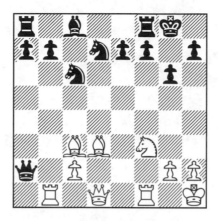

Black to play

Now Black is ahead three pawns, but White has massive compensation (almost two pawns worth, according to *Rybka*). Sure, a computer or a grandmaster might hold Black's position, but it's tough playing when your opponent has all the attacking chances. The following is a helpful heuristic: *If you fianchetto a bishop, castle on that side, and then trade it off while your opponent still has a queen and a bishop of that same color, you are often asking for trouble!* Here Black's kingside is suffering such a fate.

16...Qd5

16...Nc5 is again better.

17 Rb5

White plays energetically.

17...Qd6 18 Qd2

Heading for the weakened dark squares.

18...a6??

Missing the threats; 18...f6 was necessary. Black goes from better to lost, which is very easy to do in this type of position.

19 Qh6

Threatening the basic pattern mate 20 Qg7 mate.

19...f6

Trying to plug the holes, but it is too late.

20 Bxg6 1-0

According to *Rybka*, White mates in nine moves. After 20...hxg6 21 Qxg6+ Kh8, White can save his attacked rook with 22 Rh5 mate.

Lesson learned; if you can learn from others' mistakes without repeating them, you are a rare player indeed...